The Classical Art of Command

JOSEPH
ROISMAN

The Classical Art
of Command

Eight Greek Generals Who
Shaped the History of Warfare

OXFORD
UNIVERSITY PRESS

OXFORD
UNIVERSITY PRESS

Oxford University Press is a department of the University of Oxford. It furthers
the University's objective of excellence in research, scholarship, and education
by publishing worldwide. Oxford is a registered trade mark of Oxford University
Press in the UK and certain other countries.

Published in the United States of America by Oxford University Press
198 Madison Avenue, New York, NY 10016, United States of America.

© Oxford University Press 2017

Library of Congress Cataloging-in-Publication Data
Names: Roisman, Joseph, 1946– author.
Title: The classical art of command : eight Greek generals who shaped the
  history of warfare / Joseph Roisman.
Other titles: Greek generals who shaped the history of warfare
Description: New York, NY : Oxford University Press, [2017] | Includes
  bibliographical references and index.
Identifiers: LCCN 2016019526 (print) | LCCN 2016019663 (ebook) |
  ISBN 9780199985821 (hardback) | ISBN 9780190641931 (online) |
  ISBN 9780199985838 (Updf) | ISBN 9780199985845 (epub)
Subjects: LCSH: Greece—History, Military—To 146 B.C. |
  Generals—Greece—Biography. | Command of troops—Case studies. |
  Leadership—Greece—History—To 1500. | Leadership—Case studies.
Classification: LCC DE88 .R65 2017 (print) | LCC DE88 (ebook) |
  DDC 355.0092/238—dc23
LC record available at https://lccn.loc.gov/2016019526

9 8 7 6 5 4 3 2 1
Printed by Sheridan Books, Inc., United States of America

To Hanna, Elad, Helaina and Talia, Shalev, Diana and Noa

CONTENTS

MAPS AND ILLUSTRATIONS

Maps

Illustrations

PREFACE

F ROM VIDEO GAMES to detailed scholarly publications: ancient Greek warfare is not a subject that has suffered from experts' or laypersons' neglect. It comes as somewhat of a surprise, then, that there are very few monographs, if any, that focus on Greek generalship, especially during the golden age of ancient Greece. This book strives to partially fill the void. It aims to inform readers who are new to the subject about the varied nature of the Classical art of command. It is also hoped that scholars or other experts may find some of the analyses and observations offered here useful or different from the familiar. To make the narrative accessible, there is an effort to avoid professional jargon or overly technical descriptions, while the documentation favors (though not exclusively) the ancient sources and recent publications in English.

For the present author, this book constitutes a regression of sorts. My first book was on the Athenian general Demosthenes, and since then I have pursued other interests, although I polyamorously kept succumbing to the appeal of military history. Fortunately, my departure from the field helped in deepening and improving my understanding of it.

There were many who helped me in this project. First among them is my friend Ian Worthington, who generously agreed to read and comment on the manuscript. The usefulness of his criticism can only be matched by his joy of making it. Gregory Nagy deserves special thanks for allowing me to return to the Center of Hellenic Studies and use its incomparable resources and gain the help of its dedicated staff thirty years after being a junior fellow there. Victoria Pagan and Ann Mary Eaverly were gracious hosts during a partial sabbatical spent in the Department of Classics at the University of Florida.

Finally I owe a debt of gratitude to the editorial stuff of OUP and especially to Stefan Vranka for his sensible advice, patience, and careful attention to the project.

All dates in this book are BCE unless noted otherwise, and all translations are from the Loeb Classical Library unless noted otherwise, with some translations slightly modified. The index does not cover the footnotes.

—Joseph Roisman

LIST OF ABBREVIATIONS

AHB	*Ancient History Bulletin*
AC	*L'Antiquité Classique*
AJA	*American Journal of Archaeology*
AJP	*American Journal of Philology*
AncW	*Ancient World*
Ath. Pol.	Aristotle? or [Xenophon], *Constitution of Athens*
BNJ	*Brill New Jacoby*: http://referenceworks.brillonline.com/browse/brill-s-new-jacoby
BSA	*Annual of the British School at Athens*
CAH	*Cambridge Ancient History*
C&M	*Classica et Mediaevalia*
ClAnt	*Classical Antiquity*
CPh	*Classical Philology*
CQ	*Classical Quarterly*
CR	*Classical Review*
Diod.	Diodorus of Sicily
FGrHist	Jacoby, F. 1923–1958. *Die Fragmente der griechischen Historiker.* Berlin.
G&R	*Greece and Rome*
GRBS	*Greek, Roman, and Byzantine Studies*

Hdt.	Herodotus
IG	*Inscriptiones Graecae*
JHS	*Journal of Hellenic Studies*
LCL	Loeb Classical Library, Cambridge, Massachusetts
ML	Meiggs, R., and D. Lewis, eds. 1969. *A Selection of Greek Historical Inscriptions to the End of the Fifth Century B.C.* Oxford.
Plut.	Plutarch
RhM	*Rheinisches Museum für Philologie*
RSA	*Rivista Storica dell'Antichita*
SEG	*Supplementum Epigraphicum Graecum*
Thuc.	Thucydides
Xen.	Xenophon

The Classical Art of Command

Introduction
Greek Generals and Warfare in the Classical Age

Eight Greek Generals

This book is about eight generals from Classical Greece (500–323 BCE) who left a distinct mark on Greek history and its art of command. The earliest is the Spartan king Leonidas. He and his fellow combatants won lasting fame for their fight to the death at Thermopylae against an invading Persian army. That battle was the final test of Leonidas' leadership, coming after struggles with recruitment, topography, morale, and tactics. Next is the wily Athenian general Themistocles, who earned his reputation as the architect of Athens' maritime power and as the leader of the Greeks to victory over the Persian navy at Salamis. We shall examine the challenges he faced in implementing his military plans and the effectiveness of his leadership and solutions. The next general to be considered, Pericles, was Athens' most prominent political and military leader when the city was at the zenith of its power. He led a hard-won campaign against the island of Samos, where he introduced a new siege technology. Even more significant was his problematic strategy against Sparta in what is known as the Peloponnesian War, a conflict also central to the career of our fourth commander, the Athenian general Demosthenes. Demosthenes believed that military surprise was the key to victory, and came up with the novel idea of establishing an offensive fortified base on Spartan territory. Demosthenes won some spectacular victories but was also responsible for the worst defeat Athens ever suffered on land, thus inviting an examination of the causes of his success and failure. Since antiquity, the Spartan Lysander has had a place among Greece's leading generals for his naval victory over Athens that decided the Peloponnesian

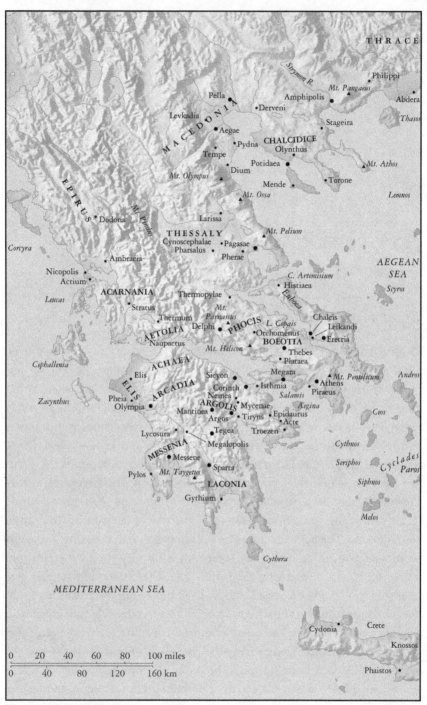

THRACE

Philippi

Strymon R.

Mt. Pangaeus ▲   Abdera

Pella   Amphipolis

Levkadia   • Derveni   Stageira   *Thasos*

MACEDONIA   Aegae   CHALCIDICE

• Pydna   Olynthus   *Mt. Athos* ▲

Tempe   Potidaea

Dium   • Mende   Torone

Mt. Olympus ▲   *Lemnos*

Mt. Ossa ▲

Corcyra   EPIRUS   Larissa   *Mt. Pelium* ▲

Dodona   THESSALY   AEGEAN
    Cynoscephalae   • Pagasae   SEA
    Ambracia   Pharsalus   • Pherae   *Scyros*

Nicopolis   *C. Artemisium*
Actium   • Histiaea

Leucas   ACARNANIA   Thermopylae   *Mt.*
    Stratus   *Parnassus*   Chalcis
    Thermum   Delphi   PHOCIS   *L. Copais*   Lefkandi
    AETOLIA   • Orchomenus   Eretria
    Naupactus   BOEOTIA

Cephallenia   *Mt. Helicon*   • Thebes
    ACHAEA   • Plataea
    Elis   Sicyon   Megara   *Andros*
    ELIS   ARCADIA   Corinth   • Isthmia   *Mt. Pentelicum* ▲
Zacynthus   Pheia   Nemea   Athens
    Olympia   Mantinea   ARGOLIS   *Salamis*   Piraeus
    Argos   Mycenae   *Aegina*   *Ceos*
    Tegea   Tiryns   Epidaurus
    Lycosura   Troezen   Acte   *Cythnos*
    MESSENIA   Megalopolis   *Seriphos*   *Cyclades*
    Messene   *Siphnos*   *Paros*
    Pylos   *Mt. Taygetus* ▲   Sparta
    LACONIA   *Melos*
    Gythium

    MEDITERRANEAN SEA

    Cythera

    Cydonia   Crete

    Knossos

0   20   40   60   80   100 miles

0   40   80   120   160 km   Phaistos

MAP 1 Ancient Greece.

War. No description of his generalship would be complete, however, without an analysis of his later failure to mold the postwar Spartan empire and of the campaign in Boeotia that ended in his death. Dionysius, the ruler of Syracuse, was one of the busiest military leaders in the Classical age and one of the keenest to develop new military technology. His conflicts with Carthage and with Greek and native communities in Sicily and southern Italy greatly expand our knowledge about the running of big and small operations, sieges, and the coordination of land and sea attacks in Greek warfare. Our last generals to be considered, Epaminondas and Pelopidas, were chiefly responsible for making their native city of Thebes the strongest military power in Greece, if only for a relatively short time. They provide a unique opportunity for observing two major generals working in partnership. Both of them, and in particular Epaminondas, are credited with introducing innovative tactics and with leading campaigns and devising a strategy that ended Sparta's military hegemony.

Some readers may wonder about the grounds for selecting only these eight generals when there are many more candidates for examination. In particular, what about Alexander the Great, arguably the best of all ancient commanders? I do not believe that there is room for another analysis of Alexander's generalship when there are so many available already. Moreover, the generals of this book better represent Greek warfare in the Classical age than Alexander's unique campaign in Asia. I shall also not plead editorial and space considerations or insist that both ancient and modern authors agree on the importance of the aforementioned leaders, convenient and justified as those arguments may be. The selection is subjective: I regard these generals as leaders in their field, and find them particularly interesting and highly illustrative in their achievements as well as their imperfections. Yet the choice could be justified on less personal grounds. The generals discussed here responded to ancient expectations of Greek commanders, and their careers inform us, not just about their individual performance, but also about those expectations themselves. In addition, they represent, not only the two most famous Greek cities, Athens and Sparta, but also Thebes and Syracuse, which had their own particular challenges. These eight generals also added something new and gave their personal stamp to the conventional Greek art of command. Finally, they inspired later commanders in antiquity and beyond, or were thought to be their models. Thus it has been common to compare the Scots leader William Wallace to King Leonidas as two freedom fighters, or Churchill to Themistocles as leaders of great strategic insight who could identify a danger and prepare for it long before it became imminent. German historian Hans Delbrück thought that Fredrick the Great of Prussia during the Seven

Years' War (1756–1763) used a strategy of attrition and avoiding direct conflict with superior military force that resembled Pericles' strategy during the Peloponnesian War and Fabius' Maximus' strategy against Hannibal in the Second Punic War. The centrality of military surprise to the generalship of Demosthenes of Athens (not the orator) made him a precursor of the strategy of indirect approach recommended by the well-known British strategist B. H. Liddell Hart. Dionysius I of Syracuse probably imitated Demosthenes' and Lysander's tactics in their respective campaigns, and was praised together with a later Syracusan tyrant, Agathocles, by Scipio Africanus the Elder, the conqueror of Hannibal, as the best in effective administration and in daring tempered by intelligence (Polybius 15.35.6; cf. Nepos, *Of Kings* 2.2). Roman orator Cicero and American general George Patton believed that Epaminondas of Thebes was the greatest of all the Greeks. Apparently there is much to learn from the eight generals of this book.

The following chapters will evaluate the nature of these generals' military leadership and their impact on Greek history. The present chapter aims to provide background information on what Greek generals did and were expected to do, and the military contexts in which they operated. The following two examples of generals in combat will serve as an introduction to these subjects.

Two Generals in Action

The conflict of Athens and her allies with Sparta and hers, known as the Peloponnesian War (431–404), was one of the most important events in ancient Greek history. It was a long, drawn-out contest, on land and sea and in a theater that stretched from Asia Minor in the east to Sicily in the west. One of its leading Athenian generals was Demosthenes, son of Alcisthenes (Ch. 4). In 426, this young man was active in western Greece, and after suffering defeat in his first encounter with local enemies, he found himself a few months later engaged in another battle, near the city of Olpae on the Ambraciot Gulf (Map 9, p. 131). Two coalition armies faced each other across a ravine. On one side was Spartan general Eurylochus, who commanded an army of 6,000 hoplites (heavy infantrymen), half of them local Ambraciots and mercenaries, and half troops from the Peloponnese. On the other side was Demosthenes with an unknown number of hoplites and light infantry, mostly javelin throwers, from western Greece, along with a modest force of Athenian hoplites and archers. Demosthenes had the advantage of camping only three miles from friendly Amphilochian Argos, while an Athenian fleet of twenty ships prevented the enemy from bringing aid by sea, or escaping to it. Yet the Peloponnesian-Ambraciot army enjoyed numerical superiority in heavy infantry.

In typical large land battles, the troops were massed facing each other, and the burden of the fighting rested on the hoplites.[1] The strength of the army usually lay in its right wing, which fought the enemy's weaker left wing. It was also common for a larger army to use its numerical superiority to outflank the opposition's left wing in order to attack its vulnerable flank or rear. At Olpae, both sides deviated from these practices, though to different degrees. Spartan general Eurylochus intended to use his larger numbers to outflank Demosthenes' stronger *right* wing. For that purpose, he placed himself on the far left of his own left wing in order to lead the attack and the flanking maneuver against the Demosthenes and his hoplites. Demosthenes commanded the customary right wing, but, being short on heavy infantry, he was forced to use mostly light infantry in his left wing against the enemy's better-protected and deadlier heavy infantry. Yet he anticipated the enemy's tactics and countered them with a stratagem, hiding 400 local hoplites and lightly armed troops in a sunken road with overgrown vegetation and ordering them to attack the enemy rear when it tried to outflank him. Eurylochus and his men were thus crushed between Demosthenes' anvil and the ambuscaders' hammer. The Spartan general, his second in command, and the troops around them were all killed. The rest of the army fled the battlefield, some in more orderly fashion than others.[2]

Demosthenes displayed a number of qualities of good generalship in this battle. Although the troops under his command came from different places and had different military skills, he successfully established his authority over them and effectively combined their proficiencies. He designed a battle plan that worked by correctly predicting the enemy's movements. He used the topography to his advantage and coordinated and timed an attack of two different forces that resulted in a deadly surprise. He thus won a victory against an army with superior strength in hoplites.

Next we take a chronological leap to another general discussed in this book, Dionysius I (Ch. 6). He ruled Syracuse in Sicily from 408 to 367, and throughout much of his reign, he aimed to extend his dominion over Sicily and southern Italy. In 394, he marched against Tauromenium, a local Sicel city a few kilometers north of Naxos, in an effort to secure his hold over

1. Below, pp. 14–17.
2. The battle: Thuc. 3.106.1–108.3; Polyaenus 3.1.2 (300 men in the ambush); Hammond 1966, 245–256; Pritchett 1965–1992, 8:1–78; my p. 150 below.

eastern Sicily (Map 14, p. 229). It was not an easy undertaking, because Tauromenium and its citadel were situated on a hill, surrounded by tall walls, and its defenders were highly motivated to fight for their freedom. Dionysius camped south of the town and carried on a siege that the locals' successful opposition extended into the winter. Disappointed with the siege, he now set his hopes on a surprise attack, for which he picked what looked like optimal conditions. At the winter solstice (around December 21), he and his troops, probably hoplites, stole toward the town's citadel under the cover of a moonless, stormy night. The bitter cold and the defenders' confidence in their fortifications made them negligent in their duties. Dionysius approached the fortifications where they were tallest and hence thought least vulnerable. His force struggled against the rough terrain and the deep snow, and he himself suffered from severe frostbite and poor vision. Nevertheless, he mastered a peak from which he entered the settlement. His success was short-lived: the defenders quickly recovered, launched a counterattack, and ejected him and his companions. It appears that Dionysius was now joined by units from his camp down the hill, who could not help much because the locals used their advantage of elevation to descend on them and probably to shower them with missiles. Dionysius lost 600 men and all his arms except for his body armor, and was almost captured alive. His defeat also encouraged the cities of Messina and Acragas to drive out his supporters.

Unlike Demosthenes' at Olpae, Dionysius' surprise attack failed and produced harmful repercussions. Nevertheless, he showed traits of good generalship in this operation. He displayed personal courage and endurance that reflected his physical fitness (he was then in his mid-thirties). The night operation was based on good intelligence about the terrain, the fortifications, and the enemy's guarding routine. He chose the right time for the attack and even established good communications with the forces that were left behind and joined him later. He may also have tried to apply lessons learned from his past experience. If the assault and the fighting occurred at dawn, as was often the case with Greek night attacks, it is possible that Dionysius' success in an earlier operation, where he surprised Carthaginian forces near Syracuse at dawn in 395, encouraged him to extend that tactic to this mission. The difficulties of urban combat and the enemy's topographical advantage explain his failure. In 392, Dionysius retuned to Tauromenium and captured it (we are not told how), replacing its Sicel population with mercenaries loyal to him.[3]

3. Diod. 14.88.1–5; 96.4; my p. 260. Dawn attack at Syracuse: pp. 256–257 below.

These instances of generals in action represent only a sample of the Greek battle experience. Nevertheless, the two episodes illustrate some of the major expectations of Greek generals and their responses to military challenges. At most times, a Greek general was expected to lead his troops in person and participate in the fighting. Not all generals were engaged with both strategy and tactics, but Dionysius represented the military leader who played the double role of strategist and tactician. Thus the campaign against Tauromenium was part of a greater plan to expand but also defend his power against rivals such as Carthage in western Sicily and Rhegium across the Straits of Messina. Both Demosthenes and Dionysius showed how the general planned, took charge of, and coordinated the attack in a way that was designed to maximize his strengths and exploit the enemy's weaknesses, including its expectations of him. The general was also called on to adapt the fighting to the terrain, season, and time of day, and either to use conventional tactics or to resort to surprise and stratagems. He commanded forces made up of fellow citizens, allies, and mercenaries, over all of whom he was supposed to establish his authority in spite of their different relationships with him. The examples of Demosthenes and Dionysius suggest that a general was also supposed to be equally comfortable leading heavy and light infantry and, as we shall see, cavalry and ships, too. He was expected to be a man of many military parts: commander of an army in a pitched battle, manager of a siege, leader of a stealth operation, and a soldier like the rest.[4]

Greek Generals: Responsibilities and Personality

Many of the above qualities were presumed to produce victory, which was what generals were supposed to achieve. In the Classical period that frames this book, there was a growing interest in the education of a successful general and in what was expected of him. Military instructors taught individual fighting skills and drilling, and military manuals instructed their readers in such lessons as how to survive a siege or how to use and improve the Athenian cavalry. The fourth-century historian and soldier Xenophon wrote a fictional-historical work on the education of young Cyrus (the Great) before he became the king of Persia in the sixth century, the *Cyropaedia*, which

---

4. For additional expectations and the nature of Greek generalship, see Anderson 1970, 67–83; Wheeler 1991 (*contra*: Pritchett 1994, 111–144); Boëldieu-Trévet 2007; Wheeler 2007; Moore 2013.

is full of practical advice about how to train and run an army. It includes, among other things, instructions in drilling and selecting troops for battle, choosing a site for and building a camp, and adapting the army's march to the terrain and local opposition. It also discusses caring for the soldiers, keeping them fit, making them obedient and motivated, dealing with allies, and the like. Xenophon's and other Greeks' emphasis on the practical responsibilities of generalship persisted into later periods and can been seen in Polybius. This Hellenistic Greek historian argued that success depended largely on preplanning and selecting men to execute the plan. A general was expected to know the conditions—geographical, seasonal, etc.—under which he operated, and to have good military intelligence about the enemy and an effective communication system. He was also encouraged to be knowledgeable in ancillary arts that could help his planning, such as military history, astronomy, and geometry.[5]

Scholars see these and similar expectations as a reflection of the growing professionalism of Greek generalship that took place no later than the Peloponnesian War (below, pp. 9–11). It is noteworthy, however, that our ancient sources on Greek generals, including the ones discussed in this book, tend to ignore these aspects of generalship. Historians and biographers, who constitute the vast majority of the sources, deal mostly with the generals' plans and actions rather than with the practical preparations for them or with the finer details of their execution. The reason seems to go beyond the conventions of the literary genre, which deemed the latter sort of information uninteresting and generally undeserving of attention. The Greeks, it appears, believed that there was more to military command than craftsmanship and practical knowledge. To the ancients, personality and character were at least as important, if not more so.

Xenophon's characterization of good generalship in his memoirs of Socrates well illustrates this emphasis. Xenophon's *Memorabilia* is a tribute to his teacher, the philosopher Socrates, in the form of recollections of Socrates' conversations with various Greeks. One of them was an aspirant to the office of general in Athens. He studied with an instructor who claimed to teach generalship but in fact taught what the Greeks called "tactics"; that

---

5. Military instructors and manuals: e.g., Xen, *On the Cavalry Commander*; Aeneas Tacticus, *How to Survive Under Siege*; Wheeler 1983; Campbell 1987; Whitehead 2001, 34–42. Good generalship: Xen. *Cyropaedia* 1.6.9–46; Polybius 9.12–21; cf. Plato *Laches* 181c–184c; Xen. *Memorabilia* 3.1.7, 2.1–4, 4.1–12, 5.22–23; Wood 1964; Hutchinson 2000. Isocrates' definition of good generalship is tailored to fit the career of his favorite pupil, Timotheus: 15.104–127.

is, the training and ordering of troops. Socrates claimed that generalship was much more:

> For a general must also be capable of furnishing military equipment and providing supplies for the men; he must be resourceful, active, careful, hardy and quick-witted; he must be both gentle and brutal, at once straightforward and designing, capable of both caution and surprise, lavish and rapacious, generous and mean, skillful in defense and attack; and there are many other qualifications, some natural, some acquired, that are necessary to one who would succeed as a general.[6]

Socrates' ideal general possesses a range of mental capacities and characteristics that enable him to deal effectively with ever-changing military situations. Most of these qualities belong to the category of personal traits. As we shall see, the ideal of the general who could oscillate readily between opposing methods and attitudes was never attained, because certain personality traits tend to be dominant over others. For example, the Athenian Demosthenes and the Theban Pelopidas were more daring than the cautious Pericles. In any case, personality mattered, and this book deals with this often neglected feature of Greek generalship, in addition to its other aspects. For generalship was shaped, not just by military, political, and other environments, but also by the leader's character, which influenced his reaction to them. Any discussion of the Greek art of command will be deficient if it fails to deal with the individual styles of its practitioners. This book accordingly consists of chapters on individual commanders instead of a general investigation of the nature or models of Greek generalship. Nevertheless, a brief survey of the history of Greek military leadership, its prerequisites, and its offices will be helpful in understanding their careers.

What Generals Did, Their Qualifications, and Their Offices

The pre-classical general led armies by virtue of his high political and socioeconomic status and his military record.[7] After arranging his men for battle, he led them personally against the opposition, joining their ranks. He was

---

6. Xen. *Memorabilia* 3.6.1.
7. For the following section, see the works cited in note 4, above.

not expected to be a tactical innovator but to be courageous, crafty, physically fit, and ambitious for honor and fame. The demands of the role became more complex as early as the Peloponnesian War, in which generals might change tactics in mid-battle and use more stratagems and surprise. They coordinated and integrated movements of forces from different directions. They increased their reliance on light infantry and cavalry, whose contribution to victory in earlier times was largely secondary, and they strengthened the cooperation of such troops with heavy infantry. They also made more extensive use of mercenaries, in conjunction with or separately from citizen armies, and became greater users of war technology, particularly in sieges. Many scholars regard these developments as signs of the growing professionalism and expertise of Greek generalship.[8]

This transition or transformation, however, was anything but complete. There were many persistent attributes that can be traced back to earlier times, even all the way to Homer (c. 800). The general of the Classical age, like his forerunners, participated in the fighting, where he was expected to show personal courage. Like the Homeric hero, he was competitive and strove for excellence (*arete*), although more for the sake of the state than for himself. Indeed, most Greeks knew the Homeric epics, whose tales of heroic valor and its social and material rewards must have inspired many men, especially from the élite, to seek military distinction and leadership. The sources are regrettably scant on their motives in doing so. Yet, in addition to patriotism, public esteem, and profit, aspirants to the office must also have been moved by ambition to prove their worth as leaders, fighters, and men. We shall see that generals such as Demosthenes, Dionysius, Pelopidas, and Epaminondas even thought that they could achieve victory through personal feats of valor. The last two paid for that belief with their lives.[9]

Moreover, before and during the Classical age, commanders moved comfortably between leading large armies and commanding small operations. Up to the fourth century, there was no clear divide between military and civilian leadership, and even in later times, generals continued to play an important role in political institutions such as the popular assembly. As in the past, a general served both as a director of military policies and as a tactician arranging and leading troops in battle. He also continued to function as a provider of care for the troops and as their motivator. Often he enjoyed

8. E.g., Lengauer 1974; Wheeler 1991; Sage 1996, 65–66; Boëldieu-Trévet 2007.
9. See pp. 6, 164–165; pp. 320–321, 334–335. Homeric leadership and martial value: e.g., van Wees 1992.

a ready-made loyalty because he and his family were well known to his troops before he assumed command. Some of his distinguishing privileges of office, such as his distinctive armor and his greater material rewards and honor, were also legacies of earlier times. Personal character continued to be relevant. Onosander, the first-century CE author of a treatise on generalship, describes the good general in a way that earlier Greeks would have largely accepted:

> I believe then, that we must choose a general . . . because he is temperate, self-restrained, vigilant, frugal, hardened to labor, alert, free from avarice, neither too young nor too old, indeed a father of children if possible, a ready speaker, and a man with a good reputation.[10]

In short, generals of the Classical age resembled their predecessors in many ways, including their lack of military specialization.[11]

The prerequisites for Classical generalship differed from one state to another, but included some common qualifications. In most cases, the general was an adult citizen who was politically involved, enjoyed public visibility, and preferably had military experience. Xenophon describes an Athenian who ran for the office of general and boasted that he had held lower-ranking commands in the past and suffered wounds in service. He complained, however, that he had lost to someone with no military experience. Sore loser or not, the speaker suggests that a general was expected to have previous combat experience, but also that it was not a prime consideration. The ancient Greeks had no military academies or special courses of education to prepare commanders for the role. The aforementioned military instructors and manuals had limited use and appeal, though one speaker in a Platonic dialogue believed that a man could progress from the mastery of individual fighting to that of tactics and then to generalship. A motivated man could ask generals in his family or city about their experience, and ancient military authors recommended learning from historical examples. As we shall

---

10. Onosander, *The General* 1.1. The general's privileges and appearance (to which should be added his riding a horse): Wheeler 1991, 141–143.

11. Keegan's *The Mask of Command* (1988), which has influenced many military historians, deserves a special note. He sees the key to military success in the commanders' relationships with the troops and the kind of bonds that tied the troops together. Keegan also discusses the evolvement of military leadership from the heroic type, to a more managerial commander, to the professional, and culminating in a leader who combined all of these traits. However, the usefulness of his book for this study is limited, because we know only little about the relationships between our generals and their followers, and even less about the troops. In addition, our eight military leaders do not fit well Keegan's typology of commanders.

see, however, many generals learned on the job, for there was no more influential teacher than personal experience.[12]

We know relatively little about the qualifications or experience of the eight men described in this book before they became generals, but it is possible to describe the nature of their office. Athenians Themistocles, Pericles, and Demosthenes held the office of a *strategos* (general). In democratic Athens, there was a board of ten such generals who were elected annually, at first one per tribe (an administrative, recruiting, and voting unit), and later by the entire citizen body. Unlike many other Athenian magistrates, generals could be reelected to office, and this possibility, as well as the generalship's material and symbolic rewards, made it a coveted and influential position. Generals were often involved in domestic and foreign policy and were therefore potentially influential beyond the military sphere. Depending on the campaign, the general might be its sole leader or manage it with colleagues who could constrain his actions. In addition, the Athenian general was answerable to the popular assembly, which decided the goal of the campaign and what forces he could employ. He was also accountable in the law courts for his handling of the monies at his disposal and for his general conduct in office. Indeed, many Athenian generals whose performance was deemed unsatisfactory were put on trial and, when convicted, were fined, exiled, or put to death. Pericles, for example, was heavily fined in 430 for allegedly embezzling money and deceiving the people, and in a notorious miscarriage of justice in 406, the Athenians condemned to death six generals for failing to collect the dead and survivors of a naval battle. Lastly, the Athenians under arms could be undisciplined and argumentative. The general derived his authority over them from his office, including the legal power to punish misconduct, but also from his personality, social status, record, reputation, and handling of the troops.[13]

Pelopidas and Epaminondas of Thebes held the annual office of Boeotarch, the chief magistrate and commander of the Boeotian confederacy. The Boeotarch's power and its limitations resembled those of the Athenian general.[14]

The authority of Spartan Leonidas came largely from his position as a king who was the army's chief commander. Sparta in fact had two kings, but to

---

12. Xen. *Memorabilia* 3.4.1–12; Plato *Laches* 182c. Learning by enquiry: Xen. *Memorabilia* 3.5.22–23; Polybius 9.12–21. Military manuals: see note 5 above.
13. Athenian generals: Fornara 1971; Hamel 1998; Crowley 2012, 121–125. Pericles' trial: p. 138 below. The generals' trial: p. 197 below.
14. Pp. 19–20.

prevent paralyzing disputes between them, they were not allowed to co-lead the same campaign. Their authority, both at home and abroad, was derived from their royal and military rank, the belief that they were Heracles' descendants, and a collection of honors and privileges, including heroic death rites. As members of the Spartan Council (see below) and as generals, the kings had a say in foreign affairs. But Spartan monarchical power was checked by other political institutions and by the kings' accountability for misconduct or failure, which could result in their exile and other penalties. The Spartan Council or *gerousia* (28 elders with the two kings) sat in judgment of the kings. It also supervised the agenda of the popular assembly that elected officials, legislated, and sanctioned war or peace. There were five annual officeholders, called *ephors*, who might join the kings on campaign and were involved in foreign policy. All these limits on royal power, as well as its accountability, explain why Aristotle called the Spartan kingship a "hereditary generalship" (*strategia*), meaning that it was more a magistracy than a typical monarchy. But in Sparta as elsewhere, it was often the man who made the office, and strong Spartan kings could dominate political and military affairs beyond their prescribed powers. This was true also for Spartan general Lysander, who was not a king but held the annually elected office of *nauarchos* or admiral. In that capacity, he led naval and land forces or served as an adviser to the king. The nauarch ranked below the kings in authority, yet as long as Lysander did not conflict directly with them, he wielded power and prestige that exceeded theirs.[15]

Dionysius I of Syracuse was elected first as a general, Athenian style, and then as a supreme commander. He was commonly identified as a tyrant who disregarded the formal limitations of his office and the city's constitution. This characterization did not mean that he was unaccountable for his poor performances, only that reactions to them came in the form of political protests, conspiracies, and attempts on his life. His authority and legitimacy were largely anchored in his personality and his almost-ceaseless military activity, both as an aggressor and in defense of his city.[16]

Before we turn to these commanders, the next sections will offer a necessary but brief introduction to Greek warfare in the Classical age. They deal with the types of soldiers and styles of fighting that Greek land armies had in common: heavy infantry (hoplites), light infantry, and cavalry. They also

---

15. Spartan royal power: Hdt. 6.56–59; Xen. *The Constitution of the Lacedaemonians* 15.6–9; Aristotle *Politics* 3.9.2, 1285a; Thomas 1973. Spartan government: Andrewes 2007; Cartledge 1987, 116–132. Nauarch: pp. 189–190.
16. See Ch. 6.

describe the armies of the cities of the generals in this book, as well as those of two of their chief enemies, Persia and Carthage. Lastly, they outline the major attributes of the Greek battleship (trireme) and of the navies that used it.[17]

LAND WARFARE

Scholars are divided about when the Greeks fully adopted the use of heavily armed infantry, and even about its exact nature. The view taken here follows the "orthodox" school that places the full adoption of hoplite weapons and tactics in the sixth century and emphasizes fighting in mass formation.[18]

The hoplite (*hoplites*, lit. "armed man") wore a crested bronze helmet that exposed only the eyes, mouth, and chin, but in later times might cover just the crown of the head (Figure 1 below). He protected his upper body with a bronze corselet or, more commonly, a cuirass made of stiff linen and leather that might be covered by bronze scales. Bronze greaves protected the legs. The hoplite carried a circular, concave shield, about one meter in diameter, made of wood and covered with a thin layer of bronze. He used it for shoving the enemy, but primarily for protection that could be increased by forming a wall of overlapping shields. Up to the fourth century, the shields were often individually emblazoned (except for those of the uni-formed Spartans). The main offensive weapon was a spear, about two to two and a half meters long, with a wooden shaft tipped with a spearhead and a spike butt. For hand-to-hand combat the hoplite also used a roughly sixty-centimeter slashing sword that replaced the former cut-and-thrust kind. It has been estimated that a full set of hoplite armor weighed in total about 23–30 kilos and clearly affected endurance and mobility. As time progressed, hoplites gave up on some of their body protection for greater freedom of movement, although many of the above-described components did not substantially change.[19]

There was no rigid pattern of hoplite fighting, but the battle normally commenced after both armies had picked a (preferably) level field. They

---

17. For ancient Greek warfare, see Pritchett 1965–1992; Hanson 2004; van Wees 2004; Rawlings 2007; Sabin et al. 2007.

18. For the traditional view on hoplite warfare, see Hanson 1991 and 2009; Schwartz 2009; cf. Crowley 2012; Kagan and Viggiano 2013, 1–56. *Contra*: Krentz 1985b and 2002; van Wees 2004, 47–60.

19. Hoplite armor and reassessment of its weight: Krentz 2010, 188–197 (who estimates that the total armor weight was at most 23 kg and more probably 13 kg); Viggiano and Van Wees 2013.

FIGURE I *Hoplites in combat.* A late seventh-century Corinthian vase depicting individual hoplites in combat, each with a differently emblazoned shield. A wounded hoplite is lying with blood dripping from his unprotected thigh. His shield is commonly concave. Note the archer on the right, who equally commonly seeks protection behind the hoplites.
© *RMN-Grand Palais/Art Resource, New York.*

formed a phalanx in files, often eight men deep, that were supposed to stand or move in orderly fashion. Much of the fighting was carried out by the first three ranks, which clashed with their opponents, using the shields for shoving and the spears for stabbing, while the men in the rear joined the fighting as needed (Figure 2 below). The breakup of the formation resulted in hand-to-hand combats, and the flight of the enemy marked the end of the battle. In the Classical age, winners claimed victory by setting up a trophy on the battlefield and by granting the enemy the request to collect its dead and wounded.[20]

The following additional characteristics were common to many battles. Commanders tended to put their best units on the right wing of the phalanx, which was also the place of honor. It faced the enemy's weaker left wing, which in turn was supposed to hold on until its right wing decided the battle or came to the rescue. It could happen that both right wings won

20. See the previous last two notes, as well as Rawlings 2007, 81–103.

FIGURE 2 *Hoplite group formation.* The battle scene in this figure was drawn by a Corinthian painter c. 640 on what is known as the Chigi Vase, found in Etruria, Italy. It shows two rows of heavily armed men about to engage in battle or to hurl their spears at each other. The group at the center has ten legs but four spears, probably to suggest a longer line of men. On the left is a group of soldiers coming to enforce its side. The boy piper is either playing a marching rhythm or sounding the alarm.

© *Scala/Art Resource, New York.*

their contests and then opted either to continue fighting or to join the flight of their comrades. The phalanx was most vulnerable at its unprotected flanks and rear, which were also the preferred targets of outflanking maneuvers. Finally, the hoplite general's duties included choosing the battlefield, performing certain religious duties associated with war, and exhorting the troops before fighting began. He also arranged the lines of battle and then joined the troops as a soldier-general, normally on the right wing. The casualty rate of generals was relatively high, and their death could result in the defeat of their armies. Prior to Leonidas' time, the military commander had largely avoided directing movements of units and the battle in general after it began. This pattern would change when generals introduced more complex tactics and exercised greater control over how the battle evolved. They were assisted by lower-ranking officers, including commanders of units within the phalanx and leaders of the files.[21]

Lightly armed soldiers such as archers, slingers, and javelin-throwers could mingle with the hoplites, but were more often used separately for skirmishes, raiding, harassment, scouting, pursuing fleeing troops, and similar assignments. Their light armor, loose formation, and lack of protection restricted their close combat to fighting similar forces. But under resourceful generals, in greater numbers, or on certain kinds of ground, they could be more than a match for heavy infantry. Two types of light infantry had a significant impact on battles that will be analyzed in this book. The *peltasts* (from *pelte*, a crescent-shaped shield that later became round) stood somewhere between the lightly and heavily armed soldiers. The light infantry's shields were smaller and their spears or javelins shorter than those of the hoplites, and they had no body armor or helmets. Yet they proved their effectiveness under Demosthenes against the Ambraciots in western Greece and against a Spartan hoplite force on the island of Sphacteria near Pylos in Messenia. The *hamippoi* were light infantry who fought in conjunction with the cavalry and who in 362 helped the Theban Epaminondas win the battle of Mantinea. Light infantry came largely from the poor or from relatively marginal states, and hence enjoyed low prestige. Their inferior image and limited military role, along with the privileging of hoplite warfare, explain why many sources do not even mention them.[22]

Greek cavalrymen enjoyed greater respect, thanks to the long-established link between horse breeding and élite status. Their overall military contribution, however, seems to have been limited until the late fifth century. They rode a relatively small horse with no stirrups and carried javelins as missiles and a spear and a sword for closer combat. For protection, they wore a helmet, body armor, and boots, and they protected their horses with bronze face and chest pieces. On the battlefield, they traditionally safeguarded the phalanx on its flanks, where they grouped in diamond, wedge, or (more commonly) rectangular or square formations. They engaged the opposite cavalry, pursued it wherever it fled, and then returned to dismount and join the mêlée. We shall see that generals such as Dionysius, Pelopidas, and Epaminondas integrated them more fully into the battle against hoplites, because horses (contrary

21. Hoplite generals: Wheeler 1991; Hanson 2009, 107–117; Boëldieu-Trévet 2007; cf. Pritchett 1994.
22. Light infantry and peltasts: Lippelt 1910; Best 1969; Anderson 1970, 111–138; Sekunda and Burliga 2014. *Hamippoi*: p. 332 below.

to prevalent belief) could be trained to overcome the fear of attacking the phalanx frontally. Beyond the battlefield, the cavalry fulfilled missions that resembled those of light infantry.[23]

Mercenaries came from every corner of the Greek world and its neighbors, and they served in all military capacities. Generals such as Lysander, Dionysius, and Epaminondas made wide use of them in battle, in raiding expeditions, and in more sedentary roles such as garrisons. The sources mention them only sporadically, partly because of their secondary contribution to the fighting and their engagement in mundane military activities, and partly because of a bias against soldiers for hire. But their loyalty to their employers was not as unstable as is generally believed, and they seldom changed sides under the command of the generals discussed here.[24]

The Armies of Sparta, Athens, Boeotia, Syracuse, Persia, and Carthage

We shall leave the particulars of the army commanded by each of the generals of this book for the chapters devoted to them. This section provides a general survey of army organization and related topics.

The core of the Spartan army led by Leonidas and Lysander comprised Spartan citizens, a group that increasingly became its officer class as the number of citizens declined. Each citizen-soldier had the Greek letter lambda (Λ, for Lacedaemonians, after the region of Lacedaemon where Sparta was located) emblazoned on his shield, and was supposed to return home "with the shield or on it." It is impossible to say how far Leonidas' army resembled the hierarchical military organization of the later Spartan army, with its lower-ranking commanders over units of fluctuating size. The army also included *perioeci*, "dwellers around," men from communities, especially in Laconia, who enjoyed civil but not political rights and who commonly fought as hoplites. Members of Sparta's semi-servile class, the helots (p. 26), were also drafted and served mostly as arms carriers, light infantry, and servants of the Spartan hoplites. In addition, Sparta stood at the head of an alliance of states known as the Peloponnesian League, whose coalition army was led by the Spartan king. His authority over this army varied greatly, but the Spartans

---

23. Spence 1993; Gaebel 2002.
24. Parke 1933; Trundle 2004.

themselves, as opposed to their allies, rarely showed a reluctance to fight.[25] Indeed, the Spartans instilled in their men and women from youth the values of discipline, valor, fear of shame, and esteem for death in battle, which earned the fallen an immortal fame. These were ideals that other Greek hoplites readily adopted, but the Spartans were deemed their best practitioners.

The Athenian army of the Classical age, led by Themistocles and Demosthenes (among others), was organized into ten tribal regiments (*taxeis*), whose size changed according to the demands of the mission and the availability of recruits. At the head of the Athenian chain of command were ten annually elected generals (p. 12), who ranked over elected regimental commanders, the *taxiarchs*, who in turn were superior to their appointees, the leaders of companies (*lochagoi*). After the popular assembly authorized a campaign and decided the strength of the force to be used, the generals recruited citizens and resident aliens according to catalogues of those who were qualified to serve as hoplites. They normally included men from draft-age groups who owned property and were physically able. The generals also drafted a force of cavalry and mounted archers, as well as units of light infantry such as peltasts and foot archers. When Pericles and Demosthenes were active, allies from within and outside the Athenian Empire made invaluable contributions to the manpower, equipment, and budget of the Athenian army and navy.[26]

The army commanded by Epaminondas and Pelopidas came from the city-states of Boeotia in central Greece. They formed the Boeotian League or Confederacy—a somewhat unusual organization for the independent-minded Greeks—which was dominated by Thebes. The membership and administration of the League changed over time, as did the obligations of its members, but it was led from early on by officials called Boeotarchs, who functioned as generals and chief magistrates. An ancient account of the League's political and military structure in the 390s suggests Theban control. Thebes provided more Boeotarchs, councilmen, troops, and money to the federation than any other member, and the federal council met in its citadel, the Cadmeia. The same account reports that that each of the eleven districts that composed the League was expected to send about a thousand hoplites and a hundred cavalrymen to the federal army. It is uncertain whether the drafting quotas, which amounted to a sizable army of 11,000

25. The Spartan army and its organization: Lazenby 1985. See also pp. 284, 292 below for its subunits. Helots in the Spartan army: Hunt 2006. The Peloponnesian League: de Ste. Croix 1972, 101–124; Bolmarcich 2005.
26. Burckhardt 1996; Christ 2001; Crowley 2012, 22–39; Bugh 1988 (cavalry).

troops and 660 cavalry, were mandatory or desirable, and filling them probably depended on the Boeotarchs' ability to enforce them. The careers of Epaminondas and Pelopidas indicate that the generals needed considerable negotiating skills to persuade their constituencies and colleagues to adopt their plans. These two generals were also associated with a Theban élite crash unit called the Sacred Band that was instrumental to their victories in some decisive battles.[27]

The army of Syracuse, the native city of the tyrant Dionysius, was not substantially different from other Greek armies. About two generations before Dionysius took power, another Syracusan tyrant, Gelon, reportedly made an unsuccessful offer to lead the Greek war against the Persian invasion, promising to bring 20,000 hoplites, 2,000 cavalry, 2,000 slingers, 2,000 archers, and 200 ships. The size of the Syracusan army and navy could change dramatically from one war to another, but these elements were largely regular components of its armed forces. For both its army and navy, Syracuse recruited citizens (including enfranchised, sometimes forcibly transplanted residents), slaves, freed slaves, allies, and mercenaries. Its troops came largely from Sicily and Italy and offered a variety of military skills. We shall see that Dionysius introduced new armaments to land and sea warfare and greatly improved the city's defenses.[28]

Two invading enemy forces also deserve a brief description. The larger was the Persian army, which included contingents of infantry and cavalry from lands ranging from India to Asia Minor, and was frequently led by the Persian king. The Asian infantryman on average was not as well protected as the Greek hoplite, though he had the advantage of pelting the enemy from a distance with bows, slings, or javelins (Figure 3 below). The historian Herodotus describes his arms and dress in his account of the army that the Persian king Xerxes took to Greece:

Here are the peoples which made up Xerxes' army. First, there were the Persians, dressed as follows. On their heads they wore *tiaras*, as they call them, which are loose, felt caps, and their bodies were clothed in colorful tunics with sleeves and breastplates of iron plate, looking rather like fish-scales. Their legs were covered with trousers, and instead of normal shields they carried pieces of wickerwork. They had

27. *Oxyrhynchian Greek History* 16.3–4. Boeotian government: Buckler 1980; Buck 1994, 6–10; Beck 1997; Buckler and Beck 2008, 127–198. Sacred Band and a map of Boeotia: (Map 11): 169, 281–282.
28. Gelon: Hdt. 7.156–162. Syracuse's army and navy: Finley 1979, 51–52, 66–70; Caven 1990, 243–247; Morrison 1990.

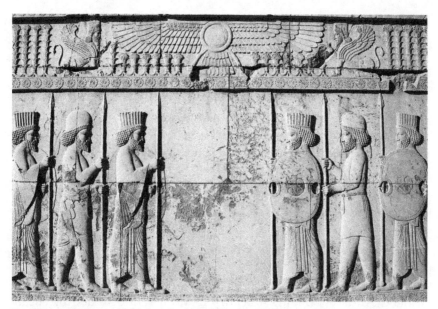

FIGURE 3 *Persian soldiers from Persepolis.* The Apadana was a sixth–fifth-century, monumental royal reception building in the Persian capital, Persepolis. It included reliefs of Persian and Median (recognized by their round hats) soldiers. Some scholars identify them with The Immortals. They hold a spear and the so-called eight-shaped or waist shield.

quivers hanging under their shields, short spears, large bows, arrows made of cane, and also daggers hanging from their belts down beside their right thighs.

The Persian infantry included an élite unit called the Ten Thousand Immortals, of which 1,000 "bravest and noblest Persians" accompanied the king. The Persian cavalry force specialized in shooting arrows at the enemy. It included a picked cavalry unit of 1,000.[29]

Carthage, Dionysius' chief military adversary, was a Phoenician colony in North Africa (now Tunisia) that was founded around 800. It had an oligarchic government, and its wealth came from extensive maritime trade and from exploitation of material and human resources in Africa and in Carthaginian colonies and trading posts. The city could mobilize large

29. Quote: Hdt. 7.61, Waterfield trans. ("and breastplates" is an emendation). The 1,000 and the Ten Thousand Immortals: Hdt. 7.41, 83 (who wrongly describes them as separate units), 103; Heraclides, *FGrHist* 689 F 1. The Persian army: Hignett 1963, 40–55; Dandamaev and Lukonin 1989, 222–237; Sekunda 1992; Cawkwell 2005, 237–254. Cf. Khorasani 2010; Charles 2011.

armies, cavalry forces, and navies made up largely of mercenaries and allies but commanded by Carthaginian generals and officers. The Carthaginian heavy infantry fought and were armed much like the Greek hoplite phalanx, with the Iberian troops using a cutting and stabbing sword. The light infantrymen, like their Greek counterparts, used small shields, javelins, arrows, and slings, while the cavalry used spears and swords. Also like Greek lightly armed units, they often commenced battle with skirmishing and then retreated to let the heavy infantry decide the conflict, while the cavalry engaged its counterpart in the wings or attacked the flanks of the infantry.[30]

Greek Battleships and Navies

The trireme or *trieres* ("three-rower") was the most common battleship in the Classical era (Figure 4 below). It was designed to destroy enemy ships with its protruding, half-submerged ram made of wood sheathed in bronze. About 170 rowers provided the power for the ship's movements and ramming. They sat on three stacked, crowded levels under the ship's deck, and included citizens, resident aliens, hired foreigners, and slaves. These humble origins (many of the citizen rowers came from the lower classes) gave naval service a lower place in public esteem than that of hoplites and cavalry. On the deck were twenty marine hoplites, a few archers, other seamen, a pilot who directed the ship with two steering oars at the stern, and the ship's captain or *trierarch*, a wealthy Athenian responsible for the ship's equipment and upkeep. It has been calculated that the trireme measured about 40 meters long, 5.4 meters wide, and 2.4 meters above the waterline. The ship had two masts with sails that were removed before battle.

The trireme used two primary offensive tactics: sailing through or between enemy ships (*diekplous*) and sailing around them (*periplous*). The purpose of both movements was to ram an individual enemy ship, often in the stern, or to shear off its oars. Such tactics required training and expertise, and if executed improperly could fail to incapacitate the enemy ship or result in getting dangerously entangled with it. Additionally, marines, archers, and javelin throwers on deck used their weapons against

---

30. The evidence on the Carthaginian army is fuller for later periods than for Dionysius' era, but may be applied to it. The Carthaginian army: Ameling 1993, esp. 67–118, 155–182; Lazenby 1998a, 6–8; Koon 2011, esp. 79–80.

FIGURE 4 *The Athenian trireme.* The *Olympia*, a twentieth-century reconstruction of an Athenian trireme.

© *The Trireme Trust*

the unprotected enemy rowers or boarded the enemy ship to eliminate them.[31]

The Athenian and other Greek navies used also *penteconters* (fifty-oared ships), rowed by twenty-five men on each side. Yet the trireme was the warship preferred by Greeks, Persians, and Carthaginians alike. The main difference between the Greek ships and their Phoenician counterparts, which composed a significant part of the Persian navy, was that the latter were taller, lighter, and had bulwarks, a difference that played a part in their defeat by the Greeks at Salamis. Dionysius of Syracuse used triremes, too, but he added new types of ships, the "four" and the "five."[32]

These descriptions of Greek and non-Greek armies and navies, far from exhaustive as they are, should be sufficient to acquaint readers with the military and cultural realities that framed the performance of our eight Greek generals.

31. The Athenian trireme: Wallinga 1993; Morrison, Coates, and Rankov 2000.
32. Carthaginian navy: Lancel 1995, 125–131; and see note 30 above. Persian navy: Wallinga 2005, esp. 32–46, 94–107; and see Ch. 2 on the battles of Artemisium and Salamis. Dionysius' ships: pp. 244–245 below.

| Leonidas of Sparta
The Lion at the Gates

Leonidas' Sparta and His Military Challenges

The reign of the Spartan king Leonidas (I), son of Anaxandridas, was relatively short, about ten years long (490/89–480). Nevertheless, he was arguably the most famous of all Spartans because he represented his countrymen's heroism in the battle of Thermopylae against the invading Persian army. His role and death there overshadowed everything else in his career, with the result that we have little information about his earlier life.

Leonidas was born probably around 540 to King Anaxandridas of the Agiad house. (Sparta had a dual kingship from two royal families, the Agiads and the Europontids.) He succeeded his half-brother, Cleomenes I, who was one of Sparta's more formidable kings. Cleomenes made numerous enemies, both at home and abroad, and they often paid a heavy price for opposing him. Leonidas, however, appeared to be spared Cleomenes' animosity, and even married his only child, Gorgo, thereby strengthening his claim to the throne and to Cleomenes' inheritance.[1]

The reconstruction of the history of Leonidas is challenged by the ancient evidence about him that is not always relaible.[2] It is further complicated by

1. For the chronology followed here, see Lazenby 1993; Cartledge 2006. Leonidas' birth and marriage: Hdt. 5.41, 7.239. Leonidas and the battle of Thermopylae: e.g., Lazenby 1993, 117–114; Hammond 1996; de Souza 2003; Holland 2005, 260–306; Cartledge 2006; Fields 2007; Matthew and Trundle 2013; cf. Whatley 1964.
2. The chief source is Herodotus. See Bibliography, "The Main Ancient Sources," under "Herodotus," "Diodorus," "Justin," and "Plutarch." The non-Herodotean sources on the Persian War: Flower and Marincola 2002, 31–35.

ancient accounts of his native land during his lifetime or earlier. Although Sparta had its critics, ancient works more commonly praise it, resulting in what modern historians call the "Spartan mirage": an idealized image of Spartan people and practices that still captivates modern readers. It depicts a society of equals, or "similar ones" (*homoioi*), who were fiercely loyal to the state and its way of life, ranking them above family and even their own lives. Both Spartans and non-Spartans believed that Spartans excelled all other Greeks in government, customs, and especially martial prowess and courage. Leonidas' last stand at Thermopylae against an overwhelmingly larger force made an invaluable contribution to the image of Spartans as honorable men who preferred to die rather than surrender. Scholars have long shown the disparity between Spartan ideology and the messy reality of a less-than-egalitarian society of citizens who did not always live up to the martial and societal standards expected of them. Nevertheless, the power that Spartan ideals and legacies exerted on both countrymen and outsiders was real enough.[3]

In spite of our deficient sources, it can be said that the Sparta of Leonidas' time was a militaristic, somewhat-xenophobic state that demanded strict obedience and discipline of its citizens. To a large extent, the Spartans' subjugation of the non-Spartan population in the southern Peloponnese contributed to this character (Map 2, below). These formerly independent people, largely Messenians, were given the status of helots ("captives"), a position somewhere between those of slaves and of serfs. The helots tilled lands that now belonged to their Spartan landlords, and shared their crops with them. The Spartans were a minority, and their need to control the far more numerous helots, along with their fear of insurrections from within and inimical neighbors from without, accounted for their cultivation of communal solidarity and their wish to maintain military supremacy. Conversely, the helots' labor and production allowed the Spartan men to dedicate much of their time to military training and activities, resulting in what may be called the only professional army (apart from mercenaries) in fifth-century Greece.[4]

The foregoing survey is designed to provide the necessary background to the nature of Leonidas' generalship and the tasks he faced. His greatest challenge was fighting a Persian army that was much larger than his own. This

---

3. Recent works on Sparta and its image: Flower 2002; Cartledge 2004; Whitby 2002; Hodkinson 2009; Kennell 2010.
4. Helots: Ducat 1990; Luraghi and Alcock 2003; Luraghi 2008.

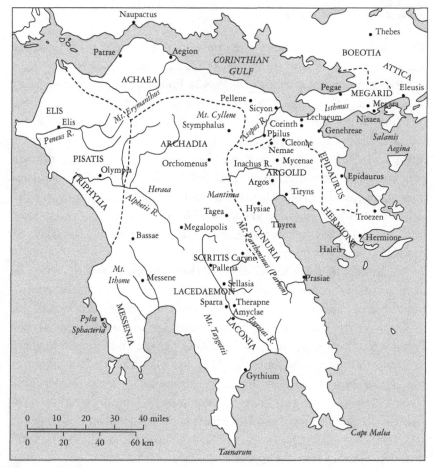

MAP 2 The Peloponnese.

difficulty was recognized even before he got to the pass of Thermopylae, when he had to convince the Spartans and others that defending it with the available force was a viable plan. He then had to reconcile conflicting agendas among his allied contingents and establish their trust in him. He also had to deal with their fear of the enemy and to organize an effective defense of his post and a successful use of his hoplites. When threatened by the Persians from the front and the rear, he was confronted with the dilemma of how to deal with allies who were reluctant to stay, and with how to resist the enemy in spite of the impossible odds. As we shall see, Spartan culture, political and tactical considerations, leadership skills, and his own personality all contributed to the way that Leonidas met these and similar challenges.

The Threat of War

The conflict between the Greeks and the Persians, in which Leonidas played his celebrated role, began in 500, when Greek cities in the eastern Aegean and Asia Minor rebelled against the Persian Empire in what is known as the Ionian Revolt (500–493). The revolt failed, and the Persians reestablished their rule in the region, even extending it to islands in the Aegean and to northern Greece. Sparta, led by Cleomenes I, kept itself out of the conflict, but around 492–491, when the Persian king's ambassadors asked for symbols of submission, the Spartans famously killed them in violation of religious and diplomatic custom. (The Athenians treated the envoys sent to them similarly.) It was a loud proclamation of independence and an anti-Persian stand from a state that was the most powerful in Greece and therefore had no reason to welcome a greater power.[5]

We hear nothing about Leonidas until the eve of the great Persian War. Its main historian, Herodotus, however, recounts a story of questionable authenticity about Leonidas' wife, Gorgo. It tells that she was the only person able to decipher a secret message sent by the exiled Spartan king Demaratus from Persia about Xerxes' preparations to invade Greece. The Spartans hastened to inform the other Greeks about it. They also consulted the Delphic oracle, which gave them the horrible answer that they would lose either their country or their king in the war. The oracle that foretold Leonidas' death, and the positive portrayal of Gorgo and Demaratus (although Herodotus is uncertain about his goodwill), suggest attempts by the Spartans and others to shape historical memory after the event. In addition, Herodotus is unclear about the chronology of the Spartans' consultation of Delphi, which he dates to the beginning of the war (480) but also connects with Xerxes' earlier preparations, which lasted a few years.[6]

It was Xerxes, in any case, who left the Spartans no option but to go to war (Map 3 below). He did not even ask them or Athens to give him earth and water as tokens of submission, as he did with other Greeks. Moreover,

---

5. The Ionian revolt and Sparta under Cleomenes: Georges 2000; de Ste. Croix 2004. The treatment of Persian envoys: Hdt. 7.133.
6. Sparta, Demaratus, Gorgo, and the oracle: 7.220, 239; Justin 2.10.12–17 (mistaking Gorgo for Leonidas' sister), and 2.11.8–9; Cawkwell 2005, 89. The oracle as an *ex eventu* tale: Hignett 1963, 125, 371; Fontenrose 1978, 77–77. In favor of its authenticity: Green 1996, 67–68; Hammond 1996, 6–7; Pomeroy 2002, 8, 146; Cartledge 2006, 127–128. Xerxes' preparations: 7.20, with Lazenby 1993, 97; Wallinga 2005, 22–26.

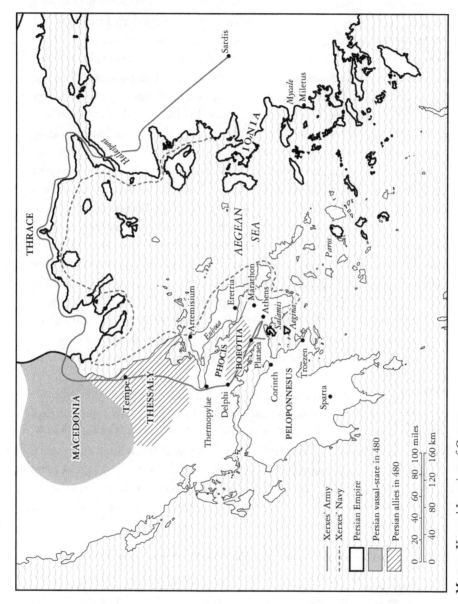

MAP 3 Xerxes' Invasion of Greece.

the presence in his court of the disgraced and exiled Spartan king Demaratus portended ill for Leonidas' co-king Leotychidas, who was Demaratus' enemy, and even for Leonidas himself.[7]

The arrival of Xerxes and his army at Sardis in Asia Minor in 481 moved the Greeks intending to oppose him to form what modern historians call the Hellenic (Greek) League. Their representatives met in a council on the Isthmus of Corinth, probably in the autumn and in the temple of Poseidon. The identity of the Spartan delegates is unknown, but they probably did not include Leonidas, because the Spartan kings did not normally go on diplomatic missions of that sort. The council made several operational and strategic decisions, of which the most pertinent to Leonidas' story was to appoint Sparta the leader of the war on land and sea. The Greeks also sent envoys to persuade uncommitted but potentially useful Greek states to join their alliance.[8] But the attempts to expand the anti-Persian front failed. According to Herodotus, both Argos and Syracuse, who were requested to join the Greek coalition, would agree only on condition that Sparta share or concede its leadership, a condition the Spartans firmly rejected. Their reaction went beyond considerations of power and prestige. It meant that they knowingly and courageously put themselves at the top of the Persian king's enemy list. As the leader of the coalition forces, Leonidas stood there, too, since throughout the war, his co-king, Leotychidas, got military commands of lesser honor and significance. Xerxes showed the personal cost of such a position when he mutilated Leonidas' dead body after the battle of Thermopylae.[9]

Among the decisions that the Hellenic Council made was to send spies to Sardis to collect information on the invading army. It is reported that the spies were captured, and that the Persian king, out of self-confidence, but also in order to use the size of his army as a psychological weapon, showed his forces to them before sending them back to tell the tale. We are not told what effect his ploy had on the Greeks, although they were fully aware of the Persians' numerical superiority. Modern scholars still

---

7. Demaratus' conflicts at home and exile: 6.61–71. Xerxes' request for submission: 7.32, 133.
8. For these and other decisions, see 7.132.1-2145.1–2, 149, 150–162, 172.1; Diod. 11.3.3, and see also p. 65 below. Date of the meeting: Lazenby 1993, 104; Cartledge 2006, 99. Its location: Macan 1908, 2:219; Hignett 1963, 98n1; Cartledge 2006, 99–102. Hellenic League: Brunt 1953–1954.
9. Spartans' insistence on leading: see the previous note, and Diod. 11.3.4–5. Leotychidas' inferior status: Lewis 1977, 45–46. Xerxes and Leonidas' body: 7.238, and p. 52 below.

struggle to assess the size of the Persian force. The sources are murky, for the ancients had difficulty estimating the size of large groups reliably, and tended to inflate or deflate the numbers of the warring parties in order to either glorify the victor or explain defeat. Herodotus' figures for the Persian forces are too high: 1,700,000 for the land army before it reached Europe, and over 5,283,000 with additional European troops, as well as 1,207 battleships. Many historians cut the numbers down to around 100,000 infantry and 600 ships, which still make it the largest force ever to come to Greece. The Greeks, if we accept Herodotus' figures, marshaled 38,700 hoplites and about 70,000 light troops at the last land battle of the war at Plataea in 479, and 366–378 battleships at the Battle of Salamis in 480.[10]

Numbers, of course, can be a crude index of strength, especially since both armies included many more light-armed than heavy infantry. Nevertheless, the size of the enemy force is said to have played a role in the first and failed Greek attempt to stop Xerxes. The northern Greek region of Thessaly was dominated by rival ruling families, and one of them, the Aleuadae of Larissa, was actively pro-Persian. Their opponents appealed to the Greeks to save Thessaly for the alliance, and their timing after the recent failure to enlist more Greeks to the cause could not have been better. An expeditionary force of 10,000 hoplites arrived at the pass of Tempe on the road from Macedonia to Thessaly in the hope that it could check Xerxes' advance (Map 3). Shortly afterwards, however, the Greeks decided to return to the Isthmus of Corinth without waiting for the Persians, who were still in Asia. The reasons for the retreat cannot be safely ascertained, but lack of confidence in the loyalty of local Thessalians and the fear of being trapped in Tempe must have played a role. More relevant to our subject is the identity of the leaders who made the decision to leave. Unlike the Athenians, who sent to Tempe their arguably most prominent politician and general, Themistocles (Ch. 2), the Spartans were commanded

10. Greek spies: 7.146–147. Problems of ancient estimates: Rubicam 2003. Persian infantry: 7.60.1, 186; Diod. 11.3.7, 5.2; and Justin 2.10.18 (1,000,000); Ctesias *FGrHist* 688 F 13.27 (800,000); cf. Isocrates 6.100, 12.49 (700,000). Herodotus also mentions (questionably) 80,000 cavalry including an élite unite of 1,000: 7.41, 87.1. Persian navy: 7.89.1; Aeschylus *Persians* 341–343; cf. Diod. 11.2.1, and Lysias 2.27 (1,200 ships); Isocrates 4.93 (2,000); Ctesias *FGrHist* 688 F 13.27 (1,000). Modern estimates: Grundy 1901, 222; Hignett 1963, 345–355; Cawkwell 2005, 243–252; Cartledge 2006, 109–118; cf. Burn 1962, 322–332; Green 1996, 60–62 (c. 1,200 military and non-military vessels). Plataea: 9.28–30; Hignett 1963, 435–438. For the Battle of Salamis, see the next chapter. Manipulating numbers: Flower and Marincola 2002, 192.

by the otherwise-unknown Euaenetus, a *polemarch* or officer of the rank that in later times allowed its holder to command a *mora*, one-sixth of the Spartan infantry. Even if the nature of this command changed after the Persian War, Euaenetus was clearly inferior in rank and prestige to Leonidas, the commander of the Spartan army, of the Peloponnesian League, and indeed of the entire Greek army. Rightly or wrongly, the Spartans seemed to view the Tempe expedition as affecting the Thessalians more than other Greeks including the the Spartans, and spared their king for missions they deemed more important.[11]

Preliminaries to the Battle of Thermopylae

In actuality, the retreat from Tempe worsened the Greeks' situation because it conceded northern and part of central Greece to the enemy. Two major city-states, Thebes and Athens, were now on Xerxes' marching route, and, unlike Thessaly, they were too important for the Greeks to sacrifice. The Greek council at the Isthmus decided to meet Xerxes on land at Thermopylae and at sea at Artemisium in Euboea, keeping the Greek navy and army in touch with each other, because the victory or defeat of one would affect the fortunes of the other.[12] We shall focus on the preparations for the stand at Thermopylae and the battle there in full awareness that the extant ancient accounts were written without the benefit of eyewitness testimonies and after considerable passage of time, and that they were dominated by the mythology of Leonidas' and the Spartans' heroism.

Leonidas was appointed to command the forces at Thermopylae, and his first task appears to have been persuading other Greeks and even his countrymen to agree on the mission. It was not an easy task, because there appeared to be opposition or alternative plans to it. Indeed, when Herodotus says that the proposal to guard Thermopylae "won" in the deliberations of the Greek council, he suggests that its members were not of one mind about it. Those most likely to oppose or question the plan were the Peloponnesian states,

---

11. The Tempe campaign: 7.172–175; Diod. 11. 2.5–6; Plut. *Themistocles* 7; Westlake 1936, 16–19; Hignett 1963, 102–104; Robertson 1976; Lazenby 1993, 109–114; Green 1996, 84–87; Blösel 2004, 108–120; Strauss 2004, 14–15. The Spartan *polemarchos*: Lazenby 1985, 5, 6, 10, 84. Diod. 11.2.5 calls him "Synetus." See the next chapter (2) for Themistocles in Tempe, and p. 284 below, for the Spartan *mora*.

12. Communication between Thermopylae and Artemisium: 7.175.

and possibly some Spartans. Not long afterwards, when the Greek force was already at Thermopylae, Leonidas' Peloponnesian troops suggested retreating and protecting the Isthmus of Corinth instead. The Peloponnesians had in mind a defense line not unlike the one at Thermopylae and Artemisium, with the Greeks waiting for the Persian army behind an Isthmian wall while the Greek ships awaited Xerxes' navy on the water. That the idea of an Isthmian wall was already current is suggested by the swift commencement of its building shortly after Thermopylae.[13] I am well aware that Herodotus was convinced by the Athenian argument that the Isthmian defense was a bad idea militarily and morally. He presents it as motivated by fear and as a betrayal of Greece and especially of Athens. The plan was also ineffective, he thought, because the Persians would have used their naval supremacy to land behind the defenders of the wall, detach Peloponnesians from the coalition, and eventually force the Spartans to die nobly or surrender. The clear message is that the true, unselfish savior of Greece was Athens, not Sparta. Yet the Peloponnesian scheme was neither narrow-minded nor egoistic; Herodotus himself admits that it was motivated by concerns for the whole of Greece, and even regards Peloponnesians who did not participate in the building of the wall as traitors.[14] More important, the plan was in tune with the Spartan strategic vision.

Unlike the Athenians, the Spartans did not seek so much to defeat the Persians as to frustrate their advance and make them realize that the invasion had failed and would be better called off. This outlook can be discerned at Tempe and Thermopylae, and it lies behind the Isthmian wall project. Even the many apocryphal stories about Leonidas and the Spartans who went knowingly to their death show them thinking in terms of obstructing the enemy. In contrast, the Athenians, both during and after the war, thought that they should defeat and destroy the Persians. Although the Spartans changed their mind in 479 in favor of deciding the war with the battle of Plataea, they would revert later to a more defensive mode and leave to the Athenians the campaign against the Persians in the Aegean and beyond.[15]

13. The council's deliberations: 7.175. Retreat to the Peloponnese: 7.207, 8.71; Lazenby 1993, 137, as well as the next note and below. Questionable Spartan wish to retreat from Artemisium: Plut. *Themistocles* 7; cf. 8.4, and my next chapter.
14. The Isthmian wall: 7.139, and 8.40, 49, 56, 60, 71–74, 79, and 9.7–9; cf. Bowie 2006. Thuc. 1.73.1–74.4 suggests the Athenian origins of the claim that the Spartan strategy was selfish.
15. For the following, see also Evans 1964; Evans 1969, 393–394.

Leonidas appeared to support the Spartans' limited objective, but unlike the Peloponnesians, he believed it could be achieved in central Greece. Therefore he had to win them and the Spartans over to his way of thinking. He was successful, thanks to his royal authority and to his plan that initially called for a relatively small Spartan force to be sent to Thermopylae (before a larger army arrived there). The core of the army he took with him was made up of 300 citizens, whom he picked personally and who were fathers of sons. The group was modeled after, though not identical with, an élite Spartan infantry unit called "cavalrymen" (*hippeis*), which also numbered 300 and served as the king's bodyguard, among other functions.[16] Herodotus provides no reason for the choice of hoplite-fathers because it was obvious to him and to the other sources that the Spartans who went to Thermopylae knew that they were about to die, and that Leonidas wanted to make sure that their family line was secure. The motive of self-sacrifice is corroborated by the Spartan glorification of "beautiful death" in battle for the sake of the *polis*, which the seventh-century Spartan "national" poet Tyrtaeus celebrated in his poems.[17]

> When this (courageous) man falls in the front ranks and loses the life dear to him, he brings glory to his city, his people, and his father, with many wounds to the front, through his chest, his bossed shield, and breastplate. Young and old alike grieve for him, and the whole city mourns, sorely missing him.

Yet death in battle and its valorization were not the only option in the Spartan military book. The same poem of Tyrtaeus that lauds fallen warriors also praises the living troops who return victorious from battle:

> And if he avoids the doom of death that lays a man out, and with victory has his prayer for glory in battle fulfilled, all men ... honor him.... As he ages he enjoys distinction among the people of his town.

Leonidas' picking of men whose progeny was assured did not mean that he and his recruits resolved to die, but only that they knew that they *might*

---

16. The 300 as an advance force: Hdt. 7.206. (7.205) actually says that Leonidas took the "usual" 300 *and* fathers of sons, but it makes sense to identify the 300 as fathers, too: 7.202; Macan 1908, 1: 307. The 300 and the "cavalrymen": Lazenby 1993, 135–136; Cartledge 2006, 129; Figueira 2006, 61–62.

17. Rationalizing Leonidas' choice: e.g., Green 1996, 111; Lazenby 1993, 136. Thermopylae as a doomed mission: esp. Cartledge 2006, 130–132. The following and the next quotation: Tyrtaeus F 12, Yardley trans. Spartan "beautiful death" and its later decline: Loraux 1995, 70–73; Piccirilli 1995.

die. They might also come back to Sparta triumphantly. The fact that the group of men he picked was relatively small in number and that they had already fulfilled their family and national duty to procreate also made it easier for him to "sell" his plan to the Spartan authorities and public. A similar reproductive expectation of women is reflected in an apocryphal saying attributed to Leonidas. When his wife, Gorgo, asked him for instructions before he marched to Thermopylae, he told her to marry good men and bear good children. Leonidas, in sum, knew how to persuade the Spartans to agree to his plan.[18]

Although Herodotus mentions just 300 recruits from Sparta, other sources report that they were joined by an additional 700 Lacedaemonian hoplites, probably *perioeci* (p. 18), and an uncertain number of helots. Leonidas also led Peloponnesian contingents that included 2,120 hoplites from different Arcadian communities—400 from Corinth, 200 from Phlius (Argolis), and eighty from Mycenae. A total force of 3,800 troops from the entire Peloponnese was modest by any measure, but it was meant to be augmented later by reinforcements from the Peloponnese and central Greece.[19]

A greater challenge awaited Leonidas in urging states around Thermopylae to help in its defense. The Persians' expected arrival there made the locals fearful, and they were strongly influenced by the neighboring Thessalians, who supported the enemy. He was successful, especially in Locris and Phocis, mostly because, as a Spartan king, he was living proof of his polis' commitment to fight the Persians. Helpful, too, were the Greek coalition's promises to these states that the Greek navy destined for Euboea would protect them, and that more troops were coming. The result was that Leonidas augmented his force by adding to it 700 Thespians, 1,000 Locrians, 1,000 Malians, and c. 1,000 Phocians. For some of these states, the contribution constituted the bulk of their armies.[20] Of special note was an additional contingent of 400

18. Leonidas and Gorgo: Plut. *Moralia* 225a. Hindsight lies behind other traditions about Leonidas and his troops and their departure from Sparta: Diod. 11.4.2–4; Plut. *Moralia* 866b; Green 2006, 55n27.

19. One thousand Lacedaemonians, who probably included the 300 Spartans: Diod. 11.4.2, 5; Isocrates 4.90, 6.99; with Flower 1998, 367–368. Helots in the Spartan army: Hunt 2006. Peloponnesian allies: Hdt. 7.202, 205; followed by Pausanias 10.20.2. Expected reinforcements: Hdt. 7.206, and below; cf. Lysias 2.31. 7.228 and Diod. 11.4.5–6 mention 4,000 troops under Leonidas' command. The conclusion reached here is an attempt at a compromise among the varying sources.

20. The Greeks' promise to Locris and Phocis: Hdt. 7.203, 205; Diod. 11.4.6. The contingents from central Greece: Hdt. 7.202–203; Diod. 11.4.7; Pausanias 10.20.2 (who guesses around 6,000 Locrians); and see below.

Thebans. Herodotus depicts them as partly hostages and partly bound to be traitors, probably because Thebes turned out to be the most notorious collaborator with the Persians after the Greek defeat at Thermopylae. The later author Plutarch, who came to the defense of his fellow Boeotians, charged Herodotus with personal animosity against Thebes and with distorting its history, even calling the Theban warriors at Thermopylae Leonidas' "friends." By all appearances, the Theban unit was at the center of a feud over their city's image, with detractors, mainly from Athens, besmirching it, and others, even before Plutarch, defending it. Closer to the pro-Theban position is a (probably invented) tale about Leonidas' visit to Thebes on his way to Thermopylae. The king was accorded the exceptional privilege of sleeping in Heracles' temple, where dreams had a prophetic quality, and where he dreamt about the future rise and fall of Thebes, probably in the fourth century. Admittedly, 400 warriors were just a fraction of the Theban army, but the fact that they stayed with Leonidas until the last day of fighting, and even after other Greeks left him, suggests that Plutarch was closer to the truth than Herodotus in characterizing them as loyal to the Greek cause. Indeed, one source says that Thebes was then split between pro- and anti-Persian factions and that the Thebans who went with Leonidas belonged presumably to the latter faction.[21] The king's success in obtaining Theban troops thus illustrates his ability to negotiate among, or impose his will on, conflicting sides and interests. He would soon deal with similarly opposing wishes when he decided to stay at Thermopylae against the opinion of his Peloponnesian allies and in support of Phocis and Locris.

Leonidas in Thermopylae

According to our sources, then, Leonidas took around 8,100 troops to Thermopylae, a sizable force in Greek terms, but comparatively small enough to raise the question of how he, or the Greek coalition, thought it could withstand the onslaught of the much larger Persian army.[22]

21. Four hundred Thebans and their depiction: Hdt. 7.202, 205, 222, 233; Diod. 11.4.7, and see Hammond 1996, 16, but also Hignett 1963, 371; Green 1996, 140; Keaveney 1996, 42–43. Plutarch on Herodotus: Plut. *Moralia* 864d–867c. Leonidas' dream: Plut. *Moralia* 865f. Divided Thebes: Diod. 11.4.7. Thebes in the Persian War: Demand 1982, 20–27.

22. Notes 19–21 above. Herodotus' figures for Leonidas' army add up to a total of 5,200 troops in addition to an unspecified number of Locrians. Diodorus' figures add up to 7,400 troops, including 1,000 Locrians, but he omits Herodotus' 700 Thespians.

Herodotus, who gives Xerxes at Thermopylae an impossibly large army of 5,283,220, was well aware of the disparity, which probably moved him to elaborate on the rationale of defending Thermopylae. He describes the topographical features of the place (on which, see pp. 38–39 below), which undermined the enemy's superiority in numbers and cavalry. He also mentions Thermopylae's proximity to the Greek warring states, the accessible local provisions, and the Greeks' ignorance at that time of a path that would allow the pass to be outflanked. To all of this should be added Herodotus' assertions that Leonidas' army was supposed to be only an advance force, and that additional Spartan and Peloponnesian reinforcements were expected to arrive in its support. They were delayed, however, by the need to celebrate local festivals, and then forestalled by Xerxes' quick victory. Leonidas' force was small, then, because it was believed that, together with local troops, it would be sufficient to hold the enemy off until reinforcements arrived.[23]

This premise had to be modified upon Leonidas' arrival at Thermopylae, where he found out about a path called Anopaea that offered a way for the enemy to outflank his position from the rear. We are told that a force of 1,000 Phocians volunteered to guard the path. One wonders how much choice Leonidas had in giving this assignment to them and not to other contingents, because the Phocians were intent on defending not only him but also, and even more urgently, their country. The two purposes may not have been compatible, as suggested by the Phocians' later abandoning of the path for a better defensive position when under attack, and by their not joining Leonidas even after the Persians moved away from them (pp. 43–44 below).[24] Their guard duty also depleted Leonidas' army at Thermopylae, an effect that, together with seeing the mighty Persian army at close range for the first time, put fear in the hearts of his allies. It was not without reason that

Pausanias (10.20.2) reproduces Herodotus' figures and adds the unlikely estimate that Leonidas also got c. 6,000 Locrians. The total of 8,100 troops reached here is the sum of Diodorus' figures plus the 700 Thespians whom he mentions later, not giving their number: 11.9.2. For different estimates of the number of Leonidas' troops: e.g., Hignett 1963, 117–119; Lazenby 1993, 134–135; Mathew 2013, 65–71. Herodotus on the size of the Persian army: 7.186.

23. Expected reinforcements: Hdt. 7.206. Scholarly doubts about their historicity and the reasons of their failure to arrive are unjustified: see Macan 1908, 1:309b, 2:269; Hignett 1963, 121–127; Cartledge 2006, 126–128. On the adequacy of Leonidas' force: e.g., Hammond 1996, 16; McInerney 1999, 333–339; Matthew 2013 (who adds the naval forces at Artemisium to his defense).

24. The Phocians' conduct at this point and later: Hdt. 8.30–32; 9.31; McInerney 1999, 154–185.

the Peloponnesian contingents now proposed a return to the Isthmus (p. 33 above). Leonidas decided against them, and so mollified the local Locrians and Phocians, who justifiably felt betrayed. His decision demonstrated his ability to exert authority over the reluctant Peloponnesian troops, but it also reflected his dependence on the local Greeks, making him the first general in this book whose military planning, and even success and failure, were related to his cooperation with allies. Leonidas also tried to correct his deficiency in numbers by sending messengers around to request reinforcements. At this juncture, the Spartan king had to worry about the enemy and his own army, which was too small and included units with conflicting agendas and low morale.[25]

Leonidas also faced the challenge of organizing the defense of the pass of Thermopylae, for which he used topography and a wall to counter the enemy's advantage in size and mobility. Roughly speaking, the site was bounded by the sea and the mountains, and the pass was no wider than around 15 meters, and even narrower in places. Reconstructing the features of ancient Thermopylae is complicated by great changes to the coastline since antiquity; the Malian Gulf has receded, and the plain between it and the mountain has grown from silting. Herodotus, who visited the site, provides a useful account of the pass as it then appeared:

> As for the pass through Trachis, it is, at its narrowest point, only half a plethron [ca. 15 meters] wide. In actual fact, though, this is not the narrowest part of the region thereabouts; both before and after Thermopylae the pass narrows even further, until at Alpeni, which is after Thermopylae, it is no more than a cart-track, and before it, at the Phoenix River near the town of Anthelia, it becomes a mere cart-track again. The western part of Thermopylae is a tall, sheer, inaccessible cliff which stretches away to Mount Oeta, while to the east of the road there is only marshland and the sea. In this pass there are warm bathing-pools, which the local inhabitants call "Pots," and the altar to Heracles is located there. There was once a wall built across the pass, with a gate added a long time ago.[26]

Although Herodotus' direction is wrong—the pass runs from east to west and not from north to south—modern inspections of the site

---

25. Leonidas and the local Greeks: Hdt. 7.212–218; Hignett 1963, 119; Cartledge 2006, 139; cf. Cawkwell 2005, 93–96, 118n19, who disputes the Greeks' dismay.
26. Herodotus on Thermopylae: 7.176, Waterfield translation; cf. 7.198–199.

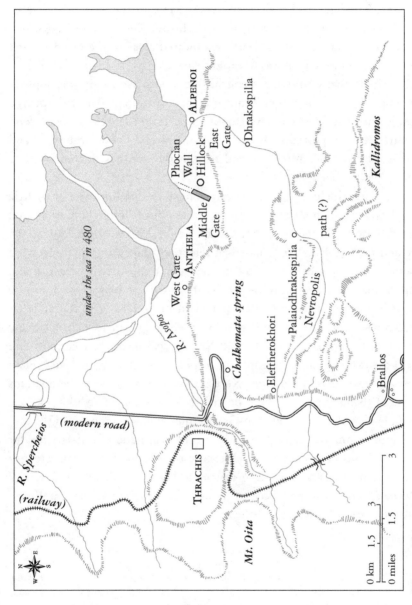

MAP 4 Thermopylae.

have given no reason to doubt his accuracy. Historians, and especially G. B. Grundy, usefully note the West, Middle (mentioned by Herodotus), and East Gates in the wall that had been built by the Phocians (Map 4). They fell into disrepair before Leonidas' arrival and were restored by his men. The hot springs that gave their name to the pass, *Thermopylae*, or "Hot Gates," played no role in the fighting. The little hill on which the last defenders met their death was located close to the Middle Gate. Generally, Leonidas' plan was to exploit the narrow terrain in order to neutralize the Persians' superior strength. But he also had to give his hoplites some open space where they could use their advantage over the enemy's lighter-armed and less cohesive troops and execute, as we shall see, a false retreat. He thus posted men both in front of and behind the wall, and instructed those manning the wall to join the hoplites in front to help them repel the enemy.[27]

Herodotus includes in his description of the preliminaries to battle an episode that, intentionally or not, evokes the tale of the Greek spies captured by the Persians at Sardis. To recall, Xerxes showed them the size and might of his army and then sent them home to report. Now, at Thermopylae, he sent a scout to find out about the Greeks' strength and dispositions. It happened to be the Spartans' turn to be stationed outside the wall, and the Persian scout watched them exercising in the nude (as Greeks were wont to do) and combing their long hair (which not many other Greeks sported). When he told Xerxes what he saw, the curious king asked the exiled King Demaratus, his expert on things Spartan, to explain their behavior. Demaratus told Xerxes that it was the way the Spartans prepared themselves to kill and be killed. Xerxes was incredulous, as one might expect of a barbarian (non-Greek) ruler who was ignorant of the idea of gaining immortality through a beautiful death and of self-sacrifice for freedom. Thus both tales about observing the enemy pit Persian strength in size against Spartan strength in spirit. The story about the Spartans' readiness to die is suspect because it anticipates their fate, but it well prepares the reader for what comes next.[28]

---

27. The battle site: Grundy 1901, 277–291, followed by Hignett 1963, 127–131; Rapp 2013. Against the view of Szemler, Cherf, and Craft 1996 that the fighting actually took place at the Dhema pass leading to Phocis, see Lazenby 1998b; Cawkwell 2005, 273–276.
28. Hdt. 7.208–209; cf. 7.102–104, with Dillery 1996, 238–239. Diodorus' report of the Spartans' rejection of Xerxes' offer to let them surrender their arms and leave Thermopylae does not inspire confidence: 11.5.4–6.2; cf. Plut. *Moral.* 225d.

Xerxes waited four days before launching his attack. Herodotus is probably right in assuming that the king delayed because he expected the Greeks to flee. After all, before reaching Thermopylae, he had encountered no armed resistance, and he had used the size of his army as an effective psychological weapon before. On the fifth day, allegedly in a frustrated rage, Xerxes sent his troops against the defenders of the pass in three waves of attack. First came the Medians from Iran, and when they failed, Xerxes sent in the Cissians of Susiana and possibly the Scythian Sacae, too. The Medians and the Cissians were ranked below the Persians in national prestige and probably in military quality, but except for the Cissian headdress, they resembled the Persians in armor (for which, see pp. 20–21 above). The Sacae were Scythian people from central Asia armed with Scythian bows, daggers, and battle-axes. When these attacks failed, Xerxes threw in what he thought was his ace card: the Ten Thousand Immortals (p. 21 above). These were a select Persian unit, and each of them was allegedly eager to face three Greeks in battle. As it happened, there were not enough Greeks to accommodate their wish—which was not the reason they also retreated. The Persians also changed the formation of the attacking units in a failed attempt to meet the unique circumstances of the battle. The sources tell us, however, that the Greeks were able to repel and inflict losses on the enemy thanks to the narrow confines of the battlefield and their larger arms and closed-ranks fighting that gave them better cover.[29]

It is worth remembering that many ancient historians tended to attribute victory more to moral superiority, including martial spirit, than to technology. Nevertheless, historian Diodorus notes the Persian disadvantage due to their lighter arms, and Herodotus mentions that their spears were shorter than the Greeks' and opines elsewhere that the Greeks won because of their heavier weapons and better protection. Indeed, fighting in a phalanx or individually, the Greeks could inflict greater harm on the enemy than the enemy could on them. Their discipline and cohesiveness gave them an offensive and defensive advantage over looser formations. Their shields were bigger and more durable than the Persian wicker or hardened-leather shields, and their primary offensive weapon, a c. 2–2.5-meter spear, could reach an opponent earlier than Persian arms. Their tactics were effective, too. The men

29. Diod. 11.7.3; cf. Polyaenus 1.32.1. Xerxes' pre-battle expectations: Hdt. 7.210. Persians, Medians, Cissians, and Sacae: 7.61–62, 64, 83; Diod. 11.6.3–7.4. See also Ctesias *FGrHist* 688 F 13.27, who confuses the name of the Persian general. There was a storm in the region (Hdt. 7.188; 8.13-14), but the tale that the Persians were defeated because they were scared by it (Polyaenus 1.32.2) is supported by no other source.

who bore the brunt of the fighting were rotated among different divisions to avoid exhaustion. At one point, the Spartans feigned a retreat, encouraging the enemy to pursue them in a disorderly fashion only to be slaughtered when the Spartans turned around to meet them. Leonidas, who must have coordinated the rotation and the false retreat, thus showed that he was capable of both leading and directing the battle and that he had more than a death wish on his mind. The result was that many more enemy fighters died than Greeks.[30]

The sources do not report, however, how the Greeks defended themselves against the Persians' primary weapon of bows and arrows. An anecdotal tale recounts that when someone claimed the Persians had so many arrows that they hid the sun, the Spartan Dieneces, said to be the bravest of them all, retorted: "We shall have our battle in the shade." Although the fighting took place during the hot month of August, when shade would have been much appreciated, the story is *ben trovato*, if only because it suggests that the Greeks simply ignored the danger. It has been speculated that the Spartans dealt with the archers by tempting the Persians to attack them at close range, where they could be easily defeated, or by the aforementioned fake retreat. It has also been suggested that the Spartans attacked the archers with their front ranks, who then rejoined the phalanx. No less likely, however, is the possibility that Leonidas, whose Greek army included light-armed troops, especially from Locris and Malis, and probably helots, used them against their Persian counterparts. That they are not mentioned in the battle narratives is hardly surprising: our sources allow the Spartans to hog the limelight, and ancient writers often overlooked the contribution of light infantry in combat.[31]

The second day of fighting produced identical results, although Xerxes sent in picked units, motivating them with promises of rewards and punishments, and then prevented them by force from leaving the battlefield. The sources describe a Persian king who jumped three times

30. Hoplite weapons: p. 14 above. Greek advantage in weapons: Hdt. 5.49; 7.211; 9.62–63; Diod. 11.7.3; cf. Aeschylus *Persians* 239–242. Weapon technology and victory: Rey 2010, 25–26. Rotation: Hdt. 7.212. Diodorus 11.8.2 distinguishes the Spartans for *not* rotating their front ranks. Feigned retreat: Hdt. 7.211, and possibly Plato *Laches* 191c, if the speaker misattributed the tactics to the battle of Plataea: Lazenby 1993, 250.
31. Fighting in the shade: Hdt. 7.226; Plut. *Moralia* 225b, who attributes the saying to Leonidas. Persian bows: Dandamaev and Lukonin 1989, 225–226. Spartan tactics against arrows: Grundy 1901, 297; Lazenby 1993, 138; Ray 2009, 73–74.

off his throne in alarm about his troops on the first day, and was at a loss for what to do on the second day. Although Xerxes' despair may have been exaggerated for dramatic purposes, there is little doubt that what came next was a turning point for him and his opponents. The Greek Ephialtes of Malis offered Xerxes a way to victory and thereby put his name at the top of the Greeks' list of infamy.[32] Ephialtes offered to guide a force through the Anopaea path, which snaked around the pass of Thermopylae, first west and then south, and ended at the East Gate (Map 4 above). The existence of the path was no secret, at least to Xerxes' Thessalian allies, but whether or not Xerxes had heard of it before, he was ready to use it in order to outflank the enemy after two days of futile fighting. The mission was given to Hydarnes and "his command"; namely, the Immortals, although it is uncertain if the entire complement of 10,000 went with him.[33]

The Persians used the cover of night and of oak woods to hide their march from the defenders of Thermopylae and the Phocians, who guarded the path. By dawn, they reached a high point on the mountain where the Phocians were camped. According to Herodotus, both sides were taken by surprise. The Phocians found out about the Persians only when they heard the rustling of the marchers' feet on the ground covered with dry leaves, and barely had time to arm themselves. The Persians, for their part, did not expect to find enemy troops there, and when they did, Hydarnes thought that they were Spartans. Neither side had reason to be proud of its military intelligence. The Persians recovered first and showered arrows upon the Phocians, who fled to the top of the mountain, where they organized themselves for defense. With more than a touch of irony, Herodotus says that the Phocians fled because they thought they were the Persians' main targets, but that the Persians ignored them and hurried toward Thermopylae. By all signs, Leonidas did not hear about this encounter in "real time." It happened at dawn, and he learned only from his day watchers that the Persians had taken the path (see below). It is fair to assume that there

---

32. Second day of fighting, and Xerxes' reactions: Diod. 11.8.1–4; 7.212–213; cf. Justin 2.11.3. Ctesias, *FGrHist* 688 F 13.27, counts an improbable 50,000 Persian troops in the charge. The sources name other Greeks who offered Xerxes similar advice and guidance, but many agree with Herodotus, who insists that Ephialtes was the sole culprit: 7.213–214; Diod. 11.8.4; Ctesias *FGrHist* 688 F 13.27.

33. The Anopaea path: Hdt. 7.213–215, with Wallace 1980; Sánchez Moreno 2010: *The Leonidas Expedition*; Diod. 11.8.4; Pausanias 1.4.2, 10.2–8. Hydarnes' command: Hdt. 7.215. Diod. 11.8.5 and Justin 2.11.5 give him 20,000 troops, and Ctesias, *FGrHist* 688 F 13.27, 40,000, but neither version appears credible: Green 2006, 45–46.

was no Spartan liaison in the Phocian camp or effective communication between Leonidas and the Phocians to apprise him of the situation. By contrast, the Greeks pre-arranged communication between Thermopylae and Artemisium.[34]

Although Leonidas was ignorant of what happened on the path, he knew the Persians were there. Deserters came to him during the night, and day lookouts posted on the heights arrived at dawn to tell him the same bad news. It is at this point that the so-called puzzle of Thermopylae demands the most attention. We know that many Greek troops soon left the pass and that Leonidas remained there with the rest to defend it against all odds. What is unclear and greatly debated are the motives and reasoning of all actors involved, and even what happened after the Greeks' departure.

The sources differ on the details but agree that the Greeks met in council to discuss the question of whether to abandon Thermopylae or to stay and defend it.[35] They similarly agree that many left, but are unclear about the identity and number of those who remained with Leonidas. This uncertainty is unfortunate, because the size of the remaining force is relevant to the question of their reasons for staying. After the other Greeks' departure, according to Herodotus, Leonidas' force consisted of Spartans, Thespians, and Thebans, who originally and respectively numbered 300, 700, and 400 hoplites. To these should be added 700 Lacedaemonians, probably perioeci, whom Diodorus includes in the army that marched to Thermopylae. If we take into consideration the sources' report of only a few Greek casualties during the first two days of battle, we may conclude that Leonidas had at his disposal around 2,000 hoplites (in addition to lightly armed helots) after the other Greeks' departure. This was about a quarter of his original force, but it still gave him a better fighting chance than the ancient sources would allow him.[36]

The Greeks who left Thermopylae, then, consisted of Locrians, Malians, and Peloponnesians, and there are two rival traditions about the cause of their departure. The more common one is that Leonidas told

---

34. The attack on the Phocians and Leonidas' day watchers: Hdt. 7.217–219. Attack at dawn: Hdt. 7.217; Beloch 1914, II² 2:91–105. Communication between Thermopylae and Artemisium: Hdt. 8.21.

35. Greek informants: Hdt. 7.218–219; Diod. 11.8.5 (probably based on Ephorus: Burn 1962, 416–417). The time of the council's meeting: Hdt. 7.219 (dawn) and Diod. 11.9.1 (around midnight), and see Hignett 1963, 371–378. I follow Herodotus' version.

36. Number of soldiers who stayed with Leonidas: Hdt. 7.222 (1,400); Diod. 11.9.2 (over 500); Justin 2.11.5 (600). The last two authors depend on Ephorus' problematical version of events (below). Pausanias (10.20.2) adds the Mycenaeans, originally eighty in

them to leave, either because he wanted to spare their lives, perhaps so they could fight another battle, or because he knew that they lacked the courage and the sense of honor that staying at Thermopylae now entailed. Herodotus, however, mentions an additional, alternative version, which he rejects, and which suggests that those who didn't wish to stay left on their own.[37] Because both praise and blame were liberally attributed to the actors at Thermopylae after the event, we can only surmise what happened that fateful morning. But an assessment of the situation—not from the Spartan perspective that governs ancient and modern accounts, but from the allies' point of view—makes their leaving either independently of Leonidas' wishes or with his reluctant approval both possible and less reprehensible. We have already seen that not all Peloponnesians agreed about the benefit and wisdom of defending the pass, even before the battle. The local Greeks were in a much tighter spot because, unlike the Peloponnesians, they had no second line of defense. The Malians' land was already under Persian occupation, and the Locrians had every reason to assume that theirs would be occupied next if Thermopylae fell. In addition, the Persian outflanking maneuver meant that it would be hard, if not impossible, to replicate the success of the previous two days, because any sortie out of the wall would be exposed to attack from both front and rear. Finally, in an anecdote of questionable historicity, the Greeks heard from the reputable Acarnanian seer Megistias that the omens predicted they would meet death in the morning. Altogether, these dire prospects weakened the Greeks' resolve and their rationale for remaining with Leonidas.[38]

Herodotus refuses to believe that the allies left without Leonidas' permission and gives the example of the seer Megistias, whom Leonidas generously allowed to go home. The seer, however, sent back his son instead and stayed to die in battle. The anecdote probably comes from an assembly line of similar heroic stories about men who could have avoided the last stand at Thermopylae with Leonidas' permission, but did not. These

---

number, to his force. Four thousand dead were found on the site (including Thespians and helots): Hdt. 7.228; 8.25; Diod. 11.33.2. Few Greek casualties in the first two days: Hdt. 7.211–212; Diod. 11.7.4; Ctesias *FGrHist* 688 F 13.27. One thousand Lacedaemonian dead in Thermopylae: Isocrates 4.90; 6.99; cf. Diod. 11.4.2, 5. Flower 1998, 368, thinks, however, that Leonidas let the perioeci go.

37. Leonidas' dismissal of the allies: Hdt. 7.220–222; Diod. 11.9.1–3 (who has them leave at night); Justin 2.11.5–7. Their leaving on their own: Hdt. 7.219; Plut. *Moralia* 864e. See also Evans 1964, 237; Green 1996, 139–140.

38. Megistias' prophecy: Hdt. 7.210.

include Spartan seer Themisteas, whom Leonidas wished to spare by sending him home to deliver a message. Themisteas refused, saying: "I was sent out to fight, not to carry messages." Two other Spartans were discharged for health reasons, but one of them returned to die on the battlefield. Even if we accept the historicity of these tales, they involved individual discharges, not entire contingents, and in a way they disprove Herodotus' point, because they suggest that the Greeks who left could have disobeyed Leonidas' evacuation order without protest on his part. Finally, I am unfamiliar with any other example of Spartans, before or after Leonidas, who showed a similar consideration for non-Spartan contingents or nobly spared them the risk of dying in battle. Either the allies at Thermopylae took off without Leonidas' permission, or he gave them his blessing to save face. They must have departed early in the day and surely before the Persian force arrived from Anopaea.[39]

Arguably, a more intriguing question than the allies' reasons for leaving concerns the motives and the rationale of those who stayed. For the ancient sources, the answer was clear: the defenders were willing to die for home, Greek liberty, eternal glory, and, in the case of the Spartans, conformity with their ideals and norms of conduct. This Spartan motive is expressed by the famous epitaph on their burial ground at Thermopylae, written perhaps by the poet Simonides:

> Stranger, tell the people of Lacedaemon
> that we who lie here obeyed their commands.[40]

Elsewhere, Herodotus has the exiled king Demaratus articulating the Spartan military collective's ethos:

> The point is that although they're free, they're not entirely free: their master is the law, and they're far more afraid of this than your {i.e., Xerxes'} men are of you. At any rate, they do what the law commands, and its command never changes; it is that they should not turn tail in battle no matter how many men are ranged against them, but should maintain their positions and either win or die.[41]

---

39. Megistias: Hdt. 7.220–221, cf. 7.228; Plut. *Moralia* 866c. Themisteas: Plut. *Moralia* 221d; cf. 225e, 866b–c. Two ill Spartans: Hdt. 7.229–231, and below. Against the interpretation offered here, see, e.g., Hope Simpson 1972, 1–5.
40. Epitaph: Hdt. 7.228 = Simonides F 22b (Page); Waterfield trans.
41. Demaratus on the Spartans: Hdt. 7.104, Waterfield translation, and see also Hdt. 7.220.

The Greeks believed that fate decided who died in battle, but Leonidas and the Spartans chose their own fate, displaying heroic character and manly self-control. The theme recurs in various forms in the sources, including mention of Leonidas' macabre advice to the troops to have an early breakfast because they would all have dinner *chez* Hades (freely paraphrased). It is even suggested that Leonidas wished to keep the glory of dying for country and Greece to himself and the Spartans alone. On the personal level, and as already mentioned, Leonidas reportedly intended to save Sparta by dying and so fulfill an oracle that predicted the demise of either a Spartan king or his state.[42]

These and similar motives were based on hindsight and a patriotic agenda, yet we should not discard them as pure invention. A strong belief in the cause of defending one's native city and Greece, and the expectation of gaining fame through death in battle, were in evidence before and after the Persian War, and not just in Sparta. Indeed, the sources suggest that the Thespians and even the Thebans who went to Thermopylae were strongly motivated to fight the Persians. Equally influential was the competitive notion of excellence, or *arete*, that can be traced back to the Homeric epics (p. 10 above), and that guided Leonidas, the Spartans, and most likely the other warriors. Giving up on Thermopylae without a fight meant loss of honor and worth, but dying in battle was a proof of courage, manliness, and prowess superior to those of the Persians and even of other Greeks. It made the warrior *kalos kagathos*, lit. "beautiful and good," as a Greek two generations later would remind the Spartans who violated this ideal and surrendered to the enemy.[43]

The sources allow us to deduce additional considerations in favor of staying. If we are correct in estimating the strength of Leonidas' force at around 2,000 hoplites and an unknown number of light-armed troops, the idea of holding the passage was less desperate than it is often portrayed. There was also the expectation, which is often ignored, that reinforcements

---

42. Omens and oracle foretelling Leonidas' and the Spartan fates: Hdt. 7.219, 220–221; Justin 2.11.8. Fighting and dying for country and Greek freedom: Diod. 11.4.3, 5, 6.2, 7.1, 11.9.4; Plut. *Moralia* 225b–c; Justin 2.11.5–7, 8–10. Dinner in Hades: Diod. 11.9.4; Plut. *Moralia* 225d; Cicero *Tusculan Disputations* 1.42.101; cf. Seneca *Suasoriae* 2.12. Keeping glory for Sparta alone: Hdt. 7.220; Diod. 11.9.1.

43. Thespians' motives and participation: 7.132, 202, 222; 8.50; 9.30 (suggesting that they lost most of their hoplites at Thermopylae). Thebans' motives: Diod. 11.4.7; Plut. *Moralia* 865e–f. Spartan ambition for excellence, and its weakening later: Hdt. 7.220, 223; Diod. 11.4.4–5, 9.1–3, 11.1–6 (Diodorus' own platitudes); Plut. *Moralia* 225a; Justin 2.11.9–1; Thuc. 4.401–2, and note 17 above; p. 162 below.

would arrive from Sparta and other Peloponnesian states. These newcomers, and especially the Spartans among them, would have improved the Greeks' odds of survival. The personal relationship between Leonidas and the non-Spartans mattered, too. The epitaph on the tomb of seer Megistias of Acarnania states that he refused to desert the Spartan leaders, and it is possible that the commanders of Thespian and Theban units were Leonidas' friends or admirers as well. Camaraderie forged among the Spartans and other Greeks during the wait for the enemy and the actual fighting could also have played a role. Herodotus says that the Thespians refused to leave Leonidas and those about him. Lastly, there was the power of Leonidas' personality.[44]

It is close to impossible to penetrate the thick, glorifying layers that surround the personality of Leonidas. Without exception, all sources describe him as a man of valor who intended from the start to die for his country and for Greek freedom. He is also described as ambitious for fame and intent on proving that he and the Spartans were foremost in courage, honor, and leadership. Although many of the above-mentioned attributes are typical of idealizing portrayals, there is no reason to question the personal courage of Leonidas or his readiness to put his and others' lives on the line. It was reported that, in response to Xerxes' demand that Leonidas surrender his arms, the latter invited him to "come and get them" (*molon labe*). Leonidas must have set a personal example to all troops, not just the Spartans. He is said to have believed that respect for his royal rank motivated troops to fight the enemy. Under the difficult circumstances of Thermopylae, however, royal authority was not enough. While the loyalty of his handpicked Spartans and the other Lacedaemonians was largely guaranteed, the Greek allies stayed with him for the reasons mentioned above and because of his ability to impress upon them, emotionally and cognitively, that it was the right choice. It took strong personal leadership to get such results.[45]

44. Planned reinforcements: p. 37 above. Non-Spartan commanders: Demophilus of Thespia (Hdt. 7.222) and Leontiades or Anaxander of Thebes (Hdt. 7.233; Plut. *Moralia* 867a; Keaveney 1996, 44n8). Megistias' epitaph: Hdt. 7.228. Thespians and Leonidas: Hdt. 7.222. For the following, see also Lazenby 1993, 144–145; Green 1996, 139–140.
45. See note 40 above, as well as Hdt. 7.220; Diod. 11.4.2; Plut. *Moralia* 225a–d. Rejecting surrender: Plut. *Moralia* 225c–d. Difficulties of uncovering Leonidas' personality: e.g., Evans 1991, 74. Herodotus' heroic depiction of Leonidas: Munson 2001, 176–178; Baragwanath 2008, 64–78.

Nevertheless, the idea that Leonidas and his troops ended up acting essentially like men on a suicide mission, intending to harm but not defeat the enemy, has troubled modern scholars attempting to rationalize their last stand. They make his position less hopeless by placing the allies' retreat not before the battle, but during it. Others argue that Leonidas sent these troops to stop Hydarnes' advance over the Anopaea Pass, but that they deserted or were defeated. It is also claimed that Leonidas stayed in order to allow the retreating Greeks or those facing the Persian navy at Artemisium more time to accomplish their goals, but that he then fell in battle.[46] A major flaw in such suggestions is that they either directly contradict the ancient evidence or overburden it with speculative reconstructions. And although all of the surviving ancient accounts of Leonidas are favorable, none compliments him for staying to protect the retreating Greeks.

Even the very different version of the events found in other sources has its advocates. Unlike Herodotus, who places the last fighting during the day and around the wall, this tradition recounts that when the Greeks learned of the Persian outflanking movement, they decided to raid the Persian camp at night, aiming in particular to kill Xerxes and willing to die trying. They destroyed anyone they encountered and were greatly helped by the panic of the Persians, who killed each other in their confusion. The Greeks then burst into the royal tent, looking for Xerxes, but he was out searching for them. When dawn arrived, the Persians discovered how few the attackers were and killed them all with arrows and javelins.[47]

Although many commentators reject this version, others argue that the story of the night attack was based on a poem by the contemporary poet Simonides, whose authority was equal to that of Herodotus' sources. Night operations were not unknown to the Spartans, who selected young men to kill helots at night (or during the day) in what is known as the *krypteia*, or "secret service." It has been suggested, therefore, that Leonidas sent or led a picked unit to the Persian camp to assassinate Xerxes, and that the survivors of the raid came back to fight the last battle described by Herodotus. This view is favored by the Greeks' difficult circumstances, which made such a desperate move conceivable, and by the Homeric tale of a night raid on the enemy camp by two Greek heroes, which may have

46. Not much has changed since Hignett surveyed and criticized these and similar views: 1963, 371–378.
47. Diod. 11.9.3–10.4; Plut. *Moralia* 866a; Justin 2.11.15–18. Their version probably went back to fourth-century historian Ephorus: Hammond 1996, 1–4; Flower 1998.

inspired the attack or those who wrote about it.[48] Several considerations, however, argue against this tradition. The sources describing the night attack agree that it was the work of the entire Greek force and not of a selected group of warriors, and that it ended when exposed in the Persian camp and not later. Furthermore, a *krypteia*-like mission and weapons were not good preparation for a full-scale night attack. The Spartans' meager record of night attacks (of later times) also fails to support a night operation at Thermopylae and shows that they, like many other Greeks, did not prefer it as a way of fighting. But even this small record reveals an unexpected finding. When the Spartans attacked at night, they did so chiefly at sea, against enemy ships or in seaborne raids. Their only known night attack on land was a failed attempt by the Spartan commander Sphodrias in 378 to raid the Piraeus from Thespia in Boeotia, in which it is unclear whether he used Spartan troops. It is true that anecdotal evidence describes a nighttime destruction of enemy property by Leonidas and his men that ended in the acquisition of booty. Even if authentic, this raid involved no fighting, and although scholars have tried to date it to the pre-battle stay at Thermopylae, the tale does not even name the enemy. The Spartans could march by night, but they normally waited for dawn, at the earliest, before launching their attacks. A night attack such as the one attributed to Leonidas appears not to have been in their DNA.[49]

We are left, therefore, with Herodotus' tale of events. He says that Xerxes ordered the attack when "the market (*agora*) is full," probably 9:00–10:00 a.m. His reasons for not attacking earlier are left unstated. Possibly he waited for the allies to complete their departure or expected Leonidas and his troops to do the same. At the same time, Herodotus implies that the king anticipated that the force from Anopaea would arrive shortly. The historian then tells us that the Greeks and the Persians met at a broader space than before, the former fighting with reckless disregard for their lives

48. Linking the night attack to Simonides' poem, the Spartan *krypteia*, and the Homeric raid, especially in *Iliad* 10: Flower 1998, 374–375, who believes, however, that no reconstruction of the last battle in Thermopylae is possible. In favor of a Greek night raid: Green 1996, 139; 2006, 61–62n43; cf. Ray 2009, 80.

49. For additional objections to the tradition of a night attack, see Obst 1913, 112; Hammond 1996, 8; and other scholars cited in Flower 1998, 366n9. Spartan night attacks: Thuc. 2.93.1–94.4; Xen. *Hellenica* 1.6.28–33; 5.1.8–9; 5.4.20–21 (Sphodrias). Leonidas' night plunder; Polyaenus 1.32.3; Lazenby 1993, 136–137. For Greek night operations, see Sheldon 2012, 72–87.

and the latter under their commanders' whips, trampled underfoot by their comrades.[50]

Even if the Greeks realized they were about to die, Herodotus' account of the movements of Leonidas and his followers suggests they did not seek death. At first, the Spartan king went to the more open space, probably around the Middle Gate, because it advantaged his hoplites and their longer spears. His giving up on the defense of the wall and the narrower pass suggests an offensive purpose such as blunting the Persian attack or breaking through the Persians before their outflanking movement was completed. Then conditions worsened. The Greeks' spears were broken, they were reduced to fighting with their swords, Leonidas fell, and Hydarnes' and Ephialtes' force completed their outflanking movement and arrived at the scene. The remaining Greek soldiers retreated to the narrow part of the path and then to a hillock behind the wall, trying to optimize their protection rather than heroically standing their ground. This is not to detract from their courage but only to suggest that their desire to survive was stronger than their wish for fame. Herodotus describes the Greeks' last stand:

> The Persians and the Lacedaemonians grappled at length with one another over the corpse of Leonidas, but the Greeks fought so well and so bravely that they eventually succeeded in dragging his body away. Four times they forced the Persians back, and the contest remained close until Ephialtes and his men arrived. With their arrival, the battle changed: as soon as the Greeks realized they had come, they regrouped and all (except the Thebans) pulled back past the wall to where the road was narrow, where they took up a position on the spur—that is, the rise in the pass which is now marked by the stone lion commemorating Leonidas. Here the Greeks defended themselves with knives, if they still had them, and otherwise with their hands and teeth, while the Persians buried them in a hail of missiles, some charging at them head on and demolishing the wall, while the rest surrounded them on all sides.

It should be said in reference to Herodotus' description that the lion statue honoring Leonidas has since disappeared and been replaced by a modern reproduction of the Spartans' inscribed epitaph, quoted above

---

50. Time of attack: Hdt. 7.223; Hignett 1963, 147, 376. For Xerxes' additional possible considerations, see Hope Simpson 1972, 9. Fighting outside the narrows: Hdt. 7.223, 225. For Leonidas' movements, cf. also Lazenby 1993, 146–147.

(p. 46 above). The hillock, however, was identified by the Greek archaeologist S. Marinatos, who found there many bronze and iron arrowheads, which he attributed to Xerxes' army. There is no archaeological confirmation or refutation of Herodotus' claim elsewhere that in the battle of Thermopylae the Persians suffered 20,000 losses as opposed to the Greeks' 4,000.[51]

The contest over Leonidas' corpse has been doubted because no one survived to tell the story and because the scene recalls Homer's *Iliad*, in particular the heroic fight over the body of Achilles' friend Patroclus. Yet Homeric allusions are insufficient to make the story fictional, and the presence in Xerxes' army of Greeks who visited the battlefield shortly thereafter and may have questioned participants suggests possible sources for the story. According to the Greek protocol of war, possessing the enemy's bodies confirmed his defeat and the possessor's victory, and the Greeks around Leonidas' body were unwilling to concede defeat, even in their desperate hour. It was also a demonstration of their personal loyalty to the dead king. We shall see how their conduct inspired later Spartans to attempt imitating them, although not always wisely.[52]

The Aftermath

After the battle, Xerxes inspected the dead and ordered that Leonidas' head be cut off and impaled with his body. It was a common punishment for enemies of the Persian crown and the royal family, but for the Greeks it was a shockingly impious act that marked the barbarians' difference from them. Herodotus, who thought that the mutilation of Leonidas' body was actually out of character for the Persians, tells nevertheless about Xerxes' later macabre exhibition of the Greek dead. He invited Greeks serving in his fleet, anchored then at nearby Histiaea in Euboea, to come and look at the battle scene. The demand for the tour was so high that there were not enough boats. Herodotus also says that Xerxes tried unsuccessfully to trick the visitors by leaving only 1,000 of his own dead on the ground and hiding the other

---

51. Hillock: Marinatos 1951, 61–69; but see also Flower 1998, 377–378. Losses: Hdt. 8.25.
52. Homer and Leonidas' body: Flower 1998, 374–376; Gainsford 2013, 118–120. Homeric allusions there and elsewhere: Boedeker 2003, 34–35; Lendon 2005, 65–67; Pelling 2006a, 92–93; Foster 2012, 202–204. Greeks at the site: Hdt. 8.24–25, and below. Fighting over the dead leader: pp. 224, 295, 321 below.

19,000 in covered trenches. In contrast, he piled 4,000 Greek dead in one place. The reported disparity in losses flatters the Greek side and is too large to encourage confidence.[53]

As expected, the Greeks had the last word, even about Leonidas' remains. The second-century-CE traveler Pausanias describes two monuments, opposite the theater in Sparta, of Leonidas and Pausanias, who was Leonidas' half-brother and who led the Greeks to a victory over the Persians in Plataea in 479.

> Every year they deliver speeches over their monuments, and hold a contest in which none may compete except Spartans. The bones of Leonidas were taken by Pausanias from Thermopylae forty years after the battle. There is set up a slab with the names, and their fathers' names, of those who endured the fight at Thermopylae against the Persians.[54]

Given that the Greeks regained Thermopylae only a year after the battle, one may hope that Leonidas' body was correctly identified before his bones, or perhaps his image, were carried to Sparta. Archaeologists found no tomb at the Spartan site but uncovered a Hellenistic temple and a fifth-century torso of a helmeted figure, which has been popularly identified as Leonidas (Figure 5). The Spartans also instituted a festival called the Leonideia that was celebrated as late as the Roman period.[55]

Additional contemporary or near-contemporary memorialization of Leonidas and his Spartans included epitaphs inscribed on steles at Thermopylae, poems composed in their honor, and stories about individual Spartans and their alleged sayings. Many of these tales revolve around the themes of courage, solidarity, and their opposites.[56] As if in a zero-sum game, the memory of Leonidas and the Spartans came at the expense of the other Greek troops. No source quotes an epitaph commemorating the

---

53. Impaling Leonidas' body: 7.238. Persian mutilation of enemies: Bosworth 1995, 2:44–45; Llewellyn-Jones 2013, 139. Touring the battleground: Hdt. 8.24–25; cf. Bowie 2007, 116–117.
54. Quotation: Pausanias 3.14.1 (translation slightly modified).
55. There are chronological difficulties with dating the burial forty years after Thermopylae, for which see Pritchett 1974–1991, 4: 242; Jung 2011; Low 2011; Gengler 2009. Burial and the king's image: Hdt. 6.58. See also Low 2006, 99–101.
56. Epitaphs and poems on the fallen: Hdt. 7.228; Diod. 11.11.6. Stories of valorous solidarity and deviations from it: Hdt. 7.229–232; 9.71; Brown 2013; cf. Baragwanath 2008, 74–78. Sayings: Plut. *Moralia* 225a–e; 866b; cf. Diod. 11.5.4–5.

FIGURE 5 *"Leonidas" bust.*
© *Vanni Archive/Art Resource, New York.*

Thespians, who may have lost most of their hoplites at Thermopylae. The Thebans' reputation fared the worst. According to Herodotus, they separated themselves from the Greek retreat to the hillock, and in a shameful, abject manner begged the Persians to spare them because they were their friends and had been compelled to fight against them. A strong believer in the principle of retribution, Herodotus makes them pay for their action by reporting that before the Thessalians intervened on the Thebans' behalf, the Persians killed some of them, and that they later branded the rest. Justice was also meted out to the Theban general whose son was killed in an attempt to capture the city of Plataea years later (in 431). Plutarch, who criticized Herodotus' history, strongly protested against what he regarded as Herodotus' besmirching of the Thebans' "great and noble deed" at Thermopylae. He sensibly questions the logic of Leonidas' keeping 400 reluctant warriors almost to the bitter end, and mocks and denies the story about the Thebans' supplication and branding. The two contradictory traditions are hopelessly biased, but Plutarch's criticism appears justified, at least in part. That the Thebans waited almost until the last moment before surrendering argues against their unwillingness to fight. Other sources' silence about the controversy also suggests its marginality: from the classical period to the modern era, Leonidas and the Spartans have dominated the memory of Thermopylae.[57]

Conclusion

Although the ancient sources on Leonidas at Thermopylae insist on making him a hero, it is possible to offer an alternative perspective. Stripped of his glorification, Leonidas was a failed general. His defeat allowed the Persians to take Boeotia and Athens, and except for standing for Greek pride, he made no military contribution to the final Greek victory, which was attained later at sea at Salamis and on land at Plataea. It is true that he tried to make the most of the difficult circumstances at Thermopylae. He reconciled the different interests and agendas of his Greek allies, and he made successful use of the terrain, the wall, and his hoplites against a superior enemy. But his military intelligence was inadequate—he learned of the circuitous Anopaea path only upon his arrival—and to judge by the result, he dealt with it ineffectively. This failure contributed to his inability to hold off the enemy for more than three days. Even his control over the allies was incomplete, and, if the interpretation suggested previously is correct, he was unable to persuade them to stay when it really counted. The net result was a Greek defeat at Thermopylae of which Leonidas cannot be fully exonerated.

Yet such a bottom-line approach is misleading and too narrow, because a general's contribution to the Greek art of command lay, not just in tactical innovations or even in producing victories, but also in how he was perceived. Leonidas represented the belief that the true measure of a general and his army was courage, perseverance, and dedication to an ideal that was greater than the self or the final result.[58] He also stood for the concept of honorable

---

57. Thespians' likely loss of hoplites: Hdt. 9.32. Thebans: Hdt. 7.233; Plut. *Moralia* 864c–867c; and see pp. 35–36 above. Keaveney 1996, 47–48, however, accepts the tradition of their branding. Thermopylae's legacy: Albertz 2006; Cartledge 2006, 177–198; Brown 2013.

58. See, for example, Diodorus' paean to the Spartans at Thermopylae, which ranks intentions above outcome, and the defeat over the Greek victories that followed it: 11.11.1–5.

defeat, which allowed people to deal psychologically with the pain of losing men, a battle, or even an entire war. These attributes explain the universal appeal of Leonidas then and now. Yet once Leonidas and his companions became an ideal, their example became unattainable. Either because the Spartans feared the risk of again losing so many men in one battle, or because of the decline in the ethos that Leonidas embodied, there would be no second Thermopylae for Sparta.

| Themistocles of Athens
The Clever Counselor

Themistocles, His City, and His Military Challenges

The Athenian general and politician Themistocles was best known for making Athens into a maritime power and for leading the Greeks to a decisive naval victory against the Persian invaders. Historian Diodorus even eulogized him as a man who singlehandedly saved Athens and Greece from the Persians. The historian's evident bias illustrates how favorable (or unfavorable) traditions can stand in the way of reconstructing the nature of Themistocles' military leadership. The ancient sources on the general and the events in which he was involved raise problems because they reflect different accounts of the war and conflicting attempts to shape its memory and legacy. Themistocles was a controversial figure who had both admirers and detractors, and their views of him complicate the ancient sources' descriptions of his actions and policies. But what kind of general was he?[1]

If there is ever a sculpture gallery of ancient Greek generals, the statues of the two heroes of the Persian War, Leonidas and Themistocles, should be standing next to each other (Figure 6). But then the visitor may wish to compare

---

1. Diod. 11.59.1–3. For the ancient sources on Themistocles, see my Bibliography, "The Main Ancient Sources," under "Cornelius Nepos," "Herodotus," "Plutarch," "Thucydides," and "Timotheus." For the "Themistocles Decree," see pp. 66–67 below. Modern treatments of the Persian War include discussions of Themistocles: e.g., Grundy 1901; Burn 1984; Lazenby 1993; Green 1996; and the literature cited in this and the previous chapter. More specifically: Podlecki 1975; Lenardon 1978; Blösel 2004.

them, and the temptation to make them perfect opposites will be almost irresistible. The ancient evidence on the Spartan king is unanimously laudatory, while the Athenian has a more ambivalent reputation. In Homeric terms, Leonidas was Achilles, the straight shooter and ultimate warrior, but Themistocles was more of an Odysseus, the consummate trickster, a wily tactician, but also a thoughtful strategist. The Spartan was a hoplite general, and Themistocles an admiral. Leonidas embodied his country's martial courage and archaic values, while Themistocles stood for Athenian ambition, resourcefulness, and democracy. Leonidas died in battle, heroically defending Greece against the Persians, while Themistocles died in exile under the patronage of the Persian king. In truth, the differences between the two were often a matter of degree. Although Themistocles excelled in the art of persuasion, Leonidas, as we have seen, could also be diplomatic and persuasive, and both men were patriots, though in different ways. This chapter focuses on the generalship of Themistocles, who was among the most individualistic and politically minded of all the commanders dealt with in this book.

Because generalship in fifth-century Athens was both a military and political office, and because Themistocles was very active politically, a few broad observations about the nature of Athenian democracy in his times are in order. The most powerful institution in Athens was the popular assembly (*ecclesia*), which legislated and decided issues pertaining to public affairs, including war, peace, and finance. A council of 500 members, the *boule*, prepared the agenda for the assembly and had a number of administrative and judicial responsibilities. Nine Athenian annual archons (chief magistrates), selected by lot since 487–486, were in charge of the city's administration, religion, army, and judicial affairs. The Athenian citizen body was divided into ten groups called tribes, each drawn from dispersed counties. Each tribe sent fifty annual members to the council and a tribal regiment to the army, and elected a general (*strategos*) for one-year term that could be repeated (see p. 12 above). A democratic judicial process relevant to Themistocles' career was ostracism (*ostrakismos*), which could send a leader into a ten-year exile by popular vote. There was more than one attempt to ostracize Themistocles, but only the last, around 471–470, was successful (Figure 7).[2]

The nature of Athenian democracy and its offices affected the challenges Themistocles faced and explain why his generalship was inseparable from, and often dominated by, his skills as a politician and negotiator. Both as

---

2. Athenian democracy: e.g., Sinclair 1988; Carey 2000; Lewis 2004; and in later times: Hansen 1991. Ostracism: Forsdyke 2005.

FIGURE 6 *Themistocles' bust.* A Roman bust from Ostia of Themistocles, possibly based on a fifth-century original.
© *Werner Forman/Art Resource, New York*

an archon and as a general, he derived his authority less from his rank than from his ability to persuade the citizens to accept his policies, such as building a large navy or dealing with the Persian threat. This was also true in his relations with his colleagues and other Greeks. Themistocles' city had the biggest war fleet in Greece, but this advantage was not always sufficient to induce other Greeks to follow him or his plans. Therefore, he was compelled to adapt Athens' interests and strategy to those of other Greeks, to overcome their distrust of him and his city, and, when possible, to force them to follow an Athenian agenda. Both inside and outside Athens, Themistocles contended with crises that originated in fear of the mightier Persian enemy and in the Greeks' low morale. All these difficulties complicated his greatest military challenge: defeating an enemy that had more ships, occupied the shore that protected its navy, and was on a winning track.

Themistocles' personality had much to do with his successes and failures in meeting these challenges and with his military leadership in

FIGURE 7 *Themistocles' potsherd.* Voting to exile a person by ostracism was done with inscribed *ostraka*, potsherds. The potsherd in the picture, whose exact date is unknown, is inscribed with "Themistocles (of the deme) Phrearrhoi."
© *Album/Art Resource, New York*

general. He was very clever (and was the first to tell people so), highly ambitious for himself and his city, and often stubborn in resisting initial setbacks and opposition. He was also an astute reader of other people's minds, whether they were Athenians, other Greeks, or even the Persian king. This insight helped him in persuading the masses and fellow commanders to adopt his military plans, as well as in formulating his strategy for the war and especially for Athens' future, although ancient and modern observers may have exaggerated his visionary powers. Themistocles was also too competitive for his own good and for Athens', with a self-confidence that added to his authority but also led him astray and made him enemies.

Themistocles and the Athenian Navy

Themistocles was born around 525. His father was Neocles, of whom nothing is known except that he resided in the township, or *deme*, of Phrearrhoi in southern Attica. The family belonged to the Athenian élite, although not its highest rank. Stories about Themistocles' youth and education are suspect because they retrospectively highlight characteristics that he became known for only later. Nevertheless, they suggest personality traits that were relevant to his leadership, such as his unbounded ambition, obsessive interest in public affairs, fierce competitiveness, native intelligence, and corruptibility. Little is known of his early political connections, perhaps because he was often a loner.[3]

Around 493–492, Themistocles was selected as an archon. Ancient historians, followed by modern interpreters, associate his archonship with the fortification of the Piraeus harbor and the buildup of the Athenian navy, but on a speculative if not anachronistic basis. Better attested to is his participation in the land battle of Marathon in 490, in which the Athenians and their Plataean neighbors defeated a Persian expeditionary force. He is reported to have been stationed next to his political rival Aristides and to have fought valiantly, but it is unclear whether he was there as a general, a commander of his tribal unit, or an ordinary hoplite.[4]

Themistocles' most important act before the Persian War was initiating the construction of a large number of battleships or triremes (on which, see pp. 22–23 above). The project illustrated his characteristic combination of political action and strategic planning that distinguished him from other generals of the time. A fourth-century work known as *The Constitution of the Athenians* (*Athenaion Politeia*, commonly abbreviated by scholars as *Ath. Pol.*), which a number of scholars attribute to Aristotle, describes Themistocles' naval bill:

> Two years later, in the archonship of Nicomedes (483–482), in consequence of the discovery of the (silver) mines at Maronea (Laurium in Attica), the working of which had given the state a profit of a hundred talents, the advice was given by some persons that the money

3. Themistocles' birth date, family background, and education: Plut. *Themistocles* 1–3; Nepos *Themistocles* 1; Podlecki 1975, 1–3; Frost 1998, 54–66; Marr 1998, 68–72.

4. Themistocles' archonship: Dionysius of Halicarnassus *Roman Antiquities* 6.34.1; Thuc. 1.93.3; Podlecki 1975, 6–8, 49; Develin 1989, 55; Hornblower 1991–2008, 1:138–139. Fortifying the Piraeus and the so-called first naval bill: see below. The claim that Themistocles' sponsored Phrynichus' play *The Sack of Miletus* to warn Athens of Persian aggression has little support: Hdt. 6.21; Roisman 1988; Rosenbloom 1993. Themistocles at Marathon: Plut. *Aristides* 5; *Themistocles* 3; Frost 1998, 65–66.

should be distributed among the people; but Themistocles prevented this, not saying what use he would make of the money, but recommending that it should be lent to the hundred richest Athenians, each receiving a talent, so that if they should spend it in a satisfactory manner, the state would have the advantage, but if they did not, the state should call in the money from the borrowers. On these terms, the money was put at his disposal, and he used it to get a fleet of a hundred triremes built, each of the hundred borrowers having one ship built, and with these they fought the naval battle at Salamis against the barbarians. And it was during this period that Aristides son of Lysimachus was ostracized.

Other accounts mention the building of 200 ships, yet the figure of 100 is more reasonable for the core navy and better attested. The assertion that Themistocles concealed the aim of his financial scheme and bamboozled the Athenians into letting him build them a larger fleet is implausible: such a major project could not be implemented without public debate and support, and it is unclear why it had to be secret. Apparently it was difficult for some ancient authors to believe that Themistocles could get people to do what he wanted without tricking them. Ancient and modern historians are also divided on the purpose of the plan. Some believe it was designed to decide Athens' ongoing war with the neighboring island of Aegina, while others, including the source quoted here, suggest that the ships were built in preparation for the coming war with Persia. The historian Thucydides is probably right in stating that the project took place during the war with Aegina *and* in anticipation of the Persian War. Lastly, Themistocles and his audience must have been aware that the projected fleet would make Athens the greatest maritime power in Greece. His naval bill, then, suggests a combination of short- and long-term strategic objectives, although the evidence discourages the conclusion in hindsight that he was already thinking of using Athens' new power to rule over other Greeks.[5]

Themistocles' naval plan demanded much of his fellow Athenians, who should be commended for their sacrifice. They gave up immediate rewards in favor of a program that involved heavy expenses beyond the initial

5. Quotation: *Ath. Pol.* 22. Themistocles' proposal: Hdt. 7.144 (200 ships); Thuc. 1.14.3 (no figure); Plut. *Themistocles* 3–4 (100 ships); Nepos *Themistocles* 2 (confusing Aegina with Corcyra and adding unattested details); Polyaenus 1.30.6; Justin 2.12.12 (200 ships); and see the next note, and Schreiner 2004, 69–98, who doubts the scope of the project. Athens and Aegina: Podlecki 1976; Haas 1985; Strauss 2004, 80.

investment. A trireme was a costly affair in terms of manufacturing, equipment, maintenance, and the rowers' wages, which were covered by revenues from the mines and possibly private sources. The project was also exacting in manpower: with about 200 sailors per trireme, the planned 100 new ships required 20,000 men. The number of male citizens in the Athens of the 480s is a matter of speculation, but it is highly unlikely that there were enough to man the ships fully. Possibly, and as is attested for later times, the rowers included non-citizens and even slaves. The Athenian collective effort aside, Themistocles was indeed the architect of their naval power. His visionary strategy distinguished him from Leonidas and some other generals discussed in this book, who were better known for their personal performance in battle or their innovative tactics.[6]

Themistocles and the Persian War Till the Battle of Artemisium

In 483–482, the same year that Themistocles proposed his naval bill, he also took an active part in the ostracism of his main political rival, Aristides. Although the two men agreed on how to deal with the Persian enemy, they differed over domestic affairs and the leadership of Athens. The ostracism of Aristides made Themistocles the most prominent general in the city, a position he retained even after the recall of Aristides about two years later.[7] His authority is shown in the role he played in the deliberations over Athens' response to Xerxes' looming invasion of Greece. The Athenians knew well that Xerxes aimed to punish them for helping the Ionians in their revolt against Persia in 500–498. As was customary in such situations, they consulted the oracle of Apollo at Delphi. The god gave the delegation a horrifying, almost angry response, advising the Athenians to flee to the ends of the earth and predicting that they would experience doom, fire, bloodshed, and the destruction of the city and its temples. Taking the very unusual step of rejecting the answer, the Athenian envoys returned to the oracle as suppliants and threatened Apollo

---

6. Themistocles' naval plan: Holladay 1987; Lazenby 1993, 83–85; Green 1996, 53–56; Hale 2009, 15–28. Ancient, elitist responses to it: Plut. *Themistocles* 4; Plato *Laws* 706c–d; Frost 1998, 72–79.
7. Aristides' ostracism: *Ath. Pol.* 22 (quoted above); Plut. *Themistocles* 5, 11; *Aristides* 7–8, 25. For Aristides' recall, see later in this chapter. Plut. *Themistocles* 6 includes unreliable anecdotes related to Themistocles' career in 483–480; see Frost 1998, 84–90; Marr 1998, 84–86.

with a sit-in till death unless they got a better prophecy. They were rewarded with a sliver of hope:

> No, Pallas Athena cannot placate Olympian Zeus,
> Though she begs him with many words and cunning arguments.
> I shall tell you once more, and endure my words with adamant:
> While all else that lies within the borders of Cecrops' land (Attica)
> And the vale of holy Cithaeron is falling to the enemy,
> Far-seeing Zeus gives you, Tritogeneia (Athena), a wall of wood.
> Only this will stand intact and help you and your children.
> You should not abide and wait the advance of the vast host
> Of horse and foot from the mainland, but turn your back
> And yield. The time will come for you to confront them.
> Blessed Salamis, you will be the death of mother's sons
> Either when the seed is scattered or when it is gathered in.[8]

Historians are divided between those who regard both oracles as later, anachronistic inventions and those, including the present author, who see them as largely authentic. Indeed, it did not require great deal of imagination at the time to anticipate destruction and defeat for Athens, or even for the enemy, at Salamis. More important, what often mattered was not the words of oracles, but how were they interpreted, and in Athens these particular oracles were understood according to people's preconceived ideas about how to meet the Persian invasion. Athenians in favor of leaving the city and avoiding confrontation could find support for their position in the frightening aspect of the message. Those who preferred to fight the Persians could conveniently ignore most of the prophecy and hang on to its only positive line, which offered help behind a wooden wall. But within the latter group there was disagreement about what this "wall" meant, i.e., about where and how to face the enemy. The more elderly citizens preferred to stay and defend the city, and accordingly interpreted the "wall of wood" as a reference to a stockade around the Acropolis. Those who favored evacuating the city and fighting the enemy at sea interpreted the phrase more metaphorically, but equally freely, as a reference to Athenian battleships. Themistocles successfully argued for the latter course by forcing ambivalence on the line "Blessed Salamis, you will be the death of mother's sons" and reading it as a prediction of a Persian rather than a Greek defeat. This interpretation, and his earlier

---

8. Oracles: Hdt. 7.138–144; Plut. *Themistocles* 10; Justin 2.11.13–16. Quotation: Hdt. 7.141, Waterfield trans.

ability to persuade his Athenian audience to support his naval bill, mark him as more politically astute than most Greek generals of his age. In practical terms, the decision led to the building of additional ships, on which the Athenians' chance of survival now depended. The mass evacuation of Athens and the confrontation at sea could wait until they became more urgent.[9]

Later in the summer of 481, Greek representatives of the anti-Persian coalition met in a common council at Corinth, described in the previous chapter. Biographer Plutarch credits Themistocles with being primarily responsible for the Council's call to end all intra-Greek wars, including the one between Athens and Aegina. While there is no good reason to question Themistocles' role as a peacemaker, the cessation of such conflicts was in the interests of all present.[10]

The issue of who should lead the Greek coalition was more controversial. While it was agreed that Sparta should command the joint Greek army, "there was talk," says Herodotus, probably in reference to the Athenians, that Athens should command the Greek navy. The delegates, however—many of them from the Peloponnese and Sparta's allies—adamantly opposed the idea and even threatened to withdraw from the coalition unless Sparta led both land and naval forces. We are told that Athens nobly gave up for the sake of Greek unity, and that Themistocles helped in the process. The truth is that the Athenians had little choice. The great loser was Themistocles, who would probably have been the chief admiral of the Greek fleet, but was now left with secondary power and prestige. The demotion must have hurt this highly ambitious man, whose legendary ability to get what he wanted was more powerful at Athens than elsewhere, as we shall see.[11]

The council at Corinth also tried to retain the loyalty of Thessaly, which lay on Xerxes' invasion route through northern Greece. The Greeks sent an army to the Tempe pass between Thessaly and Macedonia to stop the Persian army on its way from Asia Minor. We have already dealt with this failed operation from the Spartan perspective (pp. 31–32), but what were the Athenian expectations of Tempe? Obviously it was in Athens' interest to draw the Greek line of defense as far north of Athens as possible; Athens' trust in her navy did not preclude a wish to stop the enemy on land. Athens'

---

9. The debate on the oracle's authenticity and Delphi's position: Hignett 1963, 439–447; Hands 1965; Lazenby 1993, 98–102; Blösel 2004, 64–107.

10. Themistocles and Greek peace: Plut. *Themistocles* 6; cf. Aelius Aristides 2.248; *Suda*, s.v. "Aneilen."

11. Hdt. 8.2–3; Plut. *Themistocles* 7 (erroneously postdates the episode a year later); Podlecki 1975, 15–16; cf. Marr 1998, 88.

seriousness about the expedition to Tempe is shown by Themistocles' presence among the Greek commanders and by the contribution of an unknown number of Athenian hoplites to the Greek force of 10,000. Athens possibly also provided the ships that ferried the troops to Alus in Achaea, whence the army marched on to Tempe. Not long after, however, the Greeks aborted the mission, discouraged by the lack of local Thessalian support and by the poor defensibility of the pass. Their retreat to the Isthmus left Athens more vulnerable to the invaders than ever and more dependent on Leonidas' success to stop them at Thermopylae. But it also strengthened Themistocles' position of relying chiefly on the navy for salvation.[12]

Some historians date the so-called Themistocles Decree to the time between Themistocles' return from Tempe and the first naval battle of the Persian War at Artemisium, i.e., spring–August 480. The decree was included in a third-century inscription from Troezen in the Argolid that purports to reproduce the Athenian original. It records a motion by Themistocles, adopted by the Athenian assembly, that called for the evacuation of noncombatant Athenians to Aegina and the island of Salamis, except for a few religious officials who were to stay on the Acropolis. The other citizens and residents of Athens were asked to man 200 ships, and each ship got a *trierarch* (captain), ten marines, four archers, and special crewmen. There were instructions on how to assign men to the ships and what religious sacrifices to make. The decree then ordered 100 ships to sail to Artemisium in Euboea, and the remaining 100 to stay around Attica and Salamis. It also allowed exiles by ostracism to go to Salamis until their fate was decided later (the text breaks off here).

The decree has been subjected to vigorous debate between the readers who acknowledge that the inscription includes unoriginal features but regard it as a largely faithful reproduction of one or more authentic decrees, and other scholars, who firmly reject its historicity and see it as a later, probably fourth-century, fabrication. I shall not enumerate the many arguments for and against its authenticity, but shall only state my opinion that the problems of establishing an exact date for the decree/s (if authentic), the difficulty of correlating it to the narrative of Herodotus and other sources, and its anachronistic features all make supporting its authenticity more difficult than rejecting it. In truth, even if we acknowledge the decree's historicity, it adds little to our assessment of Themistocles' generalship. Firstly, the

12. The transport of troops: Blösel 2004, 114, with n. 42. Plut. *Themistocles* 6–7 is chronologically confused regarding the background to Tempe.

extant inscription is probably a compilation of several decrees, and there is no assurance that he authored all of them. Secondly, the provisions dispatching the ships to different destinations could not have been drafted without consulting other Greek allies, and therefore reveal little about how much he contributed to the war plan. Thirdly, the decree's arrangements for manning the ships suspiciously resemble much later ones, and, even if authentic, may be attributable to established practices rather than to Themistocles' organizational skills. Finally, the fact that the Athenians ended up sending more than the decreed 100 ships to Artemisium shows that the decree was temporary. Indeed, there is less disagreement among historians that, after Tempe, the Athenians discussed blueprints for future evacuation and uses of the fleet, all subject to change.[13]

Themistocles in Artemisium

In August 480, the Greeks decided to stop the advancing Persian invasion with an army at Thermopylae and with a navy at Artemisium in Euboea (Map 5). It is often assumed that the primary goal of this arrangement was to enable the land and naval forces to help each other, but this view should be qualified. Artemisium is about 60 kilometers east of Thermopylae, too far to give Leonidas quick support or to receive it from him. Although the outcome of a battle in one place could affect the other, the best help that the Greek army and navy could render each other was to win their battles and so prevent their Persian counterparts from cooperating. The related view, that Themistocles was responsible for the choice of Artemisium as the Greeks' base, is ill supported. The only source for it is the late-Roman author Cornelius Nepos, who says that Themistocles picked Artemisium for the narrowness of its straits, which disadvantaged the larger Persian navy. Though Artemisium has other strategic and topographical advantages, its straits are in fact about 16 kilometers wide. Nepos seems to confuse Artemisium with Themistocles' later advocacy of a battle in the

---

13. Themistocles' Decree: *SEG* 30.384; translation: Fornara 1983, no. 55. Its authenticity and date: Jameson 1960 (summer, 480); Podlecki 1975, 14–15 (autumn, 481); Frost 1998, 94 (May–June 480); Hammond 1988b, 559–563 (September 481); Green 1996, 98–101 (after Tempe); cf. Lenardon 1978, 70 (either before or after Tempe); Strauss 2004, 61–62 (summer 481). A fabricated document: e.g., Habicht 1961; Hignett 1963, 458–468; Lazenby 1993, 102–105; Johansson 2001; Blösel 2004, 247–254. (I have changed my opinion about the decree's authenticity since Roisman 2011, 231).

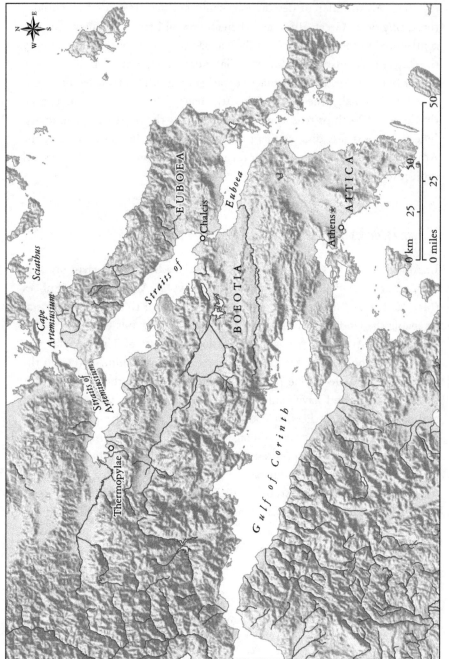

MAP 5 Artemisium.

narrow straits of Salamis. In any case, Herodotus tells us that about 330 Greek ships faced about 700 Persian ships (discounting earlier losses, chiefly from a storm) in three days of battles, the last of which ended indecisively.[14]

Before the first main battle, there was a small skirmish between Greek and Persian scout ships, and the Greek fleet changed its anchorage from Artemisium to Chalcis in Euboea, and then back again. The Persians arrived in full force at Aphetae in Magnesia, across the straits from Artemisium. It is said that when the Greeks saw the great size of the enemy fleet, they panicked and wanted to sail to the Peloponnese. The local Euboeans got wind of the plan and asked the Greek commander-in-chief, the Spartan Eurybiades, to give them a short time to transfer their families and slaves elsewhere, but he refused. The Euboeans then gave Themistocles thirty talents, of which he gave five to Eurybiades and three to a Corinthian commander as a bribe to stay, while he pocketed the rest. Those who were corrupted thought that the money came from Athens for the purpose of preventing their departure.[15]

The tale should not be construed as critical of Themistocles, since his bribes stopped the disintegration of the Greek navy and saved the plan of meeting the enemy around Euboea—outcomes that go far towards excusing his methods and his profit from the transaction. But there are several considerations that argue against accepting the story. Even if we ignore its suspicious similarity to many other anecdotes about Themistocles' use of bribery, it cannot be easily dissociated from the Athenian patriotic traditions that portrayed the Spartans and other Greeks as more fearful and selfish than the courageous and selfless Athenians. Later, on the eve of the Battle of Salamis, Themistocles persuaded Eurybiades to reconsider a plan to retreat to the Peloponnese under more difficult circumstances, and without a bribe, making it unlikely that he bought Eurybiades' agreement for the same purpose here. Especially questionable is Eurybiades' alleged disregard of the adverse impact that a retreat would have had on Leonidas

---

14. Artemisium and Thermopylae: Hdt. 7.175; 8.21. Mutual-help strategy: e.g., Evans 1969; Green 1996, 100; but see the reservations of Hignett 1963, 152–154. Themistocles' choice of Artemisium: Nepos *Themistocles* 3.3; Grundy 1901, 269–270; cf. Hignett 1963, 153. Artemisium's advantages: Strauss 2004, 15–16. The number of ships: Hdt. 8.1, 11, 14, 43–47, 82; and below.
15. Hdt. 7.179–183, 192; 8.4–5; Plut. *Themistocles* 7; with Marr 1998, 88–89. Plutarch criticizes Herodotus for tainting the Greek victory with this tale (*Moralia* 867b–c). In *Themistocles* (7) he adds an anecdote on how Themistocles also tricked and threatened an Athenian captain into staying.

and his force at Thermopylae. Although the Greek navy was not sent to Artemisium to assist Leonidas directly, a retreat would have exposed him to Persian attack from land and sea and undermined the resolve of his local allies, whom the Greeks had promised to defend with their navy. The idea, then, that Eurybiades was willing to ignore and even desert his king is unlikely. It appears that Eurybiades was used as a foil for the glorification of Themistocles and his city, and not for the last time, as we shall see. The important fact was not that Eurybiades took a bribe, but that he stayed at Artemisium. The sources offer no shred of criticism of his generalship there, and their silence shows that the Athenians' earlier demand to lead the joint navy was more about prestige than about improving the Greeks' chances of victory.[16]

I shall describe the Battle of Artemisium only briefly, because, except for the historian Diodorus (below), no other source mentions Themistocles' role in it. Shortly after the Persians' arrival at Aphetae, they sent 200 ships to encircle Euboea and trap the Greeks between their fleets. The Greeks sailed against a fleet coming from Aphetae, formed a protective circle, and then successfully attacked the Persians who were trying to surround them. At night the Persian fleet that went around Euboea suffered heavy losses from a storm. The second day of the battle was marked by the arrival of fifty-three more ships from Athens and the sinking of some enemy ships. On the third and last day, the Persians made another attempt to encircle the Greek fleet near Artemisium. It was followed by a mostly even combat in which the Persians suffered more losses. The result of the entire battle was inconclusive.[17]

Herodotus, our chief source for the battle, is silent about Themistocles' contribution to it, suggesting that the general did not even distinguish himself in combat: that honor went to the entire Athenian contingent, and within it to another Athenian, Cleinias. We hear that half of the Athenian fleet was damaged in the engagement, probably because of their

---

16. See the previous note, and Baragwanath 2008, 291–294; cf. Pelling 2007, 159–160. On stereotypical portrayals of Themistocles, including his bribing methods: e.g., Pelling 2007, 157–162. Themistocles, Eurybiades, and Leonidas: Hdt. 8.58, 203. Lazenby 1993, 128–130, defends the story; *contra*: Blösel 2004, 132–135. Diodorus on Themistocles and Eurybiades: 11.12.4. Eurybiades' portrait: cf. Blösel, 2004, 200–204.
17. Artemisium: Hdt. 8.1–21; Diod. 11.12–13; Hignett 1963, 149–192, 386–392; Lazenby 1993, 152–188, 251–260; Blösel 2004, 132–185; Hale 2009, 43–54, and see the next note.

zeal and central role in the fighting, although credit should also be given to the Persians' capabilities. But Diodorus, probably following the fourth-century historian Ephorus, greatly praises Themistocles by way of denigrating Eurybiades. He presents the latter as the chief admiral in name only after he allegedly conceded the actual command to Themistocles. In addition to key differences between Diodorus and Herodotus about the chronological order of the battle and the size and movements of its opposing navies, Diodorus says nothing about its second day, and his description of the last day lacks real substance. Of the two reports, Herodotus' is the more reliable, by the consensus of most scholars. Indeed, it is possible that Diodorus' source, Ephorus, in an effort to rival Herodotus' story, based his version on a poem by Simonides on the prowess of the Athenians at Artemisium.[18]

The inconclusive results of the battle of Artemisium were attended by news that Thermopylae had fallen into enemy hands, which led to a general Greek retreat to the Saronic Gulf between Attica and the Peloponnese. Even before they left, Themistocles called a meeting of the Athenian commanders and told them that he had a secret plan to make Xerxes' Greek allies rebel against him (p. 72 below). He also instructed them to slaughter local Euboean herds, which would be better eaten by Greeks than by the enemy. He asked the commanders to light fires to mislead the enemy into thinking they would stay, and promised to lead the fleet back to safety. Many of his pronouncements were designed to raise Athenian morale after the depressing news from Thermopylae and the even more depressing prospect of having to abandon Athens to Persian occupation and to meet the enemy at sea again. The Euboeans should have been the most disgruntled: Themistocles allegedly charged them thirty talents to prevent an earlier retreat (p. 69 above), killed their sheep and goats, and now left them defenseless to face the Persian invaders. It is not uncharacteristic of our source to ignore the cost of Themistocles' ploys to other Greeks.

Yet not everything went Themistocles' way. Among the instructions he gave the Athenians was the order not to leave before he told them to. In fact, the timing of their retreat was dependent on the other fleets and had to be coordinated with them, as is shown by the Athenians'

---

18. Diod. 11.12.1–13.4. Honors for excellence: Hdt. 8.11, 17. Diodorus and Ephorus: my Bibliography, Part A, under "Diodorus of Sicily." Simonides on Artemisium: esp. F 3 W²; Kowerski 2005, 22–33, 58–61. Simonides and Ephorus: Flower 1998, 370. Green (1996, 109–149) and Strauss (2004, 15–30) try to reconcile Diodorus' and Herodotus' narratives.

sailing in the rear of the retreating Greeks. This necessity was a reminder that Themistocles' desire to control actions and events often exceeded his power.[19]

Similarly unsuccessful was his secret plan to incite the Ionians (i.e., the Greeks from Asia Minor and several Aegean islands) to desert Xerxes. He inscribed a message next to every drinking place in Artemisium, and at other places of supply and shelter, that encouraged them, and through them the Carians, to desert to the Greek side, to remain neutral, or at least to under-perform in battle. Herodotus considers it a win–win ploy: either the Ionians would change sides, or Xerxes would distrust and not use them. The results, however, were highly disappointing. Only two Ionian ships deserted Xerxes, who went on to deploy the Ionians in the subsequent Battle of Salamis, where only a few of them neglected their duty. This should not have come as a sur-prise; at Artemisium, only one Ionian ship changed sides, and before Salamis, the Persians were winning the war. The story shows that Themistocles was a clever trickster who tried to weaken the enemy, but his tactic was ineffective (and not for the last time).[20]

The Battle of Salamis

The sources report that after the Greeks' retreat from Artemisium to Salamis, the Athenians began evacuating their city in anticipation of the Persians' arrival. They put their women, children, the elderly, slaves, and property on boats that took them to Aegina, Troezen, and Salamis. Historians have largely agreed, however, that the complex project of a mass evacuation must have begun some time before Artemisium; otherwise the Athenians would have had less than a week to complete it. Apparently the tales about Athenian resistance to leaving the city at this stage and about Themistocles using oracles and other divine messages to persuade them to do so belong, at best, to earlier events, perhaps including the aforementioned debate about the oracle and the wall of wood (pp. 64–65 above). Even more

---

19. Hdt. 8.19, 21; Blösel 2004, 145–158; and see the next note.
20. Retreat from Artemisium: Hdt. 8.19, 21. Message to the Ionians: Hdt. 8.22; Plut. *Themistocles* 9; Justin 2.12.1–7; Polyaenus 2.13.3. Ionian defections and performance at Salamis: Hdt. 8.11, 82, 85, 90; cf. 7.52; Diod. 11.17.3–4; Justin 2.12.25. Bowie's objections to the story are surmountable: 2007, 113. The Athenians later regarded Artemisium as a victory: Plut. *Themistocles* 8; cf. Hdt. 8.76.

questionable is the story that Themistocles used the pretext of inspecting the baggage of the evacuees for a missing Gorgon's head from a statue in order to take their money to pay the Athenian rowers. An alternative version states that the campaign was financed by the Areopagus, a council of former archons (including Themistocles). All these stories were probably products of a later rivalry over who deserved credit for helping in the evacuation and of the commonplace image of tricky Themistocles. Themistocles, however, was surely instrumental in making this strategic retreat successful.[21] Finally, Plutarch claims that Themistocles initiated the recall of his rival Aristides and other ostracized Athenians from exile, because the people wanted them back and were afraid that they might join the enemy. It is hard to accept Plutarch's version because he post-dates the recall of the exiles from 481–480 to late summer of 480, and because no other source on the exiles' return credits Themistocles with it. Yet even if Themistocles was not the proposer, he probably supported the motion, which contributed to Athenian unity and allowed him to join a popular cause and reconcile with an influential leader, soon to be elected general. Here again he blended political and military leadership.[22]

It was now well into September of 480, and the Greek fleet at Salamis was augmented by contingents that had not fought at Artemisium. The best authorities for the size of the fleet are the contemporary poet Aeschylus, who described the battle of Salamis in his play *The Persians*, and the later historian Herodotus. Their versions differ, however. Aeschylus mentions 300 or 310 ships, depending on the reading of the text of *The Persians*. Herodotus reports a total of 378 triremes and five *penteconters* (a fifty-oared battleship), but the sum of the individual contingents he lists is only 366 ships. These figures and those of other sources are open to question, but Herodotus' detailed list of the individual states' contributions amounting to 366 ships suggests a research effort and so a safer estimate. The fleet anchored on the eastern shore

---

21. Of the sources, only Plutarch (*Themistocles* 10) reports Themistocles' role in, or Athenian opposition to, the evacuation of the city; and see Graninger 2010. Chronology: Lazenby 1993, 153–154; Strauss 2004, 59–66, 81; Green 2006, 66n58. Financing Salamis: *Ath. Pol.* 23.1–2; Plut. *Themistocles* 10; Rhodes 1993, 287–289.

22. Themistocles and Aristides' recall: Plut. *Themistocles* 11. Yet *Ath. Pol.* 22.8; Andocides 1.77, 107; Nepos *Aristides* 1–2, and even Plut. *Aristides* 8, fail to mention Themistocles' authorship of the decree. The recall's date: Rhodes 1993, 281. Marr 1998, 96–97, however, supports Plutarch's version. See p. 87 below for Aristides' command at Psyttaleia.

of Salamis, chiefly in the harbor of the town and probably in other anchorages north and south of it.[23]

The size of the Persian fleet is equally uncertain. Aeschylus mentions 1,000 ships and 207 fast ships, which were probably part of the 1,000. Herodotus, possibly influenced by Aeschylus, estimates that the Persians had 1,207 ships, while later sources mention 1,000 ships. Scholarly estimates range from around 340 to 1,207 vessels, including inactive ships. Crediting the figures of 1,000–1,207 ships depends on accepting Herodotus' claim that Xerxes succeeded in replenishing all of his losses, which many scholars are inclined to doubt. A suggested estimate of 600–700 ships may upset fewer historians.[24]

The commanders of the Greek fleet met to discuss the situation, which did not look good. The Persian fleet was anchored or expected to arrive in nearby Phaleron, and during the meeting (or the next one), news of Xerxes' occupation and destruction of Athens arrived. There was real danger of a split in the Greek camp. The prevailing view in the council was stated by the Peloponnesians, who favored retreating to the Isthmus of Corinth and fighting the enemy on land and sea there. In fact, they had already began building an Isthmian defensive wall as soon as news of the defeat at Thermopylae reached the Peloponnese. The Athenians opposed this plan, or at least viewed it with great apprehension. After the defeat at Thermopylae, they rightly or wrongly expected the Peloponnesians to defend them across the border in Boeotia, and felt betrayed when they did not. Now they would have to evacuate their people once again from Salamis. They also suspected another betrayal, believing that a retreat to the Isthmus would result in the return

23. The Greek fleet: Aeschylus *Persians* 338–340, with Garvie 2009, 175, defending the reading of 300 ships; Hdt.: 8.43–48. Two deserting ships joined the Greeks later: Hdt. 8.82. See also Thuc. 1.74.1 (400 ships); Ctesias *Persica* 23, and Plato *Laws* 699b (1,000 ships); Hyperides *Against Diondas* 145v–144r (360, including 220 Athenian ships). 310 ships: Hignett 1963, 209–210; Lazenby 1993, 172–173; Green 1996, 162–163. 366 ships: Strauss 2004, 78–70. 380 ships: Morison et al. 2000, 56–57. 375 ships, of which only 300 were used: Wallinga 2005, 60, cf. 113, 134. The location of the Greek fleet: Lazenby 1993, 180; Wallinga 2005, 58.

24. The Persian fleet: Aeschylus *Persians* 341–343; Hdt. 7.89, 184; 8.66. 600–700 ships: Lazenby 1993, 173–174; and cf. Strauss 2004, 104 (c. 650 ships). Hignett 1963, 208–209: 340 ships. About 1,200 ships, but only 207 fought: Wallinga 2005, esp. 42–43, 57: cf. Morrison et al. 2000, 57. Potter 2006 estimates that each side sent 150–200 ships into battle.

of the Greek contingents to their homes.[25] Herodotus even reports that the Greek generals panicked when they heard the news about the fall and destruction of Athens, and that some rushed to their ships in preparation for departure even before the rest voted to leave. Dramatic and biased as this account is—Herodotus' Athenian informants tended to portray other Greeks, especially Peloponnesians, as full of fear in the face of adversity and bad news—it is to the historian's credit that he does not, like Plutarch, depict the chief admiral Eurybiades as a cowardly commander who wanted to beat a hasty retreat. In Herodotus, the Spartan general seems to favor a retreat to the Isthmus, but also encourages people to speak their mind; that is, to suggest other options.[26]

Moreover, Herodotus suggests that even Themistocles accepted the council's decision to defend the Peloponnese from the Isthmus. According to the historian, it was Themistocles' friend, Mnesiphilus, who warned him to reject the plan, because each Greek contingent would sail to its respective home once they left Salamis. He advised him to appeal to Eurybiades to reverse the decision, and Themistocles liked the idea and acted upon it. In a composition criticizing Herodotus, Plutarch dismisses the story as an invention designed to detract from Themistocles' glory, and several modern scholars have joined him in questioning the episode. There are good reasons, however, to accept it. First, Themistocles had accepted the other generals' decision to retreat before (in Tempe and again at Artemisium), and may have yielded to them again. Second, the historical existence of Mnesiphilus and his association with Themistocles is attested elsewhere. Indeed, denying Mnesiphilus credit while giving Themistocles exclusive rights to every good idea in the conflict is both conventional and improbable. Yet, once Themistocles took ownership of the idea of foiling the retreat, he deserved full credit for implementing it.

Themistocles took a boat to Eurybiades' ship and argued against leaving Salamis, using the aforementioned scenario of the disintegration of the fleet, among other persuasions. The likelihood that the fleet would actually break up is unknown, but it was an Athenian fear that must have been shared by

25. Building the Isthmian wall: Hdt. 8.50, 71; 9.7; Plut. *Themistocles* 9; Diod. 11.16.2; p. 33 above. Expected defense in Boeotia: Hdt. 8.40; Plut. *Themistocles* 9; Cawkwell 2005, 105–106. Expected disintegration of the fleet at the Isthmus: Hdt. 8.57.

26. Debate in council: Hdt. 8.49–50, 56–57; cf. Strauss 2004, 82. Plutarch on Eurybiades: *Themistocles* 11.

Eurybiades. Nevertheless, it took leadership and even courage on Eurybiades' part to call another council to reconsider the retreat in the face of the expected opposition.[27]

The credibility of Herodotus' description of the subsequent debate in the Greek headquarters is questionable. It is full of literary devices such as direct speech, aphorism-like repartee, personal characterizations, and arguments that betray both hindsight on the war and an Athenian bias. At its core, however, Themistocles' argument was that meeting the Persians in the open sea near the Isthmus, instead of in the narrower channel at the island of Salamis (about a mile from the Attic shore), would disadvantage the heavier and less numerous Greek ships. Retreat to the Isthmus would also mean the loss of Salamis with its Athenian refugees, as well as neighboring Aegina and Megara with their fleets. The way would then be clear for a Persian invasion of the Peloponnese by land and sea. In other words, Themistocles claimed that fighting around Salamis was good for the *Peloponnesians*. In addition, he waved the proverbial stick by threatening that if the Greek fleet left Salamis, the Athenians would leave with their ships for Italy.[28]

Themistocles' reasoning was not without flaws. Nowhere did he address the question weighing heavily on the Peloponnesians' minds: What would happen if the Greeks lost at Salamis? At best, such a loss would have greatly undermined a second line of defense in the Isthmus, and at worst it would have trapped the fleet at Salamis. Conversely, a naval defeat near the Isthmus would be less detrimental because the Peloponnese could provide shelter and aid with their Isthmian wall (under construction), land forces, and fortified places. Against the fear of defeat at Salamis, Themistocles raised the greater fear that had convinced Eurybiades that he should recall the council, this time in the form of the possibility that the Athenians rather the other Greeks would leave. Such a prospect meant certain naval defeat at both Salamis and the Isthmus: out of the 366 Greek ships present,

27. Mnesiphilus: Hdt. 8.57; and see also Lazenby 1993, 257–258. Doubting the story: Plut. *Moralia* 869c–e; Grundy 1901, 363–364; Hignett 1963, 203–204; and for more references: Blösel 2004, 187n9. Themistocles' persuasion of Eurybiades: Hdt. 8.58; Nepos *Themistocles* 4.1–2.

28. Hdt. 8.59–64; Plut. *Themistocles* 11–12; Diod. 11.15.2–4; Lazenby 1993, 154–163; Green 1996, 166–171; Strauss 2004, 84–89; cf. Bowie 2007, 144–146. Herodotus' description of the Greek ships as heavier than the Persian ships contradicts Plutarch's description of them as lighter and lower: *Themistocles* 14. Therefore, it has been suggested that Herodotus' text be amended from "heavier" (*baryteras*) to "slower" (*bradyteras*). See Cawkwell 2005, 270n11; Wallinga 2005, 94–107.

Eurybiades could lose 180 Athenian as well as thirty Aeginetan and twenty Megaran ships. We do not know if Themistocles bluffed or was sincere when he threatened to leave, but neither did Eurybiades. In sum, the Athenian leader may have been a great strategist, but he was an even greater manipulator.[29]

It helped Themistocles that Eurybiades' voice in the council carried weight. Indeed, it would have been easier for the Spartan to agree with the Peloponnesians' plan and blame Themistocles for any of its adverse effects. But he supported Themistocles, both because he saw the merits of his position and because he did not want to lose the Athenian and possibly other fleets. We may also presume that a greater solicitude for the fate of Greece lay behind these concerns; it was not only the Athenians who were selfless Greek patriots. There may have been a personal consideration as well. In Herodotus' account, Themistocles tells Eurybiades that "if you stay here, you are a courageous man (*aner agathos*), but if not, you will destroy Greece." The words are probably Herodotus' rather than Themistocles', and yet the idea that Salamis provided an opportunity to display exceptional courage on the sea, as Leonidas had done on land, would have appealed to the Spartan leader.[30]

The Greeks prepared themselves for battle and, according to our sources, received favorable omens in the form of an earthquake, an apparition, and even an owl that perched on Themistocles' masthead. But enemy movements had a greater impact on their behavior. The Persian navy sailed toward Salamis and took up a battle formation as their army marched toward the Peloponnese. All the misgivings about Themistocles' and Eurybiades' plan and the hopes for the alternative Isthmus defense now resurfaced, especially among the rowing masses. According to Diodorus, they completely ignored Eurybiades' and Themistocles' orders and exhortations and were ready to sail to the Peloponnese. It was the first time for Eurybiades, though not for Themistocles, that his authority and persuasive efforts failed him. The popular protest forced the Spartan admiral to call a new meeting of the Greek commanders, who decided to retreat from Salamis in spite of the opposition of Eurybiades, the Athenians, the Aeginetans, and the

---

29. See also Pelling 2006b, 110–112. Peloponnesian concerns about Salamis as opposed to the Isthmus: Hdt. 8.49, 70; Diod. 11.15.3. The Athenians are said to have 200 ships, of which they gave 20 to Chalcidian crews: Hdt. 8.44, 46, 61; Plut. *Themistocles* 11, 14 and see also Nepos *Themistocles* 3.2, and the Themistocles Decree. Aeginetan and Megaran ships: Hdt. 8.1, 45–46.
30. In Hdt. (8.63–64, 74) Eurybiades has the final say; cf. Plut. *Themistocles* 11–12; Diod. 11.15.4. Quotation: Hdt. 8.62.

Megarans.[31] These were the circumstances that prompted Themistocles' most celebrated ploy.

Under the cover of night, he sent his loyal slave Sicinnus on a boat to the Persian camp with a secret message to the Persian commanders and probably also to their king. In it, Themistocles affected sympathy for the Persian cause and claimed that the frightened Greeks were planning a retreat. He urged the Persians to seize the opportunity to prevent the Greeks' escape, and suggested that, rather than resist the enemy, the Greeks who were divided between sympathizers and enemies of Persia would fight each other.[32]

Like many other successful deceptions, Themistocles' message mixed truth with lies. The Greeks' internal division, their fear of the enemy, and their wish to leave Salamis were authentic and largely verifiable. Themistocles' and other Greeks' hidden intention to change sides was either a lie or unverifiable wishful thinking by the Persians. In any case, the impact of Themistocles' trickery on the Persian battle plan was not as decisive as has been claimed. He did not make Xerxes fight in or around Salamis: the king had intended to do it anyway. It was not in Xerxes' interest to allow the Greeks to leave and thus postpone the final decision to the Isthmus, where they could get better support on land. Moreover, according to Herodotus, the Persian war council had already endorsed the idea of meeting the Greeks at sea. Even before Themistocles sent his message, Persian ships sailed toward Salamis and took up battle formation, but postponed fighting until the next day because they ran out of daylight. (Presumably the fleet returned for the night to Phaleron.) After Themistocles' message and around midnight, the Persians sent troops to occupy the island of Psyttaleia between Salamis and Attica, and ships both to Salamis and to guard the straits between the island and Attica. It appears, then, that Themistocles' message had its greatest effect on the timetable of Xerxes, who moved the dispatch of the fleet from morning to midnight. The king

---

31. Favorable signs: Hdt. 8.64–65; Plut. *Themistocles* 12; cf. 15. Reactions to the Persian movements: Hdt. 8.70, 74; Plut. *Themistocles* 12; cf. Diod. 11.16.1–17.1 and Marincola 2007, 118–119, for Diodorus' differences from Herodotus.

32. Hdt. 8.75. In Aeschylus' version (*Persians* 353–371), Themistocles is not mentioned, the messenger is a nameless Greek, and the emphasis is on the Greeks' wish to escape that night. Aeschylus' and Herodotus' reports are preferable to Plut. *Themistocles* 12; Diod. 11.17.1–2; Nepos *Themistocles* 4.3–5; and Justin 2.12.18–21. Lazenby 1993, 167–172, and Wallinga 2005, 68–69, accept the Sicinnus tale against the objections of Hignett 1963, 403–408; cf. Marr 1998, 100–103.

may also have added to his original plan the dispatch of 200 Egyptian ships to guard the western exit between Salamis and the Megaran coast, in order to prevent a possible Greek escape there. It is true that Themistocles' message made the Persians surprised to find the Greeks ready for battle instead of flight, but even Aeschylus, who dwells on the Persians' fear and shock at this discovery, suggests that they quickly recovered and switched to a belligerent mode. Themistocles' trickery was instrumental, in sum, in strengthening the Persians' desire to fight at Salamis and in their adjusting their battle plan.[33]

According to the sources, Xerxes played into Themistocles' hands by fighting in the straits between Salamis and Attica, which were more favorable to the Greeks than the open sea. Historians have wondered why the king made this choice. The question betrays a Greek or more accurately an Athenian perspective, according to which the Persians were more likely to lose in the narrows than on the open sea. For the Persians, however, the open sea was not so attractive. Artemisium showed that a larger space did not favor them *ipso facto*, and fighting would take place in the open only with the Greeks' consent. More important (and perhaps to state the obvious), the choice of narrows or high seas was only one important factor among many, including naval technology, tactics, fighting skills, and adaptability. Xerxes had more ships, and they were manned with skilled crews—especially from Phoenicia, Ionia, and Caria—whom he could trust to win a victory in the narrows. That Themistocles took credit for tricking the Persians into battle and forcing the Greeks into it is hardly surprising. The Greeks were receptive to this claim because it enhanced their victory and sense of superiority over the barbarians.[34]

Reconstructing what happened that night and the day after is complicated by the need to reconcile divergent evidence, identify uncertain locations,

33. Persian plans and movements before and after Themistocles' message: Aeschylus *Persians* 363–370, 382–391; Hdt.: 8.67–70, 76; and see the previous note. Egyptian ships: Diod. 11.17.2; Hdt. 7.89; cf. Plut. *Themistocles* 12; *Aristides* 8. Lazenby 1993, 174–175, and Strauss 2004, 134, dispute Diodorus' report about the Egyptian squadron, but see Wallinga 2005, 71n9. For the original Persian plan, see also Wallinga 2005, 68–81. Persian surprise at Salamis: Aeschylus *Persians* 391–407; Green 1996, 187; Strauss 2004, 206.
34. Crediting Themistocles for Salamis: Hdt. 8.80; Thuc. 1.74.1; Plut. *Themistocles* 12; Nepos *Themistocles* 4.4. Morrison et al. (2000, 59) think that Xerxes made the mistake of fighting at Salamis through overconfidence. See Lazenby 1993, 163; cf. Bowie 2007, 186, against the tradition that Xerxes planned before the battle to build a mole between Attica and Salamis, as claimed by Strabo 9.1.13 and Ctesias *Persica* 26, and supported by Green 1996, 172–173.

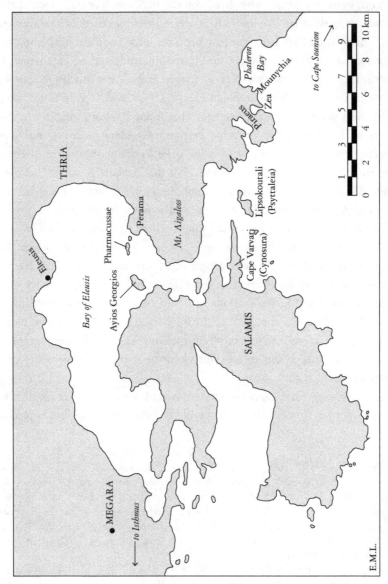

MAP 6 Salamis.

E.M.L.

and establish a timeline for the movements of both Persians and Greeks. It also requires ascertaining the battle lines and navigating among widely different modern interpretations of the sources. The following reconstruction deals with the above problems only when they are directly relevant to Themistocles' generalship.

Our reconstruction begins with establishing the Persians' positions and missions to which Themistocles' battle plan responded. The playwright Aeschylus says that Xerxes ordered the Persians that night "to arrange the mass (or the main body) of their ships in three lines and guard the exits and the surging straits, while stationing others so as to surround the island of Ajax (Salamis) completely." He goes on to describe the manning of the ships, and adds that, "all through the night, the masters of the fleet kept the whole naval host sailing to and fro." Herodotus, relying partly on Aeschylus, says that "the western wing of the (Persian) fleet sailed on a wide curve for Salamis, while the second section, consisting of ships stationed near Ceos and Cynosura, blocked the whole channel all the way to Munichia." Xerxes also sent troops to occupy the island of Psyttaleia, who were supposed to rescue crews from his battle-damaged ships, and kill those of the enemy.[35]

Scholars disagree about the location of Ceos, where the Persian "second section" was stationed, and I find the view that identifies it with the harbor of Zea in the Piraeus peninsula more convincing than other possibilities (Map 6). Less in dispute are the identifications of Munychia on the eastern Phaleron Bay, of Cynosura as Cape Varvari on Salamis, and of the island of Psyttaleia (Lipsokoutai) across from Cynosura. Even so, there are difficulties in reconciling the reports of Aeschylus and Herodotus with each other as well as with Diodorus, who is the only source for the dispatch of an Egyptian fleet to the western straits separating Salamis from Megara. A reconstruction that keeps as close as possible to the ancient accounts suggests that the Persians sent naval contingents to guard both the western Megaran straits and the eastern straits between Cynosura and Psyttaleia. Their mission was secondary in importance to that of the main Persian force, which sailed north through the eastern straits between Psyttaleia and the Piraeus in the direction of the Bay of Eleusis, intending to engage

35. Quotation from Aeschylus: *Persians* 364–383 LCL, Sommerstein trans.; from Hdt.: 8.76, Waterfield trans. Persian movements: Aeschylus *Persians* 447–454; Hdt. 8.71, 76; Diod. 11.17.1–2. For Herodotus' partial use of Aeschylus: Parker 2007a.

the Greeks in battle and to prevent their retreat to Eleusis Bay from their anchorages on the Salamis shore north of Cynosura. Aeschylus' statement that the Persians arranged their ships in three lines is unclear, but also less than crucial for understanding the battle. It could mean that they advanced in three columns or ranks, or that they sent the main body to sail into the channel and two other contingents on guarding duty, or a score of other possibilities. In addition, the Persians stationed land troops on the mainland coastline toward the Peloponnese. Their role resembled that of the troops on the island of Psyttaleia: to support and rescue their ships and crews and to kill enemy crewmen in case they reached land.[36]

The sources suggest that what finally persuaded the Greeks to stay in Salamis was the arrival of enemy ships across from them. We are told that, while the Greek commanders were still arguing about the decision to leave Salamis, the Athenian leader Aristides arrived from Aegina after successfully evading the Persian naval blockade. Perhaps guessing more than knowing, he told Themistocles that the Persians now controlled all exits out of Salamis. The two agreed to set aside their political differences, and Themistocles asked Aristides to tell the Greek commanders the news, because Themistocles' advocacy of fighting at Salamis gave him low credibility. One might add that his record of persuading non-Athenians was not very good. In spite of Aristides' reputation for honesty, he was not believed, largely because his agenda was identical to Themistocles'. Only the arrival of a deserter enemy ship from the Aegean island of Tenos, whose captain apprised the Greeks of the Persian plan, convinced the Greek generals that they had no choice but to fight.[37]

It was now dawn, and both sides must have been tired: the Persians had been rowing since midnight, with the extra effort of rowing quietly to avoid detection, and the Greek commanders had argued all night. The Greeks also suffered from a shortage of supplies and were full of trepidation.

---

36. For the interpretation offered here, see also Green 1996, esp. 181–182. Other reconstructions: e.g., Lazenby 1993, 174–181 (identifying Ceos with Zea); Strauss 2004, 126–140; Wallinga 2005, 50–53 (locating Ceos around the Megara–Salamis straits); and for a summary of scholarly interpretations: Bowie 2007, 164–166; Garvie 2009, 186–187. Persian land troops; Hdt. 8.71, 92.

37. Hdt. 8.82–83; Plut. *Themistocles* 12 (mistaking Tenedos for Tenos); *Aristides* 8. See Frost 1998, 132–133, against Diod. 11.17.3–4, where the informer is a Samian swimmer who promised a wholesale Ionian desertion during the battle (which never happened).

Then their mood changed to "courage born of necessity," as Plutarch puts it. Themistocles had a share in the transformation. He exhorted the marines assembled on the ships' decks to make their best effort. It was an important moment for him because it confirmed his transition from an Athenian general into an all-Greek leader.[38]

It is common to treat the different testimonies on the Battle of Salamis as pieces of the same puzzle, but some of them do not fit. Chief among these is the sources' disagreement on the position and orientation of the opposing lines before fighting began, a discrepancy that affects the reconstruction of the entire battle. The sources also disagree on where the Spartan fleet was stationed, who started the fighting, and how it evolved. Consequently, historians, including the present author, must resort to the less-than-ideal solution of selective reading and filling the gaps with speculations.[39]

According to historian Diodorus, Themistocles and Eurybiades established the Greek dispositions for battle. It is a rare acknowledgment that Themistocles was not solely responsible for such arrangements. The Greek navy of around 366 ships was deployed in several lines, with the 180 Athenian ships leading what Herodotus called "the western" and Diodorus "the left" wing, while thirty Aeginetan and twenty Megaran ships held the eastern or right wing. The rest of the Greeks occupied the center.[40] Herodotus places the sixteen Spartan ships on the eastern/right wing, and Diodorus, on the left wing next to the Athenians, but the question of their exact location is less important than their role in the battle, on which the sources' silence is eloquent. The Persian side of about 600–700 ships was also arranged in several lines. Its best contingents consisted of the Phoenician ships that led the Persian western or right wing across from the Athenians. Next to the Phoenicians were stationed Cypriot, Cilician, and

---

38. Lack of supply: Hdt. 8.68. A dubious tradition in Plut. *Themistocles* 13 tells us that the "violent mob" sacrificed three Persian prisoners to "Dionysius the Flesh Eater." At most, it illustrates the pre-battle terror; and see Frost 1998, 135; Marr 1998, 105–116. Themistocles' exhortation: Hdt. 8.83; Graham 1996.

39. See the following notes in this chapter. Modern discussions: Hignett 1963, 193–239; Hammond 1973, 215–310; Roux 1974; Burn 1984, 450–475; Green 1996, 153–198; Lazenby 1993, 151–197; Strauss 2004, 157–208; Wallinga 2005, 55–159; Shepherd 2010.

40. Greek battle lines: Diod. 11.18.1; Hdt. 8.83. Wings: Hdt. 8.85; Diod. 11. 18.1–2. 180 Athenians ships: Hdt. 8.44, 46, 61; Plut. *Themistocles* 11, 14, and see also Nepos *Themistocles* 3.2 and the Themistocles Decree. 30 Aeginetan and Megarans ships: Hdt. 8.1, 45.

Pamphylian ships, with the Lycians in the rear. The Ionian Greeks were in the Persian eastern or left wing.[41]

According to Aeschylus, our earliest source on the battle, one Persian force, arranged in three lines, was supposed to guard the exits, while "others" were to surround Salamis. He adds that the Persians guarding the exits and the straits were surprised when the Greeks, whom they had expected to flee, showed up ready for battle. A straight reading of the text suggests that the Persians were positioned around the eastern exits between the Cynosura Peninsula and the island of Psyttaleia, and that Aeschylus' "others" probably refers to additional forces that guarded the Megaran straits.[42] But other sources complicate the picture. According to Herodotus, the disposition of the western (right) wing of the Persians, made up of Phoenicians, and that of the Athenians who opposed them were "towards Eleusis," while the eastern (left) Persian wing, made up of Ionians, and the Spartans who faced them were "towards the Piraeus." This probably means northwest-to-southeast opposing lines, with the Persians positioned along the western Attic coast and the Greeks along the eastern coast of Salamis. Herodotus does not say where the respective lines started or ended. Diodorus, who agrees to some extent with Herodotus about the makeup of the lines, differs sharply about their orientation. He says that the Greeks sailed into battle and occupied the straits from Salamis to the shrine of Heracles. By most accounts the shrine was on the Attic shore, somewhere near modern Perama. This means that, unlike Herodotus, who envisaged Greek and Persian lines stretched along the opposite shores of the straits, Diodorus describes a Greek line from east to west *across* the straits. I am less than fully certain in my preference for Herodotus' version over Diodorus', but the former's account is more compatible with other accounts of the battle. By this interpretation, the Greeks were originally arranged in a line that stretched from the southwestern shore of the bay across from Ayios Georgios (St. George) Island to the tip of the Cynosura promontory. The western point of the Persian battle lines was around the Pharmacussae Islands (Ayios Georgios) and a nearby reef that was a small island in antiquity, while their eastern point was near Cynosura. Unlike the Greeks, the Persians continued to send ships into the straits, perhaps accounting for Aeschylus' description of the Persians' first guarding the

---

41. The Spartan fleet: Diod. 11.18.1; Hdt. 8.43, 85. Persian dispositions: Hdt. 8.85; Diod. 11.18.1, 19.1.

42. Aeschylus *Persians* 361–398. For this and other interpretations of the "others," see Garvie 2009, 186–187.

straits and then meeting the Greeks there. Each fleet was backed by troops on the shore it held.[43]

Both the Greeks and the Persians arranged their ships several lines deep. There is little benefit in speculating how deep, because the depth depended on too many unknown or conjectural factors, such as where exactly they fought, the depth of the sea along the coast, the minimal distance required between ships, and how many ships could be squeezed into the straits under these conditions. Since there is no indication that the Persians tried to outflank the Greeks, it appears that the opposing front lines were at first fairly equal in length.[44]

The ancient accounts also differ on when and how the conflict began and how it evolved. Instead of preferring one source to the exclusion of another, I offer the following description, on the premise that the sources can be largely reconciled if we assume that they cobbled together (not necessarily in strict chronological order) actions that took place in different locales and stages of the battle. Our description will be followed by examinations of selected, disputed aspects of the battle and of Themistocles' role in the fighting.

The battle started at dawn and lasted as long as there was light. The Persians attacked first, and the Greeks, led by their right wing, backed water toward the shore until one of their ships charged an enemy ship and got entangled with it, whereupon the Greeks came to its rescue.[45] It is possible that the Greeks delayed their counterattack until a blowing wind destabilized the Persian ships, and credit was given to Themistocles for choosing this timing. The battle then devolved into mostly single encounters

---

43. The directions of the lines: Hdt. 8.85; Diod. 11.18.2. For Heracles' shrine, which is related to the point from which Xerxes' viewed the battle: Hdt. 8.90; Plut. *Themistocles* 13; Lazenby 1993, 185–186; Frost 1998, 133. My interpretation is closer, though not identical, to Lazenby, Strauss, and Wallinga than to Roux, Burn, Hammond, and Green (add Green 2006, 71n74), who rely largely on Diodorus.

44. See the previous note and note 24, above. Depth of the lines: Aeschylus *Persians* 365; Hdt. 8.89; Plut. *Themistocles* 15; Diod. 11.18.4. Equal length of lines: Plut. *Themistocles* 15. It is likely that the 207 Persian fast ships, mentioned by Aeschylus *Persians* 341–343, were positioned at the front. Wallinga 2005, 57–58, thinks that only these ships were sent into the straits.

45. Conflict at dawn and the Greek right wing in the lead: Aeschylus *Persians* 384–385; Hdt. 8.83. Persian attack, Greek withdrawal, and the charge of the single ship: Hdt. 8.84; Aeschylus *Persians* 408–411; Plut. *Themistocles* 15. Diodorus, too, gives the first blow to a Persian admiral who died valiantly in combat: 11.18.5.

between opposing ships, which took place simultaneously in roughly two locations: along the straits between the Cynosura Peninsula in the southeast and the Pharmacussae islands in the northwest, and around the exits to the Saronic Gulf (especially the more easterly exit) created by the Cynosura Peninsula and the island of Psyttaleia. In the straits, the Persians suffered from confusion created by the flight of some of their ships and the attempts of others to take their place. The Athenians used the Persian disorder and the impact of the wind to ram the enemy ships, at times first shearing their oars. Victorious, they pursued the Phoenician and Cypriot ships to the Attic shores and then returned to continue fighting, mostly around the exits from the straits.[46]

At the eastern exits, the Aeginetans and fellow Greek squadrons fought the Persian left wing, which suffered from lack of order throughout the day. The traffic of incoming ships through the exits forced the Persians to rearrange their lines, causing confusion that was compounded later by the movement of fleeing ships in the opposite direction. Diodorus adds that the death of the Persian admiral (probably Ariabignes, Xerxes' half-brother and the commander of the Ionians and the Carians) at the beginning of the battle caused his subordinates to give conflicting commands. The Aeginetans defeated their opponents and then sought to destroy ships that had managed to escape the Athenians. It is likely that Aeschylus' description of a Greek encirclement of the Persians refers to this stage of fighting. This is how the stage character of a Persian messenger to the royal court describes the events:

> At first the streaming Persian force resisted firmly; but when our masses of ships were crowded into a narrow space, they had no way to come to each other's help, they got stuck by their own side's bronze-pointed rams, they had all of their oarage smashed, and the Greek ships, noticing it, surrounded them completely and went on striking them. The hulls of our ships turned keel-up, and the sea surface was no longer visible, filled as it was with the wreckage of ships and slaughter of men; the shore and reefs were also full of corpses.[47]

46. Wind effect: Plut. *Themistocles* 14, and below. Persian confusion in the straits and the Athenian reaction to it: Hdt. 8.89; Diod. 11.19.1, 18.5–6. The sources never precisely place the "narrows" that confounded the Persians. Burn and Green, however, suggest that the fighting took place around the Pharmacussae islands: n. 39 above. Athenian pursuit and return: Diod. 11.19.1–2.

47. Quotation: Aeschylus *Persians* 412–421, Sommerstein trans. The Aeginetan fleet: Hdt. 8.91; Diod. 11.19.1. Persian movements around the exits: Diod. 11.18.4; Hdt. 8.91–92. The Persian admiral: Diod. 11.18.5, with Hdt. 7.97; 8.89. Green 1996, 192, places him at the head of the Phoenicians on the other wing in order to accommodate

Against this description of the Persians busily bumping into each other or fleeing the scene, it should be said that by most accounts they continued to fight in spite of the difficulties. In addition, some Persians who lost their ships survived by getting to friendly Attic shores. We do not know what role the squadrons that were originally assigned to guard the eastern and western exits played; we may assume that some of them joined the battle but that many more participated in the general flight. A great number of Persians drowned because they did not know how to swim and because the Greeks hunted them down. Aeschylus describes a gruesome scene of the Greeks using the debris of ships to kill their crews.

> Meanwhile the [Greek] enemy were clubbing men and splitting their spines with broken pieces of oars and spars from the wreckage, as if they were tunny or some other catch of fish, and a mixture of shrieking and wailing filled the expanse of the sea, until the dark face of night blotted it out.

According to Diodorus, the Greeks lost forty ships, compared to more than 200 Persian ships destroyed, discounting those that were captured.[48]

The only fighting on land associated with the battle happened on the island of Psyttaleia. Apparently during the Greek naval mopping-up operations, the Athenian Aristides took light-armed and hoplite troops (probably stationed on the Cynosura Peninsula), landed on the island, and killed most of the Persians there except for a few dignitaries. He then patrolled the shores in search of additional enemy personnel. In spite of scholars' efforts to magnify the military significance of this operation, it merely helped solidify the victory and the Greeks' control over the straits.[49]

an unreliable tradition that he was killed by the Athenian Aminias: Plut. *Themistocles* 15; Diod. 11.27.2. Aeginetans and Athenians: Hdt. 8.91.

48. Persians drowning: Hdt. 8.89; saved by land troops: 8.92. Quotation: Aeschylus *Persians* 432–428, Sommerstein trans. Losses: Diod. 11.19.3. Less reliably, Ctesias (*Persica* 30) and Plutarch (*Moralia* 349a) count 500 and 1,000 lost Persian ships, respectively.

49. Psyttaleia: Aeschylus *Persians* 447–471; Hdt. 8.76, 95; Plut. *Aristides* 9 (who gives Aristides sole credit for the idea). Hignett's (1963, 238n7) rejection of Pausanias' (1.36.2) statement that 400 enemy fighters died on the island is unconvincing. See Saïd 1992–1993; Green 1996, 196–197; Harrison 2000, 97–98; Strauss 2004, 195–196; Wallinga 2005, 87–89; Rosenbloom 2006, 72–74.

Some clarifications regarding contested events of the battle are in order. According to Herodotus, the initial Persian attack resulted in the Greeks' backing water toward the shore until one of their ships charged the enemy and the rest came to its rescue (p. 85 above). Herodotus is the sole source for the Greek withdrawal, and it has been maintained that he is here describing a tactical retreat or a ploy designed to bait or confuse the enemy. Yet Herodotus' statement that the retreating Greeks were about to beach their ships suggests that their withdrawal was not a deception, but due to fear. He had no reason to omit the presumed stratagem, which was not beyond his comprehension and would have added to the Greeks' credit.[50] Herodotus also refers to an ancient controversy over which ship attacked the Persians first. The Athenians claimed that it was one of theirs under the brave Captain Aminias, but the Aeginetans claimed the ship as their own. We should follow Herodotus' reluctance to decide between the competing claims to fame. The clash probably took place on the Athenian wing, because the Aeginetan tradition does not exclude the possibility that their ship fought alongside the Athenians rather than with the other Aeginetan ships on the other wing.[51]

Herodotus records an additional ancient controversy, reproducing an Athenian tradition according to which the Corinthian fleet, led by their general, Adeimantus, hoisted sail at the beginning of the battle and took off in the direction of Eleusis Bay. There they met a mysterious boat whose crew reproached them for running away while the Greeks were winning. The Corinthians returned to the main Greek fleet, only to find out that the battle was over. Herodotus asserts, however, that the Corinthians vehemently denied the story and argued that they were among the first to join battle, with the rest of the Greeks supporting their version. Epigraphic evidence, some from Athenian-controlled Salamis, confirms that the Corinthians and their general fought at Salamis, suggesting that the Athenian story about their escape belongs to later times when the two states were hostile to each other. Nevertheless, scholars have tried to rehabilitate the Corinthians even further. They place them initially north of the main Greek fleet and turn their to-and-fro movements into an attempt to deceive the Persians into thinking that the Greeks were fleeing or to bait them into a false pursuit. Because the evidence for the Corinthians' alleged departure and return comes

50. Hdt. 8.84. Greek feigned, tactical retreat: Green 1996, 187–188; Wallinga 2005, 129; cf. Burn 1984, 458. See also Hignett 1963, 234; Lazenby 1993, 189; Strauss 2004, 164–166.
51. Hdt. 8.84. Aeschylus *Persians* 408–411 does not identify the ship that charged first.

from a discredited source, it is better to assume that the Corinthians never left their post, which was probably next to the Athenians'.[52]

Lastly, Plutarch's biography of Themistocles credits the Athenian general with using nature to battle the enemy. He skillfully picked the time of attack when a breeze blew in and the waters swelled. This did not affect the lighter and lower Greek ships, but it slewed around the heavy Persian ships with their high sterns and raised decks and made them present their broadsides to the Greeks. The latter rushed upon them while keeping an eye on Themistocles, who knew what was best for them.[53]

Plutarch's version combines the credible with the less so. Nowadays a breeze called the *Aura* starts blowing through the Salamis straits between 8:00 and 10:00 a.m., sometimes making the sea choppy. A study of ancient Phoenician ships confirms that they were tall and had bulwarks, which would make them more vulnerable to the effect of the wind than the heavier (*pace* Plutarch) or slower Greek ships. Conversely, Herodotus argues that the Phoenician ships handled better than the Greeks', and all sources, including Plutarch, indicate that the Persians did not merely offer their broadsides to the attackers but continued to fight. Moreover, the claim that the Greeks waited for the wind before attacking contradicts both Aeschylus and Herodotus, who time the beginning of the conflict earlier, at dawn. It also challenges Herodotus' report that the Persians attacked first. A plausible compromise can be reached if we assume that the Persians charged first, shortly after dawn, and that the Greeks retreated in fear before changing direction in an attempt to rescue the Greek ship that turned around. Some time later, they timed their attack with the wind and the swell. It is also possible that Themistocles gave them the signal, yet Plutarch's claim that the Greeks won because Themistocles picked the place and the time of battle is exaggerated. At best, he led his wing, but not the entire Greek line; while the wind did not win the battle for the Greeks, but only gave them a non-decisive advantage. It was the Persians who made the greatest contribution to the Greek victory.[54]

---

52. The Corinthian controversy: Hdt. 8.94. A Corinthian maneuver: Burn 1984, 458–460; Green 1996, 186–187; Strauss 2004, 152, 163, 200–203; Wallinga 2005, 125–129, but see Lazenby 1993, 189–190. Epigraphic evidence exonerating the Corinthians: Plut. *Moralia* 870c–871a; *ML* no. 24. Plut. *Moralia* 870e suggests they were on the left wing.
53. Plut. *Themistocles* 14; cf. Aelius Aristides 2.282.
54. Accepting Plutarch's version: Green 1996, 190; Strauss 2004, 145, 152–154, 164–166. Rejecting Plutarch: Hignett 1963, 233; Frost 1998, 138–139; Lazenby 1993, 186; Wallinga 2005, 96–97. The structure of the Phoenician ships: Hdt. 8.10; Basch 1969; Wallinga 2005, 94–107.

All sources agree that the Greeks enjoyed superior order and discipline. The sources differ about the causes of Persian disorganization, perhaps because they, and even contemporaries, were unsure how to account for it. Thus we hear that the Persian confusion was due to their conflicting wishes to flee and to continue fighting (Herodotus), to the wind (Plutarch), to the death of their admiral (Diodorus), and to their inability (in various forms) to deal with the narrows (Aeschylus, Diodorus, and Plutarch). In other words, the Persians' defeat was the result of their tactical and organizational incompetence in overcoming these challenges, compounded by Greek discipline and fighting skills.

The last point is relevant to the way the battle was fought and to Themistocles' generalship. In a naval battle, cooperation among the crewmen of an individual ship was much more essential to success than that between a ship and its sister ships. A ship might help another in distress, but the brunt of the battle was borne by single vessels that chased and attacked their counterparts wherever they found them. It meant that collective action, the domain of the general, was limited. He set up lines that served a mostly defensive purpose. With the attack, however, the lines dissolved into individual encounters, as is reflected in many accounts of Salamis, including Aeschylus', which says that "each captain chose a different enemy ship at which to run his own." Herodotus individualized the fighting even more, not just for the sake of recording fame and enlivening the narrative, but because that was the nature of the battle. The story of Xerxes' ally, the wily Carian queen Artemisia, exemplifies individualism in battle. Pursued by the Athenian captain Aminias, she rammed and sank a fellow or neighboring Carian ship, as if she were fighting on the Greek side. Her action duped her Athenian pursuer, who left her alone, thinking that she was either a Greek or a defector (and thus losing the 10,000-drachma bounty on her head). She also deceived Xerxes, who saw her from afar and praised her action. Aminias started from a position across from the Persian right wing. We cannot be certain about Artemisia's original position, but if the placing of her fellow Carians and the Ionians under joint command the year before is an indication, she probably fought next to the Ionians on the Persian left wing. Either she or Aminias left their original positions to fight on their own. There are additional illustrations of the fluid, even chaotic nature of the battle.[55]

The Battle of Salamis was won by a common rather than a coordinated effort of the Greek captains and crews. Themistocles' role as general was

---

55. Aeschylus quotation: *Persians* 411. Artemisia's ploy and position: Hdt. 7.97; 8.87–88, 93–94. Examples of single, at times fluctuating, encounters: Hdt. 8.90; Pausanias 10.9.1; Plut. *Moralia* 869d = Simonides Fr. 19, Campbell.

prescribed by such circumstances. It is explicitly attested for the pre-battle stage and included arranging the lines, instructing the marines, and timing the Greek attack with the blowing of the wind. There were additional group actions, such as the Athenians' return from pursuing the enemy to rejoin the battle, the Aeginetans' patrolling the exits, and the Greeks' surrounding Persian ships in the narrows. But we should respect the sources' silence about Themistocles' role in any of them.[56]

One last episode in Herodotus throws additional light on Themistocles' contribution to Salamis. While an Aeginetan ship rammed and captured a Phoenician vessel, Themistocles was sailing by in pursuit of an unidentified ship. The Aeginetan captain, Polycritus, recognized the Athenian flagship by its insignia and taunted Themistocles with the Aeginetan victory over the enemy ship, using it to refute charges made by Athens in the past against Aegina's and Polycritus' father for their collaboration with the Persians. The Athenian–Aeginetan rivalry aside, the incident shows how Themistocles' role as general changed into that of a ship captain once the battle moved beyond its initial stage.[57]

Themistocles after Salamis

Salamis was Themistocles' finest hour. Many Athenians—Themistocles most of all—believed victory could not have been achieved without him and his fellow citizens. Other Greeks begged to differ. They awarded the prize for valor and excellence among cities to Aegina, and recognized among individual captains the aforementioned Aminias of Athens and Polycritus of Aegina. We are told that nobody won the award for "the Greek who excelled all others" in the war, because every general put himself first, and many of them, Themistocles second. A second place could be excused as due to envy or even as a consolation prize, but it was still not as good as being proclaimed the best.[58] Themistocles did not settle for such a disappointing result, and advertised his exploits with monuments and word of mouth. He also received special honors in Sparta. He was invited there, perhaps on Eurybiades' initiative, and was awarded

---

56. Lazenby's comment (1993, 196) on the Greek victory is apt: it was "won not by tactical brilliance . . . but by hard fighting."
57. Hdt. 8.92. Charges against Aegina: Hdt. 6.49–59, 73.
58. Second place: Hdt. 8.93, 123–124; Plut. *Themistocles* 17; Diod. 11.27.2. Justin 2.14.10–11 and Aelius Aristides 13.1.224 wrongly award Themistocles the first prize.

the prize for wisdom and cleverness, while Eurybiades got the award for valor. The Spartans would not concede military excellence to others, but in this case they may have been right in distinguishing between military and advisory skills. They then gave Themistocles a beautiful chariot and sent him away escorted by a special infantry unit, traditionally called "the Cavalrymen," that normally surrounded the Spartan king. Their intention was to acknowledge his and Athens' role in the war and to gain their gratitude. Little did they know that, in later years, the Athenians would construe their gesture as a Spartan concession of Athens' primacy in saving Greece.[59]

In spite of the honors, Themistocles' career after Salamis was marked by a downward trajectory. At home, other leaders such as Aristides, Xanthippus (father of the future leader Pericles), and Cimon (son of Miltiades of Battle of Marathon fame) were edging him out, and soon Sparta would put him on its enemies' list. Since we are interested mainly in Themistocles' generalship, we shall limit our examination to that aspect of his later career.

After his defeat at Salamis, Xerxes decided to retreat to Asia Minor by land and leave part of his land forces in Greece to continue the war under the general Mardonius. He instructed his fleet to sail toward the Hellespont and to guard the bridges there in expectation of his crossing back into Asia. The Greeks missed the departure of the Persian navy because they expected the king to offer another naval battle or to build a mole for a land attack on the island of Salamis. On realizing their error, they pursued him, but, unable to catch the enemy ships, they stopped at the Cycladic island of Andros to discuss their next step. At the generals' council, according to Herodotus, Themistocles suggested that the Greek navy sail to the Hellespont and destroy the bridges there. The Spartan admiral Eurybiades opposed him, arguing in favor of letting the Persians go because trapping them in Greece could result in its devastation and perhaps a reconquest. The Peloponnesian generals supported Eurybiades' suggestion, which carried the day.

It is easy to agree with the Spartans' wounded- or caged-animal rationale for not obstructing the Persian retreat. But there was more to the debate than that. It confirms Themistocles' poor record of persuading Greeks other than his fellow Athenians, and shows how the Athenians and the Spartans

---

59. Themistocles' self-promotion: Plut. *Themistocles* 18; Pausanias 1.36.1. Honors for Themistocles: Hdt. 8.124; Plut. *Themistocles* 17; Diod. 11.27.3; Jordan 1988. Athens' view of the honors: Thuc. 1.74.3.

differed over the goals of the war. As the previous chapter argues, in Spartan eyes, the war was fought to defend Greece and expel the Persians, while for the Athenians it was also (and perhaps more) about defeating and destroying them. This is why the Athenian captains at Andros did not want to let Xerxes and part of his army leave and planned to defy the Council's decision by sailing to the Hellespont and destroying the bridges. But Themistocles was unwilling at this stage to fracture the Greek coalition. He was probably also less confident than his fellow Athenians of their ability to defeat the Persian navy singlehandedly. Therefore, he used Eurybiades' reasoning to persuade them to give up their plan.[60]

According to Herodotus, Themistocles tried to gain personally from the decision not to sail to the Hellespont. He once again sent his loyal emissary Sicinnus on a secret mission to Xerxes, who was still in Attica, to tell the king that he had done him a favor by stopping the Greeks from pursuing his fleet and destroying the bridges. Other sources credit him with the worthier motive of trying to scare the king into hastening his retreat to Asia and leaving only part of his army in Greece, thereby making the later Greek victory over the Persians at Plataea more feasible. Historians have rejected the story, chiefly from disbelief that Xerxes would trust Themistocles a second time. However, as with his first message to the king, he was only encouraging Xerxes to stick with his original plan of leaving Greece, and Themistocles' message, whether he believed it or not, confirmed the danger to his way out of it. There was nothing unpatriotic in Themistocles' taking credit for something that the Greeks did not do.[61]

With the mission to the Hellespont aborted, the Greek fleet turned to punishing Greek cities for their "Medism" (collaboration with the Persians). Herodotus, who presents Themistocles after Salamis mostly in a negative light, now portrays him as an avaricious bully. Unbeknownst to the other

---

60. Hdt. 8.108–109, whose version is preferable to Plut. *Themistocles* 16; *Aristides* 9; cf. Aelius Aristides, 2.293. Podlecki's skepticism (1975, 25) of the debate is justified for some of its details but not for the entire episode: see Strauss 2004, 231–233, and cf. Hignett 1963, 241–243; Baragwanath 2008, 289, 298–300.

61. Themistocles' message: Hdt. 8.110; Ctesias *FGrHist* 699 Fr. 13.30; Diod. 11.19.5–6; Plut. *Themistocles* 16; *Aristides* 9; cf. Thuc. 1.137.4; Nepos *Themistocles* 5.1–2; Pausanias 1.30.4; Justin 2.13.5. Xerxes' retreat plans: Hdt. 7.107. Rejecting the story: Marr 1995b; Blösel 2004, 265–284. Crediting it to varying degrees: Lazenby 1993, 199–202; cf. Podlecki 1975, 26–27; Frost 1998, 147–148. As it happened, a storm destroyed the bridges, and the Persians crossed to Asia on boats: Hdt. 8.117.

Greek commanders, he extorted money from Cycladic cities on the charge of helping the Persians. Themistocles was not averse to personal profit, but it is much likelier that the Medized cities could not have been fined or besieged unless the other Greeks approved. If he was the leading general in these operations, he was also chiefly responsible for the failed sieges of the island of Andros and of the city of Carystus on Euboea.[62]

Themistocles disappears from history until about the winter of 479–478. Other leaders led the Athenian contingents in the battles that concluded the Persian War, on land at Plataea and at sea across from Samos at Mycale. There is little profit in speculating why he was not among these generals or whether he participated in these battles at all. It is more fruitful to examine two postwar strategic projects that he initiated: the building of the city walls, and the development and fortification of the harbor of the Piraeus.[63]

The Persian occupation of Athens had left most of the city in ruins, and the Athenians began restoring and fortifying it. According to historian Thucydides, our chief informant on how Themistocles tricked the Spartans into complying with the operation, the Spartans did not want any city to be fortified, and their allies were afraid of Athens' navy and confidence. So a Spartan delegation asked the Athenians to stop the constructions and even join them in destroying walls of other cities outside the Peloponnese under the pretext that, if the Persians returned, they would not have any fortified place for a base. In contrast, the Peloponnese could provide a shelter and a base of operation for any Greek attack.[64] Themistocles responded with a conceal-and-delay tactic. He told the Spartans to go home and wait for an Athenian embassy that would discuss the issue. But before he and other envoys left for Sparta, he instructed the Athenians to mobilize every pair of hands at their disposal, women's and children's included, in order to build the walls in haste, using whatever came handy. A portion of Athens' ancient wall has been identified as "Themistocles Wall," because, unlike the usual cut and well-assembled stones, it uses blocks of different sizes, including broken statue bases and

---

62. Hdt. 8.111–112, recapitulated by Plut. *Themistocles* 20; Bowie 2007, 202; cf., however, Baragwanath 2008, 289–322.
63. Except for a wall around the Acropolis and a sacred ground on its slope, there is no archaeological evidence for a prewar city walls: Papadopoulos 2008. Vanderpool 1974, however, argues for their historicity.
64. Thuc. 1.90.1–2.

FIGURE 8 *"Themistocles' wall."*
Photograph by Alaniaris, Wikimedia.

reliefs (Figure 8). Nevertheless, the roughly 6.5-kilometers-long wall was soundly constructed.[65]

Once in Sparta, Themistocles kept avoiding the subject of the wall, and when reports on the building in progress kept coming, he advised the Spartans to send envoys to check the situation for themselves. He also secretly told the Athenians to keep the Spartan envoys tactfully in Athens until he and his colleagues returned, fearing that the Spartans would not let them go. When he finally learned that the walls had reached a desirable height, he delivered a proud address to the Spartans in which he stressed Athens' independence. He argued that for Athens to have walls was in both her own and other Greeks' interest, adding that "an equal and fair contribution to decisions on common policy could only be made from a position of equal strength." Thucydides says that the Spartans concealed their anger and told the Athenian envoys that Athens was their friend and that their original

---

65. Thuc. 1.89.1–93.2. "Themistocles' Wall": Boersma 1970, 154; Wycherley 1978, 7–25. It is possible, however, that some of the tombs' remains incorporated into the wall belonged to a later period; and see Blösel 2012, 220–221, against associating this portion of the wall with Themistocles.

suggestion to halt the fortifications was made for the good of all Greeks. They then sent the Athenian delegation home.

This story has its share of problems. It is unclear why the Athenians had to build the walls clandestinely and under a ruse if the Spartans did not prohibit it or threaten Athens with sanctions. Sources later than Thucydides add (probably to solve this puzzle) that Spartan delegations ordered the Athenians to stop the work and even warned them of potential punishment. This is unlikely. While the Spartans had their differences with Athens during the war, they understood their limited power to dictate to the Athenians what to do. Equally dubious are stories that attempt to explain Themistocles' success in duping and persuading the Spartans. They report either that he pleaded a long illness to delay his arrival in Sparta, or that he bribed its magistrates not to oppose the project.[66] Indeed, all our testimonies on the affair reflect a biased perspective that highlights the Athenians' patriotism, independence, and superior intelligence. It is better to distinguish between the Spartans' actions (and even their words) and the motives ascribed to them. Sparta and its allies were no doubt interested in leaving Athens unfortified and therefore dependent on their goodwill and power. But this desire complemented rather than contradicted their stated argument against fortifying Athens, which made good military sense. There was a real fear that the Persians would try to avenge their defeat with a second invasion, and their reoccupation of Athens was not a far-fetched prospect. The Spartans' offer of the Peloponnese as a refuge was also in line with their pre-Salamis strategy of fighting the invaders from there. In short, even if Sparta was concerned about Athens' rising power, it viewed the Persian threat with equal apprehension. I suggest that it was Themistocles who perceived the Spartan appeal as an ultimatum and an insult, because he saw Sparta more as a rival than as an ally. He also persuaded the Athenians that Sparta would take action to prevent the building of the walls unless the Athenians did it secretly and in a hurry. Perhaps he reminded them of how King Cleomenes I of Sparta had expelled families from Athens about a generation earlier

---

66. Diod. 11.39.1–40.5 (Spartan orders and threats); Plut. *Themistocles* 19; Nepos *Themistocles* 6.2–7.6; Justin 2.15.1–2; Polyaenus 1.30.5; Frontinus *Stratagems* 1.1.10 (excusing delay due to illness); cf. Demosthenes, *Against Leptines* 20.73. Bribing the Spartans: Andocides *On the Peace* 3.38; Theopompus *FGrHist* 115 F 85; and rejecting this allegation: Marr 1998, 118–119.

(508–507) and then had mobilized a Peloponnesian army in an attempt to invade Attica and overthrow its democracy. Another unwarranted fear was that the Spartans would not release him after discovering the truth. The Athenians held Spartan envoys in Athens as hostages, but that is not why the Spartans failed to detain him: the idea that Themistocles and his fellow envoys would be detained was his, not the Spartans', and in one version of the story, he even offers himself to the Spartans as security for the safe return of their envoys from Athens. It is also hard to see the Spartans holding Themistocles under guard just because he lied to them, or really believing that keeping him would stop the Athenians from building the walls. It has been argued that Themistocles knowingly sacrificed his good standing in Sparta for the sake of his city. It is equally likely that his trickery was ill conceived and that he unnecessarily introduced tensions into the Sparta–Athens relationship.[67]

The conspiratorial dimension of Themistocles' leadership recurs in another tale. Allegedly, he plotted to remove all rivals to Athens' naval power by destroying the Spartan fleet or the entire Greek navy, only to be stopped by the more fair-minded Aristides and the Athenian people. The story has less to do with history than with the traditional images of Aristides as just and of Themistocles as a no-holds-barred schemer. But there is little doubt that Themistocles continued to antagonize the Spartans. The Amphictyonic League was an organization of states associated with the sanctuary and oracle of Apollo at Delphi, and in 478, Sparta proposed to expel from it states that cooperated with the Persians. This move would have increased Spartan power in the League, and Themistocles successfully opposed it, thereby doubtless earning for himself and Athens the gratitude of Thessaly, Thebes, and Argos, who were the candidates for expulsion. The incident followed other disagreements with Sparta concerning the Hellespontine bridges, the walls, and how to help the Ionians still under Persian rule. It did not mean that Themistocles foresaw the escalation of Athenian–Spartan rivalry into a full-scale Peloponnesian War a generation later. More probably, he aimed to make Athens an alternative to Sparta as leader of Greece. It was now, at the

---

67. Cleomenes and Athens: Hdt. 5.67–76. Themistocles' serving as security: Diod. 11.40.2–3. Themistocles' sacrifice: Podlecki 1975, 32. *Pace* Blösel, 2012, 216–223, the problems with the story are insufficient to discredit it wholly. For the affair, see also Hornblower 1991–2008, 1:135–138. For erroneous ascriptions to Themistocles of the building of the Long Walls between Athens and the Piraeus, see Constantakopoulou, 2007, 139–142.

latest, that the Spartans became hostile toward him and supportive of his rival, Cimon.[68]

Themistocles also transformed the Piraeus, about eight kilometers from the city, into Athens' chief harbor and fortified it. Since antiquity, the project has been considered one of his crowning strategic achievements. The most authoritative informant on the project is Thucydides, who believes that Themistocles had already started it in his archonship of 493–492 and that he continued to build it, probably around 477. The historian claims that Themistocles was the first Athenian leader to tell his countrymen to seek their future in the sea, and that he regarded the Piraeus as even more important than the upper city. A fortified Piraeus with strong, thick walls freed able men to serve in the navy, which was the foundation of Athens' maritime power and empire. The harbor and the navy also defended Athens from enemies who might threaten it by sea or land, and even allowed it to counterattack them. Taking their cue from Thucydides, other sources made Themistocles the architect of the Athenian Empire (on which see Ch. 3). They also claimed that he strengthened the political power of the common people, the *demos*, who rowed the boats.[69]

It is difficult to accept these assertions at face value. Thucydides' report says much about Themistocles' thoughts and intentions, to which he was not privy. In addition, his assertions (echoed by other sources) seem tainted with anachronism when they attribute to Themistocles later developments such as the growth of Athenian democracy and naval power, or even preparations for a future invasion of Attica. In fact it was not so much Themistocles but his political rivals, Cimon and Aristides, who set up the Attic-Delian League that later turned into an Athenian empire. Nor was Themistocles involved in any of the anti-Persian operations that characterized and legitimized Athenian imperial hegemony. Finally, the fortification of the Piraeus, like the rebuilding of Athens' walls, suggests a defensive rather than an expansionist

---

68. Alleged plan to destroy the Greek navy: Plut. *Themistocles* 20; or the Spartan fleet: Cicero *De Officiis* 3.49; Valerius Maximus 6.5. ext. 2; and see Podlecki 1975, 117; Marr 1998, 123–124. Themistocles and Delphi: Plut. *Themistocles* 20. The Ionian question: Hdt. 9.106.

69. Thuc. 1.93.3–7. Themistocles and the Athenian Empire and democracy: Plut. *Themistocles* 19; Diod. 11.41.1–43.3. The tradition that he hid the plan from both the Athenian Assembly and the Spartans is unlikely: Diod. 11.42.1–43.2, with Podlecki 1975, 96. At present, there is almost no archaeological evidence of the Piraeus' walls from Themistocles' times: Podlecki 1975, 179–181; Garland 1987, 14–22, 162–165. See also Constantakopoulou 2007, 139–140.

strategy. Nevertheless, Themistocles' role in the buildup of Athens' naval capability was revolutionary in an era that sought power and honor mostly from land warfare. For this innovation, he deserves full credit.[70]

The rest of Themistocles' career will be described here only briefly and for the sake of rounding up his story. He was ostracized from Athens in 470–471 after losing his popularity. He later became a man on the run until he settled in Asia Minor under the royal protection of Xerxes' successor. He died in the 450s at the reported age of 65. One questionable but patriotic tradition claims that he killed himself by drinking ox blood rather than assist the Persians in a campaign against the Athenians. If other uncertain traditions are to be believed, he did not rest in peace. It is said that his bones were secretly smuggled into Athens for burial, and many years later, a tomb near the Piraeus (appropriately enough) was identified as his.[71]

Conclusion

Undoubtedly Themistocles had many merits, some of which reflected his character. He demonstrated courage, gumption, and intelligence when he stood against a numerically superior Persian force at sea and prevailed by using the Greeks' maritime skills, geography, and nature. He was ambitious for himself and his city and could translate his ambitions into far-reaching projects. His naval bill, the Piraeus project, and his successful resistance to Sparta showed his strategic vision for Athens as a Greek leader. He was highly competitive and knew how to win, as he showed by prevailing over opposition to his war plans at home and among Greek allies. He was very good at manipulating people's fears, discerning their desires, and then using persuasion, deception, and other means to get their cooperation. He was resourceful and flexible, but also highly determined to stick to his plans even if he failed at first to realize them. These political skills often overshadowed his generalship when he was in command.

70. Thucydides, Themistocles, and the Piraeus: Blösel 2012, 222–223. On ancient critics of Themistocles and the demos: Frost 1998, 158–159; Marr 1998, 120–122. Diod. 11.43.3 reports that Themistocles persuaded the people to build 20 new triremes every year and give tax-free status to resident aliens and craftsmen who could help with the naval project. Since craftsmen, and especially resident aliens, continued to pay taxes, neither motion can be verified.

71. Themistocles' exile: Thuc. 1.135.2–138.6; Diod. 11.54.1–58.4; Plut. *Themistocles* 22–32; see Keaveney 2003. On the traditions about his death, see Marr 1995a.

Yet, before this summary turns into another paean of Themistocles, his accomplishments should be put in perspective. He was nothing like Leonidas or some other commanders discussed in this book, who distinguished themselves as warrior-generals. Even his notorious cunning and powers of persuasion failed more than once to get results. If the interpretation offered here is accepted, one of his greatest claims to fame—baiting Xerxes to fight at Salamis—was largely self-aggrandizement. His pursuit of honor and his self-perception as a farsighted man who could outsmart individuals, groups, and states blinded both contemporary and later observers. Views of him as the visionary founder of the later Athenian Empire are poorly substantiated. His fierce competiveness could be just as harmful as beneficial. It contributed to the rivalry with Sparta, which was unnecessary and even counterproductive. Cimon, the general who replaced him at the center of Athens' foreign and domestic policy, showed that Athens could grow in power while remaining Sparta's friend. There is a story that Themistocles wanted a colt from a horse breeder, apparently for free. When he was refused, he threatened that he would leave a wooden (Trojan) horse in the man's house; that is, encourage lawsuits within his household. In a way, this bully politician-general left a Trojan horse in Athens, in the form of uncompromising competition with Sparta.[72]

72. The horse breeder: Plut. *Themistocles* 5.

CHAPTER 3

Pericles of Athens
The Magisterial Commander

Pericles, Athenian Democracy, and His Military Challenges

Nothing is reported about the relationship between Themistocles, the subject of the last chapter, and Pericles (c. 495/90–429 BCE), the most famous of Athens' democratic leaders. Yet the two must have known each other because Pericles was Themistocles' younger contemporary. From the historian of the Peloponnesian War, Thucydides, onward, many writers have also presented Pericles as Themistocles' political and strategic heir. There are indeed close similarities between them. Both men improved the defense of the city and its harbor, developed its maritime power, and clashed with Sparta over Greek supremacy. In each man's generalship, military and political considerations were closely intertwined, and they both experienced ups and downs in their careers. The impact of both on Athens and Greece outlived their careers.[1]

Pericles was born between 495 and 490 to a family from the first ranks of the Athenian élite. His father, Xanthippus, was an active politician before the Persian War and a general during it. His mother, Agariste, came from the aristocratic and highly influential Alcmeonid family, which produced a

---

1. Pericles and Themistocles: Podlecki 1998, 11–16. For the ancient evidence on Pericles, see my "Bibliography, The Main Ancient Sources," s.vv. "Thucydides," "Diodorus," and "Plutarch"; and generally, Samons 2007, 1–4. Modern discussions of Pericles are numerous. Among the more recent monographs are Kagan 1991; Schubert 1994; Podlecki 1998; Will 2003; Lehmann 2008; Tracy 2009; Azoulay 2014. See also the following notes in this chapter.

FIGURE 9 *Pericles' bust.* A Roman copy of a Greek bronze original statue, now in the Vatican Museum. Contemporary comic authors had a field day with Pericles' heavy, elongated head, calling him a "squill" or (sea) onion head, and Plutarch (*Pericles* 3) claims that artists tried to hide it with a helmet.
© *Author*

number of leading politicians, including Cleisthenes, the father of Athenian democracy.[2]

The Athens of Pericles' day was more democratic and more powerful than in Themistocles' times. After the Persian War, the Athenians and Greeks from the Aegean formed the so-called Attic-Delian league, whose purpose was to continue the war against the Persians and liberate Greeks under Persian rule through the use of a common navy. Under the leadership of Cimon, son of Miltiades, the Athenians gradually turned the league into an Athenian empire and many of its members into tribute-paying subjects. The Spartans did not interfere much in this process, because they had no maritime ambitions and because they trusted their friend Cimon not to jeopardize their interests and

2. Pericles' family background, birth, and appearance: Hdt. 6.131; Plut. *Pericles* 3, 7; Stadter 1989, 62–68.

their hegemony on land. Cimon's political orientation was traditionalist, but leaders such as Ephialtes and Pericles pushed successfully for greater democratization of Athens. Thus Athenian democracy and imperialism went hand in hand, although it is debatable that they were causally linked.[3]

Pericles' public career stretched over a generation, roughly from the late 460s to his death in 429. As a general he encountered a variety of challenges, some common to the other commanders discussed in this book, others unique to his career. Like other generals, he was expected to lead both armies and fleets. He had to deal with an opposition that on land ranged from regular Greek armies to raiders and barbarians, and at sea from Greek fleets to pirates. Pericles was also significantly involved in siege warfare, both defensive and offensive. At times he was simultaneously engaged on more than one front and had to decide where to fight or whether to split his forces, sometimes on the basis of military intelligence that he knew was inadequate. The Athenian Empire presented him with the problem of rebel allies (including powerful ones, such as Samos, that had their own allies) and the need to settle their affairs in a way that would deter them from rebelling again. Loyal and new allies had to be defended from inimical neighbors, which meant expanding Athens' military commitments. Pericles' greatest test, however, was planning and directing the war against Sparta, a task that called for preparing the city militarily and mentally for a conflict he expected to be long and trying. He had to persuade the Athenians to agree with his strategy, which involved making difficult decisions, such as how to deal with the larger and better Peloponnesian army (he refused to engage it in battle) and how to reconcile the defense of Attica with that of the empire (he prioritized the latter). There were also unexpected hardships that emerged during the war, including a devastating plague and, apparently, depleted assets. Pericles met some of these challenges more successfully than others, as we shall see.

Pericles' Generalship Prior to the War Against Samos (463/2–441)

Our information about Pericles' military career up to the Samian revolt in 441 is sketchy. His first known command came in 463–462, when he led a fleet off the southern coast of Asia, but the purpose of the mission

---

3. The Athenian Empire: Meiggs 1972; Osborne 2000; Low 2008. I use "empire" for the Greek *arche* ("hegemony" or "control"): see Ma et al. 2009. Empire and democracy: Raaflaub 1994; Rhodes 2007; Brock 2009; cf. Foster 2010.

is unclear.[4] In 457, Pericles took part in the battle of Tanagra in Boeotia, between the Athenians with their Argive allies and the Spartans with their Peloponnesian allies. The Spartans won and went home, but a few months later, the Athenians returned to Boeotia and established their power there. Plutarch says that Pericles fought in Tanagra with vigor and bravery, but does not tell if he served as a soldier, a unit commander, or a general. As it happened, Tanagra was the only time that Pericles met in person a Spartan-led Peloponnesian army on the battlefield. Perhaps the memory of the defeat had something to do with his avoidance of the Peloponnesian armies that later invaded Attica, first in 446, and then in the early years of the Peloponnesian War.[5]

Around 454, Pericles led an expedition into western Greece (see Map 9, p. 131). The year before, the Athenian general Tolmides had led a highly successful campaign in that area, winning over cities on the Ionian islands of Zacynthus and Cephallenia, and settling Messenian refugees who had rebelled against Sparta in Naupactus on the northern shore of the Corinthian Gulf. Tolmides also captured the Corinthian post of Chalcis west of Naupactus, and concluded his term by winning a battle against Sicyon, Corinth's western neighbor. In comparison to Tolmides' exploits, Pericles' gains were relatively modest. He left the Megaran harbor of Pegae with a thousand hoplites and fifty (or 100) triremes, and he raided the Peloponnesian coast. He then invaded Sicyon and defeated its army, but was unable to capture the city. From Sicyon, Pericles sailed to neighboring Achaea, where he may have established an Athenian post. He reinforced his army with local troops and crossed over to Acarnania, which threatened Athens' ally Naupactus. Pericles converted many Acarnanians to the Athenian side and pillaged the land of others, but was unable to take the important city of Oeniadae, which remained hostile to Athens. He then returned home. It is possible that among the nine trophies that Pericles set up in the course of his career, one commemorated his exploits in this campaign. Yet his failure to take the cities of Sicyon and Oeniadae suggests why more important military assignments at that time went to other generals, such as Tolmides or Myronides.[6]

---

4. Pericles' early career: Bloedow 2011. His first command: Plut. *Cimon* 13 = Callisthenes *FGrHist* 124 F 16.
5. Pericles in Tanagra: Plut. *Pericles* 10; Fornara 1971, 46 (as a commander); Podlecki 1998, 44 (somewhat skeptical of Plutarch's report). For the battle, see Roisman 1993a.
6. Tolmides' campaign: Thuc. 1.108.5; Diod. 11.84.1–8; Pausanias 1.27.6; Scholion Aeschines 2.75 = Fornara 1983 no. 84; Lewis 1992a, 117–118. Pericles' expedition:

Pericles' involvement in military and international affairs intensified in the 440s. Around 450–449, he is said to have proposed the so-called Congress Decree, which invited Greeks from Asia and Europe to Athens to discuss Persian impiety during the Persian War, the oaths the Greeks took when they fought them, and how to secure safe sailing of the seas and peace among the Greeks. The authenticity of the decree is a subject of scholarly debate, but I agree with historians who regard it as genuine. It appears that Pericles, like Themistocles, vied with Sparta over the leadership of the Greek world, causing Sparta to oppose the decree and so discouraging other Greeks from showing up. But the two powers were not inevitably destined to fight each other, as the Second Sacred War of 449 or 448 demonstrates. This conflict revolved around a dispute between Phocis and Delphi over the control of the highly important temple and oracle of Apollo at Delphi. A Spartan army put Delphi in charge of both, and left the region, allowing Pericles to arrive with an Athenian army and transfer the temple to Phocis' control. Each power wanted to include the Delphic oracle in its sphere of influence, yet stopped short of an armed conflict. This mutual understanding would last for almost two decades before Pericles contributed to its breakup.[7]

Around 448, if not earlier, Pericles was reportedly involved in several colonization projects. Since the early days of the Attic-Delian League, Athens had been settling Athenians on foreign lands, where they retained their Athenian citizenship and helped in bolstering the security of the empire in a variety of ways, including checking allies' rebellions. Pericles led 1,000 settlers to the Thracian Chersonese, an important economic and strategic region that also helped ensure the security of ships importing grain to Athens from the Black Sea. The Chersonese was suffering from depredations by pirates and neighboring Thracian tribes, and Pericles built fortifications at its neck to defend the local settlements. He is also said to have been involved in setting Athenians on Naxos, on Andros, and among the Thracian Bisaltians.

Thuc. 1.111.2–3; Diod. 11.85.1–2 (50 triremes), 88.1–2; Plut. *Pericles* 19 (100 triremes). See p. 148 below, for the regional politics in western Greece. Frontinus' *Stratagems* 1.5.10 may refer to the Sicyonian campaign. Pericles' nine trophies: Plut. *Pericles* 38; *Comparison of Pericles and Fabius Maximus* 2. The number could include more than one victory in a single campaign.

7. The Congress Decree: Plut. *Pericles* 17; Meiggs 1972, 512–514; Munn 2006, 287–289; Kagan 2010, 43–45. The Second Sacred War also involved the Boeotians: Plut. *Pericles* 21; Thuc. 1.112.5; Philochorus *FGrHist* 328 F 34; the *Suda*, s.v. "Hieros Polemos"; Sánchez 2001, 106–111; Bowden 2005, 136–137; cf. Hornblower 1992, 178. Green 2006, 164n345, dates Pericles' intervention in Phocis to 455.

The last-mentioned settlement was perhaps the colony of Brea in the rich Strymon region.

Projects such as these must have confirmed Pericles' view that Athens' safety and prosperity were inseparable from those of its empire. They should have also made him popular in Athens and its new colonies.[8]

In 447–446, Athens and Pericles had to deal with dangers to Athenian control over territories closer to home. There were simultaneous threats to Athenian domination in Boeotia and Euboea from local opposition, while the strategic city of Megara changed sides to join the Spartan alliance. The Athenians succeeded in confining Megaran opposition to within the city walls, but an army sent to Boeotia under the general Tolmides was ambushed at Coronea by a coalition of Boeotian exiles, Euboeans, Locrians, and other foes. Tolmides and many Athenians died, others were captured, and Athens had to cede control of Boeotia to its local enemies.[9]

Pericles did not participate in the Athenian expedition to Boeotia and had advised against it. The biographer Plutarch commends his caution in wishing to avoid a battle that involved uncertainty and considerable risk. He depicts Pericles as trying unsuccessfully to curb the belligerence of the Athenian people and their generals, including Tolmides, yet the results of Cornoea proved his wisdom and patriotism. Plutarch was correct about the cautious nature of Pericles' military leadership (see pp. 141–142 below), but he does not make a good case for it in this campaign, failing to clarify the risk the Athenians took in Boeotia and how Pericles' recommendation to wait before marching could have reduced it. Scholars have tried to attribute Pericles' caution to a temporary shortage of manpower and the need to wait for more troops, but that suggestion is based on the unproven premise that the army sent to Boeotia was too small. In fact, Tolmides reinforced his hoplite army with volunteers, and in Greek warfare, ambushes such as Coronea were often used successfully by smaller forces against larger ones. We do not know why Pericles opposed the campaign, but Plutarch, who probably did not

8. Settlers in the Chersonese: Plut. *Pericles* 11, 19; Diod. 11.88.3 (dates the settlement to 453); cf. *IG* I3 1162 = *ML* no. 48 (in 447). Settlers to Naxos and Andros: Plut. *Pericles* 11; Green 2006, 170n364 (in 453). Bisaltae in Thrace: Plut. *Pericles* 11. Brea: *IG* I3 46 = Fornara 1983, no. 100.

9. Athens' expedition to Megara: Diod. 12.5.2; *ML* 51 = Fornara 1983 no. 101; Meiggs 1972, 177–178; Legon 1981, 192–199. The battle of Coronea and its background: Thuc. 1.113.1–4; Diod. 12.5.1–6.2; Plut. *Pericles* 18; Pausanias 1.27.5; Meiggs 1972, 176–177; Buck 1979, 150–153.

know the reason either, may have turned Pericles' opposition into a virtue in hindsight.[10]

The defeat at Coronea strengthened the opposition to Athens in Euboea, and much of the island revolted (446). The importance of Euboea to Athens cannot be overstated, since it contained Athenian settlements, was close to Attica, and could threaten Athenian imports, including grain. Tolmides' death left a vacancy, which Pericles now filled by leading an army to Euboea. But the Euboeans were saved for the moment by the clearer and more present danger of a Peloponnesian invasion of Attica. The Athenian loss of control over the Megarid allowed a Peloponnesian army led by the Spartan king Pleistoanax to march freely into Attica and to reach Eleusis and nearby Thria. The conjunction of the revolts in Megara, Boeotia, and Euboea with the Peloponnesian invasion strongly suggests a coordinated effort. Athens' ignorance of it was a serious intelligence failure.[11]

The Athenians had to react quickly, and Pericles took his army back to Attica. No battle took place, however, because the Peloponnesian army went home after devastating some land and besieging a local fort. The sources credit its retreat to Pericles' bribing of King Pleistoanax or his adviser, Cleandridas, both of whom were in fact indicted in Sparta for bribery and sent into exile. But did they take a bribe or withdraw because of it? It is impossible to confirm or deny the allegation of a transaction that took place in private. The Athenians liked to believe that the Spartan authorities were corruptible, as in their tales about Themistocles, Pericles' supposed role model, who allegedly bribed Spartan commanders and officials during and after the Persian War (pp. 69, 96 above). One source even goes as far as to claim that Pericles sent the Spartans an annual bribe of ten talents to keep them from starting a war. But even if money changed hands on this occasion, it did not have to be the only or the chief reason for the retreat, because Pleistoanax' march accomplished several goals. It temporarily relieved Athenian military pressure on Sparta's allies in Euboea and,

10. Pericles' caution and opposition: Plut. *Pericles* 18, cf. 21; Polyaenus 3.1.3. Presumed shortage of men: Buck 1979, 152. Diod. 11.84.4–5, however, dates Tolmides' request for volunteers to an earlier campaign; and see Stadter 1989, 211. Greek ambushes: Sheldon 2012.

11. Euboea's revolt, Megara, and Pleistoanax' march: Thuc. 1.114.1–3, 2.21.1, 5.16.3; Plut. *Pericles* 22–23; Diod. 12.5.2, 7. Our description tries to reconcile Thucydides' apparent dating of the Euboean revolt to 446 with Diodorus' dating its beginning to 448; see Green 2006, 185n27.

for a longer period, in Megara and even Boeotia. The Spartan expedition also showed the Athenians and their allies that deployment of the Athenian army outside Attica could put their homeland in danger. All these goals were attained without risking a battle. Thus it is ironic that caution and prudence were praised in Pericles but perceived as corrupted and reprehensible in his Spartan counterpart. That the Spartans at home had higher expectations of the campaign and punished their king for its results does not mean that they were more realistic than he was. Moreover, it is highly likely that the experience of the Peloponnesian invasion of Attica played a role in the Athenians' decision shortly afterward to sign a treaty with Sparta (the so-called Thirty Years' Peace) that would preclude such invasions. Another lesson was that the Athenians should be better prepared for future Spartan invasions. It was probably this encounter that inspired Pericles' war strategy, which relied on the city's fortifications for protection, avoided open battle with the Peloponnesians, and employed the navy to raid their territory.[12]

The removal of the Spartan threat allowed Pericles to go back to Euboea with fifty ships and 5,000 hoplites and subjugate the island with a vengeance. He expelled the wealthy élite of Chalcis (known as the *Hippobotae*), banished the people of Histiaea to Macedonia, and founded an Athenian colony on their land. The Spartan invasion of Attica made it vital for Athens to show its allies that it was as powerful as ever and that there was a price to pay for a revolt.[13]

The victory in Euboea must have made it psychologically easier for the Athenians to sign the Thirty Years' Peace treaty with Sparta (446), which was not very favorable to Athens. For, in spite of the good results of Pericles' generalship, Thucydides was right to note that Athens was in a position of relative weakness at the time, giving up positions in the Peloponnese (including the Megaran harbors of Nisaea and Pegae), Troezen, and Achaea, the last of which had been gained for Athens by Pericles in 454 (p. 104 above). We are not told where he stood on the treaty, but there was nothing in its terms

12. Bribing the Spartans: see the previous note (11) and Aristophanes *Clouds* 858–859, 115, with Ephorus *FGrHist* 70 F 193 = Fornara 1983 no. 104; Diod. 13.106.10. Meiggs 1972, 181–182, attributes the retreat to a preliminary agreement on the terms of the Thirty Years' Peace later that year, but may confuse causes with results; see also de Ste. Croix 1972, 196–200.
13. Pericles in Euboea: Thuc. 1.114.3; Plut. *Pericles* 23; Diod. 12.7, 22.2; Strabo 10.1.3. Two decrees about Athenian regulations in Eretria and Chalcis have been dated to this time: Fornara 1983, nos. 102–103; Ostwald 2002; or to the 420s: Paparzarkadas 2009, 73–75.

that was incompatible with his policies so far, including his preference for avoiding a military conflict with Sparta. The Thirty Years' Peace collapsed after fifteen years, and some ancient sources blame Pericles for its failure (see below).[14]

It is likely that the Spartan invasion of 446 raised concerns in Athens about the inadequacy of her defenses and gave impetus to the building of the so-called Middle or South Long Wall (Map 7 below). Many scholars date the beginning of its construction to 446, after the signing of the Thirty Years' Peace. Athens already had "Long Walls," one running from the city to the Piraeus, and another to its other harbor in Phaleron. The Middle Wall, which Pericles is said to have planned and supervised, paralleled the Piraeus or North Wall at a distance of about 180 meters. A late source explains that it was designed to provide a second line of defense in case the more southerly Phaleron Wall fell into enemy hands. It is also possible that Pericles concluded that it would be easier to guard and defend walls that were closer to each other than the original, more widely separated walls. Strategically, the project was a sequel to Themistocles' fortification of the city and the Piraeus. It also adopted the original purpose of the Long Walls (for which no source gives Pericles the credit): to secure traffic and supplies between the harbors and the city. But there was a difference in the execution of the two projects. While Themistocles' fortification of Athens was completed with record speed, we hear of contemporary complaints that Pericles' wall was made of words instead of stones and that its builders made no progress.[15]

Following the ostracism of Pericles' major political rival, Thucydides, son of Melesias (i.e., not the historian), in 444–443, Pericles was elected general consecutively for the next fifteen years (444–429). His supremacy moved historian Thucydides to describe Athens as a democracy in name but really a

14. The Thirty Years' Peace: Thuc. 1.35.2, 44.1, 45.3, 67.2–4, 115.1, 144.2; 4.21.3; Plut. *Pericles* 24; Diod. 12.7; Andocides 3.6; Lewis 1992c, 136–138.
15. The Middle Wall and its rationale: Plato *Gorgias* 455e; Scholion on Plato *Gorgias* 455e = Fornara 1983 no. 79; Plut. *Pericles* 13; cf. Andocides 3.7; Aeschines 2.174; Gomme in Gomme et al. 1945–1981, 1:312–313; Lewis 1992c, 138–139; Conwell 2008, 74–78. For its date after 446/5, see the literature cited in Conwell 2008, 67n12, which prefers a broader range of 452–431: Conwell 2008, 65–72. Complaints about construction delays: Cratinus F 326 K–A = Plut. *Pericles* 13; Plut. *Moralia* 351a. Conwell (2008, 72–74) is skeptical about their validity. Bugh (1988, 49) and Spence (2010, 118–123) suggest that a reform that more than trebled the number of cavalrymen came in response to the invasion and was designed to protect the countryside. Yet attributing it to Pericles goes beyond the evidence.

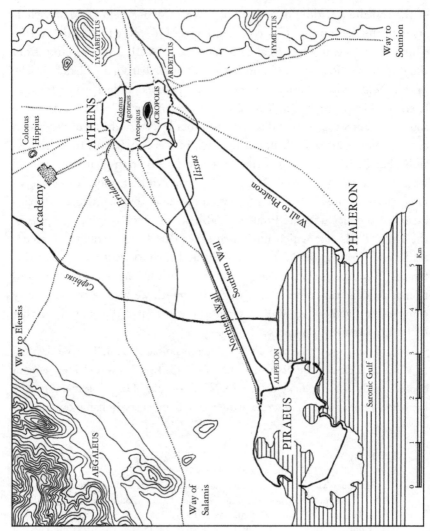

MAP 7   Athens' Long Walls.

city ruled by its "first man."[16] Although the evidence on Pericles as a general during these years has many gaps, his putting down of a revolt on the island of Samos in 441–439 provides a better view of his art of command than any event discussed so far.

The Samian Revolt

The origins of the Samian revolt lay in a dispute with the city of Miletus over the control of Priene in Asia Minor (see Map 13, Aegean Greece, Ch. 5, p. 190 below).[17] Samos was a fairly wealthy and powerful island ruled by an oligarchy. It enjoyed the privileged status of an independent member in the Attic-Delian League, to which it contributed ships instead of money. It seems to have been more loyal to Athens than the nearby city of Miletus on the mainland of Asia Minor, which had perhaps revolted in the past and been punished with an Athenian intervention and a change of government from oligarchy to democracy. After its defeat by Samos in 441, Miletus asked the Athenians to intervene in their conflict over possession of its neighbor Priene. Athens told the Samians to stop the war and bring their case for arbitration by Athens, but the Samians declined the offer. In response, Athens launched a campaign against Samos, which Pericles advocated and led.

Our extant, largely pro-Athenian sources explain the Samian rejection of Athenian arbitration by pointing out that Samos had the upper hand in the war against Miletus, and that Samians believed Athens sided with Miletus in the dispute. Unlike Samos, Miletus was a democracy, and the presence in Athens of Samian exiles who sought to change the oligarchic government of their island and supported the Milesian complaint could indeed have made the Samian authorities fear that Athens' plans for Samos went beyond putting an end to the war. In truth, Athens, as a hegemonic

16. Pericles and Thucydides, son of Melesias, were divided on many issues, but not on strategy: see esp. Plut. *Pericles* 8, 11, 14, cf. 12; Andrewes 1978; Krentz 1984; Kallet-Marx 1989. Plut. *Pericles* 11 is the only source that associates Pericles with the establishment in 444 of an all-Greek city in Thurii, southern Italy, for which see Rutter 1973. Pericles' fifteen years of generalship: Plut. *Pericles* 16; Stadter 1989, 163, 196–197. Thucydides on Pericles' rule: 2.65.9, expanded with much flourish by Plut. *Pericles* 16.

17. The Samian revolt: Thuc. 1.115.2–117.3; Diod. 12.17.1–28.4; Plut. *Pericles* 24–28; Scholia on Aristophanes' *Wasps* 281–284; Kagan 1969, 170–178; Fornara and Lewis 1979; Shipley 1987, 113–120; Stadter 1989, 232–263; Rood 1998, 219–222; Wecowski 2013, 157–166.

state, was expected to stop wars among her allies, and Pericles justified the campaign against Samos by its refusal to end the war. But that is
unlikely to have been his only motive. To begin with, Athens could not
afford to allow Samos to change the balance of power in a strategically sensitive region near Persian-held territory. There was also the broader issue
of Athens' relationship with her allies. Later, in 431, when Athens was at
war with Sparta, Pericles regarded keeping a tight grip on the allies as one
of the Athenians' cardinal interests. It was a policy he adhered to in prewar times as well. The allegation that Pericles advocated the war for the
sake of his lover, Aspasia, who came from Miletus, was libelous. Yet if the
rumor dates to the time of the Samian campaign, it suggests that the war did
not enjoy universal support at home.[18]

Pericles sailed to Samos with forty ships, a medium-sized force, which
suggested that he did not expect strong opposition there. The democratic
foes of the Samian government who were in Athens at the time may have
promised him local support. In addition, the Athenian declaration of war
on Samos was one-sided, because Samos formally declared war on Athens
only later in the conflict. Apparently the Samians were hoping for a non-
military solution, and Pericles, who was aware of their desire, hoped to
catch them unprepared. The results justified the expectation of an easy
campaign. After landing on the island, Pericles entered the city unopposed
and changed its government to a democracy. He also sent fifty boys and
fifty adult men of the local élite as hostages to an Athenian settlement on
the island of Lemnos in the northern Aegean. He then put a garrison in the
city of Samos, collected a fine, and sailed home a few days afterwards with
his fleet.[19]

If the scholarly interpretation of a highly fragmented inscription is
correct, the expedition was not cost-effective. Athens spent 128 talents on
it, while Pericles is said to have fined the Samians only eighty talents. At
the end of the Samian war of 441–439, the Athenians demanded that Samos
pay 1,200 talents in indemnities, having themselves spent a little more than
1,400 talents on the entire campaign. Yet in ancient Athens, as in modern

18. For the origins of the Samian revolt, see the previous note and Quinn 1981, 11–12;
Krentz 1984, 500–501. Athens and Miletus: Meiggs 1972, 562–565; Gorman 2001,
216–236. Samians in Athens: Thuc. 1.115.2; cf. Aristophanes *Wasps* 281–285. Athens
and wars among her allies: Thuc. 6.76.3; de Ste. Croix 1972, 121. A tight grip on
allies: Thuc. 2.13.2. Aspasia and Samos: Duris *FGrHist* 76 F 5; Plut. *Pericles* 24; Henry
1995, 72.

19. Diod. 12.27.1–2; Thuc. 1.115.2–3; cf. scholion on Aristophanes *Wasps* 283. Samos'
later declaration of war: Diod. 12.27.3; Thuc. 1.115.5.

times, security often trumped budgetary considerations. Such priorities are suggested by flattering stories about Pericles, who reportedly rejected attempts by the Samian hostages, local oligarchs, and a neighboring Persian *satrap* (provincial governor) to bribe him. Possibly the payments offered to him, if historical, were not bribes, but ransom in return for more lenient treatment of the oligarchs and the city.[20]

Pericles' measures of taking local hostages, changing the government, planting a garrison, and indemnities payments were tried and familiar measures against miscreant allies. Yet Samos did not respond well to this "one-size-fits-all" punishment, and Pericles' settlement failed. After his departure, the city descended into civil strife between democrats (probably aided by the Athenian garrison) and oligarchs. Some oligarchs crossed over to Asia Minor and asked Pissuthnes, the Persian satrap in Sardis, for help, thereby offering him and his king an opportunity to regain influence in a region they had lost to Athens. Pissuthnes gave the Samians 700 mercenaries, who stole into the city, and, helped by powerful Samians, overthrew the democratic government. The rebels exiled political opponents, delivered the Athenian garrison and officials to the satrap, and even managed to rescue the hostages on Lemnos. The stealthy capture of the city and the rescue operation suggest a Samian talent for commando-style tactics. Samos then declared open rebellion against Athens and invited any interested party to join in. The Samians also made preparations to renew their campaign against Miletus. It is hard to imagine a greater reversal of Pericles' settlement. In fact, the new situation was much worse for Athens than the situation before his advocation of a war on the island.[21]

The complex chronology of the Samian campaign makes it difficult to establish when it became more than a local revolt. In addition to getting aid from the Persian satrap and the city of Byzantium, Samos appealed at an unknown time for help from the Peloponnesian League. The Corinthians opposed their request, and their view prevailed. Yet, if the scholarly assumption that Sparta

---

20. The campaign expenditures: *IG* I³ 363–365 = Fornara 1983 no. 113, with Fornara and Lewis 1979, 9–12. Fine of 80 talents: Diod. 12.27.2; cf. Quinn 1981, 69n22; 1,400 talents: see the inscription cited here, and cf. Diod. 12.28.3 (emended); Isocrates 15.11 (emended); Nepos *Timotheus* 1 (1,200 talents). Bribes for Pericles: Plut. *Pericles* 25, with Stadter 1989, 244–245.

21. Samos after Pericles' departure: Thuc. 1.115.4–5; Plut. *Pericles* 25 (claiming, probably wrongly, that Pissuthnes rescued the hostages); Diod. 12.27.3. Pissuthnes and the Persian king in this conflict: Briant 2002, 580–581; Waters 2010, 822–823.

was among those wanting to help Samos is correct, Athens had every right to be concerned about a widening of the conflict.[22] Moreover, by the time the Athenians sent a second fleet to Samos (winter of 441 or spring of 440), they had heard that a fleet from Phoenicia might come to Samos' help. (The Persians employed Phoenician fleets in the Mediterranean.) Because nobody saw or engaged these ships in the course of the revolt, it is impossible to say whether the intelligence about them was correct, erroneous, or misleading. Nevertheless, the Athenians had good reasons to be worried about the integrity of their maritime hegemony, which it was later thought that the Samians almost deprived them of. The concern for the security of the empire accounted also for Pericles' subsequent harsh treatment of the defeated Samians and even for Athens' going to war against Sparta.[23]

We can imagine that no Athenian was more motivated than Pericles to return to Samos and deal with the consequences of his failed settlement there. However, he was not the only active general there. The entire board of ten Athenian generals went to Samos at one time or another, and their presence suggests both the magnitude of the campaign and the seriousness with which the Athenians viewed it. Among Pericles' colleagues was the famous playwright Sophocles, who clearly did more than is suggested by a story that he allegedly partied and flirted with boys while on campaign, to Pericles' chagrin. In any case, Pericles was probably the leading general of the war.[24] He sailed to Samos with sixty ships—more than the forty originally sent to Samos but still not enough, because Pericles had to let sixteen ships go elsewhere; some to Caria to look out for the Phoenician ships, and others (including Sophocles') to bring reinforcements from Chios and Lesbos. For a general who, we shall see, often sought security and victory

22. Byzantium and Samos: Thuc. 1.115.5; Lendon 2010, 83–85 (suggesting that Byzantium endangered the importation of grain to Athens). Samos and the Peloponnesian League: Thuc. 1.40.5; cf. 1.41.2, 43.1. Spartan support of Samos: e.g., de Ste. Croix 1972, 200–202; Cartledge 1982, 260–263; Hornblower 1991–2008, 1:87–88; cf. Lendon 1994.

23. Phoenician fleet: Thuc. 1.116.1; and below. Samos' depriving Athens of the sea: Thuc. 8.76.4, cited also by Plut. *Pericles* 28, and Kagan 1969, 172; but see also Shipley 1987, 118; Hornblower 1991–2008, 1:188, 3:978. Perhaps memories of the sixth-century Samian tyrant Polycrates, who reportedly wanted to rule the sea (Hdt. 3.12) added to the Athenians' anxiety.

24. Ten generals at Samos: Androtion *FGrHist* 324 F 38 = Fornara 1983 no. 110; Thuc. 1.116.1, 117.2; Lendon 2010, 85. Hamel (1998, 88–70) and Podlecki (1998, 163) question Pericles' supreme command of the war. Sophocles and the Samian campaign: Plut. *Pericles* 8; Athenaeus 13.603e–604b; Stadter 1989, 109 (with additional sources and discussion).

in numbers, this was a painful but necessary concession. Pericles hurried to the region before the situation got worse: a Samian fleet, including fifty battleships, twenty transport ships, and probably land forces, was already waging war on Miletus. News of the Athenian expedition caused the seventy Samian ships to leave Miletus, and on their way home they clashed with Pericles' fleet of forty-four ships near the island of Tragia, about 25 kilometers west of Miletus. Pericles won the battle, which was more balanced than the number of ships suggests, because it is unclear how many of the twenty Samian transport ships could contribute to the fighting. Before pushing forward, Pericles waited for the arrival of forty additional ships from Athens and twenty-five ships from Chios and from Mytilene on Lesbos. Although we do not know how many Athenian ships survived the Battle of Tragia, Pericles must now have been in his comfort zone of numerical superiority. He then landed on Samos and besieged the city by sea and land.[25]

Possibly it was now that the Athenians tattooed an owl, an Athenian symbol, on the foreheads of Samian prisoners of war to mark their transition to slaves. The story of this unusually harsh treatment suggests that the Athenians regarded the war as more than an impersonal test of power. They were angry with the Samians because, as they saw it, the island had enjoyed a preferred status in the Athenian empire but ungratefully threatened Athens' maritime rule.[26]

The besieged Samians showed no sign of giving up. They ventured outside their walls to fight the enemy, and according to one report, their general, the philosopher Melissus, defeated Pericles in a naval engagement. Five Samian ships escaped the blockade and sailed to bring over the rumored Phoenician fleet. Even if Pericles had doubts that the Phoenicians were coming, he could not afford the risk of their arrival. He sailed with sixty ships to Caunus in Caria to meet the Phoenicians, leaving behind no more than sixty-five ships. Melissus used the opportunity to attack the undefended Athenian camp by surprise—in this war, the Athenians

---

25. Thuc. 1.116.1–2; Plut. *Pericles* 25–26; Diod. 12.27.4. Sophocles in Chios: Ion of Chios *FGrHist* 392 T 5b, F 6 = Athenaeus 13.603e.

26. Tattooing captives: Plut. *Pericles* 26 (confusing the Samians with the Athenians, but he also cites an Aristophanic line that appears to confirm the punishment); Duris *FGrHist* 76 F 66 = Photius *Lexicon* s.v. "Samion ho demos"; Aelain *Varia Historia* 2.9. Karavites 1985, 54–56, rejects the story, but see Stadter 1989, 249–250. Ingrate Samos: cf. Aristotle *Rhetoric* 3.4.3 14071–13; Lehmann 2008, 183. Compare also the Athenian anger at "ingrate" Mytilene, which enjoyed a status similar to Samos' but rebelled in in 428: Thuc. 3.36.2.

fell victim to Samian surprises time after time. The Samians destroyed Athenian ships on guard and possibly ships beached at the Athenian camp, and defeated others that sailed against them. They also took many captives. It is said that they tattooed the Athenian prisoners with the symbol of the Samian ship *Samaena* in retaliation for the Athenian tattooing of Samians. Emotions seem to have run high in this conflict. For fourteen days, Samos made the Athenian nightmare of losing control of the sea come true, enjoying uninterrupted traffic of provisions to and from the city. Plutarch attributes their success to Pericles' erroneous decision to leave Samos, but the biographer's judgment is too harsh and based on hindsight. A Phoenician fleet could have decided the war, and if someone was at fault, it was the other Athenian generals at Samos, who allowed the enemy to surprise them once again. In any case, the Samian victory must have strengthened Pericles' faith in numerical superiority. With more ships at his disposal, he could have left behind a larger contingent, giving the Athenians a better chance of repelling the Samian attack.[27]

The news of the Athenian setback and the non-appearance of the Phoenician ships sent Pericles hurrying back to Samos, where he defeated Melissus in battle, thereby ending the island's brief maritime supremacy. He then renewed the siege. It was probably at his request that the Athenians sent sixty additional ships to Samos, and that Chios and Lesbos contributed thirty more. If his fleet had recovered its original numbers and no ship had returned home, he now commanded a huge force of 215 ships. By fully exploiting the empire's military and financial resources, he achieved an advantage that no surprise attack or need to split his navy would undermine. The siege itself was expertly handled. Pericles divided his force into eight sections, giving each a day's rest while the others were on active duty. He was also the first Athenian general known to use circumvallate walls and to employ a military engineer, Artemon of Clazomenae, who is said to have invented the Greek battering ram and the "tortoises" (sheds) that protected it (Figure 10). An anecdote of questionable historicity reports Pericles'

---

27. Samian offensive: Plut. *Pericles* 26; Pritchett 1971–1991, 2:140. Pericles' actions: Thuc. 1.116.3–4; Plut. *Pericles* 26; Diod. 12.28.1. According to *Suda* mu 496 s.v. "Meletos," Melissus (Meletus) fought Sophocles. The evidence is against Gomme's rejection of Melissus' victory: Gomme et al. 1945–1981, 1:353. Podlecki 1998, 120, postdates Melissus' victory to a later stage and against a different general. Tattoos: see the previous note.

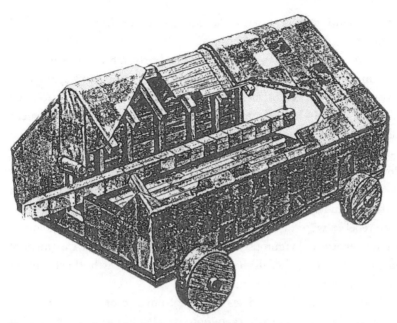

FIGURE 10 *A sketch of a siege ram with tortoise.*

resorting to trickery as well. While besieging an unnamed, stoutly defended city by the sea, perhaps Samos, he raised a tumult at one place around the walls. When the keepers of the city gates ran to the diversion, he burst in through the gates.[28]

What truly decided the war was Pericles' quantitative advantage in troops, ships, and money. These resources also explain why, by comparison to some other fifth-century sieges, his investment of Samos lasted "only" eight months. After the campaign was over, Pericles even boasted that it took ten years for Agamemnon to capture Troy but only nine months (counted inclusively) for him (or Athens) to subdue powerful Samos. Plutarch claims that Pericles preferred to spend time and money rather than blood at Samos, and one story suggests where some of the money went. We hear that Athenian

---

28. Reinforcements for Pericles: Thuc. 1.117.2; Diod. 12.28.2. Fighting in shifts: Plut. *Pericles* 27; cf. Thuc. 2.75.3; Stadter 1989, 252. Thuc. 1.116.2 mentions Pericles' use of three walls, which could mean a single wall around three sides of the city: Gomme in Gomme et al., 1945–1981, 1:353; Garlan 1974, 114; Krentz 2007, 179. Artemon and his siege engines: Plut. *Pericles* 27; Diod. 12.28.3; Winter 1971, 156–157, 307; cf. Campbell 2003, esp. 3–4. Pericles' trick: Frontinus *Stratagems* 3.9.5.

prostitutes, camp followers with the expedition, dedicated a statue of Aphrodite in Samos out of their earnings.[29]

In the end, Samos surrendered and paid dearly for the revolt. Some Samian commanders and their men were executed in a horrible way (below). The city's walls were demolished and its ships confiscated. Athens ended Samos' status as an independent ally and possibly changed its government to a democracy once again. The Samians also gave hostages and paid a 1,200-talent fine divided into annual installments. It was now or later that they lost lands to the Athenians, who dedicated them to their national deities. A fragmented inscription records a treaty between Samos and Athens that includes an oath of loyalty to Athens and her allies and a promise not to rebel in word or deed. The city of Byzantium surrendered later.[30]

Plutarch reports and vigorously denies a story about Pericles' treatment of Samian crews, now or earlier in the conflict, citing the fourth–third-century historian Duris of Samos as the source.

The latter claimed that Pericles brought Samian captains and marines to Miletus' marketplace and tied them onto wooden boards. We know from other sources that such punishment involved chaining the prisoners' wrists and ankles to a pole or a board and affixing a collar around their necks. It resulted in a prolonged and painful death, although Duris reported that, after ten days of torture, the prisoners' heads were bashed with clubs and their bodies were cast out without funeral rites. Plutarch rejects the story because it does not appear in his other sources, and because of what he regards as Duris' general mendacity, his pro-Samian/anti-Athenian agenda, and his wish to add a tragic element to his history. An additional, unmentioned reason for Plutarch to reject the episode is that it contradicts his portrayal of Pericles as a man who curbed other people's worse nature. Yet Plutarch's objections are surmountable. Strapping a person until death and prohibiting his burial were penalties known from the Athenian law code, and are therefore likely to have been used by Pericles. The place of execution adds credibility to the

29. Troy and Samos: Plut. *Pericles* 28; *Moralia* 350e; Jacoby on Ion of Chios, *FGrHist* 392 F 12. Saving Athenian lives: Plut. *Pericles* 27. Athenian prostitutes: Alexis of Samos *FGrHist* 539 F 1 = Athenaeus 13.572f.
30. Terms of surrender: Thuc. 1.117.3; Plut. *Pericles* 28; Diod. 12.28.3–4 (emended); Isocrates 15.111 (emended); Nepos *Timotheus* 1.2. An undated erection of statues of Heracles, Zeus, and Athena in the Samian temple of Hera has been interpreted as an Athenian provocation: Strabo 14.14; Wecowski 2013, 162–164. The treaty between Athens and Samos: *ML* no. 56, 151–154 = Fornara 1983 no. 115. Loss of Land: *IG* I³ 1492–9; Smarczyk 1990; Papazarkadas 2009, 68, 80n10. Change

story. Miletus was the bitter enemy of Samos, while in Athens such treatment of prisoners of war (as opposed to criminals) was unknown and might have aroused opposition. The punishment was also in line with other emotional or vengeful facets of the war against Samos.[31]

For the Athenians and Pericles, punishing the Samians complemented the celebration and commemoration of their victory at home. It was customary in Athens to honor the war dead with a collective burial in what could be described as the national cemetery in the Kerameikos district of the city. The ceremony included a public eulogy, which Pericles delivered on this occasion, thus adding to his military victory a triumph in the contest over which speaker would give the funeral oration. It is reported that when he left the podium, women shook his hand and decorated him as if he had won a wrestling match. Pericles deserved the accolades: his speech left a lasting impression, and even a few quotations have survived to this day. An anecdote of uncertain historicity reports a different but typically Greek reaction to his success in the form of an attempt to belittle it. It tells us that Elpinice, the sister of the general Cimon, who dominated Athenian affairs before Pericles, tried to spoil Pericles' victory by contrasting Cimon's loss of men in wars against the barbarians to Pericles' losses against an allied and kindred state. (The Samians were believed to have come originally from Attica.) Pericles' rebuttal was *ad hominem* and by modern standards, mean-spirited. With a smile, he softly quoted a verse of the archaic poet Archilochus: "It was not for you, old woman, to perfume yourself." Even if the story is an invention, his attitude was in character. In addition to mocking Elpenice's alleged sexual history and now-faded allure, the line told her to mind her own business. One is reminded of Pericles' advice to Athenian women in a later and more famous funeral oration, where he defined their absence from male discourse as the greatest of feminine virtues.[32]

of government: Andrewes in Gomme et al. 1945–1981, 5:44–47, but see Quinn 1981, 13–17, and Hornblower 1991–2006, 1:192–193, for the possibility that Samos remained oligarchic. Byzantium: Thuc. 1.117.3.

31. Plut. *Pericles* 28 = Duris of Samos *BNJ* 76 F 67. For the punishment and its likely authenticity, see Meiggs 1972, 191–192; Stadter 1989, 258; Green 2006, 220n138; Pownall, "Duris of Samos"; *contra*: Karavites 1985, 48–53.

32. Pericles' eulogy: Plut. *Pericles* 28. Quotations from it: Aristotle *Rhetoric* 1.7.35 1365a31–33; Plut. *Pericles* 8, 28; *Moralia* 350e; with Jacoby 1947, 13–15. Pericles and Elpinice: Plut. *Pericles* 28, and see *Pericles* 10 for a similar anecdote on a different occasion; Wecowski 2013, 161n30. Pericles on feminine virtue: Thuc. 2.45.2.

Pericles' leadership in Samos was both effective and versatile. Strategically, he recognized the danger of the revolt to Athens' maritime rule and to its dominance over other allies. Tactically, he faced serious challenges, the first of which was an enemy who was powerful and resourceful on land and sea and who had an astute general. The campaign required him to be equally good as a field commander, an admiral, and a besieger. Questionable intelligence forced him to make decisions without full knowledge, such as weakening the siege of Samos in order to meet a rumored Phoenician fleet. More than once during the war, he found himself short of ships or troops. He overcame these problems largely by mobilizing the empire's large resources, including siege technology that was innovative for the times. Yet, his generalship was not free of error, as the quick collapse of his first settlement and the resultant broadening of the conflict to Persia and Byzantium demonstrate. He learned his lesson, though, and his second settlement of Samos was both harsher and more effective. It is true that discontented Samians took refuge at Aenaea on the opposite mainland and later harassed the city, even helping the Peloponnesians in their war against Athens. Yet Pericles deserves credit for Samos' loyalty to Athens through the rest of the century, even after the island reverted to an oligarchic government in 412.[33]

Pericles' military activity up to the eve of the Peloponnesian War goes unmentioned by the sources, except for Plutarch, who reports on his expedition to the Black Sea, probably around 437. He took a large, splendid fleet and treated Greek allies with friendliness and kindness but cowed their barbarian neighbors. This characteristic preference for a large force and the help given to colonies by fighting non-Greeks appeared elsewhere in Pericles' career. Also familiar was his aid to the people of Sinope in changing their government to one friendlier to Athens, and his settlement of Athenians there. It is commonly speculated that, in addition to demonstrating Athenian power in the region, he sought to control maritime routes and secure resources such as grain, minerals, and lands.[34]

---

33. A very positive assessment of Pericles at Samos: Kagan 1991, 141, cf. Lehmann 2008, 189–190. Samian exiles and oligarchy in 412: Thuc. 4.75.1; 8.21.
34. Pericles and the Pontus: Plut. *Pericles* 20. An Athenian casualty list was linked to this campaign: *IG* I³ 1180a; Stadter 1989, 216–219. See also Gomme in Gomme et al. 1945–1981, 1:367–368; Podlecki 1998, 130–131; Moreno 2007, 164–166; Braund 2005. Tsetskhladze 1997 is skeptical of the historicity of the expedition and even of Athens' significant economic interests in the region in this period.

Pericles' Strategy of the Peloponnesian War

The Peloponnesian War pitted Athens and her allies against Sparta and hers in what many consider one of the most important conflicts in ancient Greek history. The war was divided into three parts: the Archidamian War (431–421), named after the Spartan king Archidamus (II); an uneasy peace from 421 to 413; and the Decelean War (413–404), named for Spartan-occupied Decelea in Attica. Although Pericles died in the autumn of the third year of the war, 429, his impact on the conflict preceded and postdated his death. Some of his contemporaries even blamed him for it, and according to Thucydides, he was the architect of the Athenian war strategy, at least in its early stages. This section deals with the so-called Periclean strategy and the campaigns he initiated or led. As elsewhere in this chapter, the discussion focuses on events for which Pericles' involvement is not merely presumed, but directly attested.[35]

The question of Pericles' responsibility for the war is not directly relevant to his generalship. Thucydides largely impersonalizes this issue and instead famously distinguishes between the "truest" or underlying cause of the war, which in his opinion was Sparta's fear of Athens' growth in power, and the more immediate or triggering causes. The latter included a conflict between Corinth—a major Spartan ally—and the island of Corcyra, a new Athenian ally on whose behalf Athens sent a fleet that engaged the Corinthians in battle. Another conflict arose between Athens and the tribute-paying city of Potidaea in Chalcidice, which rebelled against Athens and received aid from Corinth. Another cause (and in non-Thucydidean sources, a central one) was complaints that Aegina made to the Peloponnesians about Athens' violation of Aegina's autonomy, and by Megara about the so-called Megaran Decree, by which Athens imposed harsh economic sanctions on Megara. Pericles is said to have been uncompromising about punishing Megara, and he probably supported Athens' heavy-handed treatment of Aegina, too. Yet Plutarch's claim that he was directly responsible for sending fleets to Corcyra's aid against Corinth is supported by no other source. Even more dubious are ancient conspiracy theories charging Pericles with instigating the war for personal reasons, such as helping his mistress Aspasia in her alleged quarrel with Megara or averting forthcoming legal action against his friends or

---

35. Spence (1990) opposes calling Pericles a "strategist" and prefers to see him as a skilled, adaptable tactician, but see Hunter 2005, and especially Platias and Koliopoulos 2010, for the opposite view.

even against himself.[36] This much is certain: he was convinced that going to war was justified on military grounds, because Athens was superior to Sparta in resources and other capabilities. The war was also justified on moral grounds, because Sparta had broken the Thirty Years' Peace treaty by refusing a prescribed arbitration of its dispute with Athens. In Pericles' view, the only way out of the conflict was for Sparta, not Athens, to make concessions.[37]

Thucydides praises Pericles' leadership and foresight, believing his strategy could have won the war if his successors had been better leaders and less prone to mistakes. Intentionally or not, Thucydides' narrative is geared to prove this thesis. As if such tendentiousness were not enough, Thucydides presents Pericles' strategy mostly in the form of direct or indirect speeches made by Pericles himself. As the historian says about the speeches in his work, "My method in this book has been to make each speaker say broadly what I suppose would have been needed on any given occasion, while keeping as closely as I could to the overall intent of what was actually said." This is not the place to join the ongoing debate over the authenticity of speeches in Thucydides. My point is that Pericles' description of his strategy in Thucydides is influenced by the specific historical moment in which the speech was given, and that changing circumstances affected, not just the presentation of the strategy, but also the strategy itself, causing even Pericles to deviate from it.[38]

The fundamental facts that shaped Pericles' strategy were established before the war and were known to both sides. Athens' strength lay in its navy and the empire that provided it with financial, material, and other

---

36. Thucydides on the causes of the Peloponnesian war: 1.23.4–89.1. The scholarship on the causes is vast. See, e.g., Kagan 1969; de Ste. Croix 1972; Badian 1993, 125–162; Lazenby 2004, 16–30; Rhodes 2006, 80–89; Tritle 2010, 4–43. Pericles, Megara, Aegina, and Corcyra: Thuc. 1.139.1–144.2; Plut. *Pericles* 8, 29–31 (whose claim about Pericles' involvement in the Corcyran affair is supported by Bloedow 1994 and Cawkwell 1997, 26); Diod. 12.39.4–5; Andocides 3.6–8. Pericles' personal motives: Aristophanes *Acharnians* 513–539; *Peace* 605–618; Plut. *Pericles* 30 (Aspasia), and 32 (pending trials); Diod. 12.38.2–39.4.

37. Pericles and Spartan concessions: Thuc. (e.g.) 1.127.3, 140.1, 5, 144.1–2; and cf. Fornara and Samons 1991, 145–146.

38. Thucydides on Pericles and his successors: 2.65.6–13, and below. See Mann 2007 for criticism of Thucydides' view. Quotation: Thuc. 1.22, Hammond trans. For Thucydides, Pericles' strategy, and speeches in Thucydides, see the following notes as well as the literature cited in the note appended to "Thucydides" in my Bibliography, under "The Main Ancient Sources." See also, e.g., Wet 1969; Cawkwell 1975; Ober 1985b; Foster 2010; Taylor 2010, 49–52.

resources. Sparta's strengths were its superior army and the large forces of its Peloponnesian allies. The ways in which each side sought to utilize these advantages were predictable. The Spartans rejected the advice of their king and general, Archidamus, to postpone the war until the Peloponnesians were closer to the Athenians in naval power and riches. Instead, they looked to their past military conflicts with Athens as their guide, chiefly the battle of Tanagra in 457 and Pleistoanax' ill-fated invasion of Attica in 446 (see pp. 104, 107–108 above). Like Pleistoanax, they would invade Attica and avoid besieging the well-fortified city of Athens, but unlike him, they would stay for a while and devastate the land. Their presence would provoke the Athenians to come out and fight them as they did at Tanagra, and they would be similarly defeated. The Spartans imagined they would win the war within few years.[39]

Thucydides succinctly describes Pericles' strategy for Athens:

> The Athenians should prepare for war and bring in their property from the country; they should not go out to battle, but come inside the city and defend it; they should maintain their fleet, which was where their strength lay, equipped and ready; and they should keep a firm hand on the allies. Athenian power, he told them, depended on the revenues received from the allies: and wars were mostly won by sound strategy and financial reserves.[40]

Thucydides provides additional information on Pericles' strategy elsewhere in his narrative. The leader's premise was that the war would be demanding and protracted. Because Athens' and Sparta's strengths were so mismatched, Athens should not meet Sparta on land, and Sparta was incapable or unwilling to meet Athens at sea. The result would be a prolonged war with victory eventually coming for the side that was better equipped, materially and mentally, to sustain such a conflict. Athens had a number of clear advantages. At sea, it had a huge navy of 300 triremes operated by skilled and experienced crews. On land, the city was well protected and could field 29,000 hoplites, who served abroad or on guard duty in the city, as well as 1,200 cavalry and 1,600 mounted archers.[41] Steady income

---

39. Archidamus' failed advice: Thuc. 1.80.1–87.2. Spartan expectations of victory: Thuc. 4.85.2, 5.14.3, 7.28.3. Spartan strategy: Brunt 1965; Kelly 1982; Cawkwell 1997, 40–43.
40. Quotation: Thuc. 2.13.2, Hammond trans; cf. 2.65.7. See note 38 as well.
41. Thuc. 1.140.1–144.4; 2.13.1–9; Plut. *Pericles* 21. Hansen (1981) argues that there was no official list (catalogue) of hoplite recruits, but see Christ 2001. For a discussion of the validity of Thucydides' figures, see Pritchard 2010, 21–27.

from the empire, along with ample public and private money at home, would enable Athens to maintain and field these forces for a long time. The enemy, in contrast, had no strong navy and little wealth, and their soldiers, who were also farmers, could serve only for a limited time. Their army was too diversified and decentralized for effective common action. Pericles believed Athens' unsurpassed assets meant that the war was not for Sparta to win, but for Athens to lose. Hence the city should avoid taking unnecessary risks, such as expanding the empire and its military commitments while at war, or confronting the Peloponnesian invaders on land. This strategy required the Athenians to rely on their self-control, good judgment, and wise leadership (i.e., Pericles'), and on their ability to sustain temporary harm with a view to victory in the long run. Athens would win when Sparta realized that it could not.

On the tactical level, Pericles believed Athenian operations should largely consist of defensive or preventive measures. The Athenians would meet the Spartan invasion by taking shelter behind the city walls and declining open battle. If the Peloponnesians tried to build a fortified base in Attica, the Athenians would stop them or answer them in kind in the Peloponnese. They would also prevent any Spartan attempt to build up a viable naval force. Such are Pericles' pronouncements about his war plans in Thucydides, to which we should add the historian's account of Athenian measures against the invasion. These included opposing it at selected fortified sites, especially on their borders, and employing cavalry to contain the damage. Athens also raided Peloponnesian shores from the sea, in retaliation for the devastation of Attica.[42]

The general orientation of Pericles' strategy and tactics, then, was conservative and defensive. He had shown that he could be aggressively expansionist in his past campaigns in the Corinthian Gulf, Boeotia, the Chersonese, and the Black Sea. But the wider scope, higher stakes, and more powerful enemy in the Peloponnesian War evoked lessons from different past experiences. Pericles had been cautious in dealing with the Peloponnesian invasion of 446, and reliant on the empire's might in the Samian War. Now he also had to persuade the skeptics and encourage the believers in his policies, necessities that may explain why he did not always tell the whole truth in the speeches that Thucydides attributes to him. A speech dated to the summer of 431 details Athens' financial

---

42. Athenian forts: Ober 1985a, 192–193; Ober 1996, 80–81. See pp. 129–132 below on the Athenian cavalry and seaborne raids.

resources. Pericles wanted to impress his audience with Athens' riches, which were supposed to make it prevail over the enemy in the long run. We should not expect Pericles or Thucydides to submit a complete list of revenues and expenses, but it is notable that, except for 600 talents in annual tribute from the allies (rather a high figure), all the other assets he named were not renewable and therefore did not suggest that Athens' economic power would be long-lived. Also conspicuously absent from his account were the projected expenditures of the war, at least for 431. In Thucydides, we recall, speakers' statements correspond to the occasion on which they spoke, and this was not a good time to raise doubts about Athens' financial strength.[43]

Pericles also had to defend himself against personal attacks at home and from Sparta. In Athens, he was charged with seeking war for selfish reasons (see pp. 121–122 above), while the Spartans demanded that Athens expel "the curse of the goddess" from the city, referring to an old "pollution" charge that Pericles had inherited from his maternal ancestors. The demand was rejected and countered with a charge of Spartan impiety, but the threats to Pericles' position continued. On the eve of the Peloponnesian invasion of 431, he proclaimed his property outside the walls public, lest the Spartan king Archidamus, who was his "guest-friend" (*xenos*), should spare it in order to discredit him at home. In spite of personal attacks, Pericles continued to dominate Athenian affairs up to at least 430. But his strategy faced serious challenges as soon as the Peloponnesians invaded Attica in the summer of 431.[44]

Pericles and the Peloponnesian War: The Limits of His Strategy

In preparation for the invasion, the Athenians transferred their domestic animals to Euboea and other islands, while people who lived in the countryside moved to the city with whatever they could bring along. Thucydides and the comic poet Aristophanes describe the psychological and physical

43. See also Kallet-Marx 2008, 194–197; Foster 2010, 184; and for an opposite interpretation: Will 2003, 234. Divided Athens about going to war: Thuc. 1.139.3. Athens' financial resources: Thuc. 2.13.3–8; cf. *Ath. Pol.* 24.3; Diod. 12.40.1–5; and see Hornblower 1:252–255; Kallet-Marx 1993, 96–107; Blamire 2001, 106–107.
44. Pericles and the curse: Thuc. 1.126.1–127.3; Plut. *Pericles* 33. Spartan impiety: Thuc. 1.128–135.1; and see van Wees 2004, 20. Archidamus and Pericles' estate: Thuc. 2.13.1; cf. Plut. *Pericles* 33; Justin 3.7.8–9; Polyaenus 1.36.2.

difficulties entailed by their change of abode and lifestyle, which forced them to live in crowded conditions and public places. It seems that Pericles, who had called upon the Athenians to ready themselves for the war, had not made adequate preparations for the influx of the refugees. No public help was extended to them, not even in allocating space, and each family had to fend for itself.[45]

The city did better with its military preparations, which included gathering allied contingents and making ready an expedition of 100 ships around the Peloponnese. The outfitting of the ships was preceded by Athenian enquiries into the willingness of western allies in Corcyra, Cephallenia, Acarnania, and Zacynthus to help Athens blockade the Peloponnese. Because all these activities took place even before the Peloponnesians came to Attica, Pericles' description of his strategy in the Assembly was puzzling. He discussed the use of the Athenian navy primarily for defensive purposes and in a reactive manner (above), but a plan to blockade the Peloponnese even before the war started suggested a more ambitious and offensive approach, even if a blockade meant disrupting maritime traffic to or from the Peloponnese at selected times and places. Pericles, it appears, curbed Athenian belligerence more at home than abroad. Nevertheless, the Athenians seem to have had less trouble than modern historians in reconciling the defensive and offensive aspects of his strategy.[46]

Spartan king Archidamus marched into Attica in the summer of 431 at the head of a large Peloponnesian army, which by a common scholarly estimate numbered around 30,000 troops (Map 8 below). He besieged the fortified Athenian site of Oenoe on the Boeotian border but was unable to capture it. The Peloponnesians then turned southeast to Eleusis and the nearby Thriasian plain, where they destroyed the crops, and where the Athenians sent cavalry against them, but apparently with little success. From there, the invaders marched northeast to Acharnae, where they proceeded to destroy the

---

45. See also Schubert and Laspe 2009, 381–384. Conditions in the city: Thuc. 2.14.1–17.3; Aristophanes, esp. *Acharnians* 32–36; *Cavalrymen* 792–794; *Peace* 550–604; 632–635; cf. [Xen.] *Ath. Pol.* 2.16; Plut. *Pericles* 34; Conwell 2008, 90–92. Pericles and preparations: Thuc. 2.13.2; Allison 1989, 45–65.
46. Preparing the fleet: Thuc. 2.17.4. Enquiries in the west: Thuc. 2.7.3; with Hornblower's interpretation of the action as a blockade: 1991–2008, 1:244. Westlake 1945, 77–78, shows the difficulties of a maritime blockade rather than its improbability; cf. Lazenby 2004, 13. Athens also unsuccessfully sought a Persian alliance: Thuc. 2.7.1.

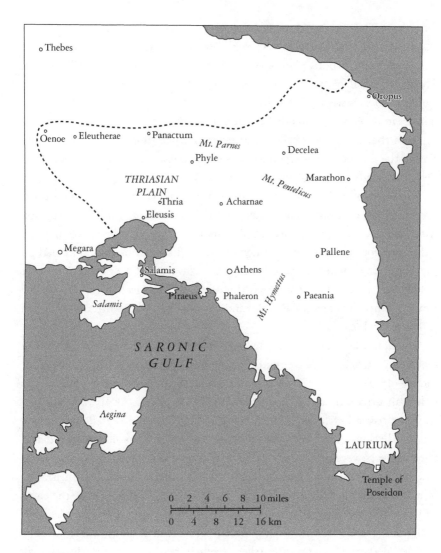

MAP 8 Attica.

fields, waiting for the Athenians to engage them. Archidamus hoped, says Thucydides, that the more bellicose young men in the city would push for battle along with the Acharnaeans, who included a large number of citizens and so could influence the vote. The Spartan commander believed he could at least create dissention in Athens. In this he admirably succeeded, but not in the greater goal of provoking the Athenians to fight him. Disappointed and running out of supplies, the Peloponnesians moved out after fewer than forty days. They retreated toward Boeotia, laid waste to land around Oropus in northern Attica, and then dispersed towards home.[47]

Pericles stuck to his plan of avoiding battle, but not without difficulties. The sources tell of Athenians who, unlike their all-knowing and self-controlled leader, were surprised by the enemy movements, or could not contain their anger and demanded confrontation with the invaders. Thucydides explains that the post–Persian War generation had not known the destruction of the homeland experienced by their parents, while many expected the Peloponnesians to go no further than Eleusis, where the previous invasion under Pleistoanax had stopped. Such attitudes, and the wish to avenge a perceived insult to personal and collective pride, contributed to the frustration with Pericles' strategy of restraint. Apparently, his mental preparation of the Athenians for the invasion had not worked. His inaction was ridiculed on the comic stage, where he was depicted as a coward and hypocrite. The latter charge was an occupational hazard for any Athenian leader, but it recalled similar complaints against Pericles and the building of the Middle Wall (see p. 109 above).[48]

There may have been additional reasons for the discontent. Pericles spoke repeatedly of Athens' power and the superiority of her resources to those of the enemy. But if the city was well protected, its navy unconquerable, its riches unsurpassed, and it had about 30,000 hoplites, cavalry, and archers, why not risk a battle on the fields of Attica? It is true that Pericles made dire predictions about the consequences of a defeat, but neither the defeat nor its effects were predetermined. The failure of the Athenian leader Nicias to deter the Athenians from going to war in Sicily in 415 is illustrative in this regard. He hoped to dissuade the people by claiming that the campaign would require large forces and much money, but they thought that, with a large armada and their resources, they could actually win. Similarly, Pericles' depiction of a mighty Athens seemed inconsistent with the strategy

47. Invasion: Thuc. 2.10.2, 18.1–23.3. Plut. *Pericles* 33; *Moralia* 784e (which mentions an unlikely invading force of 60,000). 30,000 troops: Busolt 1850–1920, 3.2:854–867; Kagan 1974, 19n9; Stadter 1989, 310.

48. It is often claimed that the damage the invaders caused was largely psychological in aim and effect: Ober 1985a, 34–37; Foxhall 1993, 142–143; Hanson 1998, esp. 42–76, 131–173; Hanson 2005, esp. 35–37, 52–57; Lendon 2010, 119–122. See, however, Thorne 2001, arguing for more substantial material damage. Attacks on Pericles: Thuc. 2.21.1–3; Plut. *Pericles* 33; Rusten 1989, 129–128; McGlew 2006; Christodoulou 2013, 232–239.

of waiting the invaders out, and it is possible that his rhetoric undermined its own purpose.[49]

Pericles did not react to the protest by bringing his strategy to open debate: he refused to call a meeting of the assembly or any other deliberative body. His political supremacy allowed him that liberty, as did the rarity of his public appearances and his cultivation of an authoritative demeanor. At the same time, he sent Athenian cavalry against advance enemy forces that were raiding in the vicinity of the city. Scholars have argued that the use of such a "mobile defense" constituted an important and under-emphasized offensive strategy. Even if correct, the evidence suggests that during the Archidamian War the cavalry was employed mostly around the city. Pericles emphasized the defense of the empire, but the invasion brought to the forefront the need to better protect the city itself.[50]

The Athenians also dispatched a large fleet around the Peloponnese while the enemy was still in Attica. Preparations for the expedition were made before the invasion, with the ambitious goal of blockading the Peloponnese (see p. 126 above). Now it was scaled down to more manageable seaborne raids, which the Athenians had used in the past. Their military rationale can be found in a (probably contemporary) work on the Athenian government, which has been misattributed to the Greek historian Xenophon, and whose anonymous author is commonly, though inaccurately, known as the "Old Oligarch." The author favorably contrasts the advantages of a maritime power over a land power, as shown in their use of seaborne raids and land invasion, respectively:

> Moreover, the rulers of the sea can do just what rulers of the land sometimes can do—ravage the territory of the stronger. For wherever there is no enemy (or wherever enemies are few), it is possible to put in along the coast and—if there is an attack—to go on board one's ship and sail away; one who does this is less badly off than one who comes

---

49. Pericles' predictions (some proven wrong): Thuc. 1.114.5. Nicias and the Sicilian expedition: Thuc. 6.19.1–24. On Pericles' advocacy of his strategy before the public, see also Ober 1985b, 173–176; cf. Taylor 2010.
50. Pericles' declining public deliberation: Thuc. 2.22.1; Plut. *Pericles* 33. Other officeholders could request a meeting, but were perhaps afraid of losing the debate; see also Kagan 1974, 55–56; Bloedow 1987; Hamel 1998, 8–12; Christodoulou 2013, 250–252 (complimenting Pericles on averting strife). Pericles' demeanor: Plut. *Pericles* 8–9. Athenian cavalry in the Archidamian war: Thuc. 2.19.2, 22.2; 3.1.2; Ober 1985b, 176–181; Bugh 1988, 79–80; Spence 1990; Hunter 2005.

to help with infantry. Further, the rulers of the sea can sail away from their own land to anywhere at all, whereas a land power can take a journey of only a few days from its own territory. Progress is slow, and going on foot one cannot carry provisions sufficient for a long time. One who goes on foot must pass through friendly country or else fight and win, whereas it is possible for the seafarer to go on shore wherever he has the stronger power and not land where he is weaker, but to sail along the coast until he comes to a friendly region or to those weaker than himself.[51]

To the aforementioned merits of seaborne raids, the Athenians added the satisfaction of tit for tat. The expedition around the Peloponnese consisted of 100 ships, 1,000 hoplites, and 400 archers. It was led by three generals other than Pericles, and it was highly successful. The fleet sailed along the coast of the Peloponnese, where it was joined by fifty Corcyran ships and other allies (see Map 2, p. 27, and Map 9 below). They attacked Acte in the Argolid, raided Peloponnesian lands, and then sailed to Messenia, where they failed to take the walled town of Methone. From there, the fleet sailed to Pheia on the western coast of Elis, where it defeated a local force of 300 men but also had to evacuate the town shortly after its occupation. The fleet then ravaged other places in Elis and turned north to capture the Corinthian town of Sollium, giving it to its inimical neighbors and Athens' allies, the Acarnanians of Palara. The Athenians also expelled a tyrant from Astacus in Acarnania and added that city to their alliance. Turning south, they took the island of Cephallenia without opposition and made it an ally, too. They then returned to Aegina on their way home.[52]

Although Pericles did not lead this campaign, some of our sources make him responsible for it, and, indeed, it bears his fingerprints. The force operated in territories familiar to him from his campaign in 454 (p. 104 above). The Athenian navy retaliated for the damage caused by the Peloponnesian invaders, just as he had promised before the war. The 150-ship expedition

---

51. Quotation: [Xenophon] *Ath. Pol.* 2.4–5, LCL trans. (modified). For the work, see conveniently, Osborne 2004. Seaborne raids in the Peloponnesian war: Westlake 1945.
52. The campaign: *IG* I³ 365; Thuc. 2.23.2–3, 2.25.1–5, 2.30.1–2; Diod. 12.43.1–5; Plut. *Pericles* 34; Polyaenus 1.36.1 (undated). Corinth restored the tyrant of Astacus later that winter: Thuc. 2.33.1–2. See p. 134 below for the fleet's later joining a raid on the Megarid. Busolt (1850–1920, 3.2:912–915n) estimates that the voyage lasted about four months.

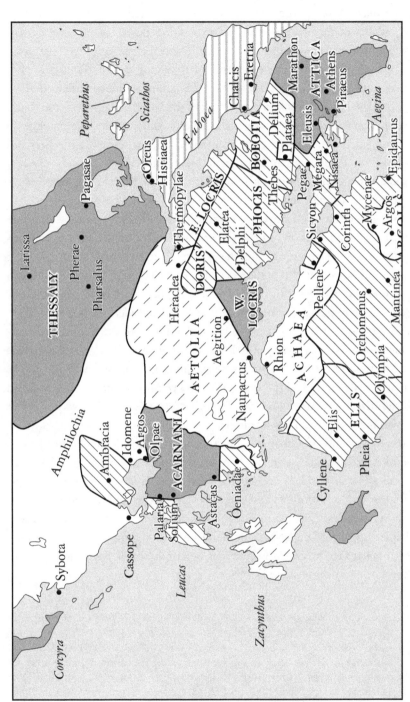

MAP 9 Central and Western Greece.

recalled his prediction that the Peloponnesians would do nothing against a large fleet. A large force was also in keeping with his desire to reduce risk and his preference for using overwhelming power against the enemy, as he had done at Samos. Additionally, the expedition was a demonstration of Athenian power, like those he had led to Samos and the Pontus region, but now for an audience of Athenians and Spartans. It showed them that, in spite of Athens' passive acknowledgment of the Spartans' superiority on land, the Athenians were strong, active, and able to inflict retributive damage on the enemy. Contrary to ancient and modern claims, however, the fleet did not cause the Peloponnesian invaders to leave Attica and go home—the real reason for their withdrawal was dwindling supplies. There is also no evidence that the expedition sought to destroy the enemy, as has been argued.[53]

But, although the campaign conformed to Pericles' strategy in some ways, it deviated from it in others. Pericles had counseled against expanding Athenian hegemony during the war for fear that new acquisitions or allies could endanger the preferred status quo. The addition of Astacus in Acarnania and of the island of Cephallenia to the Athenian alliance did not follow this advice. It was not so much that the leaders of the expedition defied him, as that the situation on the ground did not easily admit of management from Athens. Much of Athenian military activity in western Greece was directed against Corinth and her allies and in support of Athens' friends. This strategy required adding new allies and commitments in order to build and stabilize a pro-Athenian bloc. The other side of this policy was to inflict on Sparta what Athens herself feared at the hands of the enemy: attacks on its weaker allies. This was what the above-mentioned expedition did in Elis and around Acarnania, and what other Athenian forces concurrently did against Spartan allies in Potidaea and Locris. Moreover, Pericles and other generals had added and aided allies and fought those of the enemy before the war. In short, Pericles' call not to widen Athenian rule was not a dogma, and Athenian operations under his command were not a complete break from the past. It is hard to imagine him standing on the dock and wagging a scolding finger at the returning ships.[54]

53. Pericles on Peloponnesian fear of a large fleet: Thuc. 1.142.7–8; and on retributive devastation: Thuc. 1.143.3; for which, see Lendon 2010, 122–123. The expedition as the cause of the Peloponnesians' departure: Diod. 12.42.5–8; cf. Plut. *Pericles* 34, but see Thuc. 2.23.3. Seaborne raids and destroying the enemy: Westlake 1945.
54. Not expanding the empire: Thuc. 1.44.1, 2.65.7; Holladay 1978, 400. Fighting in and around Locris: Thuc. 2.9.2, 26.1–2, 32. Athens also made new allies in Thrace and Macedonia: Thuc. 2.29.1–6. I am not untroubled by the possibility that Pericles' warning against expanding Athens' rule originated in Thucydides' wish to show

The Athenians also expelled the residents of Aegina and colonized the island over the busy summer of 431. The refugees were settled by Sparta in the Argolid or went elsewhere in Greece. The sources explain the Athenian action as retaliation for Aegina's complaints against Athens, which were perceived as one of the causes of the war. It was also thought safer to settle the island with Athenians in view of its proximity to the Peloponnese. One ancient author even claims that Pericles wished to placate Athenians who were angry about the invasion by giving them Aeginetan land. Pericles' reported description of Aegina as "the eyesore of the Piraeus" further suggests his support of the project. In a strict sense, the expulsion and the colonization of the island stood in contrast to his rule of not augmenting Athens' hegemony during the war. Yet, as in the western campaign, Pericles' strategy had to be modified as events unfolded. The Spartan invasion raised concerns about the security of Athens and its territory, which had to be defended not just on land but also at sea. Converting Aegina into an Athenian possession was supposed to make it harder for the enemy to use seaborne attacks against the city and its hinterland.[55]

Other measures taken in the wake of the invasion reflected the same concern. The Athenians established guard-posts to watch for the enemy on land and sea. They also set aside a special fund of 1,000 talents to be used exclusively for dealing with attacks from the sea. They even designated 100 of their best ships as a reserve for just this purpose. Nowhere in his speeches does Pericles discuss the defense of Attica from maritime attacks, probably because he assumed that the Athenian naval supremacy was overwhelming enough to deter them. He also thought that the city and its harbor were well protected, and that Athens should be most concerned about defending its empire. After the invasion, and perhaps under popular pressure, he had to adjust his strategy toward defending the homeland and allocating military and financial resources for the purpose. Scholars who deem the keeping of 100 good ships in reserve as wasteful or misguided fail to appreciate the Athenians' practical and emotional need to defend their home. Their concern proved justified in the winter of 429, shortly after Pericles' death, when a Peloponnesian force tried unsuccessfully to attack the Piraeus by stealth.

Pericles' prescience of later events, such as the failed expedition to Sicily in 415–413. Schubert and Laspe 2009 even claim that Thucydides may have invented Pericles' war plans, but see the interpretation offered here.

55. The Aegina settlement: Thuc. 2.27.1–2; cf. Diod. 12.44.1–3. Pericles and Aegina: Plut. *Pericles* 8, 34; Figueira 1990, 17–19.

The daring attempt surprised the Athenians, who consequently improved the defenses of their harbor.[56]

The Athenian offensive of 431 ended with a raid on the Megarid in the autumn, this time under Pericles' direct command. His troops from the city were joined by men from the fleet that had returned from western Greece and learned about the invasion at its anchor in Aegina. The combined force was the largest Athenian army ever to march out during the war. It consisted of 13,000 hoplites—10,000 Athenians and 3,000 *metics* (resident aliens)—along with many light infantry. The invaders devastated most of the Megarid and took much booty before returning home. Pillaging was a common means of waging war, but the campaign had goals beyond profit and destruction. Before the Thirty Years' Peace of 446, Athens controlled Megara and its two strategic harbors on the Saronic and Corinthian gulfs. The raid of the Megarid pressured Megara to reconsider its alliance with Sparta, and the Athenians continued to invade the Megarid annually with cavalry or other forces until they captured the port of Nisaea in 424 (the city itself remained pro-Spartan). The raid had also a retributive dimension, because Megaran complaints about the Athenian economic blockade of their city topped the Spartan list of grievances that led to the war. Pericles, who was associated more than any other Athenian with the Megaran embargo, may have been especially motivated to attack the city. The campaign had several attractive features: it was short, close to home, against a weak enemy, and in a territory raided by Athenian armies in the past. Its spoils provided some compensation for those who had suffered losses in the invasion of Attica. Finally, it was good for Athens' morale. After hiding behind the walls and being powerless against the Peloponnesians, the Athenian infantry could now go on the march and strut their stuff. Indeed, the army Pericles took was too large for the mission, but he wanted to make sure that many would participate in it. He was also fond of using overwhelming power to improve his chances of success.[57]

56. Land and sea guard-posts: Thuc. 2.24.1; cf. *Ath. Pol.* 24.3; Gomme in Gomme et al. 1945–1981, 2:81; Rusten 1989, 130. Financial and military reserves: Thuc. 2.24.1–2; cf. Fornara 1983, 95–96; Fornara and Samons 1991, 93–96. Criticism of the military reserve: Hornblower 1991–2008, 1:280; Rhodes 2006, 95. The financial reserve fund: Kallet-Marx 1993, 110–111, 185; Blamire 2001, 109. It was used nevertheless in 412 when Chios rebelled: Thuc. 8.15.1. Attack on the Piraeus: Thuc. 2.93.1–94.4; cf. Diod. 12.49.1–5.
57. The Megaran campaign: Thuc. 2.31.1–3; Diod. 12.44.3. Nisaea's capture: pp. 165–166 below. Raiding and morale: cf. Ober 1996, 78.

The popularity he won in the Megaran campaign may have been among the reasons he was selected as a speaker in a public funeral for the dead of the war's first year. His eulogy, as reported by Thucydides, is one of the most famous speeches in all antiquity, but I shall mention only its few references to the war strategy. Pericles returned to the idea of the empire as the key to Athens' survival in war and peace. He presented its preservation as a moral imperative because it was an ancestral inheritance. He also described Athens' power as unique because, unlike Sparta, it could fight its neighbors without allies (as it had done recently in the Megarid), and because its combination of navy and infantry made it formidable. Athens' power was also just and acknowledged everywhere. Hearers of the speech were thus encouraged to believe that all was well with the war and that they were bound to win it.[58]

Thucydides follows the idealized depiction of Athens in Pericles' speech with a description of a plague, perhaps an ancient variant of typhoid, that hit Athens hard in the summer of 430. It claimed many dead in the city and among its armies abroad, and destroyed the social and moral fabric (or façade) of the community, according to Thucydides. Pericles paid a personal price in the death of both of his sons, with whom he had strained relationships. But he persuaded the Athenians to allow him to recognize Pericles the Younger, his child from the alien Aspasia, as his legitimate son in spite of a law (introduced by Pericles himself) restricting citizenship to those with two Athenian parents. The plague also harmed him politically, being one of the miseries of the war for which many blamed him. It made the city a death trap, now more crowded than ever with people fleeing a second Peloponnesian invasion.[59]

In the summer of 430, King Archidamus and the Peloponnesians invaded Attica for the second time (Map 8, p. 127 above). They laid waste to the plain in central Attica and then moved southward to the region around the Laurium mines. Their movements defied the expectation that they would destroy the same areas as in the last invasion, and made it clear that all of Attica outside the city was vulnerable. If there were Athenians who thought the invaders would hurry to leave for fear of catching the disease, they were disappointed, because Archidamus actually prolonged the campaign for forty

---

58. Thuc. 2.34.1–46.2, and especially, 2.36.3, 39.2–3, 41.2–4. On Pericles' funeral oration, see, e.g., Gomme 1945–1981, 2:94–144; Rusten 1989, 135–179; Hornblower 1991–2006, 1:292–316; Bosworth 2000.

59. The plague and its impact: Thuc. 2.47.1–54.5; Hollady 1979; Littman 2009. Pericles' personal losses also included a sister, other relatives, and friends: Plut. *Pericles* 36.

days. Perhaps he was waiting for the Athenians to sue for peace as they would try to do later that summer (below), or he may have wished to give the plague more time to wreak its havoc on the city.

In Athens, Pericles prevailed on the citizens not to confront the enemy, as he had done the previous summer. He likewise timed a second Athenian expedition around the Peloponnese to coincide with the Spartan invasion, hoping the retaliation would induce the enemy to withdraw. He also took command of the fleet, thereby identifying himself with the offensive rather than the defensive element of his strategy. The force he led was characteristically large, showing that Athens remained powerful in spite of the plague. It included 100 Athenian ships, 4,000 hoplites, 300 cavalry on transport ships, and fifty ships from Lesbos and Chios. The large infantry contingent is notable. Though Pericles refused to meet the invaders in Attica, he was ready to fight the enemy on its own land. He probably knew that the Peloponnesians had sent two-thirds of their armies with Archidamus' force, leaving only one-third at home. He had superior numbers against individual locations, especially in hit-and-run operations.[60]

As in the Megarid campaign, the results were positive but less than spectacular. The force spent most of its time in the Argolid Peloponnese. It first went to Epidaurus, a strategically important town near Corinth and across from Aegina, raiding its lands but failing to take the city. From there it sailed to despoil coastal Troezen, Halieis, and Hermione, and concluded by raiding and destroying Laconian Prasiae. When the troops returned to Attica, the Peloponnesians were no longer there. Although one source links their departure to the fleet's activity, the fact that they lingered in Attica for forty days (the longest of all their invasions) suggests additional reasons for their departure, such as exhausted supplies. The Athenian expedition itself was short in duration and range, partly because of losses from the plague, partly because its hoplites and cavalry were supposed to go to Chalcidice next. The failure to capture Epidaurus limited the campaign's gains to the destruction of the less-significant Prasiae, the devastation of enemy lands, and the taking of booty. As both the Athenians and their enemy knew, this was not the way to win the war. It happened to be Pericles' last campaign as a field commander.[61]

60. Thuc. 2.47.2, 55.1–2, 56.1–57.
61. The expedition: Thuc. 2.56.3–5, 57, 6.31.2; Plut. *Pericles* 35; cf. Cawkwell 1975, 69–70. Its effect on the Peloponnesians: Diod. 12.45.3. Reasons for the expedition's short duration: Plut. *Pericles* 35; Thuc. 2.58.1–2. Epidaurus' strategic value: Thuc. 5.53; Lewis 1992b, 398; Lazenby 2004, 39. Prasiae: Cartledge 2002, 238.

The plague that cut short the Athenian expedition also greatly handicapped both the operations in northern Greece against Chalcidician communities and the siege of Potidaea. The lack of meaningful accomplishments and the miseries caused by the disease and invasions led to harsh criticism of Pericles. The Athenians rejected his idea of a war with no end in sight, and sued for peace. Ironically, it was the Spartans who saved him by rejecting the Athenians' peace feelers, leaving Athens no alternative but to resume the war. Although the setback to his strategy was short-lived, it showed his failure to capture the hearts and minds of the Athenians. After all, much of his policy's success depended on Athenian stamina and their willingness to make sacrifices, neither of which, evidently, could be taken for granted. Moreover, the Spartans' reaction to the Athenian peace initiative belied his assumption that they would be the first to yield.[62]

Against this background, Thucydides gives Pericles his last speech. Of all his reported speeches, it is the richest in rhetorical devices and the weakest in substance, probably because of its stated agenda of defusing the Athenians' anger and distracting them from their present troubles. In addition, Pericles was concerned that the continuing hardships would revive attempts to stop the war. Therefore, he presents the alternative to war, not as peace, but as submission: Athens could choose freedom or slavery, either preserving the empire or giving it up. If the Athenians persevered, they would win, and Pericles described as groundless the fear that they would both suffer hardships *and* then lose the war. Athens was a maritime superpower, and its navy could sail anywhere, making defeat inconceivable and the present damage to property trivial.[63]

The speech follows Thucydides' own observation that Pericles' rhetoric of controlling an audience alternated between scaring them and giving them hope. This technique exploited an authentic fear that Athens' might lose its empire and maritime dominance. It appears that Thucydides well-known identification of the "truest cause" of the war with the Sparta's fear of Athens' growth in power is partial and one-sided, because it excludes Athens' fear for its own power.[64]

---

62. The plague and operations in northern Greece: Thuc. 2.58.1–3. Criticism of Pericles and the failed attempt at peace: Thuc. 2.59.1–2; Diod. 12.45.4–5; Kagan 1974, 81–85; Demont 2013, 77–87.

63. Pericles' speech and its goal: 2.60.1–65.5; Gomme 1945–1981, 2:167–183; Rusten 1989, 197–215; Hornblower 1991–2008, 1:340–349.

64. Pericles' rhetoric: Thuc. 2.65.9; followed by Plut. *Pericles* 15, and Diod. 12.39.5. Fear, empire, and the war: Thuc. 1.23.6, 75.3–4, 76.2; cf. 2.89.10; and fear in Thucydides: Romilly 1956; Desmond 2006.

If Pericles hoped to kill any peace initiative and assuage the anger against him, he was only partially successful. The Athenians returned to his war policy chiefly because they had no other choice. They remained angry with him and held him responsible for the conflict, its sufferings, and the loss of lives. The last accusation was especially hurtful because Pericles was reportedly sensitive about Athenian losses and even proclaimed on his deathbed, not without self-delusion, that no Athenian put on mourning cloth because of him. (He is also said to have acknowledged that the Athenians experienced pain but had not yet perceived the benefit.) The hostile climate encouraged rival leaders to impeach him in court for embezzlement and deceiving the demos. (Athenian courts often provided an arena for public debate and political warfare.) Pericles was found guilty and heavily fined, but the punishment did not prevent his reelection as a general for the following year of 429, partly because the trial had a cathartic effect, and partly because his long, uninterrupted service as a general had created a dependency on him. Nothing more is heard of his role in the war until his death from the aftereffects of the plague in the autumn of 429. This silence has much to do with Thucydides, who places his concluding encomium of Pericles' leadership and personality, not after his death, but more than a year earlier. Perhaps the historian did not wish to deal with Pericles' decline. As we shall see, in spite of Athens' adherence to some of Pericles' guidelines, significant changes were made in the conduct of the war while he was still alive. It is unknown whether he supported the changes, opposed them, or was too weak politically or physically to direct Athens' policy.[65]

In truth, the Athenians had more than enough reasons for discontent or skepticism about his war strategy. They resented their suffering and Pericles' cautious policy, and some of his strategic premises discussed here failed the test of time. He emphasized the need to protect the empire and Athens' maritime control, but so far, nothing had suggested these were in danger. On the contrary, it was the homeland and the city that needed protection.

65. Criticism of Pericles: see n. 62 above. Pericles and Athenian losses: Plut. *Pericles* 38. Pericles on suffering and no benefit: Thuc. 2.61.2. His trial and its aftermath: Thuc. 2.65.2–4; Plato *Gorgias* 516a; Plut. *Pericles* 35 (a 15–20-talent fine); Diod. 12.45.5 (an 80-talent fine); Hansen 1975, 71–73; Hamel 1998, 141–142. For the possibility that the fine was never paid: Stadter 1989, 332–333. On Pericles' reelection, probably in the spring of 429: Busolt 1850–1920, 3.2:963n2. Podlecki 1998, 153, assumes that Pericles took no part in the events between the summer of 430 and the autumn of 429, and Will 2003, 213–214, that he lost his influence.

The Spartans refused to see the supposed inevitability of their failure, and their alleged lack of wealth did not seem to impair their annual invasions or even shorten them. There were no signs that the enemy suffered from weak or ineffective central command. Meanwhile, the Athenians, who expected Pericles to practice what he preached, had reason to wonder why Athens continued to take on imperial commitments instead of limiting them. Yet the greatest challenge to Pericles' strategy was to its primary tenet that Athens' unmatched capabilities would decide the war.[66]

Athens' superior assets and capabilities were a leading theme in all of Pericles' addresses in Thucydides. Signs of strain on two of them—abundant resources and the ability to mount great expeditions—appeared as early as the summer of 430, a nadir in Pericles' career. In that year, Thucydides reports, Athens deployed the largest number of well-maintained ships in the war, including 100 ships on guard around Attica, Euboea, and Salamis, 100 around the Peloponnese, and fifty more in Potidaea and other places. The historian then adds that expenditures on the ships and on the siege of Potidaea drained Athenian resources. In other words, Pericles' large-scale expeditions became too expensive. The impact of a smaller purse on the way Athens conducted the war can be seen as early as the winter of 429–430, when Pericles was still alive.[67]

In that winter, the Athenian general Phormio took twenty ships to Naupactus on the Corinthian Gulf. His mission was to watch and possibly stop maritime traffic to and from Corinth and around the gulf. His other goal was to help Acarnania by preventing Corinthian and other Peloponnesian forces from crossing over to join its enemies. (In this he failed.) Phormio's assignments marked a change in Athenian conduct of the war. Pericles' prewar vision of a large Athenian fleet overwhelming the enemy and blockading the Peloponnese never materialized, and he was forced into the second-best option of sending large expeditionary forces to circumnavigate and raid selected places in the Peloponnese and western

---

66. See Stahl 2003, esp. 216–218; and cf. Morrison 2006, 264–268, for the mixed record of people's predictions in Thucydides—which does not mean, of course, that Thucydides invented such disappointments to prove his point.

67. Thucydides on Athenian deployments and money: 3.17.1–4. The chapter is placed in the narrative of the summer of 428, but many scholars agree that its contents better fit the summer of 430, and that it is not an interpolation: Adcock 1923–1925; Gomme in Gomme et al. 1945–1981, 2:272–277; Hornblower 1991–2006, 1:400–403; Kallet-Marx 1993, 130–134, 150–151. Expenditures and the treasury: Kallet-Marx 1993, 109–149, 184–206 (arguing against a significant drainage); Blamire 2001, 109–110; Lendon 2010, 168–169, 464–465n38.

Greece in 431 and 430 (see pp. 130, 136 above). With Phormio's mission, Pericles' original plan was further limited to blockading one city or region with a small fleet from a single local base. The move called for greater reliance on skill and expertise than on numbers. Phormio exploited these competences admirably, and even Pericles discussed them in one of his speeches, but he showed no inclination to use them, preferring to rely on "quantity" rather than "quality." There would be other circumnavigations of the Peloponnese in later years, but with smaller squadrons that were burdened with multiple missions. The likely reasons for the changes were financial constraints and disappointment with the results of large expeditions, such as Pericles' last.[68]

Subsequent operations in the Archidamian War reveal a composite of adherence to Pericles' strategy and deviations from it. (Athens' wars in Sicily and then the Aegean in 413–404 deserve a separate examination.) Confidence in Athens' abundance was replaced by fiscal concerns, as evinced by the dispatch of fleets to collect tribute from the allies and by the unprecedented imposition of a special war tax (*eisphora*) on the residents of Athens.[69] The Athenians also sent out smaller and more affordable forces on land and sea, thereby taking greater risks. They followed Pericles' advice of preserving the integrity of the empire which was the least controversial element of his strategy, but at the same time they made new alliances. In keeping with his policy, they continued to refrain from confronting the Peloponnesian army in Attica. They also kept sending their cavalry to prevent the enemy's light-armed troops from destroying land close to the city. Yet, when the Spartans stopped invading Attica in 425, it was not because Pericles' strategy of frustrating them worked, but because they feared for the Spartan prisoners of war Athens had captured that year (p. 162 below). This was not the only case where intended or unintended consequences failed to follow Pericles' script for the war.[70]

---

68. Phormio's mission and its background: Thuc. 2.68.1–69.1, 80.4. Pericles, blockading the Peloponnese, and Athenian skills: 1.142.6–9; 2.7.3; cf. Plut. *Pericles* 11.
69. Collecting tributes and war tax: e.g., Thuc. 2.69.1–2, 3.15.1–16.4; *IG* I³ 60; Blamire 2001, 109.
70. Athens after Pericles: e.g., Kagan 1974, 113–367. Athens' sending out its army to defeat in the battles of Delium (424) and Amphipolis (422) neither really challenged nor conformed to Pericles' strategy.

Conclusion

How did Pericles fare, then, as a military leader? Before the Peloponnesian War, his record was quite impressive. He never lost a campaign, and he successfully faced diverse opponents and challenges. He defeated regular and irregular forces and strengthened the Athenian hegemony by founding colonies, helping allies in trouble, and gaining new ones, especially in western Greece and the Pontus. In spite of his initial failure to deal effectively with the Samians, he later crushed their dangerous revolt. His punishment of renegade allies, both in Euboea and in Samos, revealed his cruel streak, but his final settlements in both places endured. In Samos and Euboea, he also faced the dilemma of two simultaneous threats, and his solution ultimately worked. He was also good at constructing and overcoming fortifications: he defended settlers in the Chersonese with walls, improved the defense of Athens, and used innovative techniques to breach the walls of Samos. But his record of taking cities by storm is more disappointing, including as it does his failures to capture Sicyon, Methone, and Epidaurus in the Peloponnese, and Oeniadae in Acarnania. The most important test of his art of command, however, came with the war against Sparta.

Pericles' preparations for the Peloponnesian War and his performance as its leader revealed the important influence of his personality on his generalship. As Plutarch says in his biography of Pericles:

> As a military commander, he was famous chiefly for his caution (*asphaleia*, "security"). He was never prepared to join battle when there was considerable uncertainty and risk, nor did he admire and model himself on those commanders who were acclaimed as great, but who enjoyed brilliant good fortune at the risk of their own lives. He was constantly telling his fellow citizens that if it were up to him they would remain immortal forever.[71]

Plutarch's observation may have been influenced by Thucydides, who presents careful planning and self-restraint as central to Pericles' policy and leadership. But the biographer was largely correct. Both as a general and as a strategist, Pericles often liked to play it safe. He avoided fighting the Peloponnesian army when they invaded Attica in 446, and later in the Peloponnesian War. His reluctance to take risks can be seen in his preference for leading or sending out large forces, at times larger than necessary. It also

---

71. Plut. *Pericles* 18, Waterfield translation.

explains his recommendation not to expand Athenian hegemony during the war, his waiting for the Spartans to give up rather than seeking a quick decision, and his statement (part personal conviction, part public justification) that his policy saved Athenian lives. His plan for victory rested on similar principles. The city would win with what it already had: the empire, a strong navy, maritime supremacy, and plentiful resources, which should not be tampered with or risked. This conservative and careful approach does not mean that Pericles lacked personal courage, but it does suggest a strong fear that something might go wrong in spite of Athens' capabilities.[72]

A general was expected to know the enemy's capabilities and weaknesses well, and to predict its war plans successfully. Conversely, a good military leader should have a good grasp of his city's strengths, know how to use them effectively, and convince his followers of the merits of his strategy. Pericles met these expectations only in part. He succeeded in frustrating the Spartan hope of deciding the war in a land battle. He also persuaded his people, with some difficulty, not to fight the invading army and to sustain the damage inflicted on Attica. He offered them security behind the city walls and employed countermeasures that involved little to no risk. His political skills and oratorical gifts, his seniority, his great intellect, and even his aloofness contributed to his leadership, both civilian and military. Also helpful were personal attributes that the public esteemed, such as his probity, self-control, and well-publicized modest lifestyle.[73]

That said, his war plans ran into serious problems. It proved difficult if not impossible to fight a war without extending the empire. After the first Peloponnesian invasion, the Athenians ranked safety of the empire (Pericles' prime concern) below defense of the city and its territory. Pericles' confidence in Athens' ample resources came from his experience in spending public money unsparingly on military expeditions and civilian projects, including the great Parthenon (he was more of an *obol*-pincher in private). Yet the city's financial and human resources were already becoming strained in the second year of the war. Pericles also thought that the side with greater

---

72. Thucydides' praises of Pericles: 2.65.6–13. For Pericles' caution, cf. Kagan 2005, 6–7. In his speeches in Thucydides, however, Pericles praises the Athenians' daring and reasoned risk-taking (Tompkins 2013, 448–451), which left him the discretion to decide when a risk was worth taking.

73. Plutarch, *Pericles*, on his self-controlled and modest demeanor (5, 36, 39; cf. *Moralia* 186c, 620c–d, 813d); aloofness and authoritarianism (7–8), which was viewed critically as arrogant and tyrannical (4, 6, 17); lavishness with public money but frugality in private (9, 11–12, 14, 16, 36); personal integrity (25; cf. Thuc. 2.60.5, 65.8); effective oratory (8, 20–21; cf. Thuc. 2.65.8–9).

tenacity and better judgment would win the war. There was no indication that the Spartans were lacking in either regard. On the contrary, the plague and other difficulties tested the Athenians' will to fight, and Pericles' anti-Spartan stand provoked questions about its wisdom and cost. Pericles then changed some of his strategy and saw others change the rest. Therefore, Thucydides seems to have been wrong in his belief that Athens could have won the war by sticking to Pericles' policy, even when Pericles was still alive.

CHAPTER 4

Demosthenes of Athens

The Master of Surprise

Demosthenes and His Military Challenges

In 432–431 BCE, the Spartans called an assembly of their allies to discuss going to war with Athens. According to historian Thucydides, the delegation from Corinth forcefully argued that Sparta should take immediate action. Among their means of persuasion was contrasting the Athenian "national character" with Sparta's in a way calculated to make the Spartans fear Athens and choose war. The Corinthians described the Athenians as full of action and energy and willing to put their minds and bodies at the service of the state. They were innovative in tactics and military thought, as well as "bold beyond reason." They were ambitious for gains and looked for them away from home. They tried to exploit their military successes fully, and when they failed in one place, they were ready to try again elsewhere.[1]

In his character and career, the Athenian general Demosthenes (to be distinguished from the famous fourth-century orator of the same name) exemplifies in many ways the character of his city as described by the Corinthians. He was very active, daring, and ambitious, dedicated to his city, and a designer of original military plans. Unlike the Athenians of the speech, however, he did not always stay sanguine in times of trouble, and tended to give up when unsuccessful, but otherwise Demosthenes fitted well the portrayal of his fellow citizens.

1. Thuc. 1.70.1–8, where the Spartans are depicted as the Athenians' perfect opposite. For their "national characters," see Luginbill 1999, who overestimates their significance in Thucydides' history.

Though some of Demosthenes' attributes also characterize Pericles' art of command, the two generals differed from each other in several important respects. Demosthenes was far less involved in the city's politics, and was more a tactician than a strategist. He was also less wary than Pericles of meeting the Spartans in battle. While Pericles shunned risks, Demosthenes appeared to court them. Whereas Pericles had to deal with the defense of both empire and city, Demosthenes spent his entire military career away from home and in different theaters of war than those Pericles had visited. The older statesman regarded Athens' navy as crucial to victory, but Demosthenes fought the enemy mostly on land. These differences from Pericles and other generals earn him a place in a book on Greek generalship.[2]

Because Demosthenes' generalship began in the sixth year of the Peloponnesian War, it will be useful to contextualize his first appearance by looking at the balance sheet of the opposing sides from its outbreak. By then, the two chief antagonists, especially the Spartans, had little to show for their efforts. The Peloponnesians' annual invasions of Attica were relatively short, and the damage they caused was insufficient to induce the Athenians to meet them in an all-out land battle, still less to capitulate. The only meaningful victory the Peloponnesians could claim was the destruction in 427 of the small city-state of Plataea, Athens' ally on its border with Boeotia.[3] The Athenians had done considerably better. Under Pericles, they had already occupied a few places in and around eastern Locris and turned the island of Aegina into an Athenian colony in 431. They also added the western island of Cephalonia to their alliance, and defeated and colonized Potidaea in Chalcidice (430–429). In the post-Periclean era, the general Phormio won two naval victories over Peloponnesian fleets in the Corinthian Gulf in 429, and Athens put down a revolt of the city of Mytilene on the island of Lesbos in 427. It also captured and colonized Notium in Ionia in 427, and occupied Minoa,

2. This chapter owes much to Roisman 1993b, updated and revised. Valuable on Demosthenes are: Woodcock 1928; Treu 1958; and Westlake 1968, 86–121; and see also Wylie 1993; Cawkwell 1997. All quotations of Thucydides are from *The Peloponnesian War*, trans. M. Hammond, Oxford, 2009. For the evidence on Demosthenes, see my Bibliography, "The Main Ancient Sources," s.vv. "Thucydides," "Diodorus," and "Plutarch."

3. Thuc. 3.20.1–24.3, 52, 68. In 427, a Peloponnesian fleet defeated a fleet of Corcyra, Athens' ally, but left the region shortly after: Thuc. 3.76.1–80.2. In 426, the Peloponnesians also founded Heraclea in Trachis (eastern Locris), which did not fare well: Thuc. 3.92.1–93.2.

opposite Megara. In the summer of 426, while Demosthenes was fighting his first campaign in western Greece, Athens won a victory over Tanagra in Boeotia.[4] Although the list looks impressive, it is also misleading, because Athens' gains were local and insufficient to move the Spartans to reconsider their strategy, to say nothing of their decision to go to war. Athens also lost many citizens in a plague, as we have seen, and its most prominent leader, Pericles. The time was ripe, then, for a general who could make a difference, and Demosthenes appears to have played this role, intentionally or not.

Nothing is known of Demosthenes' background, except for his father's name, Alcisthenes, and his membership in the large *deme* of Aphidna in northern Attica.[5] His "bursting" onto the scene in 426 was followed by two years of intense activity, in which he led campaigns against the Aetolians and the Ambraciots in western Greece, against the Spartans in Pylos and the island of Sphacteria in the western Peloponnese, and against Megara and Boeotia in central Greece. A hiatus in his career was soon interrupted by a small rescue operation near Epidaurus in the eastern Peloponnese in 418, and in 414–413, he led reinforcements to the Athenian expeditionary force in Sicily, where he met his death.

In the course of his career, Demosthenes faced considerable challenges. They included leading an army of men who were drawn from different states and included units with different proficiencies in attack and in retreat. He was forced to contend with enemies that had an advantage in heavy or light infantry and on unfamiliar terrain. He had to defend fortified sites against attacks by land and sea, but he also tried to capture walled cities in cooperation with fifth-columnists. The difficulties of his operations were exacerbated by the need to coordinate land and sea forces and to conduct simultaneous attacks from different directions. He also had to fight a naval battle in small confines. Beyond the battlefield, Demosthenes was called to mediate conflicts among allies and accommodate their diverse interests in order to obtain their help. He similarly had to persuade colleagues, and even his troops, to cooperate with him and accept his authority. Demosthenes opted for surprise attacks to meet many of these challenges, a solution that created difficulties of its own.

---

4. All citations are from Thucydides. Locris: 2.26.1–2, 32.1; Aegina: 2.27.1–2; Cephallenia: 2.30.2; Potidaea: 2.70.1–4; Corinthian Gulf: 2.83.1–92.7; Mytilene: 3.2.1–15.2, 25.1–28.3; Notium: 3.34.1–4; Minoa: 3.51.1–4; Tanagra: 3.91.3–6.
5. Thuc. 3.9.1; *IG* I^3 369.

Modern historians of the Peloponnesian War tend to give Demosthenes high marks for military leadership. They depict him as a brilliant strategist, courageous, and resourceful—someone who could "think outside the box," to use a modern catchphrase. In fact, Demosthenes had a checkered career that at times justified these praises, but at others showed him responsible for failures and even disaster.

Defeat and Victories in Western Greece

Demosthenes first operated in western Greece, where rival communities sought to strengthen their positions by making (or shifting) alliances with Athens or Sparta (see Map 9, p. 131). In general terms, communities on the northwestern shore of the Corinthian Gulf were friendly to Athens. These included the city of Naupactus, settled by Messenian refugees of the so-called great helots' revolt against Sparta in 460s and their descendants. The city functioned as an Athenian naval base. Naupactus' neighbors, the Ozolian (Western) Locrians, were Athens' allies as well. Further to the west was Oeniadae, a friend of the Peloponnesians and the target of several Athenian attacks. The belligerent Acarnanians, Oeniadae's neighbors and enemies, were Athens' friends, as were the Acarnanians' allies, the Amphilochians in and around (Amphilochian) Argos. There was bitter enmity between the Amphilochians (and the Acarnanians) and communities on the Ambraciot Gulf such as Ambracia and Anactorium, both Peloponnesian allies. The island of Leucas across from Acarnania was also a Peloponnesian ally. In short, regional rivalries supported by rival hegemonic powers created a messy situation that offered both opportunities and difficulties for Demosthenes.[6]

In 426, Demosthenes arrived in this region with the general Procles and an Athenian fleet of thirty ships, and after a short raid of the island of Leucas, he learned firsthand about the conflicting local interests. While the Acarnanians wanted him to help them in the siege of a city on Leucas, "their inveterate enemy," the Messenians of Naupactus wished him to go against *their* foes, the Aetolians in the north. Demosthenes took the Messenian offer because he thought he could integrate it into a larger plan of attacking the Boeotian confederacy centered at Thebes. Thebes and other Boeotians were among Sparta's chief allies and the most powerful of Athens' inimical neighbors. Not for last time, Demosthenes' plan showed a mixture of ingenuity,

6. See Berktold et al. 1996; Bommeljé and Doorn 1987.

risk-taking, and grand ambition that could result in great rewards but also heavy losses. The general intended to assemble a large force in order to defeat the Aetolians, who were regarded as largely uncivilized tribes, unschooled in heavy-infantry warfare. From Aetolia, he planned to march through Ozolian Locris to Phocis, a former friend of Athens that he hoped to turn back into an ally by persuasion or intimidation. Creating a pro-Athenian bloc from the Adriatic Sea to Phocis would have been a major gain for Athens and could have served as a launching pad for an invasion of Boeotia from the west.[7]

The plan proved too intricate, however, and exposed Demosthenes to many conflicting pressures. Everything hinged on first defeating the Aetolians with a blitzkrieg requiring enough light-armed troops to contend with their skilled javelin throwers. But Demosthenes' rejection of the Acarnanians' request to conduct a siege on Leucas led to their refusal to join him with their light-armed forces. The general thought he could substitute light-armed Locrians for the missing units, but fear of allowing the Aetolians time to mobilize a large force compelled him to attack them quickly without waiting for the Locrians' arrival. He was also dependent on the Messenians, who pushed him to keep marching and fed him optimistic intelligence, while his own ambition and confidence encouraged him to take the risk. He took the Aetolian town of Aegitium, but against expectations, the Aetolians came in large numbers to its rescue. They descended on the Athenians from the hills and showered them with their javelins, withdrawing or advancing according to the Athenians' counter-movements. After a long battle, the Athenians gave up. The repeated pursuits and retreats exhausted them, and the death of the commander of their archers unit and shortage of arrows eliminated the only effective weapon they had against the attackers. The lightly armed and fast Aetolians had little trouble killing the battle refugees, who were unfamiliar with the terrain. They fled right into their enemies' ranks or to dead-end ravines, with many finding shelter in a wood that the Aetolians then set on fire.[8]

Demosthenes' defeat was not inevitable, but he did much to bring it about. He yielded to the pressure of his allies and to his own belief that he could use them in a greater design of catching his opponents by surprise. His ignorance of the terrain was compounded by his underestimation of the

7. Quotation: Thuc. 3.94.2. Demosthenes' plan and campaigns in Aetolia and Amphilochia: Thuc. 3.94.1–98.5, 102.1–3, 105.1–114.4; Diod. 12.60.1–6; Pausanias 3.1.2; Pritchett 1965–1992, 7:47–82; 8:1–78; Lendon 2010, 233–245. See Rhodes 1994, 95, against the view that the attack complemented another invasion of Boeotia from the east; cf. Lazenby 2004, 61.
8. Thuc. 3.97.3–98.2.

enemy's fighting ability and willingness to fight and by the absence of lightly armed troops who might have matched the Aetolian javelin-throwers. His lack of experience showed in the conventional ways in which his hoplites tried and failed to contend with the enemy light infantry. In essence, he allowed the enemy to establish the manner of combat and take advantage of its greater mobility and knowledge of the terrain.

Demosthenes escaped to the coast, having lost many allies, his colleague the general Procles, and 120 Athenian hoplites, whom Thucydides describes as "the finest men lost to the city in the course of this war." Because the Athenians were capable of severely punishing generals for poor results, Demosthenes chose to stay in and around Naupactus rather than go home. But soon his career was inadvertently saved by the enemy that had defeated him and by the allies he had disappointed.[9]

At first, Demosthenes frustrated a combined Aetolian-Peloponnesian offensive against Naupactus by bringing 1,000 Acarnanian hoplites to its defense. Preventing the fall of Naupactus into Peloponnesian hands was in the common interest of Athens and Acarnania, and Demosthenes deserves credit for his rescue operation. Later in the winter, he commanded a mostly Acarnanian force that came to the help of the Amphilochians, the Acarnanians' allies, against a joint Peloponnesian-Ambraciot attack. In two battles, Demosthenes showed the great rewards of successful surprise tactics.[10]

The first battle, near Olpae, has been described in my Introduction (pp. 4–5 above). Demosthenes surprised a larger Peloponnesian-Ambraciot army, catching it between his Messenian hoplites and an ambush of Acarnanian hoplites and light infantry. The general had learned the lesson from his failure in Aetolia. Now he left little to chance, and his objective was more limited and better defined. He was also fortunate in having skilled troops from Naupactus and Acarnania, who, we recall, had refused to follow him to Aetolia. Finally, thanks to his local allies and his military intelligence, he could skillfully use the terrain instead of being its victim.[11]

---

9. Quotation: Thuc. 3.98.4–5, with Rhodes (1994, 255), on the Athenian losses. See Geske 2005, 63, for the military repercussions of Demosthenes' defeat. Demosthenes' official status at this point is uncertain: Hamel 1998, 105–106.

10. The exact location of these and other places in Amphilochia is a matter of scholarly debate: Hammond 1936–1937; Pritchett 1965–1992, 8:1–78; Lazenby 2004, 62–63.

11. See also Sheldon 2012, 59. Scholars have argued that Demosthenes learned in Aetolia how to use light-armed troops at Olpae; e.g., Grundy 1948, 1:259–260, 343; Maele 1980, 121; and, more generally, Hornblower 1991–2008, 2:188; 3:613. But it was mostly hoplites who decided the battle.

Demosthenes followed up the victory at Olpae by inflicting additional losses on the Ambraciots, although not necessarily by design. The Peloponnesians, who had lost two of their senior commanders, made a secret pact with him that allowed their officers, the Mantineans, and certain important Peloponnesians to retreat unharmed, leaving the rest to their fate. Their departure was very much in Demosthenes' interest because it left the remaining force leaderless and without its best troops. Thucydides also suggests that it weakened the Peloponnesians' local allies and put the Peloponnesians in bad odor with them. Seeing the Peloponnesians fleeing, their Ambraciot allies (who were ignorant of the deal) joined the flight, and in the ensuing confusion, the Acarnanians killed about 200 Ambraciots. The rest of the troops escaped and took refuge with a friendly local ruler.[12]

A more-significant and better-planned victory was won the next day, when Demosthenes took full advantage of his superior military intelligence and his allies' knowledge of the land. He found out that Ambraciot reinforcements, unaware of the defeat at Olpae, were on their way to help their countrymen. He dispatched units to ambush the roads and take control of commanding sites. When the Ambraciots arrived at a place called Idomene and occupied the smaller of two hills there, they did not know that Demosthenes' advance force was already hidden on the larger hill. Under cover of night, Demosthenes sent half of his army by a roundabout way, either to the enemy camp or to catch fleeing Ambraciots, while taking the other half on a direct route.[13] At the head of his force he placed Messenian troops, who used their Dorian dialect to mislead Ambraciot sentries (who spoke a similar dialect) into mistaking them for friendly soldiers. At dawn, he attacked the enemy and caught them completely unprepared, with the advance party on the adjacent hill presumably joining the attack. Many Ambraciots were slaughtered, and others fled straight into Demosthenes' ambushes or to unfamiliar ground, where the local and lighter-armed Amphilochians had an easy time pinning them down with their javelins. The Ambraciots who made it to the sea swam away in fear of the Amphilochians, their bitterest enemies, only to be killed by the Athenians who patrolled the water.

Thucydides was so impressed by the magnitude of Demosthenes' victory that he used it to narrate a short tragedy (or a macabre comedy) of errors played

12. Thuc. 3.109.1–111.4.
13. For a different interpretation of splitting the army, see Kagan 1974, 214. The battle of Idomene: Thuc. 3.112.1–8.

by an Ambraciot herald and an anonymous victorious soldier. The herald, knowing nothing of what had happened at Idomene, came to ask for the bodies of 200 soldiers who had died after the battle of Olpae the day before. He was puzzled by the amount of stripped arms on the ground, which suggested about 1,000 dead. The victorious soldier, who thought the herald had come to ask for the dead of Idomene, did not understand the herald's surprise. When the herald finally realized the size of the calamity, he went away, forgetting his whole mission. Thucydides adds to their dialogue the claim that this was the greatest disaster to befall a single Greek city in such a short time in the course of the war, saying that he refuses to record how many Ambraciots died lest he be disbelieved. The historian's implied sympathy for the losses of the defeated city does not negate the tribute he thus paid to Demosthenes' victory.[14] Yet, as much as Demosthenes deserved credit for his victories at Olpae and Idomene, their consequences were something of a disappointment. When he suggested to his allies that they follow up the victory with the capture of the now greatly weakened Ambracia, they refused. Thucydides sensibly suggests that they feared mighty Athens would take over the city, making it an unwelcome neighbor. What the historian does not say is that Demosthenes had to concede to the Acarnanians, because, just as in Aetolia, he was dependent on allies who would cooperate with Athenian generals only so far as it served them. Indeed, the Acarnanians and the Amphilochians soon made peace with Ambracia, which even received a garrison of 300 hoplites from Corinth, Athens' foe.[15]

The victories in northwestern Greece allowed Demosthenes to return to Athens without fear of public prosecution for his earlier failure. Three hundred enemy panoplies that survived the trip home commemorated his accomplishments in Athenian temples, and Demosthenes must have had little trouble getting choice military assignments in the future.

Astonishing Success in Pylos

Demosthenes' greatest victory was at Pylos, on the Messenian coast of southwestern Greece. There, in the face of adversity, he displayed personal courage,

14. The post-battle encounter: Thuc. 3.113.1–6. Lateiner (1977, 47–50) and Stahl (2003, 132–136) find a tragic dimension in the messenger's story. It is hard to reconcile the Thucydides' highlighting of Demosthenes' achievement with his alleged belittling of him; for which see, e.g., Wylie 1993; Cawkwell 1997, 50–55; Lendon 2010, 233 and *passim*.
15. Thuc. 3. 113.1–114.4. See, however, Lendon 2010, 244.

excellent planning skills based on good military intelligence, and a perseverance that was not one of his enduring virtues, as we shall see. This section
will attempt to describe Demosthenes' exploits at Pylos while also putting
them into perspective.[16]

In the spring of 425, an Athenian fleet of forty ships left Athens for Sicily,
where the Athenians were engaged in a local war. On the way there, the fleet
was supposed to help the democrats on the island of Corcyra, who were
under attack from Corcyran oligarchs on the mainland and a Peloponnesian
navy at sea. In charge of the mission were the generals Eurymedon and
Sophocles (not the playwright), and they were joined by Demosthenes, who
had "held no command after his return from Acarnania, but at his own
request the Athenians granted him leave to use these ships at his discretion
on their voyage around the Peloponnese." The Athenians could authorize a
military command even to men who were not elected generals.[17]

Demosthenes did not tell his fellow commanders exactly how he intended
to use the fleet, and his authority to employ it for an undisclosed mission
testifies to the trust and high repute he enjoyed in the city after his victories
in Acarnania. His characteristic recourse to secrecy, however, was in this case
directed against both the enemy and his fellow commanders. Planning to fortify
and occupy a deserted place called Pylos on the Messenian shore, Demosthenes
was apparently concerned that Eurymedon and Sophocles would refuse to
collaborate with him even before he reached his destination. These colleagues
were under pressure to reach Corcyra in order to save the democrats there,
and they were concerned about the expenditure of public money his plan
involved, as they told Demosthenes later. As discussed in the previous chapter, financial considerations played an important part in planning military
operations, and in Athens, generals were also subjected to financial scrutiny
(*euthynae*) in the form of a trial that could result in a heavy penalty for the
defendant.[18]

16. The chief source for the Pylos campaign is Thuc. 4.2.1–23.2, 26.1–41.4; cf. Diod.
12.61.1–64.5. Among the many studies of the event are the commentaries on the
relevant chapters in Thucydides by Gomme et al. 1956–1981, vol. 3; Hornblower
1991–2008, vol. 2; Rhodes 1999; Pritchett 1965, 1:6–29, and 1994, 145–177;
Wilson 1979; Strassler 1988, 1990; Lendon 2010, 249–277.
17. Quotation: Thuc. 4.2.4, and cf. 4.28.1–29.1. Demosthenes' status: Fornara 1971, 75;
but also Rhodes 1999, 255.
18. Thuc. 4.3.2–3. Money and the military: see pp. 122–125, 139–140 above, as well as
Kallet-Marx 1993, esp. 154. Financial scrutiny and generals: Hamel 1998, 126–130.
For additional concerns about Demosthenes' idea, see Roisman 1993b, 35; Lendon
2010, 252–253.

Yet Demosthenes' plan had many virtues, chief among them the innovative idea of *epiteichismos*, or establishing a permanent presence in a fortified place in enemy territory. This was to be achieved first by occupying a well-protected site at Pylos and manning it with Messenians from Naupactus: friends of Demosthenes' and former rebels (and their descendants) against Sparta in the late 460s who had found refuge in Naupactus with Athenian help. By raiding Messenian territory and (probably) encouraging insurrection among its residents, the Messenians from Pylos could inflict considerable damage on Sparta. Many of those who lived in the region and its adjacent lands were helots, people of semi-slave status who worked for their Spartan landlords and served in the army mostly as servants or light-armed troops. Their harsh treatment by the Spartans promised their cooperation with the men from Pylos (Map 10, p. 156 below). The site itself was well suited for Demosthenes' purpose, and to his credit, he must have inspected or learned about it from Messenian sources before the expedition. Pylos was also sufficiently distant from Sparta—Thucydides estimates the distance at 400 *stades*, about 70 km—to complicate Spartan communications and countermeasures. The surrounding land was deserted, and a nearby natural harbor allowed access from the sea for the occupiers and those wishing to aid them. Walls could complement the natural defenses of the place, which had an abundance of building material. There was even a small spring that could supply water for a garrison (but not many more).[19]

It has been claimed that Demosthenes' plan complicated and even violated Pericles' more conservative strategy of containing the conflict with Sparta. The reader will recall that Pericles opposed meeting the Spartans in battle and expanding Athens' military commitments. Yet as we have seen, Pericles himself departed from his own guidelines, and Thucydides goes as far as to credit him with the same idea of *epiteichismos* even before the war started. In addition, none of Demosthenes' contemporaries seemed to be bothered by his supposed deviation from Pericles' strategy: Demosthenes' colleagues, who opposed the fortification, raised no such argument.[20]

Nevertheless, occupying Pylos was not an easy sale. Demosthenes' colleagues opposed the idea when the fleet sailed by it, and they did not change

---

19. *Epiteichismos*: Westlake 1983; Treu 1956, 428–230; and see below. Thucydides' controversial assessment of Pylos' distance from Sparta: 4.3.2; Hornblower 1991–2008, 2:154. The site's topography and the likely positions of the walls: Thuc. 4.3.1–3, 26.2; Wilson 1979, 54–64; Lazenby 2004, 69.
20. Against viewing Pericles and Demosthenes as rival strategists, see Roisman 1993b, 12, 34. Pericles advocating *epiteichismos*: Thuc. 1.142.4.

their minds even after a chance storm forced them to anchor there and they could see the merits of Pylos for themselves.[21] But Demosthenes did not give up. He looked for support for his project among the lower-ranking officers and even the marines and rowers. Athenian generals and their troops were never far removed from the culture of persuasion in the popular assembly. According to Thucydides, however, what decided the issue was the impulsive initiative of the crews, who in their idleness applied themselves to fortifying the place. Since building the walls required six days of hard labor and supervision, Demosthenes may have had a hand in this outburst of activity. His dominant personality and confidence in his plan, abetted by popular support, forced his colleagues to acquiesce. Possibly they came to share his concern about being caught between the stormy sea and a Spartan offensive.[22] It helped the Athenians that the Spartans decided to wait for the arrival of their army from Attica and that the Peloponnesian fleet had to sail to Pylos from the vicinity of Leucas. Thucydides' claim that the Spartans did not take the threat seriously at first is supported by their failure to send even an improvised force to interrupt the fortification of Pylos.

With the fortification done, the Athenians left Demosthenes with five ships at Pylos and sailed toward Corcyra. By now the Spartans had mobilized their army and other Peloponnesians for an attack on Pylos by land and sea. Thucydides' description of how the Spartans intended to deal with Demosthenes and the Athenian fleet that came to his aid is beset with difficulties, perhaps even errors, some of which are due to his unfamiliarity with the locale. Less controversial is his report that the Spartans stationed land forces on the coast of Navarino Bay at an uncertain distance from Pylos, and that they sent 420 hoplites and an unspecified number of helot attendants to the uninhabited island of Sphacteria across from Pylos. The occupation of the island was part of their plan to prevent the Athenians from gaining a foothold in and around the bay. No one at the scene, however, could have foreseen that this defensive move would result in making Pylos

---

21. The literature on Thucydides and the role of chance in this episode is vast; see, e.g., Rood 1998, 138–153; Stahl 2006, 320–328.
22. Demosthenes' attempts at persuasion and the crews' initiative: Thuc. 4.4.1–3. Athenians' concern about being trapped: Lendon 2010, 253–254. The building of the walls: Wilson 1979, 62–64. Thuc. 4.4.2 notes that Demosthenes did not bring building tools with him, and scholars offer various solutions to the riddle: e.g., Strassler 1990, 113–114; Hornblower 1991–2008, 2:153; Lazenby 2004, 68. It is also possible that his planning skills were not infinite.

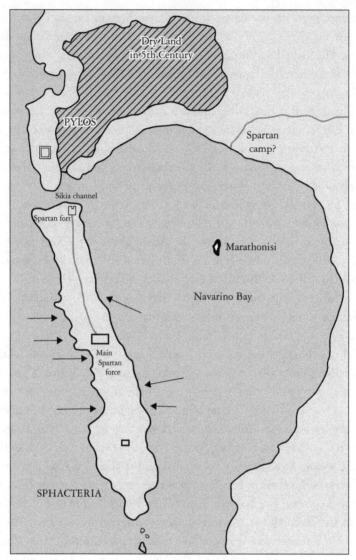

MAP 10 Pylos.

a turning point in the Peloponnesian War and would provide Demosthenes with his crowning achievement.[23]

In view of the Spartan preparations for an attack on Pylos, Demosthenes sacrificed the use of two of his five triremes in order to recall the Athenian fleet from Zacynthus. This loss was somewhat compensated by the arrival of two

---

23. Occupying Sphacteria: Thuc. 4.8.7. The Spartan measures and Thucydides' account of them: Thuc. 4.6.1–8.9; Pritchett 1965, 1:6–29; Pritchett 1994; Samons 2006.

Messenian boats carrying at least forty hoplites and a large number of wicker shields. In spite of Thucydides' language suggesting that they appeared by chance, it is more likely that the reinforcement had been coordinated in advance with Demosthenes, with only its time of arrival being unpredictable.[24] Now expecting to be attacked from both land and sea, the Athenian general dragged his triremes ashore for their protection. In the absence of good-quality weapons, he armed their crews with substandard shields, including those brought by the Messenians. He anticipated that the enemy would come in great force from the direction of the mainland, and he sent the majority of his men, with or without arms, to defend this best-fortified part of the site. He himself took sixty hoplites and a few archers to the wall that reached the sea. The rocky beach worked to his advantage by endangering any ships that landed there, limiting their movement and number.

The Spartans attacked from land and sea, but Thucydides relates only what happened on the beachfront. He shows Demosthenes' success in contending with the enemy in spite of their greater numbers, as well as the heroics of the Spartan commander Brasidas, whom Thucydides greatly admired. The historian also uses the fighting to draw attention to a reversal of roles, a recurrent theme in his work. In this engagement, the Spartans, known for their military prowess on land, fought the Athenians from the sea, while the latter, known for their naval skills, battled the enemy on land.[25] The Athenians won the battle, thanks partly to their tenacious defense and partly to Demosthenes' skillful use of the rough terrain. The defenders bravely withstood a Peloponnesian fleet of forty-three ships that carried many more marines than the Athenians'. (The sight and sound of a trireme landing could be quite frightening.) Yet it was the rocky ground that helped Demosthenes most. The Peloponnesians could land only a few ships at a time, and only where the Athenians stood. Landing on the beach also risked wrecking the ships—a sacrifice of men, equipment, and money that many of the Peloponnesian pilots and captains were unwilling to make. Even the valiant Brasidas, who called upon his fellow commanders to brave landing regardless of the consequences, was unable to disembark from his ship. (He collapsed because of his wounds and lost his shield, which the Athenians later retrieved and used for a trophy.) After two days of futile efforts, the Spartans gave up, planning to land in another spot and to use siege engines against the high wall there. But soon everything changed, thanks to the Athenian fleet.

24. Thuc. 4.9.1; and, e.g., Strassler 1990, 113.
25. Thuc. 4.12.3. For the role reversal, see Macleod 1983, 142; Boëldieu-Trévet 2007, 212–214.

Spartan neglect or lack of skill allowed the fifty Athenian ships that had come originally with Demosthenes to Pylos to return, enter the bay, and destroy or disable much of the Peloponnesian fleet.[26] Although Thucydides fails to say so, it was a most important development in the entire Pylos affair. After the Athenian victory, the Spartans lost any viable option of attacking Pylos from the sea, and, more important, they risked losing their men on the island of Sphacteria. The Athenians blockaded the island, wanting these men dead or alive, and from that point on, the warring parties' attention shifted from Pylos to the Spartans on the island.

The Spartan government was willing to go to great lengths in order to rescue these men. Sparta had just suffered a humiliating naval defeat close to home, and the prospect of losing even a few hundred men to captivity or battle was frightening to a state that already suffered from a shortage of citizens. The men on the island also included prominent, well-connected Spartans. These factors induced the Spartan authorities to accept harsh terms of truce that ensured the safety of the warriors on the island for the duration of peace negotiations with Athens. Thucydides reports a Spartan speech to the Athenian assembly on this occasion, offering to stop the war for a peace treaty. Ostensibly, the proposal suggested that Demosthenes' idea of transferring the war into enemy territory had better chance of victory than Pericles' strategy. Yet it is worth bearing in mind than no one predicted such a successful outcome of his action, not even Demosthenes himself. Moreover, while the Spartan delegates expressed concern for the men on Sphacteria, they said nothing about the occupation of Pylos. Perhaps the future of Pylos was among the points to be negotiated discreetly later. But it is just as likely that the Spartans considered the loss of Pylos less important than rescuing their men, a ranking of priorities that puts Demosthenes' hopes for Pylos' role in the war into perspective.[27]

The Athenians sought to exploit the Spartan distress and demanded concessions that Thucydides deems excessive and that Sparta rejected. With the benefit of hindsight, the historian blames the Athenian politician Cleon for spoiling an opportunity to end the war with Athens on top. After the failed negotiations, the Athenians renewed the blockade of the island with their fleet, which now grew to seventy ships, and the Peloponnesians resumed

26. Thuc. 4.13.2–14.5. For the battle and the Spartans' conduct, see Rood 1998, 33–34; Luginbill 2004–5; Samons 2006, 535–537.
27. Prominent Spartans on Sphacteria; Thuc. 5.15.1. The negotiations: Thuc. 4.17.1, 19.1; cf. 4.21.1–2. The Spartans' speech: Thuc. 4.16.3–20.4; Hornblower 1991–2008, 2:170–177; Crane 1998, 187–192; Debnar 2001, 147–167.

their attacks on the walls of Pylos, with neither effort making any progress. We do not know what Demosthenes did at this juncture, because Thucydides loses interest in him for a number of chapters. We are told that the Athenians were disappointed in their hope of starving out the men on the island, because the Spartans established a successful smuggling operation by rewarding helots and others with freedom or monetary prizes for bringing food through the blockade. Epitadas, the Spartan commander on the island, also took the precaution of conserving food by putting his men on half rations.[28]

Paradoxically, the Athenians fared worse than the besieged Spartans because they did not have enough provisions, water, or a suitable space for their big fleet. Their frustration contributed to their low morale and to their concern that the approaching winter would increase their difficulties of supply, or even force them to abandon the blockade altogether. Their hardship influenced the political scene at home, but Thucydides' account of it is so biased against the politician Cleon—whom he portrays as demagogic, insincere, cowardly, and even clownish—that the reality of the situation is almost beyond recovery. In Athens, there were clearly calls for military action and criticism of the generals at Pylos, maybe even of Demosthenes. But Thucydides provides Demosthenes with convincing reasons for not landing on the island at this point. In essence, they amount to Demosthenes' concern that fighting on the heavily wooded island would work in the Spartans' favor. The enemy could ambush the landing force, exploit their knowledge of the terrain if fighting took place in the woods, and prevent the Athenian commander from managing the battle, since he would be unable to see where reinforcements were needed or even how many losses he had suffered. Thucydides suggests that Demosthenes' concerns were directly related to his bitter experience in Aetolia, where his men had been hunted down by the locals. Equally applicable was his more positive experience in Acarnania, where he and his allies had knowledgeably exploited the terrain to inflict losses on the enemy. In any case, Demosthenes' caution now was uncharacteristic of this daring general. One reason for his eventual success at Sphacteria was that his partiality for surprise attacks was well balanced by fears of being their victim.[29]

---

28. Athenian demands and Cleon: Thuc. 4.21.1–22.3. Renewal of hostilities: Thuc. 4.23.1–2, 26.1–27.2.
29. The Spartans' and the Athenians' circumstances: Thuc. 4.26.1–27.2, 39.2. The reaction in Athens: Thuc. 4.27.1–5. Demosthenes' rationale: Thuc. 4.29.3–30.1.

What changed Demosthenes' and the Athenians' minds was a fire that largely denuded the island and exposed its occupants. Demosthenes could now ascertain how many men were on Sphacteria and their location. Thucydides says the fire was accidental, but modern scholars who think he was biased against Demosthenes, or that the latter was the best Greek general in the Peloponnesian war, credit Demosthenes with starting it. This hypothesis raises the question of what took him so long to resort to this means of exposing the enemy. It is simplest to take Thucydides at his word.[30]

According to Thucydides' description of events at Athens, the politicians Nicias and Cleon were tossing the command of the new operation at Pylos back and forth like a hot potato. It was Cleon who eventually took it, and when he promised to bring the men from the island alive or kill them there within twenty days, he seems already to have been aware of Demosthenes' new plan of attack and what troops it required. Indeed, Cleon picked Demosthenes as his colleague for this mission before leaving for Pylos with reinforcements that had assembled in Athens. These included troops (possibly hoplites) from Athenian colonies in Lemnos and Imbros, lighter-armed peltasts from Aenos in Thrace, and 400 archers. Upon arrival, the new force joined the Athenian crews and soldiers already at Pylos, as well as recruits from neighboring allies. The invasion of the island took place on the seventy-second day of the blockade.[31]

Demosthenes' and Cleon's plan of attack took into consideration the Spartans' dispositions on the island, their predictable tactics, and the terrain (Map 10, p. 156 above). The enemy general, Epitadas, assigned thirty hoplites to a post in the southern part of the island, stationed the bulk of his forces at its center under his own command, and sent a small unit to guard a makeshift fort on the northern end overlooking Pylos. Under cover of night, the Athenian commanders landed about 800 hoplites on both sides of the island. This force attacked the unprepared enemy at the southern post and eliminated them. At dawn, the Athenian generals flooded the island with

---

30. The fire: Thuc. 4.30.2. Demosthenes' responsibility for it: e.g., Woodcock 1928, 101–102; Hunter 1973, 71–72.

31. Nicias and Cleon on Pylos: Thuc. 4.27.1–29.1; Plut. *Nicias* 7 (largely based on Thucydides); Flower 1992; Geske 2005, 26–45, 85–92, 165–167. For the high likelihood that the Athenians had already approved an expedition to Pylos, see Flower 1992, 43–44; Hamel 1998, 21n50; Rhodes 1999, 225–229; but also Geske, 2005, 34–39. Cleon and Demosthenes: Thuc. 4.28.4. See Roisman 1993b, 41; and Howie 2005, 227–228, with n. 75, against their forming a political-military partnership, as claimed by, e.g., Kagan 1974, 242; Holladay 1978, 414–415, 425–427.

nearly 11,000 men, according to one estimate. These included 800 archers and 800 peltasts, as well as slingers and many other light infantry. Numbers do not always tell, but there were only 420 enemy hoplites on Sphacteria, with perhaps an equal number of lighter-armed attendants. The odds clearly favored the attackers.

As could be expected of the Spartans at the main post, they readied themselves for a hoplite battle in which they would enjoy a tactical and psychological advantage: the Spartan reputation on land was formidable. But Demosthenes was taking no chances, and he knew better than to let the enemy determine the form of the battle. He divided his troops into groups of 200 men and ordered them to seize the high points that surrounded the enemy. He then positioned his hoplites in the front, but used them more as bait for the enemy hoplites than as an offensive unit, ordering them not to advance, and sending his light-armed troops to do the fighting. Every time the Peloponnesians tried to engage the Athenian hoplites, they were attacked on their flanks by lighter troops including archers, slingers, and javelin-throwers, who shot at them from a safe distance. And when the Spartan hoplites pursued their attackers, the latter had little difficulty avoiding contact.

The more the Spartans chased the fleeing enemy and then regrouped, the more tired they grew. The din that the attackers made and the clouds of dust and ash from the fire impaired the Spartans' hearing and sight, and hence the discipline on which much of their prowess depended. It appears also that they lost Epitadas, their commander, and that his wounded deputy was presumed dead, leaving them under the command of a third-ranking, junior officer. Finally, the psychological barrier of fighting the Spartans collapsed, and with the Athenians growing bolder, the Spartans retreated to their last position in the northern fort. This move gained them only a brief respite, because a Messenian commander, with Demosthenes and Cleon's blessing, took a unit of archers and light troops and seized a higher spot at the Spartans' rear.[32]

Demosthenes and Cleon's main concern now was to prevent their spirited troops from killing these potentially precious captives. They held the army back and demanded an unconditional surrender. It appears that most of the exhausted Spartans were willing to yield, but their commander wished to consult his superiors on the mainland first. After a few comings and goings of Spartan envoys, they received these final instructions: "(T)he Spartans tell

---

32. The number of the Athenian attackers: Wilson 1979, 104–105. Fighting on the island: Thuc. 4.31.1–37.2; cf. Pausanias 4.26.1. See Debnar 2001, 164–165.

you to make your own decision about yourselves, but do nothing dishonorable." The Spartan authorities' dilemma in reconciling their men's survival, Spartan ideals, and concerns about the disastrous consequences of capitulation was understandable. Yet, if by "do nothing dishonorable" they meant surrender, the message was ambivalent, even contradictory.[33]

Two hundred and ninety men, including 120 Spartans, surrendered and were taken to Athens by Demosthenes and Cleon. The Pylos campaign had succeeded beyond expectations, including Demosthenes'. The threat of executing the prisoners prevented the Spartans' invasion of Attica, a major component of their war strategy. The victory also meant that, in the zero-sum game of national reputations, Athens' prestige went up while the Spartans' carefully cultivated ethos of courage and heroic death in battle suffered a major blow. Thucydides, always on the lookout for historical ironies, cannot resist contrasting the Spartan heroes of Thermopylae with their apparently lesser heirs:

> To the Greeks this was the most surprising event of the whole war. They had thought that Spartans would never surrender their arms, in starvation or any other extremity, but would use them to the last of their strength and die fighting. They could not believe that those who surrendered were the same quality as those who were killed.[34]

The Athenian success also encompassed the occupation of Pylos. The site was taken by highly motivated Messenians from Naupactus, who plundered Spartan fields and attracted helot deserters. Thucydides states that Spartans were very worried about the Messenians stirring up a wider helot revolt, and he mentions this fear and "the disaster on the island" as among their motives for agreeing in 421 to the Peace of Nicias, which (temporarily) ended the war. Yet scholars who congratulate Demosthenes on initiating an innovative strategy of establishing a permanent, fortified base in enemy territory (*epiteichismos*) and using it to encourage the local population to rebel, tend to ignore that it was never intended to win the war, but only to harass or at most exhaust the enemy. Moreover, the Spartans' worries about a general helot revolt were never fulfilled, and in 409, they recaptured Pylos, with little to no effect on the course of the war or their strategy.[35]

---

33. Message to the Spartans: Thuc. 4.38.3. For other interpretations, see Rood 1999, 37; Lendon 2010, 274–276.
34. Thuc. 4.40.1–2; see also 4.36.3 and cf. 5.75.3.
35. Thucydides on Pylos' impact: 4.41.1–3; cf. 5.14.3; Cawkwell 1997, 51–52. Demosthenes' new bold strategy: e.g., Hanson 2005, 111–112; but see Lendon 2010,

Demosthenes displayed commendable qualities in the Pylos campaign. He was daring and cautious at the right times, based his defense of Pylos and attack on Sphacteria on previously obtained intelligence, and took advantage of the enemy's weaknesses. He even used his favorite surprise tactics without taking great risks. No less important, he was lucky: without the storm at Pylos, the Athenians' easy defeat of the Peloponnesian navy, the fire on Sphacteria, and even the Athenian rejection of the Spartan peace offer, it is doubtful that the Pylos venture would have ended as it did.

Demosthenes may have been less successful in the competition over credit for the victory. If we believe the comic playwright Aristophanes, who was Cleon's enemy, Cleon robbed the glory of Pylos from his colleagues. The Athenians, too, made a collective claim to honor when they commemorated the campaign with a bronze statue of Victory (Nike) on the Acropolis, and the Messenians did the same at Olympia. Yet even if success has many fathers, as the saying goes, we can be certain that Demosthenes did not keep silent about his role in the affair, and that the Athenians did not forget it, since they elected him general a year later (424).[36]

Sneak Attack on Megara

Demosthenes' next scene of operation involved the city of Megara, which occupied one of the most strategic locations on the Greek mainland, a narrow isthmus separating the Peloponnese from Attica and Boeotia. Megara also had two important military and commercial harbors, Pegae on the Corinthian Gulf and Nisaea on the Saronic Gulf. Megara's relationship with Athens had its share of crises, among them the Athenian embargo against the city since 432, which was regarded, as we have seen, as a major cause of the Peloponnesian War. In the summer of 424, Megara was a Spartan ally with a democratic government. The city was under heavy pressure, both from oligarchic exiles at the harbor of Pegae, who raided Megaran territory from the west, and from annual Athenian incursions from the north. A Peloponnesian

---

254–255. See Thuc. 4.80.1 for other raids on Laconia, which were no more decisive. The Spartan fears: Boëldieu-Trevet 2007, 199–200.

36. Aristophanes on Cleon's stealing the credit for Pylos: *Cavalrymen* 54–57, 742–743; cf. 355, 392, 846, 1053, 1067; and for the honors awarded to Cleon: *Cavalrymen* 280–283, 701, 709, 1404–1405. Statue of Victory on the Acropolis: Pausanias 4.36.6. Messenian dedication at Olympia: Pausanias 5.26.1; *ML* no. 74.

garrison occupied Nisaea in order to protect the harbor and keep the democratic leaders from changing sides.[37]

Fearing the return of the oligarchic exiles to the city by popular consent, the Megaran democrats conspired with the Athenian generals Demosthenes and Hippocrates, son of Ariphron, to betray the city to Athens. Hippocrates came from a distinguished background—he was Pericles' nephew—but his hitherto-unremarkable record and Demosthenes' stature after Pylos make it likely that Demosthenes was deemed his senior. In this intrigue, however, Demosthenes played a relatively passive role, because the initiative came from Megara, as did much of the plan of attack. In order to prevent the Peloponnesian garrison at Nisaea or other reinforcements from foiling the plot, the local democrats proposed that an Athenian force launch a covert attack on the long walls, about a mile in length, that connected their city to its harbor at Nisaea. They also promised inside help in capturing the walls and occupying the city. The Megarans even told the Athenians exactly where and when to attack: they had already accustomed the commander of the guard to opening the gates before dawn for returning sea marauders, and they advised Demosthenes to rush the gates when they were opened to admit a carted boat.[38]

The plan must have been warmly endorsed by Demosthenes, if only because it resembled his successful surprise attacks at night and other subterfuges at both Amphilochia and Sphacteria. On the appointed night, Athenian ships brought Hippocrates with 600 hoplites and Demosthenes with Plataean light-armed troops and Athenian *peripoloi*—young recruits who patrolled Attica and its borders—to a nearby base on the island of Minoa. At the same time, 4,000 hoplites and 600 cavalrymen left Eleusis, Attica, for Megara, where they were meant to join these advance forces and help them take the city. Demosthenes and Hippocrates marched to the vicinity of Nisaea, where Hippocrates and his hoplites hid in a ditch not far from the gates while Demosthenes with his younger and lighter-armed troops lurked closer to the walls in order to overwhelm the gates. When the gates were opened to let in a returning boat, Demosthenes and his men rushed in. We do not know how old he was at the time—probably older than thirty,

37. Megara and its importance: see, e.g., Legon 1981, 21–30; Lewis 1992b, 387–388; Hornblower 1991–2008, 2:229–30. Athenian embargo: see p. 121 above; McDonald 1994–1995. Megara in 424: Thuc. 4.66.1–2.

38. Hippocrates was a general in 426: *ML* no. 72. He would cooperate with Demosthenes again in a plot against Boeotia: see pp. 168–171 below. The Megaran long walls: Legon 1981, 27, 185, 188–189. The Megaran plot: Thuc. 4.66.3–67.5.

the minimum age for a general—but he displayed both courage and physical fitness in being the first to enter the walls. In addition, and as shown on this occasion, in Amphilochia, and on Sphacteria, he appeared to make more frequent and better use of light infantry than other contemporary generals, because he was equally aware of their limitations in open combat and advantages in surprise attacks. He and his troops overcame the guards who offered resistance, and by the time Hippocrates' heavier-armed hoplites arrived, the gate was already secured.[39]

The success of the Athenians' operation depended on taking the long walls, and Demosthenes was helped by his enemy's conduct, as he was at Amphilochia and Pylos. The Peloponnesian guards were confounded by the night attack and feared local betrayal. They fled and shut themselves in Nisaea, leaving the long walls to the Athenians. By daylight, however, the Athenian plan had begun to unravel. Megaran collaborators were supposed to open the city gates by a stratagem, but their plot was discovered by their opponents, and the Athenians could not force their way in. Demosthenes and Hippocrates then decided to attack Nisaea, and for good reasons. Megara was bigger, better protected, and more populated than the harbor, which could easily be isolated from it. Nisaea was also defended by men who had just suffered defeat and who doubted the loyalty of the local population. The Athenians could also learn from their local friends that the Peloponnesians had little to no food reserves, and they knew that the defenders included Spartans, whose capture would have buttressed Demosthenes' fame. Finally, Demosthenes could build a siege wall with ease and expertise. There were Athenian tools and stonemasons readily available across the border, building material in abundance nearby, and—with the arrival of an Athenian army from Eleusis—plenty of working hands.

Thus, after a concerted effort of less than two days, the Athenians largely completed the building of a cross-wall that surrounded Nisaea from all directions except the sea, which was probably patrolled by Athenian vessels. The Peloponnesians were moved to surrender by low morale and expectations, the

---

39. The Athenian advance forces and their positions: Thuc. 4.67.1–2, 5, 68.5. For the *peripoloi*, see Rhodes 1999, 254; Russel 1999, 38–40. See Lendon 2010, 1–6 (cf. 297–298) for a vivid description of Demosthenes' night attack and its consequences. The minimum age of generals (with possible exceptions): Rhodes 1993, 510; cf. Hansen 1991, 231.

quick success of the Athenians, and fears of starvation and Megaran betrayal. Once again, Demosthenes was lucky, because if the guards had waited a little longer, they would have learned that a large force was coming to their rescue (below). Instead, they surrendered Nisaea, their weapons, and themselves on the condition that they be ransomed. The Spartan commander and his fellow countrymen were not given this privilege, probably because the Athenians wished to reserve the possibility of executing them if the Spartans invaded Attica. The exact number of the Spartan prisoners is unknown, but their capture made Demosthenes a champion at garnering them. If the desire for this reputation was his motive for granting the stipulated terms, he was short-sighted, because in the following winter the released guards helped the Boeotians capture an Athenian base at Delium in Boeotia.[40]

After Nisaea's surrender, the Athenians demolished the long walls between their cross-wall and Megara in order to isolate their new acquisition from the city. This act also suggested that they had given up on capturing Megara, because leaving the walls intact could have facilitated their attacking it from Nisaea. That they were leaving Megara and their partners there in the lurch became more evident in the following days, when Demosthenes and the Spartan general Brasidas met for the second time after Pylos. This time, the Spartan commander did not let the Athenian force him to fight at a disadvantage. Brasidas was in the neighborhood of Corinth, preparing for a campaign in northern Greece, but when he heard of the Athenians' occupation of the long walls he rushed to the rescue of Megara, Nisaea, and the Peloponnesians there. He assembled a force of about 3,800 hoplites, composed mostly of Corinthians, Sicyonians, and Phlians, and established a rendezvous with a Boeotian army in a village below Mount Geraneia, about 12 km west of Megara. He then hurried with 300 picked soldiers in an attempt to save Megara for the Peloponnesian cause. The Megarans, however, refused his appeal to be admitted. The city was divided between pro-Athenian democrats and pro-Spartan oligarchs, and neither side wanted to take action before seeing which invading army would prevail.[41]

Brasidas went back to his army, which a reinforcement of Boeotians had enlarged to a force of about 6,000 hoplites and 600 cavalry. The Athenians had approximately 4,600 hoplites, 600 cavalry, and an unspecified number of light

40. The guards' considerations and later fighting in Boeotia: Thuc. 4.68.1–69.4, 100.1.
41. Destroying the long walls: Thuc. 4.69.4; Rhodes 1999, 256. The Megarans would later defend their city by completing the razing of the walls: Thuc. 4.109.1. Brasidas to the rescue: Thuc. 4.70.1–71.2.

infantry. Their hoplites stood near Nisaea and the sea, and their light-armed fighters were scattered over the plain. It was now Demosthenes' turn to be taken by surprise, unprepared as he was for the arrival of enemy forces, at least at this point. An advance force of Boeotian cavalry attacked and pursued the light-armed Athenians and was checked by the Athenian cavalry in a battle that ended indecisively. Shortly afterward, Brasidas arrived with his army and, finding suitable ground, arrayed his troops for battle. At stake was the fate of Megara, and with it the ability to control the Isthmian roads to Attica, the Corinthiad, and Boeotia. Neither side went on the attack, and after an undetermined time of waiting, the Athenians retreated to Nisaea. The effect of their decision was predictable. It was interpreted in Megara either as a refusal to fight for it, as a loss, or as a show of weakness, and the pro-Spartan oligarchs became masters of the city.[42]

Thus, even though capturing Megara was the Athenians' original goal, they conceded it after little effort. Demosthenes' past record, greater prestige, and leadership of the attack on the walls makes it likely that he was chiefly responsible for the decision. Thucydides defends the choice to decline battle by saying that the Athenians risked more than the numerically superior enemy and that they had been quite successful so far. A loss could also ruin their best hoplites, while the enemy risked only fractions of their native armies. Yet this last rationale would have prevented the Athenians from ever confronting any coalition army, and can easily be refuted, like the rest of their alleged reasoning. The disparity between the opposing armies was not so great as to make the Athenian risk discouraging. The Peloponnesians had roughly 1,400 more hoplites, yet Demosthenes had faced and defeated significantly larger forces at both Olpae and Pylos. No side had an edge in the number of cavalry—both had about 600 horses—and the Athenians enjoyed the advantages of a close shelter in Nisaea, control over the sea, and proximity to home resources, including reinforcements. Thucydides suggests that the Athenian commanders feared losing what they had gained. The decision to go against Nisaea was justified under the circumstances, but Nisaea was only the byproduct of an operation whose main goal was Megara, a more significant asset. It seems that Demosthenes feared a battle because

---

42. Athenian forces: Thuc. 4.67.1–2, 68.5. Brasidas' army: 4.70.1, 72.1–2. Brasidas would later twist the truth when he claimed that he had fewer troops than the Athenians: Thuc. 4.85.6–7, 108.5; cf. Diod. 12.67.1. Demosthenes taken by surprise: Thuc. 4.72.2, but also 4.69.1. Cavalry battle: Thuc. 4.72.2–4. Thuc. 4.71.1–4 ascribes detailed reasons for both sides to avoid battle, which he is unlikely to have been privy to, especially on the Spartan side. See below for the Athenian motives.

Brasidas left him no room for the preplanning or use of surprise that had won him victories in the past. It is also possible that Demosthenes worried that a defeat in battle would devalue his success in leading the attack on the long walls (Thucydides later saw a trophy there commemorating the event) and in reestablishing Athenian control over Nisaea. It would have equally detracted from his fame as the general who kept humiliating Sparta by capturing its men. His personality may also have played a role, because setbacks often moved Demosthenes to give up, as he did when his Aetolian campaign failed, when Megara did not open its gates, and—as we shall see—in Boeotia and Syracuse. His colleague, Hippocrates, was equally motivated not to allow possible defeat to tarnish his career. And if the Athenians at home complained about the generals' failure to fight for Megara and their fellow democrats there, Demosthenes could have cited all the arguments Thucydides gives for avoiding battle, as well as a Greek proverb that ridiculed men who acted like children in risking their possession of half in an attempt to gain the whole.[43]

Coming Out Empty-Handed in Boeotia

Upon their return to Athens, Demosthenes and his colleague Hippocrates were involved in one of Athens' more ambitious war plans, this time against Boeotia. The Boeotian Confederacy was an active participant in the war against Athens, and its cavalry raided Attica during and beyond the periodic Spartan invasions. There was also a history of bad blood between these states. No wonder, then, that the Athenians welcomed a local initiative to effect a democratic, pro-Athenian revolution in two Boeotian cities.

The Boeotian conspirators, who sought Athenian aid, plotted democratic coups in the city of Siphae on the shore of the Corinthian Gulf and in Chaeronea on the western Boeotian border with Phocis. The Athenians, however, linked or subordinated these schemes to their seizing and fortifying the temple of Apollo at Delium near Tanagra in eastern Boeotia, across from Euboea (Map 11). According to Thucydides, the idea was to achieve all three

43. Nisaea and Athens: Thuc. 1.103.4, 114.1, 115.1; 2.93.1–94.4; 3.51.3–4; 4.21.3; cf. 4.118.4; 5.17.2. Nisaea as an evolved target: Thuc. 4.69.1–2. For the Athenians' considerations, see, however, Hornblower 1991–2008, 2:242–243. Trophy at Megara: Thuc. 4.67.5. Greek proverb: Leutsch and Schneidewin 1958, 1:437.7, perhaps inspired by Hesiod *Works and Days* 40.

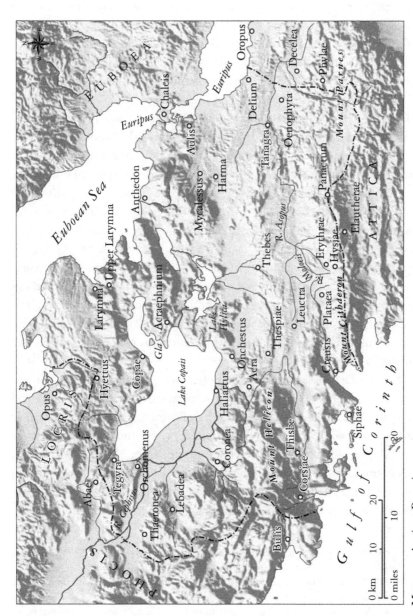

MAP 11 Ancient Boeotia.

objectives simultaneously by surprise, in the hope that splitting the Boeotian army into three fronts would prevent them from coming in full force to Delium. It was also hoped that the capture of these places would allow the Athenians to raid the region, give shelter to Boeotian opposition, and, in a best-case scenario, cause a political change in Boeotia.[44]

Generally, the plan was an expanded idea of *epiteichismos*, or the establishment of a well-protected base in hostile territory. It failed to achieve all of its goals because it was too demanding and complex and hence poorly executed. We shall focus on Demosthenes' role in the affair.

In truth, the fragmentation of the Boeotian forces would have benefitted the attacks on Siphae and Chaeronea as much as the capture of Delium. Yet Delium's greater proximity to Athens made it a prime target, at least in Thucydides' eyes. Occupying Delium was Hippocrates' mission, but Demosthenes was not relegated to the secondary role of diverting Boeotian forces. He went to western Greece because of his local connections in the region and his ability to enlist troops, especially Acarnanians, whom he had helped in 426 to defeat the Ambraciots (pp. 150–152 above). As in the past, the Acarnanians put a price tag on their assistance. After arriving at Naupactus with a forty-ship fleet, Demosthenes led the Acarnanians to victory over their northern neighbors, the Agraeans, thus expanding Acarnanian power and the pro-Athenian bloc in the region. He could now add Acarnanian and Agraean troops to the 400 hoplites he brought to Boeotia.[45]

That was Demosthenes' sole accomplishment in the campaign. For reasons that can be only conjectured, the simultaneous attacks on Delium and Siphae were postponed to the beginning of winter, increasing the chance that the plot would be discovered. Indeed, given the many people who shared the secret, including a chief conspirator from Thespia (or Thebes), plotters from Siphae and Chaeronea, Chaeronean exiles and Peloponnesian mercenaries they recruited, and men from Phocis interested in the defection of Chaeronea (not to mention Athenians in the know), it is hardly

---

44. Thuc. 4.76.4–5. See Hornblower's intriguing suggestion that, as a general that year (424), Thucydides was privy to the plan: 1991–2008, 2:249. For the plan, see Hanson 2005, 125–126; but also Lendon 2010, 301–303, who argues for a much more modest Athenian aim of assisting local rebels.

45. For Demosthenes' equality (at least) in rank to Hippocrates, see Gomme et al. 1956–1981, 3:539; Hornblower 1991–2008, 2:255; Rhodes 1999, 263. Diodorus, whose version of the event is inferior to Thucydides', is surely wrong in allocating to Demosthenes the larger part of the Athenian army: Diod. 12.69.1–2. Demosthenes and the Acarnanians: Thuc. 4.76.1, 101.3.

surprising that the plot was betrayed before the Athenian offensive began. When Demosthenes sailed to Siphae with his fleet and army, he found the city already secured by the Boeotians, who also made sure that no plot would unfold at Chaeronea. Thucydides states that a mistake or a failure caused Demosthenes to arrive at Siphae before Hippocrates left for Delium. Yet the real mistake was not his premature arrival, but the wish to coordinate the attacks in the first place. The goal of establishing bases in Boeotia could have been attained without simultaneous attacks: Hippocrates was able to occupy and fortify Delium unopposed even after the plot was uncovered and the Boeotians had returned from securing Siphae. The potential gain of surprising the enemy and forcing it to divide its force was offset by a delay in the attack that resulted in the discovery of the plot, which in turn prevented Demosthenes from taking Siphae.[46]

As it happened, the Athenian occupation of Delium led to a large battle with the Boeotians, in which the Athenians were defeated and lost their general, Hippocrates. Thucydides, rightly focusing on these more important events, provides only a short description of Demosthenes' activities, saying that, after his failure to take Siphae, Demosthenes sailed away to Sicyon. It is unclear why the general, with his large fleet and presumably adequate land forces, did not stay longer in the region to raid Boeotian lands, encourage revolutions, or draw Boeotian forces from elsewhere to himself, as was his original brief. I suggest that Demosthenes' propensity to cut losses and abort plans after a setback came into play here. He did employ the forces at his disposal for a landing at pro-Spartan Sicyon across the Gulf, perhaps intending to make raids or even an *epiteichismos* (his purpose is not reported). But the Sicyonians successfully repelled him, maybe because he landed at intervals instead of with the entire force at once.[47]

It would be unfair to blame Demosthenes alone for the Boeotian plan and its failure, because he had many partners in it. But the endeavor shares traits with his previous campaigns, suggesting his role in it. The enterprise originated in, and relied on, local initiative, planning, and resources. It

---

46. "D-Day" for the attack: Thuc. 4.77.1, 89.1. The delay from plan to execution could have been as long as three months: Gomme et al. 1956–81, 3:558. The plotters: Thuc. 4.76.1–3. For the identity of the Thespian exile: Hornblower 1991–2008, 2:249–251. The plot and its failure: Westlake 196, 116; Buck 1994, 16–18. The occupation of Delium: Thuc. 4.90.1.

47. Demosthenes' retreat and Sicyon: Thuc. 4.101.3–4. For the uncertain possibility that Demosthenes was put on trial after the Boeotian campaign, see Roisman and Worthington 2015, 89–90.

recalled Demosthenes' idea of attacking Boeotia from the west, which the Aetolians frustrated in 426. It was built on secrecy and surprise, and evinced excessive optimism and ambition, but also an inclination to give up on the original goal too quickly. It was probably public disappointment with Demosthenes and the decrease in military operations after the Peace of Nicias between Athens and Sparta (421) that were responsible for the approximately six-year hiatus in his military career. The big assignments seemed to go now to other generals such as Alcibiades, Nicias, and Laches. Nevertheless, Demosthenes was sufficiently involved in public life to serve as one of the Athenian signatories on the Peace of Nicias, and wealthy enough to function as a sponsor of performances (*choregos*) in the City Dionysia, both in 422–421.[48]

Demosthenes' next assignment paled in significance and scope in comparison with his earlier commands, and suggests a decline in his career until he was sent to Sicily in 414. In 418, the Athenians and their allies built a wall around the pro-Spartan city of Epidaurus in northeastern Peloponnese, and manned a fortress there with a garrison that included a relatively small number of Athenians. A Spartan-Argive treaty later that year included an Argive commitment to destroy the fortification around Epidaurus and to treat Athens as an enemy if she refused to abandon it. The Argives asked the Athenians to evacuate the fort, and the Athenians, who were concerned about the non-Athenian guards' reaction to the evacuation, sent Demosthenes to bring the men home. Under the pretext of an athletic competition, Demosthenes got the non-Athenians out of the fortress and then shut the gates behind them. Sometime later, when Athens and Epidaurus became friends, the fortress was surrendered to the Epidaurians.

Athens evacuated the fort because its continuing occupation would have complicated her relations with Peloponnesian allies and the cities of Argos and Epidaurus. Nevertheless, the incident was a minor affair. Demosthenes' success confirmed his reputation for cunning, and even suggested that, in the absence of great risk, he was the man for the job.[49]

---

48. Signatory: Thuc. 5.19.2, 24.1. Choregos: *IG* II² 2318.123–24. For the possibility, however, that Demosthenes signed the peace treaty as a general, see Rhodes 1999, 334–335.

49. Epidaurus: Thuc. 5.75.5–6, 77.2, 80.3. An inscription (*ML* no. 77) mentions Demosthenes' earlier activity around Argos, for which see Andrewes in Gomme et al. 1956–1981, 4:129. The evidence does not support attempts to endow Demosthenes' mission with major strategic significance: e.g., Treu 1956, 433–434; Andrewes in Gomme et al. 1956–1981, 4:137. Hornblower (1991–2008, 3:205–206) tries to put flesh on Thucydides' skeleton of a story.

Disaster in Sicily

The last and most fateful chapter in Demosthenes' career took place on the island of Sicily, and he himself was largely to blame for it. In 415, the Athenians sent a large fleet to Sicily and used it in the following summer to besiege Syracuse, the most powerful city on the island. This is not the place to discuss in detail the vagaries of what is known as the Sicilian Expedition,

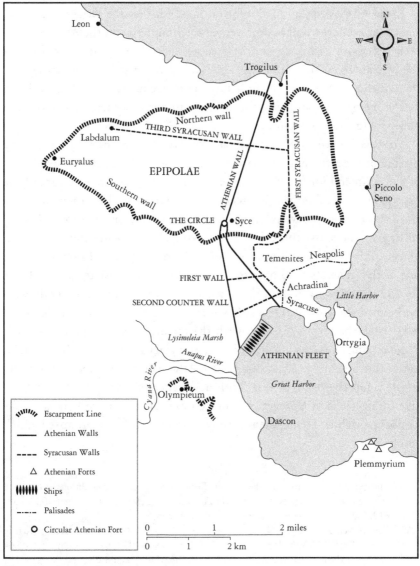

MAP 12 Ancient Syracuse.

but it is necessary to describe the circumstances awaiting Demosthenes when he arrived at Syracuse with large reinforcements in 413.[50]

Before Demosthenes' arrival, the Athenians had won consecutive victories on land and sea against Syracuse, primarily under the leadership of their experienced general Nicias. They had occupied Plemmyrium at the entrance to the Great Harbor of Syracuse, built a wall that partially surrounded the city, and gained access to Epipolae ("Overtown"), a plateau overlooking Syracuse. To the Athenians' disadvantage, however, the Syracusans had occupied Olympeium (a fort southwest of the Athenian camp in the harbor, north of River Anapos), recaptured a fort at Labdalum on the western Epipolae, and built a counter-wall that prevented the completion of the Athenian wall (Map 12 above). In addition, the Spartan general Gylippus arrived to aid the Syracusans in the summer of 414 and won a first land victory against the Athenians. He then left to collect reinforcements and allies in Sicily. Twelve Peloponnesian ships also made it to Syracuse, representatives of a newly invigorated Spartan fleet.

At this juncture, Nicias sent a letter to Athens, drawing a gloomy picture of the Athenians' situation and prospects. He asked to be relieved of his command for health reasons and offered two alternatives: recall the expedition or send large reinforcements to Syracuse. The Athenians chose the latter option. They appointed two commanders on the spot as Nicias' colleagues and substitutes if he died, giving Demosthenes and the veteran general Eurymedon the command over the new armada. Eurymedon was one of the generals who opposed Demosthenes' request to occupy Pylos (p. 153 above), and in 424, he returned from campaigning in Sicily with nothing to show for it. Demosthenes also came back empty-handed from Boeotia in the same year. Yet, with the talented Alcibiades in exile, the general Lamachus dead (shortly before in Syracuse), and the ailing Nicias away, the inventory of accomplished Athenian commanders was fairly limited. On the positive side, both new generals could use their respective connections in Corcyra, western Greece, and Sicily to help with the campaign, while Demosthenes' proven resourcefulness promised quick results.[51]

---

50. The extensive literature on the Sicilian Expedition includes, in addition to historical commentaries on the relevant chapters in Thucydides, e.g., Green 1970; Kagan 1981, 161–372; Kallet 2001. Fields 2008 has many useful images.

51. For the events described so far, see Lazenby 2004, 131–153. The Athenian decision to help Nicias: Thuc. 7.16.1; *IG* I³ 371. Eurymedon: Thuc. 3.80.2–85.1, 91.4, 115.5; 4.3.3, 46.1–2, 65.3. Athenian generals such as Conon or Thrasybulus would distinguish themselves only later.

Eurymedon left immediately for Sicily with money and a few ships, but Demosthenes waited until early spring of 413 before sailing with sixty-five ships, 1,200 Athenian hoplites, and an unknown number of allied troops. On the way to his first major stop in western Greece, he plundered Laconian land and participated in the fortification of a site on the Laconian coast across from the island of Cythera, intending to use it as a shelter for refugee helots and as a raiding base. It is unclear whether he initiated the project, but the similarity to his tactics at Pylos, noted by Thucydides, clearly suggests his endorsement. From thence Demosthenes sailed to Acarnanian and Ambraciot waters, collecting troops from allied cities on the islands and the mainland along the way, including his old friends in Acarnania and the Messenian Naupactus.[52] It was there that he heard bad news from Eurymedon, who had returned from Sicily: the Syracusans had succeeded in capturing Plemmyrium on the mouth of the Great Harbor, where Athenian grain, goods, naval equipment, and personal belongings were stored. The loss also reduced the Athenians' control over the land from which they could launch and protect ships or to which they could retreat from battle. Contributing to the Athenians' distress and low morale were the Syracusans' increased interceptions of provisions brought by sea to the Athenian camp.[53]

The worsening situation in Syracuse did not cause Demosthenes or Eurymedon to hurry there: they were busy drafting hoplites and light-armed troops in western Greece and southern Italy. Because the reported numbers of the new recruits are incomplete—we know only of 700 hoplites and 750 light infantry from Italy—they tell us little about the success of their recruiting. Yet their delayed arrival at Syracuse proved a costly risk, because it gave the Syracusans time to gain additional local allies, receive reinforcements from Greece and Sicily, and win a modest first victory over the Athenian navy in the harbor. Among their reasons for engaging the Athenian navy was their wish to forestall the arrival of the second armada. Demosthenes often relied for victory on his ability to predict and shape the enemy's response to his actions. This time, his and Eurymedon's calculated delay actually helped the enemy.[54]

52. Demosthenes' armada: Thuc. 7.20.2. Operations in Laconia: Thuc. 7.20.1–2, 26.1–3. The Athenians evacuated anti-Cythera in the following winter: Thuc. 8.4. Recruiting in western Greece: Thuc. 7.31.1–2.
53. Thuc. 7.24.3; cf. 7.36.4–6; but see also Rood 1998, 175–176.
54. Recruiting in Greece and Italy: Thuc. 7.31.1–5, 33.1–6, 35.1–2, 57.8–10. While in western Greece, the generals sent ten of their best ships to strengthen the Athenian fleet in Naupactus and made up for them with fifteen Corcyran

When the new Athenian fleet sailed into Syracuse harbor, however, it inspired disappointment, fear, and confusion in the enemy, and restored optimism and confidence to the Athenian camp. In his biography of Nicias, Plutarch describes Demosthenes' showy entrance into the harbor:

> Just then Demosthenes appeared off the harbors in a magnificent show of strength which dismayed the enemy. He had brought seventy-three ships, with 5,000 hoplites on board, and at least 3,000 others armed with javelins, bows, and slings. With his array of weaponry, with the figureheads on his ships, and the number of men employed in calling the time for the rowers and playing the pipes, he presented a fine display, designed to strike fear into the enemy.[55]

Plutarch's focus on Demosthenes is apt, because by all accounts he now dominated the scene. Thucydides ascribes to Demosthenes, not only an assessment of the situation when he arrived, but also a criticism of Nicias' management of the war so far, although it is unclear if Demosthenes made it to Nicias' face.[56] He is depicted as almost a mirror image of the more cumbersome and passive Nicias, displaying decisiveness, a knowing-best attitude, and the confidence of a man who had a quick solution for the protracted campaign. In brief terms, his plan called for an attack against the Syracusans' (third) counter-wall, which he identified as their weak spot. This was to be executed before the psychological impact of the fleet's arrival wore off. Demosthenes is also said to have predicted two opposite outcomes of his plan: the fall of Syracuse or the Athenians' withdrawal. That Syracuse did not fall and that the Athenians would withdraw only later and under worse conditions had much to do with the way he chose to implement his idea.

vessels: Thuc. 7.31.1–5. Aid to Syracuse: Thuc. 7.32.2, 33.1–2. Syracusan naval victory (including skirmishes on land): Thuc. 7.25.9, 36.1–41.4. Beloch (1914, 2.1:239–240) estimates that it took the armada about two months to get from Laconia to Syracuse.

55. Plut. *Nicias* 21, R. Waterfield, trans. Thuc. 7.42.1 gives similar figures, and Diodorus (13.11.2) mentions 80 ships. See Hornblower 1991–2008, 3:620, 1062, in support of 73 ships.

56. Demosthenes' confronting Nicias is implied by Plut. *Nicias* 21. Scholars, however, are divided on whether the criticism comes from Demosthenes, Thucydides, or both; see conveniently Kallet 2001, 106n62. Demosthenes' observations and recommendations: Thuc. 7.42.2–5.

Nevertheless, the new vigor Demosthenes brought to the campaign appeared to have an effect. The Athenians descended on Syracusan lands around the River Anapos, and the enemy's lack of response was optimistically interpreted as a yielding of control over land and sea to the Athenians. The next engagement was more sobering, however. Demosthenes used siege engines and frontal attacks against the Syracusan counter-wall but was repelled by the defenders. Under the largely self-induced pressure of having to take instant action, and with his colleagues' consent, Demosthenes turned to his favorite modus operandi, a surprise attack.[57]

He aimed to surprise the enemy on the Epipolae plateau by launching an attack from the relatively unexpected direction of the western and more accessible Euryalus Hill. More significantly, he took with him (according to one account) 10,000 hoplites and a greater number of light infantry for a full-scale night battle. There was no known precedent for fielding such a large force in a night combat, even in such bright moonlight as shone that night. The opposition consisted of a fort and sentries on the Euryalus, three fortified camps on the Epipolae, an advance guard of 600 men, and men in the city who could join the fighting.[58] At first, everything seemed to go the attackers' way. Led by Demosthenes and his colleague Menander, the Athenians went up the Euryalus, destroyed those they encountered, and took the fort there (Map 12, p. 173 above). Demosthenes, running ahead as at Megara, scattered the 600 advance guards who tried to oppose him. By now the surprise was gone, but Demosthenes and his men hurried on in order to exploit their momentum and to prevent the enemy from organizing a more effective defense. When the Syracusans' commander Gylippus and his men came out of their camps, they were beaten back. In the meantime, other Athenian troops were busy tearing down the Syracusan counter-wall, whose guards fled. Yet the Athenian wave of attack collapsed entirely when it came

---

57. Thuc. 7.42.6–43.1 is preferable to Plutarch (*Nicias* 21), who describes a debate in the generals' council in which Nicias opposed Demosthenes' plan but then reluctantly agreed to it. Lazenby (2004, 157) speculates that Demosthenes' initial actions intended to mislead the enemy before he moved against Epipolae.

58. The number of Demosthenes' troops and its plausibility: Diod. 13.11.3; Roisman 1993b, 60n121. I follow Dover's reconstruction of the Syracusan positions, which identifies the three camps as outworks to the third counter-wall: see Gomme et al. 1945–1981, 4:478.

up against its first stubborn opposition: a Boeotian unit that stood its ground and put the attackers to flight.[59]

Because Demosthenes relied on surprise and speed for victory, he had to sacrifice order and effective communication with, and control over, units that were not in his vicinity. Poor visibility hampered his ability to respond to setbacks, while speed undermined the cohesion of his ranks. These conditions allowed an unyielding unit of defenders to repel the charge and caused the fleeing Athenians to sow confusion and uncertainty among their fellow combatants. According to Thucydides' graphic account, the impaired visibility prevented the attackers from telling friends from foes, while those who kept arriving at the scene did not know where to join the battle. The only means of identification was the watchword, which the din of battle obscured, and which the enemy soon found out and used to its advantage. There were even incidents of Athenians' dying from "friendly fire" and in near-clashes among fellow soldiers. Additional problems stood out because Demosthenes should have known better. At Acarnania, Sphacteria, and even Megara, he had won largely by his successful coordination of attacks from different quarters. On the Epipolae, there seemed to be no coordinated effort, only a rush forward to meet the enemy. At Acarnania, Demosthenes had used the Dorian-speaking Messenians to mislead the Ambraciots into believing that his troops were their allies. On the Epipolae, it was his own troops who fell victim to such confusion. Thucydides says that what confounded and terrified the Athenians most was the singing of Dorian paeans, because there were Dorian Greeks fighting on both sides. Finally, at Acarnania and Pylos, Demosthenes had made good use of local intelligence and the terrain to defeat the enemy. At Syracuse, those advantages worked in the enemy's favor. Soldiers who had just arrived with Demosthenes were unfamiliar with the ground, lost their way, and were killed by the Syracusans even if they made it down from the plateau safely. In addition, the Athenians' panicked retreat clogged the only narrow path down the Epipolae, and many of them fled their pursuers only to throw themselves off the high cliffs to their death. According to

59. The night attack: Thuc. 7.43.3–45.1, summarized by Plut. *Nicias* 21; cf. Diod. 13.11.3–5. The psychological aspects of Thucydides' description: Paul 1987. It is unclear if the Boeotians, who faced the Athenians, included or were identical to c. 300 Thespian hoplites mentioned earlier in Thucydides: 7.19.3, 25.3, 43.7, 50.1–2.

the sources, the Athenians lost between 2,000 and 2,500 men on and around the Epipolae. No other land battle during the Peloponnesian War resulted in so many casualties.[60]

Like the plan of attacking Boeotia from different directions, the failure at Syracuse was not inevitable, but it could have been anticipated. Demosthenes took a gamble on surprise and lost disastrously, committing many men and assuming optimistically that shock and speed would compensate for the well-known difficulties of a night attack. His plan made it very difficult to direct the offensive and even the retreat.

The defeat had a significant impact on everyone involved, including Demosthenes. His arrival had caused fear among the Syracusans, which he wished to exploit, but now their fear changed into optimism and self-confidence, and they even used the victory to mobilize aid in Sicily. The defeated Athenians, who suffered also from unhealthy conditions in camp, grew despondent, and their leadership became divided. Demosthenes' authority as the new commander who would change the course of the campaign suffered a devastating blow. When he recommended a return home, he was successfully opposed by Nicias, who had regained the prime leadership. It appears that the other Athenian generals also deemed Demosthenes' solution of cutting their losses too radical, especially coming from the man who was responsible for the losses. Demosthenes then suggested evacuating the army to friendly Catana or Thapsus in Sicily, in order to raid enemy territory from there, or to fight at sea. Although his idea gained Eurymedon's approval, Nicias successfully shot it down. Later the Athenians changed their minds about evacuation to Catana, but a lunar eclipse was interpreted as portending disaster, and no one could overturn Nicias' decision to stay at Syracuse for twenty-seven days, as seers had prescribed. Because of my focus on Demosthenes' generalship, I shall not dwell on the motives Thucydides attributes to Nicias on this and other occasions. The historian ascribes Nicias' errors of judgment to his fear of the supernatural and of punishment at home if he returned, as well as to his belief that the Athenians could still take Syracuse. Whether Demosthenes' suggestions were sound

---

60. The battle: Thuc. 7.43.2–44.8. For the significance of the similar dialect, see also Lazenby 2004, 159. Athenian failings and their possible remedies: Sheldon 2012, 77–78. Athenian dead: Plut. *Nicias* 21; Diod. 13.11.5. See note 9 above for the apparently fewer casualties at Idomene. Hoplite casualties in Greek battles: Krentz 1985a, esp. 19. The Syracusan losses are unknown.

or not, his clouded reputation from the failed attack on the Epipolae forced him to defer to Nicias.[61]

Demosthenes appears only sporadically in Thucydides' narrative of the ensuing events. He is not mentioned among the generals who participated in the next naval battle in the harbor, though he may have fought in it. This engagement cost the Athenians their general Eurymedon, about 2,000 men, and at least eighteen ships, though they did repel a Syracusan attack on the Athenian walls. Thucydides suggests that the Athenian defeat at sea changed the Syracusan definition of victory from driving the invaders away to preventing them from escaping to a friendly base, and that they accordingly blocked the entrance to the harbor with a boom. In response, the Athenians set their slender hopes on an all-out naval battle, which, if successful, would allow them to sail out of the harbor, and if a failure, would compel them to march by land to a friendly place. They also limited their control over land to a small, fortified space next to the ships, which was easier to defend and allowed them to free troops to man the ships. The man in charge was Nicias, according to Thucydides, who credits him with a pre-battle exhortatory speech and with individual appeals to the ship commanders. Plutarch even suggests that Nicias refused to yield to the Athenians' demand to retreat by land and insisted on a naval battle.[62]

But Demosthenes' possible contribution to the Athenian plan, or at least his support of it, can be gleaned from the fact that he was one of the generals who commanded the huge Athenian fleet of about 110 ships, as well as from the tactics chosen. Victory hinged on the Athenians' numerical superiority (about 110 ships to 76) and their ability to convert the fighting into something like a land battle. The plan called for the light infantry on deck to shoot arrows and javelins at the enemy while the marines used grappling irons to prevent the enemy ships from backing away, finally boarding them to kill those on deck. Thucydides specifically mentions Demosthenes' Acarnanian recruits among the light-armed troops who fought at the harbor. Demosthenes had little experience in maritime warfare, if any, but the kind of naval battle sought by the Athenians was as close as possible to the land

---

61. Thuc. 7.47.1–49.4, 50.3–4, 60.2; Plut. *Nicias* 22–24; Diod. 13.12.1–6 (with some variations). The eclipse occurred on August 27, 413. *Pace* Kallet (2001, 158), Thucydides does not present financial concerns as the main motive for or against the evacuation.

62. The naval and land battles: Thuc. 7.51.1–54.1; Diod. 131.3.1–8. The breakthrough plan: Thuc. 7.60.1–3. Nicias' speech and appeals: Thuc. 7.61.1–64.2, 69.1–3; cf. Diod. 13.15.1–2. Plutarch on Nicias: *Nicias* 24.

fighting he was familiar with. In addition, the Athenians' use of land forces on ships copied the Syracusans' tactics, and Demosthenes had shown in the past his ability to learn from the enemy.[63]

To judge by Thucydides' description of the battle, the generals played only a limited role in it. The Athenians succeeded in breaking the barrier at the harbor mouth, but once the Syracusans joined battle, the fighting consisted largely of individual conflicts, with the generals mainly watching lest ships back away unforced from the fray. The Syracusans won because they made the Athenians fight a traditional naval battle in which the Syracusan lighter vessels enjoyed an advantage, destroying about fifty ships and losing only about twenty-five.[64] Fear now dominated the Athenian camp. The troops were so desperate to leave by land that very night that they were willing to give up collecting their dead. But Demosthenes approached Nicias with a different plan, which illustrated the essence of his generalship. The general, who recommended surprise attack as the preferred solution for most military problems, suggested that they board the remaining triremes straightway and attack the enemy unexpectedly. One may admire Demosthenes' resourcefulness in the face of adversity and his unconventional thinking, but his idea was unworkable for two reasons. The Athenians had lost faith in their ability to win at sea—understandably, in light of their two recent, consecutive defeats in the harbor. Moreover, they had only sixty ships left and about 40,000 people in camp, which meant that even a victory would give them little chance of evacuating so many people by sea, rather than by marching on land.[65]

In the end, the Athenians waited two days before starting their march away from the harbor and generally north toward Catana. They were despondent, hungry, and full of guilt for leaving the wounded and dead

---

63. Demosthenes in command: Thuc. 7.69.4. Number of ships involved: Thuc. 7.52.1, 60.4, 70.1; Diod. 13.13.4. Athenian battle plan: Thuc. 7.60.2–3, 62.2–63.2. Light-armed troops and Acarnanians: Thuc. 7.60.4, 62.2, 67.2, 70.5; Diod. 17.16.4. Demosthenes' attested prior record at sea consists of his capturing a single ship on his way to Sicily: Thuc. 7.31.1. Athenian imitation of the Syracusans: Thuc. 7.67.2.
64. The naval battle: Thuc. 7.70.1–72.2; Diod. 13.15.3–17.5. Losses: Thuc. 7.72.3; Diod. 13.17.5, 19.1.
65. Athenians' despair: Thuc. 7.72.4. Demosthenes' suggestion: Diod. 13.18.1. Sixty ships left: Thuc. 7.72.3. Forty thousand in camp: Thuc. 7.75.5. Hornblower (1991–2008, 3:1061–1066) thinks that the last figure is "impossibly high," but even if there were fewer, the ships could not have ferried out all the encamped troops. See also Roisman 1993b, 67–68. Thucydides' version (7.72.3) that Nicias agreed with Demosthenes is preferable to Diodorus' (formulaic?) story that Demosthenes' plan was rejected because of Nicias' opposition: 13.18.2.

behind. Thucydides' emotive description of their retreat and tragic end is unsurpassed. Reduced to factual terms, it tells us that the Athenians formed a hollow square, Nicias leading the van and Demosthenes bringing up the rear, with the rest of the marchers in the middle. Their pace was slow and grew increasingly slower, largely because of their short supplies and the Syracusan opposition. Intentionally or not, Thucydides' narrative of the Athenians in retreat evokes memories of the Spartans on Sphacteria, who were similarly harassed by elusive light infantry. With distress growing, the leading generals approved what would be Demosthenes' last attempt at outwitting the enemy. The Athenians lighted many fires, as if camping for the night, but left under cover of darkness, changing direction toward the southwest, away from their Syracusan pursuers and toward the sea and friendly locals. The tactic won them freedom from pursuit only till the middle of the next day. They became disoriented and very fearful, and a gap was created between the van under Nicias and the larger rear under Demosthenes. Thucydides notes that Nicias' men marched together and in good order, while Demosthenes' troops moved more slowly and in disarray. It was as if a circle closed in Demosthenes' career: his last retreat resembled his first one in Aetolia where his troops fled in disorder and suffered losses. In fairness to Demosthenes, we should note that the Syracusans attacked his men with greater frequency than they did Nicias' division. Demosthenes arrayed his troops for battle in an enclosure, but the Syracusans did not take the bait: it was easier and safer to bombard the enemy with missiles from a distance. At the end of that day, exhaustion, hunger, thirst, and many injuries led Demosthenes to surrender with 6,000 of his troops on the condition that no one would be killed. Nicias capitulated two days later after losing many more men, a carnage that justified Demosthenes' decision to spare his followers' lives.[66]

The sources are divided about Demosthenes' fate. Thucydides, our most authoritative informant, says that the Spartan general Gylippus wished to bring both Demosthenes and Nicias to Sparta as living trophies, but the Syracusans "cut

---

66. The retreat by land: Thuc. 7.75.1–87.5. There are difficulties in identifying the original direction of the march and its route: Dover in Gomme et al. 1956–1981, 4:455–460; Lazenby 2004, 163, 283n18. Similarity to Sphacteria: see also Hunter 1973, 148. Disorderly march: Thuc. 7.80.1–81.2; and in Aetolia: pp. 149–150. Capitulation: Thuc. 7.81.3–85.4; Plut. *Nicias* 27. The Syracusans imprisoned about 7,000 captives of war: Thuc. 7.87.4. Diodorus counts 18,000 losses during the retreat: 13.91.2.

RETREAT OF THE ATHENIANS FROM SYRACUSE.

FIGURE 11 *The Athenian retreat from Syracuse.* An 1890 rendition of the Athenian retreat from Syracuse drawn by Edward Ollier for the popular serial edition of the *Cassel's Illustrated Universal History.*

Retreat of the Athenians from Syracuse (engraving), English School (19th century)/Private Collection/© Look and Learn/Bridgeman Images

their throats." Other sources mention a debate in the Syracusan assembly over their fate that ended with the same result. We are even told that Demosthenes tried unsuccessfully to kill himself when surrounded by the enemy, and that later, when he and Nicias learned in prison of their imminent execution, they took their own lives. Their bodies were then exposed to public display.[67]

Conclusion

Pausanias, the Greek traveler of the Roman era, cites an Athenian inscription that commemorated the war dead, including those killed in Sicily, along with its interpretation by the Sicilian historian Philistus (c. 430–356):

> The names of the generals are inscribed with the exception of Nicias, and among the private soldiers are included the Plataeans along with the Athenians. This is the reason why Nicias was passed over, and my account is identical with that of Philistus, who says that while Demosthenes made a truce for the others and excluded himself, attempting to commit suicide when taken prisoner, Nicias voluntarily submitted to the surrender. For this reason Nicias had not his name inscribed on the slab, being condemned as a voluntary prisoner and an unworthy soldier.[68]

We don't really know why Nicias' name was not inscribed, but the contrast drawn between him and Demosthenes is surely unfair. Some scholars think that Thucydides is equally unfair in eulogizing Nicias as the man who, of all the Greeks of his age, least deserved his misfortune, saying nothing comparable about Demosthenes.[69] Clearly, the last chapter of any commander's career should not dominate the assessment of his entire generalship, but it is equally wrong to ignore it. Demosthenes was neither a hero nor a failure, but both, or one of these historical actors who do not easily fit a single category. He demonstrated original thinking and good planning skills in each of his campaigns. He was chiefly known for his victories at Pylos and Sphacteria and for establishing a permanent

---

67. Nicias and Demosthenes executed: Thuc. 7.86.1–5 (clearly disapproving of their captors); Plut. *Nicias* 28. Debate in Syracuse: Diod. 13.19.4–33.1; Plut. *Nicias* 28; cf. Thuc. 7.86.3–5. Demosthenes' and Nicias' suicide: see below, and Plut. *Nicias* 27–28.
68. Pausanias 1.29.9 = Philistus *FGrHist* 556 F 53; cf. Plut. *Comparison of Nicias and Crassus* 5.
69. Thuc. 7.86.5; Henderson 1927, 396; Cawkwell 1997, 54, 137n30 (citing Henderson).

base in enemy territory. His success encouraged imitations as early as the year he captured Pylos (425), when the Athenians set up a post near Epidaurus to raid the adjacent territory. By 413, when the Spartans similarly occupied Decelea in Attica, and when Demosthenes himself fortified a site in Laconia opposite Cythera, such projects had become quite common.[70] Demosthenes therefore deserves credit for coming up with a plan that was adopted by both his city and its enemy, although it is ironic that the Spartans made more effective use of it at Decelea than the Athenians did anywhere. In some of Demosthenes' campaigns, he used military intelligence and light infantry very effectively, although Greek antecedents of such uses suggest that he was not their originator.[71] He was a gambler who enjoyed good luck in some of his operations and suffered losses in others. He was a firm believer in surprise and deception as the best means of accomplishing his goals. His personality well suited these qualities: he was ambitious, aggressive, self-confident, daring, and a risk-taker, but also someone who tended to take failure as an endpoint instead of as a temporary setback. His impatience, however, was not as disastrous as his preference for a quick solution in the form of surprise attack, even when conditions disfavored it. With its share of successes and disappointments, Demosthenes' career shows the benefits and pitfalls of having such a general in command.

---

70. Seizing Methana around Epidaurus: Thuc. 4.45.12; Decelea: Thuc. 6.91.1–93.2; 7.18–19.3; anti-Cythera: Thuc. 7.20.2–3, 26, and above; and see Westlake 1983.
71. Antecedents of Demosthenes: Sheldon 2012, esp. 60, and see 54–59, 72–76.

| # Lysander of Sparta
The Lion and the Fox

Lysander and His Military Challenges

The biographer Plutarch begins his account of the Spartan general Lysander (c. 460–395) by correcting what he regards as a common mistake.[1] He argues that a marble statue in Delphi, which many identify with another famous Spartan general, Brasidas, is actually one of Lysander. It depicts a man with full beard and long hair, the way Spartans used to wear it. Plutarch traces the hairstyle back to the legendary Spartan lawgiver Lycurgus, who introduced it to make the handsome look better and the ugly, scarier. We do not know how good-looking Lysander was, but he could certainly be terrifying in his treatment of foes and other people who stood in his way. He was also resourceful, strong-willed, a good planner, and a military opportunist. In some of these respects, he resembled the Athenian general Demosthenes, the focus of the previous chapter. Both were determined men, fond of stratagems, who could spot an enemy's weakness and act upon it. Both overcame opponents who enjoyed superiority in either numbers or skill, and each combined diplomacy with military force in his dealings with friends and foes. They also share a record of making war on walled cities, with varying degrees of success. But Lysander was more of a strategist and political operator than the tactically minded Demosthenes, and more successful at sea. He was long remembered

---

1. For the evidence on Lysander, see Bibliography, "The Main Ancient Sources," s.vv. "Plutarch," "Xenophon" (for Xenophon on Lysander, see Westlake 1969, 216–225, but also Due 1987; Giroud 2001), "Diodorus," and the "'Oxyrhynchian *Greek History.*'"

after he died for his victory over the Athenian fleet at Aegospotami, which led to Athens' surrender and the end of the Peloponnesian War a year later. He was also famous for his involvement in the creation of a Spartan hegemony over Greece afterwards. Yet Lysander was already a controversial figure in his lifetime, and there also seems to be no modern consensus about his plans, actions, or personality.[2]

Very little is known of Lysander before 407, when he became the leader of Sparta's war against Athens in the Aegean. He was born perhaps around 460 to Aristocritus and a noble family that, like the Spartan royalty, claimed descent from the children of Heracles. The household was not rich but was well connected, with guest-friendship ties to Libya. The family's position also allowed Lysander to become the lover of the young prince Agesilaus, in whose succession to the throne in 400 Lysander would be heavily involved (p. 217 below). The tradition that Lysander was a child of lowly origins (*mothax*) who was adopted by his betters is late, and questionable.[3]

Lysander encountered great challenges in the course of his career. When he arrived in the Aegean in 407 as the new chief of Spartan operations, he had to rebuild the coalition's naval power after heavy defeats. The task involved asking for contributions from local allies who were unhappy with the Spartans' performance. He faced a highly skilled Athenian navy and a general, Alcibiades, who had a winning record. Lysander overcame these difficulties and even won a naval victory against Alcibiades' deputy at Notium, but a devastating defeat suffered by his successor in command reversed the situation. Lysander returned to the Aegean in 405 and had to again reconstruct Spartan power and alliances. Against the Athenian navy at Aegospotami, he won his biggest victory, which then presented him with two major tasks: replacing the Athenian hegemony with Spartan power everywhere, and bringing well-fortified Athens into submission as a stable Spartan ally. In dealing with these issues, Lysander had to contend with opposition to his policy both at home and abroad. Internal politics also complicated his roles as advisor and general when Sparta was involved in later campaigns in Asia Minor and in Boeotia (where he met his death). In addition to Lysander's generalship, tactics, and strategy, this chapter deals with the reasons for his uneven record of success.

---

2. Lysander statue: Plut. *Lysander* 1. On Lysander, see Lotze 1964; Bommelaer 1981; Wylei 1997; Bearzot 2004.
3. Lysander's birth, family, and status: Plut. *Lysander* 2; Phylarchus *FGrHist* 81 F 43; Aelian *Historical Miscellany* 12, 43; Bommelaer 1981, 36–39; Cartledge 1987, 28–29; Wylei1997, 76. Agesilaus' lover: Plut. *Lysander* 22.

Lysander's First Admiralship and the Battle of Notium

Between Athens' defeat in Sicily in 413, described in the previous chapter, and Lysander's first appearance in the annals of the Peloponnesian War in 407, significant changes took place. The most important from the Spartans' perspective was their opening of two fronts. After the renewal of the Peloponnesian War in 413, the Spartans established a permanent base under King Agis (I) at Decelea in Attica. Instead of making short-term invasions, as in the first years of the war, they now raided Athenian territory on a permanent basis. (The ancients, especially the Athenians, called the war of 413–404 the "Decelean War"). More relevant to the story of Lysander, and more dangerous to Athens, was Sparta's second front, an attempt to deprive Athens of its Aegean empire (Map 13 below). Sparta's success in doing so finally realized Pericles' fear for the security of Athens and for its chances of winning the war, which were based on the empire's military and financial resources. Henceforth, Athens, which in the past had expanded the war to new frontiers, was forced to fight merely to keep or retrieve its possessions.

The Spartans were encouraged to attack Athens by promises of support from rebel Athenian allies and from Persian satraps in Asia Minor. They renegotiated their alliance with the satraps and their king several times during this period, but the essence of the arrangement was Persian financial and military aid to Sparta, including the (never realized) promise of a large Phoenician fleet, in exchange for the restoration of Persian rule over the Greek cities in Asia Minor. Athenian sources allege that Persian subsidies to Sparta totaled the huge sum of 5,000 talents. Even if the figure is inflated, Persian money was crucial for the buildup and operations of a Peloponnesian navy in the Aegean.[4]

We shall discuss events preceding Lysander's first admiralship in 407 only briefly. The Spartan official in charge of the Aegean front was an elected admiral, nauarch, who served a one-year, non-renewable term. His fleet was made up of Spartan and allied contingents, and he wielded considerable authority over the territory under his control. It is likely that the qualifications for this office consisted of personal valor and of

---

4. Persian subsidies: Andocides 3.29; Isocrates 8.97. David 1979/1980 cuts the figure to 1,500–2,000 talents; and see Hodkinson's skepticism about the sources: 2000, 27–29, 155–157, 424–429.

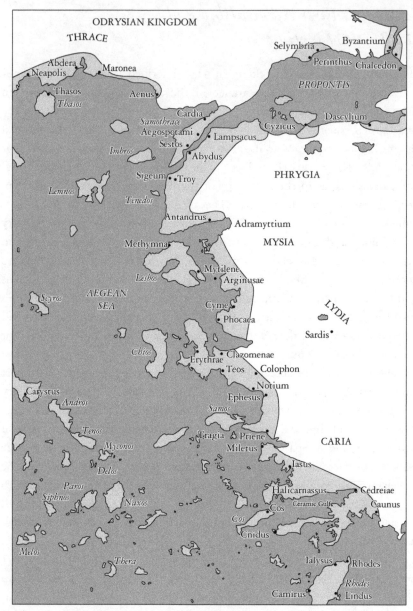

MAP 13 Aegean Greece. Gray shading indicates the Athenian Empire

experience gained mostly in land rather than in naval warfare. The admiral was also expected to have good negotiating skills for his dealings with local sympathizers. Among the reasons for Sparta's abysmal record in the Aegean before Lysander were the incompetence of its admirals and the inadequacy of its fleet. The Spartans made some gains when key

Athenian allies such Euboea, Rhodes, Miletus, and Chios changed sides. But they were not always able to keep or support their new allies, and except for one engagement near Euboea in 411, Athens won every major sea battle. A message sent to Sparta by the survivors of a heavy defeat near Cyzicus in 410 provides a dramatic illustration of the general situation: "Ships gone; (admiral) Mindarus is dead; men are starving; we don't know what to do." Of the Spartan admirals who preceded Lysander, one returned home in disgrace after a mutiny in his fleet, another died in battle, and still another was exiled. Also indicative of the Spartans' difficulties were their two failed attempts in 410 and 408 to obtain peace from Athens. Disappointed with the help they received from Tissaphernes, the satrap who controlled southern Asia Minor, they moved their operations to the northern Aegean to be closer to the territory of his rival satrap, Pharnabazus. Although the latter was more reliable ally, the Spartans failed to gain control of the region. Moreover, since 411, they had faced the best Athenian general and money-raiser of the time, the notorious turncoat Alcibiades. After a period of exile and anti-Athenian activity in Sparta and Asia Minor, Alcibiades came back to lead the Athenian war effort successfully. Yet, the Spartans' situation was not hopeless. They continued to benefit from varying degrees of Persian and local Greek support, and none of their defeats was overwhelming enough to prevent them from pursuing the war. The Spartans were especially favored by both sides' hitherto reluctance to decide the war in one big battle and their tendency to let local initiatives or developments influence their moves.[5]

The historian Diodorus states that, in spite of the Spartans' setbacks, "they did not let their spirit sink, but they chose as admiral Lysander, a man who was believed to excel all others in skill as a general and who possessed the daring that was ready to meet every situation."[6] It is likely that this depiction of Lysander is retrospective, because nothing is known of his military career to this point. Moreover, the beginning of his term marked no real change from his predecessors. It started with one more victory for Athens and Alcibiades, this time against rebel Andros, although the Athenians were unable to take the city. Lysander did nothing to help Andros and remained equally inactive when Alcibiades raided Cos and Rhodes. This was not a display of what Diodorus calls "daring." In reality, both Athens and Sparta were selective

5. Events between 413–407: Andrewes 1992, 464–489; Rhodes 2006, 142–149. Nauarchy: Sealey 1976, which dates the establishment of a one-year term to c. 412. The Spartans' desperate message: Xen. *Hellenica* 1.123; Plut. *Alcibiades* 28.
6. Quotation: Diod. 13.70.1.

about helping allies in trouble. It is also hard to fault Lysander for showing salutary caution in choosing when and where to offer battle.[7]

Lysander's reticence was due partly to the need to rebuild the coalition's navy. He took ships and troops from the Peloponnese and added forces from Rhodes, Cos, and Chios, commanding a total of about seventy ships when he anchored at the city of Ephesus (Map 13 above). He chose Ephesus as his base for several reasons. The city was loyal to Sparta and had a good and easily defensible harbor. Its location allowed him to watch closely and even disrupt movements from the nearby Athenian base in Samos. No less important, he could travel easily from Ephesus to Sardis, the seat of the new and powerful ruler in the region, Cyrus the Younger. For Lysander's arrival at the Aegean happened to coincide with a highly significant turn in the Persian–Spartan relationship. Until this point, Persian aid to Sparta had been inconsistent or meager. Now King Darius II decided to throw all his support behind the Spartans. He also sent his sixteen-year-old son Cyrus to rule over several satrapies in Asia Minor and made him a *karanos* (lord), an office that put him in charge of abundant financial resources and most of the Persian military forces on the Aegean coast.

Both Athens and a local Persian satrap hostile to Sparta asked Cyrus not to aid the Spartans. Their pressure added to his bargaining power vis-à-vis the Spartans, and Xenophon describes a lively haggling scene between Cyrus and the Spartan representatives over the Persian subsidies. Yet Lysander was an able negotiator and diplomat who could navigate his way through a maze of conflicting agendas. Eventually he came up with the winning formula of adding one *obol* to the three-*obol* daily wage for his rowers. It was highly fortunate for Sparta and Lysander that Cyrus saw it as his mission to help them so generously. The money he gave Lysander allowed the admiral to raise his rowers' wages, to pay them one month in advance, and to pay overdue wages, thereby delighting his crews and motivating them to serve him. If we can believe our sources, the subsidies also demoralized the sailors in the enemy's fleet and caused them to defect to Lysander. His visit to Sardis was the beginning of a wonderful friendship with the prince, in which Lysander often requested contributions and Cyrus granted them.[8]

The successful negotiations with Cyrus probably facilitated Lysander's Aegean networking. He called to Ephesus powerful men of oligarchic

---

7. Andros, Cos, and Rhodes: Xen. *Hellenica* 1.4.21; Diod. 13.69.4–5. I largely follow Bommelaer 1981 for the chronology of Lysander's career.
8. Xen. *Hellenica* 1.5.1–10; Diod. 13.70.1–71.3; Plut. *Lysander* 3–4.

orientation from different Greek cities in the region and encouraged them to form local political associations (*hetaireiai*). He promised to put them in charge of their cities, and they reciprocated by giving him aid. Lysander would be accused of creating a personal empire based on regional friends. Yet personal power and his state's interests were not irreconcilable, and Lysander's friendships and alliances fostered loyalty to and dependence on Sparta rather than making him a master at Sparta's expense. For example, it must have been Cyrus' money and local friends that enabled Lysander to increase his navy from seventy to ninety ships and to pay their crews. He dragged the ships ashore to dry and repair them before making his next move.[9]

Lysander's subsequent victory in the battle of Notium illustrates the opportunistic, even lucky qualities of his generalship: he won a contest that he did not initiate, and by exploiting the enemy's mistake. His victory was also augmented later by the unintended consequences of Alcibiades' leaving Athens for exile.[10]

Before the battle, Lysander showed no willingness to engage the Athenian fleet in battle. Alcibiades, who needed to show that Cyrus' backing of Sparta had done little to change the situation, arrived from Samos with eighty or a hundred ships, and waited outside Ephesus harbor for Lysander to come out and fight. Lysander declined the challenge. His best advantage lay in the safety of the harbor, and there was no point risking the new navy and the coalitions he had assembled by fighting a larger fleet led by a successful general. Alcibiades could wait no longer, needing a nearby base for his many ships, and sailed to friendly Notium, about 13 kilometers northwest of Ephesus. He then made two mistakes. He assumed that Lysander would stay put and thus allow him to deal with other affairs elsewhere. He also instructed his pilot Antiochus, whom he appointed commander of the fleet until his return, not to fight Lysander in battle. There are problems with his instructions as reported in our sources. Was Antiochus supposed to sit idle even if Lysander sailed out of the harbor? Was the charge that Antiochus disobeyed Alcibiades' orders by sailing against Lysander at Ephesus part of

9. Lysander's personal empire: Nepos, *Lysander* 1; Plut. *Lysander* 13; Wylie 1999, 79.
10. The sources on the battle of Notium disagree in details or are incomplete: *Oxyrhynchian Greek History* 4; Xen. *Hellenica* 1.5.10–15; Diod. 13.71.1–4; Plut. *Alcibiades* 35, *Lysander* 5; Pausanias 9.32.6. Bommelaer 1981, 90–95; Andrewes 1982, 15–19; Russell 1994; Lazenby 2004, 219–221; Rhodes 2011, 88–90. Like other scholarly reconstructions of the battle, the following narrative involves rejecting some details in the conflicting ancient accounts.

Alcibiades' later defense against accusations that he bore responsibility for Antiochus' defeat? Be that as it may, Antiochus gave Lysander his first naval victory.[11]

The battle evolved from a modest beginning when Antiochus sailed into Ephesus harbor with ten of his best triremes. His exact aim is unclear. He took swift ships that were suited to a hit-and-run operation, so perhaps he planned to entice and ambush only a small Spartan squadron or to drag out and destroy beached ships. He may also have imagined a best-case scenario of Lysander's fleet leaving the harbor in pursuit of his squadron; according to some accounts, he told Athenian captains to be prepared for a battle on the open sea. Lysander decided to take the risk. He had it on good intelligence that neither Alcibiades nor any other experienced general was present. He was also prepared for the possibility of an ambush, a tactic the Athenians had used in their recent victories over the Spartans and their allies. At first he sent out thirteen triremes and sank Antiochus' ship, which sailed ahead of his squadron. It was a very favorable outcome, because the fall of the chief commander constituted a severe blow in any battle and sometimes decided it. The Athenians' ships retreated hastily, and Lysander came after them with the rest of his fleet, sailing toward Notium in good order and at high speed, so as not to give the enemy time to organize. The Athenians in Notium now rushed to the rescue, but being unprepared (in violation of Antiochus' instructions?), they launched their ships piecemeal and could not form an effective line against Lysander's better-organized formation. He won the battle, but not overwhelmingly. Only fifteen to twenty-two Athenian ships were lost, and most of their crews made it to safety.[12]

When Alcibiades heard of the defeat, he rushed back to offer Lysander another battle. Lysander stayed put, however, and a frustrated Alcibiades took his fleet to Samos. The Spartan commander was wise to decline the challenge: there was now no significant disparity in the size of the opposing fleets, and Lysander no longer enjoyed the advantage of catching the enemy unprepared and without its chief commander. Moreover, it had been a long time since a Spartan admiral had set up a trophy, as he did after Notium, and there was no point in risking defeat when Sparta and its regional allies finally had a victory. Lysander's refusal to do battle robbed Alcibiades of the option of reversing the Athenian loss and led to his

---

11. Athenian fleet: Xen. *Hellenica* 1.4.21, 5.18, 20; Kagan 1987, 310 (80 ships). Alcibiades and Antiochus: Rhodes 2011, 89.
12. The view that Lysander tricked Antiochus into fighting him (see note 10) seems to transplant to Notium Lysander's later tactics at Aegospotami. See below on how Notium inspired Lysander at Aegospotami.

denouncement at home. An expert in survival, Alcibiades left for voluntary exile in Thrace, and Lysander's indirect contribution to this development must have added to Lysander's fame. If this were not fortunate enough, the defeat of his successor in command (below) would make him appear irreplaceable.[13]

As far as is known, the rest of Lysander's term as general was uneventful. Careful in picking his battles, he did nothing to help Cyme in Lydia, whose territory Alcibiades twice raided before going into exile. According to our sources, however, he tried to make the job of his successor difficult. He was replaced in the spring of 406 by the young Spartan Callicratidas, and instead of leaving him the surplus monies he had received from Cyrus, Lysander returned them to the Persian prince. He also falsely claimed that he had left Callicratidas the control of the sea, thereby burdening the latter with the impossible challenge of keeping it. (Callicratidas sarcastically invited Lysander to sail past the Athenian fleet in Samos if this were the case). In addition, Lysander's friends in camp and in the Greek cities cooperated with the new commander only reluctantly and complained that Sparta was courting defeat by sending new and inexperienced generals to the region.[14]

It is unfortunate that our sources are less interested in explaining why Lysander acted this way than in contrasting him with Callicratidas. They depict the latter as a Leonidas-like Spartan, proud and incorruptible, unlike his scheming predecessor, who fawned over barbarians. A less hostile (and less anachronistic) view of Lysander and his motives suggests he was not plotting to be recalled to the region, nor trying to sabotage the Spartan war effort. Lysander probably returned the money to Cyrus because Cyrus demanded it, and because the repayment cemented their friendship and mutual trust. Lysander's habit of mixing politics with personal friendship explains both his conduct and that of the Greeks who cooperated with him. They were not his puppets, but men with their own agenda who had now lost his personal and material support. It is understandable that they should miss Lysander and complain about Callicratidas' inexperience. But both they and Cyrus would eventually change their minds and greatly help Callicratidas.

13. The size of the opposing fleets after Notium: Xen. *Hellenica* 1.5.15; Krentz 1989, 141; Lazenby 2004, 221–222. Alcibiades' second exile: Rhodes 2006, 150, 167.
14. Cyme: Diod. 13.73.3–5; cf. Nepos *Alcibiades* 7. Callicratidas: Xen. *Hellenica* 1.5.15, 6.1–34; Diod. 13.76.1–79.7, 97.1–99.6; Plut. *Lysander* 5–7; cf. *Moral.* 222b–f. The present description is based on Roisman 1987, modified. See also Moles 1994; LaForse 1998; Pownall 2004, 94–96.

At first Callicratidas defied expectations by doing even better than Lysander. When Cyrus would not grant him an audience or money (probably hoping for more concessions from him), Callicratidas got funds from Greek allies, including Lysander's friends. (Cyrus would later reverse his decision.) Callicratidas increased the navy from Lysander's ninety to 140 and then to 170 ships. Callicratidas also sacked the Athenian fortress of Delphinium on Chios, got Chian contributions to his war fund, and plundered Teos in Ionia. He then took Methymna on Lesbos, and in the course of his blockade of the Athenian fleet in the Lesbian harbor of Mitylene, and of the city itself, he captured forty-one enemy ships. This performance gave substance to his earlier boastful message to the Athenian general Conon that he would put a stop to Conon's "adulterous" relationship with the sea, thereby proclaiming himself its "true husband" or master. His intended audience, however, was not really Conon but the Aegean Greeks, Cyrus, Sparta, and, he hoped, Lysander.

If Callicratidas could have kept his momentum going, he might have ended as one of Sparta's all-time top military leaders. All his gains were wiped out, though, by his heavy defeat and death in the naval battle of Arginusae, next to a group of small islands between Lesbos and the opposite mainland. Of his 120-ship fleet, nearly seventy were lost, including most of the Spartan squadron, as opposed to twenty-five Athenian ships out of about 150. The Peloponnesians raised the siege of Mytilene and thereby lost any chance of taking the island of Lesbos. There was even a danger of losing Chios to Athens or to hungry and underpaid troops there.[15]

Arginusae was a Peloponnesian disaster, but it also made Lysander look good. We are told that envoys of the Greek allies of Sparta and of Cyrus came to Sparta separately with the same request: to send them Lysander as the commander of the fleet in view of his victory at Notium. The Spartans granted them their wish and sent Lysander as vice-admiral (*epistoleus*, lit. "secretary"), and one Aracus as admiral because the law did not allow holding the office of admiral twice. They gave the command over the fleet, however, to Lysander.[16] Their procedural solution for Lysander's command was typical of a conflict between regulations and necessity. It also reflected the balance of power

---

15. Arginusae: Xen. 1.6.34–38, 2.1.1–5; Diod. 13.100.3–5; Lazenby 2004, 229–234; Hamel 2005, 42–57. According to a questionable tradition, the Athenians rejected a Spartan peace proposal after Arginusae: *Ath. Pol.* 34.1; Rhodes 1993, 424–425 (doubts the story); *contra:* Kagan 1987, 376–379.
16. Xen. *Hellenica* 2.1.6–7. Cf. Diod. 13. 100.7–8; Plut. *Lysander* 7; Lotz 1964, 26; Bommelaer 1981, 96.

between Sparta and its allies, in which defeat increased Spartan dependence on them and in victory lessened it. It is worth noting that no source suggests Lysander orchestrated his recall behind the scenes. The initiative came from the allies and Cyrus, and was no more Lysander's doing than their initial lack of cooperation with Callicratidas.

Victory at Aegospotami

Lysander's second term of command began, like his first one, with the task of rebuilding the coalition navy, which this time also involved restoring his network of friends and allies. In the winter of 405, he took thirty-five Peloponnesian ships and sailed to his old headquarters in Ephesus. There he assembled ships from Chios and other states, repaired some, and built others in timber-rich Antandros, across from Lesbos. Antandros was also a good launching ground for attacks against pro-Athenian Mytilene. All this activity, especially paying the sailor's wages, involved heavy expenses, which were partially defrayed by money from Sparta and from Lysander's Aegean and Ionian friends. These revenues were another illustration of how Lysander's friendships helped his city. But the big money was, as always, with the Persians. Lysander went to Sardis to ask Cyrus for funds, and Cyrus complied; after reminding him of all the large sums the Persians had so far given Spartan admirals. The message was clear: Cyrus expected Lysander to show returns for the Persian investment. He put Lysander even further in his personal debt by rewarding him with more money than was expected or agreed upon. The funds allowed Lysander to pay the crews back wages and to appoint captains for the new ships, thus ensuring loyalty to the cause and to himself. And now this lucky commander—arguably the luckiest discussed in this book—got even luckier.

In the wake of the battle of Arginusae, the Athenians condemned to death six of their generals for failing to rescue the survivors and collect the dead after the battle. By doing so, Athens shrank its pool of experienced generals to oppose Lysander even further, having already lost Alcibiades. Moreover, Cyrus was called back to his sick father, Darius II, in Iran, and was looking for all the friends and allies he could get as support in a likely contest over the throne and as protection from the new king. The situation at home made him more motivated than ever to help Sparta win the war and to strengthen his ties with the Greek city and its general. He told Lysander to be sure to have more ships than the enemy had before meeting it in battle, and he gave him additional money, including funds from his personal revenues. The result was that Lysander could command and pay a fleet that, after Aegospotami, numbered 200 ships. In this way, favorable and unexpected circumstances before the Battle of Aegospotami contributed to his victory there.[17]

An ugly affair took place in Miletus during the buildup of the Spartan armada. The city was divided between the democrats and the oligarchs, who were Lysander's allies. Lysander promised to help the latter take over the city, but the oligarchs reconsidered and opted for reconciliation with their opponents. Lysander would not hear of it and secretly reproached and probably threatened his allies, insisting that they go on with the coup. He then came to Miletus, and, pretending to be angry with the revolutionaries, he assured the democrats that he would not punish them. It was a ruse to prevent the democrats from leaving the city, and the oligarchs put many of them to the sword. Others fled inland.[18]

Plutarch shows his disgust with Lysander's subterfuge: this was not how a straight-shooting Spartan and a descendant of the children of Heracles was supposed to behave. For the biographer, the affair exemplified Lysander's habitual shiftiness and dishonorable conduct, and he cites aphorisms attributed to Lysander, such as, "Where the lion's skin will not reach, it must be patched out with the fox's," and "Cheat boys with knuckle-bones, but men with oaths." The latter line adds impiety to his faults. In fact, the career of this alleged double-crosser shows him using deceit only in a few cases, and especially sparingly in war. Moreover, Lysander's actions at Miletus must be understood in the light of Sparta's need for allies and Lysander's mistrust of local compromises as a stable foundation for Spartan power. The democrats were perceived as natural Athenian allies, while narrow oligarchic regimes were more reliable because of their affinity to the Spartan political system and greater dependence on Sparta (and Lysander) for their survival. The oligarchies also reduced Spartan dependence on Cyrus as a primary source of aid. Lysander was surely aware that such governments were unpopular, but Sparta's control of its half-servile population of helots, who greatly outnumbered its citizens, proved that the rule of a privileged minority could last for a

17. Antandros: cf. Thuc. 4.52.3. The Arginusae affair: Asmonti 2006; Hamel 2015, 71–90. Lysander, Cyrus, and the navy: Xen. *Hellenica* 2.1.5–15; Plut. *Lysander* 9 (adding that Cyrus promised to return with Phoenician and Cilician fleets); Diod. 13.103.3–4, 107.2. Kagan 1987, 382, estimates that Lysander had only 125–150 ships before Aegospotami, a figure that seems too low.
18. Plut. *Lysander* 8; Diod. 13.104.5–6; Polyaenus 1.45.1; cf. Bommelaer 1981, 80. See p. 207 below for a similar trick in Thasos.

very long time. Besides, neither Lysander nor Sparta had to bloody their hands in getting the oligarchs to power. None of these motives mean that Lysander was laying the foundations for a postwar Spartan empire: a common assumption among the sources and their modern interpreters. At this stage, he appears to have been preoccupied with strengthening his base rather than with the aftermath of a presumed victory.[19]

Along with strengthening Spartan alliances through revolutions, Lysander tried to deprive the enemy of allies. He sailed with the bulk of his navy to Caria, where he destroyed Iasus, killed 800 of its adult men, and sold its women and children into slavery. He also captured Cedreiae on the Ceramic Gulf and enslaved its population. Both towns were located conveniently south of friendly Miletus and at a safe distance from the Athenian fleet at Samos, which Lysander, cautious as ever, intended to evade at this point. The towns' capture boosted his winning record and was also profitable. Regardless of his revenue from contributions, his large fleet created a constant demand for money, and the Spartan homeland expected its share of profits, too. His murderous treatment of the defeated reflected not just his cruelty but also their impotence: he would be less harsh toward larger and more powerful cities that capitulated to him. In the case of Iasus, the population was also punished for changing sides to Athens sometime after 412.[20]

The successful campaign emboldened Lysander to cross the sea to Greece and raid Aegina and Salamis near Athens. He then landed somewhere in Attica, where he met King Agis and his troops, who came from their local base in Decelea. It is unclear what Lysander was trying to achieve here. His subsequent hurried flight from an approaching Athenian fleet suggests that he did not plan to provoke a showdown or to combine land and sea attacks on Athens. Perhaps he wished to demonstrate to both the Athenians and the Spartans that Arginusae was just a passing episode. His large fleet and his landing in Aegina, Salamis, and Attica challenged the Athenian defensive strategy that Pericles had constructed and the Athenians had improved upon (see p. 133 above). Yet the material and psychological damage he caused was limited, because he preferred to leave and fight closer to his Aegean base.[21]

19. Deceitful Lysander: Plut. *Lysander* 8; cf. *Moralia* 229b, 330f (attributed to Dionysius I of Sicily), 741c; Diod. 10.9.1; Polyaen 1.45.3; Aelian *Historical Miscellany* 7.12. Doubts about these allegations: Prentice 1934, 39.
20. Thuc. 8.28.3; Diod. 13.104.7; Xen. *Hellenica* 2.1.15.
21. Plut. *Lysander* 9; Diod. 13.104.7–8; Krentz 1989, 173–174 (Agis' idea); Kagan 1987, 384–385; Lazenby 2004, 239–240.

In the summer of 405, Lysander and his fleet sailed along the friendly coast of Ionia to the Hellespont, where he intended to seize grain ships and deal with cities that had deserted the Spartan alliance. The idea of cutting off Athens' grain imports from the Black Sea at the Hellespont could have originated in Lysander's sighting of grain ships sailing to the Piraeus when he was around Attica. He might equally have heard about them from Agis, who advocated this plan as early as 410. At that time, Spartan attempts to implement it were unsuccessful, but now Lysander had a larger navy and more allies along the coast. He must have known that even a successful blockade would not end the war quickly, because Athens had other sources of supply, a large navy, and powerful allies. Yet a blockade could damage Athens much more than the annual invasions of Attica at the beginning of the war.[22]

Predicting that the Athenians would try to oppose him, Lysander was prepared to fight them when he liked the odds. He needed a local base of operation and set his eyes on inimical Lampsacus, which had food reserves and a harbor that could shelter his fleet. In addition, Lampsacus, along with pro-Spartan Abydus to the south and the territory between them (controlled by the neighboring satrap Pharnabazus), could create a stretch of friendly land along the coast. An anecdote of uncertain date from Xenophon's history may be placed in this context. It tells that Pharnabazus slandered the Spartan governor of Abydus, Dercylidas, and that Lysander forced Dercylidas to stand guard with his shield. It was a Spartan penalty for indiscipline, considered demeaning for high-ranking Spartans, probably because it was a form of corporal punishment or because it reduced them to the status of mere sentries. Lysander's action suggests his realistic approach of choosing to appease a strategic ally over siding with a fellow countryman.[23]

Lysander took Lampsacus by storm after attacking the city from the sea and his local allies by land, an operation that required good planning and coordination against a strongly fortified city. Its capture had to be effected quickly, before the Athenians could come to the rescue. He allowed the Athenian garrison of Lampsacus to leave under truce, probably in order to save himself the trouble of besieging the citadel. He then let his soldiers loot the well-stocked city, although he spared the free residents from slaughter and captivity, as he had not done in Caria. When the Athenians

---

22. Obstructing the grain supply: Xen. *Hellenica* 1.1.35; 2.1.17; Humble 1997, 117.
23. Xen. *Hellenica* 3.1.9; cf. Hornblower 2000. Krentz 1989, 162, dates the incident to Lysander's first term in 407, but Lysander was not active in the north then.

had captured Lampsacus (then a Spartan ally) in 411, they had spared its free population, and Lysander could not afford to be harsher toward the readmitted allies.[24]

Predictably, Lysander's northern campaign greatly alarmed the Athenians. Even before he reached the Hellespont, they increased their navy in Samos and added generals to the ones already there. Yet of all their commanders, only Conon had experience and proven skills, and even he had not yet achieved his greatest successes. Pulling their resources together, the Athenians launched a fleet of 180 ships and sailed to the Thracian Chersonese. They came too late to save Lampsacus, and after two stops on the way they anchored at Aegospotami, more than 4 kilometers away. It was a problematical choice for an anchorage.[25]

Aegospotami (lit. "Goat Rivers") offered the Athenians a long, open beach for the large fleet, fresh water for the crews, and a site just across from the enemy ships and land forces at Lampsacus (Map 13, p. 190). Its greatest disadvantages were the lack of a secure harbor and its distance from the nearest reliable source of supply at Sestos (about 20 km down the coast). This latter defect complicated provisioning of the massive Athenian force and forced the men to supplement their diet and income by foraging and looting, thus shortening their time for fighting and leaving their ships unattended. The Athenian generals must have been aware of these difficulties even before Alcibiades came to point them out for them (below). But these drawbacks were outweighed, the Athenians believed, by the advantage of being close to the enemy, which saved them from the need to row at least part of the way from Sestos, thus sparing the rowers' strength for battle. Although the site was unprotected, they thought that their best defense lay in blocking and attacking the enemy on the sea. Finally, they did not expect to stay long at Aegospotami and hoped to force Lysander to a quick decision. His daily manning of the ships in the harbor and arranging them in lines of battle encouraged their expectation of an imminent clash. It is even possible that Lysander enticed them to camp at Aegospotami by refusing to venture out of Lampsacus.

Creating hardship for the enemy is always desirable, especially before a battle that could decide the war: starting with Arginusae, both sides became

---

24. Xen. *Hellenica* 1.2.15; 2.1.17–19; Diod. 13.104.8; Plut. *Lysander* 9. Athens and Lampsacus: Thuc. 8.62.2.
25. Xen. *Hellenica* 2.1.16, 20–21; Diod. 13.104, 1–2, 105.1–2; Plut. *Lysander* 9; cf. Paus. 9.32.4 (100 Athenian ships). Aegospotami's location: Strauss 1987; cf. Bommelaer 1981, 113; Rhodes 2011, 99; Robinson 2014, 13–14.

more inclined to throw into battle many more ships than in the past. Such escalation suggests not just an arms race but also a willingness to take bigger risks in hopes of a decisive win. As we have seen, the Athenians had 180 ships at Aegospotami, and after the battle, Lysander commanded 200. The Spartan leader had reasons to hope, then, that with the right preparations and tactics, he could make the coming battle his first major step toward ending the war.

The main sources for the Battle of Aegospotami are Xenophon (followed by later authors whose descriptions resemble his to varying degrees) and Diodorus. The two versions are quite different, and modern scholars tend to prefer one version, usually Xenophon's, while ignoring the other. We may use both on the assumption that they describe different events of the battle.[26]

The battles of Notium and Aegospotami were similar in some respects, and the Athenians are to blame for allowing Lysander to partly reuse his "passive-aggressive" tactics. He began the day by making sure his troops had breakfast before boarding the ships, preparing them for a waiting game:

> And after making everything ready for battle and stretching the side screens which protected the rowers, he gave orders that no one should stir from his position or put out. At sunrise the Athenians formed their ships in line for battle at the mouth of the harbor. Since, however, Lysander did not put out against them, they sailed back again, when it grew late in the day, to Aegospotami. Thereupon Lysander ordered the swiftest of his ships to follow the Athenians and, when they had disembarked, to observe what they did, and then to sail back and report to him; and he did not disembark his men from their vessels until these scout-ships had returned. This he did for four days; and the Athenians continued to sail out and offer battle.[27]

Accurate prediction of the enemy's behavior is a great advantage, and Lysander's purpose was to habituate the Athenians to a routine. Assuming he was afraid to fight, they got used to the idea that he would refuse their challenge. His restraint raised their morale and gave them the confidence to return to their mooring and leave camp in search of food and booty.

---

26. Aegospotami: Diod. 13.105.1–106.7; Xen. *Hellenica* 2.1.22–30; and cf. Plut. *Lysander* 10–11; *Alc.* 36–37; Nepos *Alc.* 8; Frontinus *Stratagems* 2.1.18; Pausanias 9.32.4, 6; Polyaenus 1.45.2; cf. 1.45.1. Some details in the ancient accounts are indeed irreconcilable. For a similar reconstruction of the battle, see Robinson 2014, who also cites earlier studies of the battle.
27. Xen. *Hellenica* 2.1.22–24.

Their commanders allowed or ignored the lack of discipline because they shared this view of the enemy, their fear of the troops, their recognition of their needs, and the lack of a harbor or a city to keep the crews in. It was now that Alcibiades came down from his fort in the Chersonese to offer the Athenian generals his help. He promised to bring Thracian troops for a land attack on Lysander at Lampsacus, or to force the Spartans to a naval engagement. He also advised the generals to move to safer and better-stocked Sestos. He was turned down, even rudely, either because of personal and political opposition or because his price (a share in command) was too high. He returned to his fort. His cameo appearance would lead to many morning-after speculations about what could have happened if his counsel had been followed.[28]

The battle of Aegospotami took place on the fifth day of the contest, when the Athenian general Philocles led thirty ships on the attack and instructed the captains of the other triremes to be prepared to join him. Like the Athenians in the battle of Cyzicus (410), or possibly at Notium, he probably hoped to lure Lysander into an ambush.[29] As at Notium, the captains failed to follow through, probably because Lysander had so far declined battle every time. Lysander knew from deserters about Philocles' plan and was well prepared for it. He came out of the harbor with his entire fleet and put Philocles to flight. It was possibly around this time that he got a signal from his scouting ships that the Athenians in Aegospotami were idle. He sped over the few kilometers to their camp, as he had done at Notium, to forestall the launch of their ships. The fighting then split into two major arenas. The land forces that he ferried aboard his ships landed on the beach and captured part of the poorly defended Athenian camp. At the same time, he and his fleet dragged beached or empty ships away from their crews with iron grapples. The Athenians frantically tried to board other ships, but there were not enough crewmen because some were away and others were fighting the enemy in the camp. Even when they managed to embark they could fill only one or two out of the three rows of benches in the ships, which were therefore slower and less maneuverable than usual, and an easy prey to Lysander's vessels. The result was an Athenian catastrophe. The largest reported number of

28. Alcibiades at Aegospotami: Xen. *Hellenica* 2.1.25–26; and for more sources and discussion, see Krentz 1989, 175–176.
29. I prefer this reconstruction to the possibility that Diodorus' ultimate source (the author of the *Oxyrhynchian Greek History?*) was guilty of duplicating events of other battles; cf. Gray 1987, 78–79; Bleckmann 1998, 115–128. Battle of Cyzicus: Xen. *Hellenica* 1.1.11–23; Diod. 13.47–51.8; Plut. *Alc.* 28.

FIGURE 12 *The Athlit ram.* A bronze ram of a trireme or a larger ship was found on the coast of Athlit, Israel, and is currently on display at the National Maritime Museum, Haifa. It weighs 465 kilograms and was made in the second century. Three-pronged rams like the one in the picture were already being used at the end of the fifth century.

Photograph by Oren Rozen.

ships that got away was twelve, out of a fleet of 180. The escapees included the state ship *Paralus*, which would bring the bad news to Athens, and nine ships that the Athenian general Conon was able to man early in the fighting. Conon's meager consolation prize was the seizure and likely destruction of the sails that Lysander had removed and left near Lampsacus before the battle. Conon then sailed with his small fleet to his Cyprian friend, King Evagoras, to offer him his services for hire, because a return home after such a fiasco would have been too hazardous. Other Athenians fled anywhere in the Chersonese or to Sestos.[30]

Aegospotami made Lysander one of Greece's most notable generals. His thorough preparation allowed him to win an easy, almost anticlimactic victory. He made excellent use of his military intelligence about the enemy's strength, its location, and its state of mind (which he skillfully manipulated). At Aegospotami he exploited on a larger and more challenging scale his

---

30. Athenian survivors: see note 26; Lysias 21.10–11; Fr. 9; Isocrates 18.59; Diod. 13.106.5–6.

previously demonstrated ability to surprise the enemy and to combine land and sea attacks. And, unlike his opponents, he was in full control of his men, despite their large numbers. Yet Lysander would not have won this victory without the "cooperation" of an enemy that suffered from poor generalship, organization, and discipline. In this piece of luck, he resembled many other great generals who benefitted from their adversaries' failings. His victory and the ways he attained it inspired imitation in other commanders, including Dionysius of Syracuse, as we shall see.

After the battle, Lysander addressed two immediate tasks: spreading the word and dealing with the prisoners. As soon as the battle was over, he sent to Sparta a fast ship decked with arms and booty to announce his victory. It arrived three days later. He also celebrated his triumphant return to Lampsacus with hymns and victory songs. His reported treatment of the prisoners was in horrible contrast. He called in his allies and asked them what to do with the Athenian captives. Since his council was made up of Athens' enemies, he must have had a good idea what the answer would be. They wanted revenge for the Athenians' drowning of the crews of two enemy ships earlier in the war. They also charged the Athenian general Philocles, now a prisoner, with proposing before the battle to cut off the right hand (or in another version, the thumb) of enemies captured alive. They voted unanimously to execute the prisoners. (Years later, in 335, Alexander the Great would similarly call the enemies of Thebes to decide its fate. They voted to destroy it, and Alexander, like Lysander, pretended to be a mere instrument in executing their verdict.) Late sources report the killing of between 3,000 and 4,000 Athenians, and add that Lysander prevented their burial. There are good reasons to suspect the largely unprecedented figures and (even more strongly) the ban on burial, yet the executions reflect the ugly temperament of the times and Lysander's cruel streak, revealed earlier in Caria. Philocles was put to the sword, but another Athenian general, Adeimantus, was spared for opposing Philocles' aforementioned motion. Unwilling to admit their own failings, the Athenians attributed Adeimantus' survival to an alleged betrayal on his part.[31]

31. Announcing and celebrating victory: Xen. 1.2.30; Diod. 13.106.7; Plut. *Lysander* 11. Treatment of prisoners: Xen. 1.2.30–32; Plut. *Lysander* 13, *Alc.* 37; Pausanias 9.32.9. Diodorus 13.106.6–7, however, reports no prisoners' "massacre," and Wylie 1986, 138–141, argues against its historicity, but see Strauss 1983, 32–34. Treachery at Aegospotami: Lysias 14.38; Pausanias 10.9.5; Rhodes 2011, 99–100 (dubious of it).

Lysander and the Spartan Empire

There would not be another great battle like Aegospotami for Lysander. From now on, his roles as general, politician, and diplomat became closely enmeshed, largely because of his involvement in the buildup and maintenance of Spartan rule in Greece and the Aegean. Since this book is focused on generalship, we shall deal chiefly with his military activity and strategic plans.

After Aegospotami, Lysander planned to starve Athens into submission by stopping its grain supply from the Black Sea. For that purpose, he took his fleet up the Propontis and received the surrender of Byzantium and Calchedon on both sides of the Bosporus straits. He also banished to Athens any Athenian garrisons or other Athenians he encountered, so that they would crowd the city and increase demand for its dwindling resources. Before sailing back to Lampsacus, he left a Spartan commander as governor (*harmostes*) in Byzantium and Calchedon, probably with mercenary garrisons. Because his welcome was not universal, at least in Byzantium, he probably initiated in both places a change of government to one friendlier to him and Sparta. Plutarch describes his general policy of treating Greek cities, which evolved over time and varied from place to place:

> He also suppressed the democratic, and the other forms of government, and left one Lacedaemonian governor in each city, and ten rulers chosen from the political associations which he had organized throughout the cities. This he did alike in the cities which had been hostile, and in those which had become his allies, and sailed along in leisurely fashion, in a manner establishing for himself the supremacy over Hellas. For in his appointments of the rulers he had regard neither to birth nor wealth, but put control of affairs into the hands of his comrades and partisans, and made them masters of rewards and punishments. He also took part himself in many massacres, and assisted in driving out the enemies of his friends. Thus he gave the Greeks no worthy specimen of Lacedaemonian rule.[32]

Plutarch's claim that Lysander created a personal empire reflects hostile interpretations of his actions by enemies at home and abroad. Lysander desired power and fame, but he was equally a Spartan patriot.[33] Friendship

---

32. Capturing Byzantium and Calchedon: Xen. *Hellenica* 2.2.1–2. Quotation: Plut. *Lysander* 13. Cf. Diod. 14.10.1 (with Andrewes 1971, 209–210, which dates the rule of ten before 404); Nepos *Lysander* 2.

33. Cf. Lotz (1964) who stresses Lysander's traditionalist ways and disposition.

with him meant friendship with Sparta, and his fostering of such ties answered an immediate strategic need. Aegospotami foretold Athens' loss of its empire to Sparta. There were two known models of Greek hegemony at the time: the Peloponnesian League and the Athenian Empire. Lysander borrowed means of control from both. Like the Peloponnesians, the new allies would follow Spartan military and political leadership, with all the obligations that it entailed, but they would also benefit from its aid and might. Like the Athenian allies or subjects, they would pay tribute, host (and pay for) mercenary garrisons with a Spartan commander, be watched over by a fleet under Spartan command, and have a government friendly to, and dependent on, the hegemon. Sparta had a history of favoring oligarchic governments, predisposing Lysander to push for a rule of ten (decarchy). The chief merit of the system was that it allowed Sparta, with its small citizen body and newly acquired maritime rule, to control a vast empire through proxies. Local opposition was expected, but it could be put down by the threat or use of force. As we shall see, Lysander was shortsighted in his view that power was the solution, and that a failure of power should be remedied by the use of greater power.

Many cities prudently opened their gates to him, especially when he came visiting with a 200-ship fleet. A few communities along the Thracian coast and in Lesbos required more forceful persuasion, however. These included the island of Thasos, across from Thrace, which the Athenians had regained for their empire in 407. Lysander called the Thasians to a local temple of Heracles (his ancestor), and promised pardon to the pro-Athenians among them. When the latter came out of hiding, he had them all executed. The incident strengthened Lysander's reputation for impiety and murderous duplicity; he had used a similar trick in Miletus (p. 198 above). The goal was to secure Sparta's friends in power, but as elsewhere, his terror tactics had a more immediate than long-term effect; in 394, Thasos restored its friendship with Athens.[34]

In 404 or 403, Lysander put the city of Aphytis in the Chalcidice under a siege but then lifted it, saying that the Libyan god Ammon told him in a dream to do so. Even if the story was a pretense, it displays a traditional Spartan sensitivity to omens and appeasing the gods. It was perhaps after this operation that he raided the territory of the Persian governor Pharnabazus, a Spartan ally. His motives were unclear, although the wish to compensate his

---

34. Thasos: Polyaenus 1.45.4; Nepos *Lysander* 2; Plut. *Lysander* 19 (probably confusing Thasos with Miletus: Bommelaer 1981, 154n225). Thasos and Athens: Buckler 2003, 159.

men was probably among them. The Persian satrap complained to Sparta, and the *ephors*—a Spartan board of annual magistrates who supervised foreign and military affairs—did not approve what Lysander did, yet he seemed to pay no price for it. Soon only Samos remained a loyal ally to Athens, and Lysander put it under siege. It was time now to end the war by bringing it to the city of Athens.[35]

The Athenians prepared themselves for a siege. They repaired the city walls and closely guarded their harbor, but they lacked the complementary strategic component of their fleet. Lysander thought he could force them into quick surrender if he exerted pressure on them by both land and sea. At his request, the Spartan king Pausanias invaded Attica with a large army and camped less than 2 kilometers from the city's main gate, while another force came from the Spartan base in Decelea. Lysander was in charge of the naval arm of the blockade. On his way to Athens, he captured nearby Aegina and raided Salamis, then anchored with around 150 ships across from the Piraeus, where he blocked traffic in and out of the harbor. Yet, in spite of the tight siege, the Athenians did not surrender. Their walls provided good protection, and they had not yet exhausted their supplies. Probably finding the siege too demanding, the Peloponnesians returned home, and the blockade continued chiefly on the sea. It was now or earlier that Lysander threatened anyone importing grain to Athens with death. Since there was not much else to do there, he left to join the siege of Samos, which he captured in the late summer of 404. He banished the local residents (or the democrats among them), recalled political exiles, and gave them the city and the new exiles' possessions. He also established an oligarchic government in the island and left a Spartan commander and garrison there. Most of these measures had been used elsewhere, and Samos was spared mass execution because of its size, prestige, and terms of surrender.[36]

Lysander's dismantling of a number of Athenian colonies was related to his policy of replacing Athenian with Spartan loyalties. At Aegina, at Melos in the central Aegean, and at Scione in Chalcidice, he brought back local residents who had been dispossessed and banished by Athenian settlers. Such actions were retributive, strategically sound, and popular with locals and other Greeks. The case of pro-Athenian Sestos was different, because

---

35. Aphytis: Plut. *Lysander* 20; cf. 16; Andrewes 1971, 217–218 (summer of 404). Pharnabazus: Plut. *Lysander* 19; Nepos, *Lysander* 3.
36. Blockading Athens: Xen. *Hellenica* 2.2.7–11 (150 ships); Diod. 13.107.1–3 (200 ships); Plut. *Lysander* 14; Isoc. 18.61 (ban on imports). Samos: Michigan Papyrus no. 5982; Xen. *Hellenica* 2.2.5–6, 3.5–7; Plut. *Lysander* 14.

Lysander (in 404?) banished, not its Athenians, but the local residents, whose lands and city he gave to senior members of his crews. It was probably this unwelcome precedent that made the Spartan government reverse his measures. This was the first time that he and the Spartan authorities had openly clashed, and his other dealings with his government suggest he must have dutifully obeyed.[37]

In the meantime, the suffering and famine in Athens intensified, but the fear that the Spartans would enslave or destroy the city deterred them from capitulating. We shall not discuss the different opinions about surrender in the city or its negotiations with Sparta, except to note that the Athenians conferred with Lysander (then in Samos) only after they had failed to get the terms they hoped for—first from King Agis and then from the ephors. The order of their appeals suggests, not that he had the final say, but rather that he stood below these officials in the Spartan hierarchy of power. Indeed, when Athens sent him the prominent politician Theramenes as an envoy, Lysander detained him for three months and refused to negotiate with him, referring him to the ephors. Whatever ultimate plan Lysander had for Athens, this man whom our sources describe as too big for Sparta and even Greece did not exceed his authority. At most, he helped in prolonging the siege so that Sparta would get the terms of peace it wanted.[38]

After about eight months of siege, the Athenians gave up. A number of Sparta's allies wanted Athens destroyed and its population enslaved, but the Spartans opposed this radical solution. The realists among them, including Lysander, argued that Sparta needed a loyal though weakened Athens to counterbalance the power of Thebes and Corinth. The terms of surrender and peace included the demolition of the Long Walls and those around the Piraeus. Thus, more than seventy years after Themistocles built Athens' walls by alleged trickery (pp. 94–97 above), the Spartans finally had their way. The irony was not lost on a young Athenian orator, who opposed the destruction of the walls in the name of the Themistocles who had built them. He was told the walls were being destroyed to save Athens, just as they had been built. Evidently Athens had its pragmatists, too. The other peace terms were designed to incapacitate Athens' hegemonic rule and make Athens friendlier to Sparta. They included the surrender of all warships

---

37. Plut. *Lysander* 14; Bommelaer 1981, 151n208; Cartledge 1987, 93–94 (dating it to 403).

38. Xen. *Hellenica* 3.2.10–18; Diod. 13.107.3–4; Lysias 12.68–70; 13.9–14; *Papyrus Michigan* 5982; Green 1991, 10–11; Wolpert 2001, 10–13. Lysander's stature: e.g., Plut. *Lysander* 19; cf. 13, 16.

except for ten or twelve, the return of exiles, a withdrawal from overseas possessions except for the islands of Lemnos, Imbros, and Scyros, an alliance with Sparta (modeled after the Peloponnesian League), and possibly the adoption of a different government vaguely described as "the ancestral constitution."[39] Then, in March of 404, came what was arguably one of Lysander's finest hours. He sailed into the Piraeus and his men enthusiastically began tearing down the walls to the music of flute-girls, "thinking that that day was the beginning of freedom for Greece." One would expect similar expressions of joy in Sparta, but the reaction was different, according to a tale that Plutarch recorded for its charm:

> It is true one hears it said by Lacedaemonians that Lysander wrote to the ephors thus: "Athens is taken"; and that the ephors wrote back to Lysander: "'Taken' were enough"; but this story was invented for its neatness' sake.[40]

Plutarch justifiably questioned the story, but it is thoroughly Spartan in spirit. In Spartan eyes, presumably, it did not matter that Lysander had brought an end to the longest and most difficult war in Sparta's history by defeating its greatest rival. What mattered was that he got an F in Laconic speech.

As it happened, the partial destruction of the Long Walls was the beginning, not of "Greek freedom," but of its suppression, starting with Athens. A group of Athenians, mostly of élite background, planned to establish a narrow oligarchic rule, known as the Thirty, which was an expanded version of the rule of ten (decarchy). Since opposition was expected, they recalled Lysander from the siege of Samos to help them. He came with 100 ships, essentially to play the role of enforcer. When there was opposition to the new regime in the Assembly, he stood up and, with his customary bluntness, blamed the Athenians for failing to demolish the walls as promised, threatening them with loss of life unless they agreed to the oligarchy. His experience with changing local governments in and around the Aegean had taught him that threats and violence got results, and the cowed Athenians acquiesced to the new regime. Yet Lysander's need to appear in person and with force in

---

39. Athens' fate and its terms of surrender: Xen. *Hellenica* 2.2.19–20, 3.8; *Ath. Pol.* 34.3; Lysias 12.70; 13.4, 34; Andocides 3.12; Diod. 13.107.4; 14.3.2; Plut. *Lysander* 14; Paus. 1.45.5; Justin 5.8.1–6; Wolpert 2001, 13–15; Bolmarcich 2005, 17–21. The claim (Pausanias 3.8.6) that Lysander and Agis advocated the destruction of Athens at the beginning of the siege is questionable, and contradicted by Polyaenus 1.45.5; see Lazenby 2004, 248, but also Powell 2006.

40. Lysander's triumph: Xen. 2.2.23. His message: Plut. *Lysander* 14.

order to coerce the settlement presaged the instability of the system he had set up for Spartan rule.[41]

After capturing Samos and settling affairs there around September of 404, Lysander disbanded the coalition navy and sailed back to Sparta with evidence of his victories, including loot and revenues. Biographer Plutarch lists the honors he received during his lifetime, all of them outside Sparta. Some were unprecedented. They included bronze statues of him and of his chief aides at Delphi and Ephesus, semi-divine honors and altars, hymns, the renaming of a Samian festival after him, and flattery from poets and musicians in his entourage. The accolades inflated Lysander's self-esteem and elevated his status at home, but they also provoked jealousy and resentment there. A similar mixture of gratitude and criticism characterized the reaction to the influx of revenues he brought to Sparta. But though Lysander may have liked the fame and honor bestowed on him, he shunned the material rewards of his position, finding the greatest value of power in its use.[42]

It was probably in late 404 that Lysander was asked to assist the Thirty once again. They wanted him to secure their government with a Spartan governor and garrison, for which they would pay. There was no opposition in Sparta to Lysander's patronage of the Thirty or to his granting of their request, because they were Sparta's friends and kept the city in check. When the Spartan force arrived in Athens, the Thirty persuaded its commander and his garrison of 700 men with words and material rewards to help them actively against people they broadly defined as a threat to them and their tyranny. Such a use of the garrison deviated from its original mission and suggests that Lysander's imperial strategy was incapable of supervising its allies and even the Spartans sent to help them.[43]

Soon, however, Sparta and Lysander had to intervene directly in Athens. In the winter and spring of 403, the Thirty suffered a series of defeats against a growing number of democratic exiles led by Thrasybulus. The exiles were helped by neighboring states such as Corinth and Thebes, who

---

41. Lysias 13.71–74; *Ath. Pol.* 34.3; Diod. 14.3.4–7.
42. Honors for Lysander: Plut. *Lysander* 18–19; *Moralia* 395d–396c; cf. Pausanias 6.3.15; 10.9.4; and for more sources and discussion, see Di Maria et al. 1997, 260–267. Lysander's fondness of fame and his poverty: Plut. *Lysander* 2, 30.
43. Garrison: Xen. *Hellenica* 2.3.13–14 (whose chronology I follow); Diod. 14.4.3–4; *Ath. Pol.* 37.2 (dating the event later); Justin 5.8.11. It is told that Lysander first refused the Thirty's request to eliminate Alcibiades in exile, but then obeyed instructions from home and asked the Persians to do it for him: Isocrates 16.40; Plut. *Alcibiades* 38; Nepos *Alcibiades* 10.

were Sparta's allies but also highly dissatisfied with its domineering position and its treatment of them. The Thirty's losses led to their removal, and they left for Eleusis. They were replaced by the more moderate but still oligarchic board of Ten and 3,000 citizens, who continued the war against the democrats now in full control of the Piraeus. In desperation, the Ten and the men from the city, as well as the Thirty from Eleusis, sent envoys to Sparta and Lysander asking for help. Lysander was already deeply involved in Athens, and now his setup of a pro-Spartan regime assisted by an armed garrison was about to collapse. Always favoring a military solution, he called upon his winning experience with blockades, at Athens and elsewhere. He arranged a financial-aid package for the Ten and persuaded the Spartans to send his brother Libys as an admiral with forty ships to shut off the Piraeus, while Lysander himself was given the rank of governor (harmost) and put in command of land operations before leaving to recruit mercenaries in the Peloponnese.[44]

The historian Xenophon claims that Lysander hoped to starve the democrats in the Piraeus into submission by cutting off their supplies on land and sea. But this aim did not exclude the possibility of reaching a quicker decision in battle. Lysander recruited 1,000 hoplite mercenaries, planning to combine his force with infantry and cavalry from the city, and then waited for a Peloponnesian army to arrive on the scene. It was the leader of that army, the Spartan king Pausanias, who would spoil his plan of defeating the democrats and saving the oligarchy.

The sources are divided about Pausanias' motives and conduct in the campaign. Xenophon, for example, thought that the king intended from the start to defeat Lysander's purpose of keeping the oligarchs in power. He pretended to fight the democrats but in fact was envious of Lysander's fame and afraid that he would again own Athens. The two leaders were certainly rivals, but other sources and Pausanias' own actions suggest that he originally agreed with Lysander's policy and only later changed his mind in favor of a settlement between the democrats and the oligarchs. Arriving in Attica with a Peloponnesian army, Pausanias marched to Halipedon, a marsh at the northern Piraeus next to the Long Walls, where he arrayed his army for a pitched battle. By all appearances he aimed, like Lysander, to end the conflict then and there. Pausanias also took the traditional leadership position

---

44. Thebes and Corinth: Diod. 14.6.1; Plut. *Lysander* 27. Lysander to the rescue: Xen. *Hellenica* 2.4.28–29; Diod. 14.33.5; *Ath. Pol.* 38.1–3; Lysias 12.58–59; Isocrates 7.68.

FIGURE 13 *The Lacedaemonians' tomb in the Kerameikos.* A number of Spartans who died fighting with Pausanias in the Piraeus were honored by the Athenians with a burial in their "national cemetery" in the Kerameikos. Their austere burial was in line with Spartan practice.
Deutches Archaeologisches Institut, Neg No D-DAI-ATH-Kerameikos 1992. Used with permission.

of commanding the right wing while Lysander with his mercenaries held the left: roles indicative of their difference both in formal rank and in genuine authority. After the democrats rejected Pausanias' call to disperse or do battle, he recalled the attack. His next moves suggest no intention to seek anything but a military solution. They will not be discussed here, however, because Pausanias used only selected units that apparently did not include Lysander and his mercenaries.

Lysander may have seen action only after Pausanias was pushed by Thrasybulus and his men from the Piraeus to a hill north of the harbor, where the king instructed the Spartans and other allies to join him. Now far outnumbering Thrasybulus' hoplites, the invaders and their allies could finally defeat him in battle. One hundred and fifty Athenians died.[45] The enemy's loss effectively strengthened Lysander's hand, because the democrats, if not already weakened, were now outnumbered and besieged by land and sea. Yet, instead of increasing the pressure on them, Pausanias chose to arrange a reconciliation between the warring Athenian parties. His decision to reject Lysander's pro-oligarchic position was undoubtedly influenced by personal considerations, among others. Pausanias wanted to increase his power and reputation and to humiliate Lysander. He was also displeased by the Thirty's actions against individual Athenians with whom he was connected. Yet there were good political and strategic reasons for undoing Lysander's settlement. Reconciliation did not make Athens less loyal to Sparta, since both democrats and oligarchs soon declared their friendship with the old enemy. Moreover, the agreement sponsored by Pausanias established a more popular government; hence, conceivably, a more stable ally. It ended a conflict that required costly and repeated Spartan intervention, and the solution was likely to please Sparta's Corinthian and Boeotian allies, who opposed the Spartan campaign and supported the exiles. It was true that the oligarchs in Eleusis and even in Athens came out as the big losers, but this byproduct hurt Lysander much more than it did Sparta. Pausanias' work behind the scenes, along with the Athenian and Spartan delegations' coming and going, hammered out an agreement that established a general amnesty in Athens. The Athenians were enjoined not to recall past wrongs, which meant that, except for a number of oligarchic officials, all the rest were exempted from punishment. Democracy was restored soon thereafter.[46]

Pausanias' solution was not universally endorsed in Sparta, and when he returned home, he was put on trial. The formal charge is unknown, and if Lysander spoke for the prosecution (as he may well have done) he suffered a second defeat, because Pausanias was acquitted by a narrow margin. About eight years later, in 395, Athens joined an anti-Spartan coalition, and it is told that Pausanias was then criticized for freeing the belligerent Athenian demos from the oligarchic constraints imposed by Lysander. Lysander also regained the reputation of using his command strictly for the benefit of Sparta. This appreciation of Lysander was more nostalgic than accurate. It ignored the weakness of Lysander's settlement and the wisdom of

---

45. Xen. *Hellenica* 2.4.28–34; *Ath. Pol.* 38.3–4; Diod. 14.33.1–6; Plut. *Lysander* 21; Pausanias 3.5.1–2; Justin 5.10.4; Krentz 1982, 70–101.
46. Pausanias and Lysander: Hamilton 1979, 82–98; Cartledge 1987, 283–286; cf. Powell 2006. The amnesty: see esp. *Ath.* Pol. 39.1–6; Loening 1987; Carawan 2013.

Pausanias' deal, which assured Sparta of Athens' friendship for much longer than Lysander's.[47]

The fall of the Thirty exposed the failings of Lysander's imperial strategy. Its major premise was that military power, which had won Sparta its empire, would also sustain it. Hence the deployment of fleets, governors and garrisons, and (if needed) armies to keep the allies in check; hence also his assistance to local oligarchies that were dependent on Spartan arms and deterrence. Complementing these means were the personal ties, political ideology, and self-interest that linked the local governments to the Spartan state or to influential Spartans like Lysander. In many of these methods, Spartan rule resembled the empire it had inherited from Athens. Yet, unlike Athens' imperial policy, Sparta's treatment of its allies benefitted just a small segment of the local population, did not provide the Greeks with economic services or incentives, and was a management style that merely reacted to local crises. In addition, Lysander ignored or failed to realize adequately that the Spartans were equally dependent on their local friends. The Athenian oligarchs were allowed to abuse their power because they fulfilled an important need, freeing the Spartans of administering the city more closely. And it was not just in Athens that Lysander's arrangement proved flimsy. In 405, Lysander was instrumental in effecting an oligarchic coup in the city of Miletus (p. 198 above). Sometime afterwards (405–403), the Persian satrap Tissaphernes helped democratic exiles return to Miletus and defended their regime from local oligarchs. It can be said to the credit of the Spartan government that it recognized the problem. The ephors abolished the rule of ten (decarchy), probably in 403, and instructed the various cities to restore their "ancestral constitutions," whatever that term meant in each case.[48]

The Fall of a Hero

The events in Athens marked a downturn in Lysander's military and political fortunes. He still moved in the highest circles, but he never again

---

47. Trial: Pausanias 3.5.2. Reactions in 395: Plut. *Lysander* 21; cf. Xen. *Hellenica* 3.5.25; and pp. 224–225 below.
48. Miletus: Xen. *Anabasis* 1.1.6–7; Hamilton 1979, 103. Abolishing decarchies: Xen. *Hellenica* 3.4.2, which appears to date the ephors' decree to 397; but see Andrewes 1971, 206–216, and Cartledge 1987, 94, for a dating to 403.

enjoyed the kind of authority that enabled him to deploy large armies and shape Greek governments. There were many reasons for his decline. Sparta had constitutional mechanisms and other regulations that limited his opportunities to hold military power over a long time. He had strong enemies at home who envied or resented his fame and power. Some Spartans disapproved of the riches he added to the city's existing economic and social inequalities, and their effect on its moral fabric.[49] Lysander's reported reaction to such enmity, then or later, was to plan a change of the Spartan monarchical government. The Spartan kings traced their lines as far back as the children of Heracles. Allegedly, Lysander wished to make kingship elective, either from all families descended from Heracles' children or from all meritorious Spartans who showed Heraclean excellence (*arete*). Either possibility would make Lysander himself a prime candidate. Nothing came of his "revolutionary" plan, and it is questionable whether he ever made it, because the evidence for it was conveniently discovered by his enemies after his death. In any case, the affair might have affected Lysander's type of command rather than its art.[50]

It is indicative of Lysander's fall from favor that the evidence for the rest of his career is episodic. Even the sources' silence in circumstances where his presence would have been expected is suggestive. Cyrus the Younger was back in Asia Minor in 401, and he covertly organized an expedition against his brother, King Artaxerxes II. He called on Sparta to return all the great favors he had done her. The city granted him an admiral with thirty-five ships for a local mission in Asia Minor, a Spartan commander who led 700 mercenary hoplites, and probably the turning of a blind eye to his recruiting of other mercenaries in Greece and elsewhere. Readers would be justified in asking, "Was that all?" Lysander, Cyrus' best Spartan friend, is nowhere mentioned in this context, and we may view both the silence about his involvement and the limited Spartan aid to Cyrus as symptoms of his weakening clout. Cyrus' expedition ended with his death in battle, which did not help Lysander's case.[51]

49. Lysander's corrupting riches: Plut. *Lysander* 16–17; Cartledge 1987, 88–89; Hodkinson 2000, 155–157, 424–429. See Smith 1948 for a different assessment of Lysander's power at this point.
50. Lysander's plan: Diod. 14.13.1–8; Plut. *Lys.* 24–26; *Agesilaus* 28; *Moral.* 212c–d, 229f (discovered speech); Nepos *Lysander* 3; Aristotle *Politics* 5.1306b. Hamilton 1979, 88–96; Bommelaer 1981, 223–225; and Cartledge 1987, 94–97, all credit the scheme; but see Flower 1991, 81–83, and Keen 1996a, who suggest its later invention.
51. Cyrus' expedition and Sparta: Diod. 14.19.2–5 (25 ships and 800 hoplites), but see Xen. *Anabasis* 1.2.21, 4.2–3; Xen. *Hellenica* 3.1.1–3; cf. Plut. *Artaxerxes* 6. Hamilton 1979, 104–106, argues for Lysander's lobbying.

In 400, Lysander saw a chance to improve his lot in the succession crisis that followed the death King Agis, who had opposed him in the past. Agis' son and designated heir, Leotychidas, was rumored to really be the son of Alcibiades, who had allegedly had an affair with Agis' wife during his exile in Sparta. Lysander supported the candidacy of Agesilaus, Agis' lame brother and Lysander's former lover. The sources are divided about the extent of Lysander's involvement, but they agree that his interpretation of an oracle warning Sparta against a "lame king" (which Lysander said was a metaphor for Leotychidas' bastardy) won the kingship for Agesilaus. The outcome was clearly favorable to Lysander. After being at odds with both Spartan kings, Lysander had now one for an ally.[52]

Three years later, that alliance was tested. The conflict between Lysander and Agesilaus took place in the context of a war between Sparta and the Persian satraps of Asia Minor that began in 400. After the failure of Cyrus' expedition, the satraps tried to reincorporate the Greek cities in and around their territory into the Persian Empire. The Greeks asked Sparta to come to their aid, and Sparta complied under the banner of championing Greek freedom. Several Spartan commanders went to Asia Minor with mercenary forces and won moderate success. Lysander's involvement in the anti-Persian operations is attested explicitly only after 396, when the Spartans heard that the Persian king had assembled a large navy, presumably for operations in the Aegean.[53]

Our major sources credit Lysander with pushing for an Asian campaign under Agesilaus' command. They say that he persuaded the king to go there, encouraged his friends in Asia Minor to request Agesilaus as the leader of the force, and detailed its composition.[54] The invading army consisted of 2,000 freed helots, 6,000 allied soldiers, and thirty advisors to the king, Lysander being the most senior. Agesilaus probably played a more active role in the affair than the accounts allow him, yet his contribution was not as problematic as the motives they ascribe to Lysander, whose reported goal was to help his friends in Asia Minor by reestablishing the decarchies, which had been disbanded by the ephors, probably in 403.

52. Lysander and Agesilaus' accession: Xen. *Hellenica* 3.3.1–4; Plut. *Lysander* 22; *Agesilaus* 2–3; Pausanias 3.8.8–10; cf. Xen. *Agesilaus* 1; Plut. *Alcibiades* 23; Cartledge 1987, 112–115; Ogden 1996, 258–259.
53. Briant 2002, 634–637; Rhodes 2006, 206–208.
54. Lysander, the war, and Agesilaus: Xen. *Hellenica* 3.4.1–3; Plut. *Lysander* 23; *Agesilaus* 6. See also Pausanias 3.9.1; Diod. 14.79.1. In his encomium of Agesilaus, *Agesilaus* 1, however, Xenophon attributes the war initiative and plans exclusively to the king.

Lysander clearly hoped to revive the decarchies, but the ancient and modern assumption that he sought thereby to rebuild the personal power he had wielded in the past is questionable. The Spartan structure of command had changed greatly. In 405 (the year of Aegospotami) and afterwards, Lysander was nominally second in command, but in actuality he ran the war and set up the client oligarchies. Now Agesilaus was supreme commander in both name and fact. As in the past, there was no real contradiction between Lysander's personal interests and those of the state. The return to decarchies, whose checkered usefulness was now ignored or forgotten, was designed to strengthen Sparta's strategic hold in Asia Minor, not just to empower Lysander. It is also doubtful that renewing the decarchies was his secret agenda. Xenophon claims that Lysander planned to do it with Agesilaus' help, suggesting that Agesilaus, too, favored the idea (although he would change his mind later). Furthermore, it is hard to imagine that the Spartans at home were unaware of Lysander's personal agenda after seeing his oligarchic Asian friends and their envoys endorsing his proposal for the expedition in public.[55]

Agesilaus presented the campaign as a new Trojan War, thereby claiming Agamemnon's position as the leader of all Greeks. In defiance of this claim, the Boeotians disturbed his sacrifice at Aulis in Euboia, which was designed to evoke Agamemnon's sacrifice of his daughter before going to Troy on an all-Greek expedition. Agesilaus never forgave the affront, and Lysander must have been equally enraged. But soon their cooperation suffered a major blow.[56]

On arriving in Asia Minor, Agesilaus pitched his camp at Ephesus and soon reached a temporary truce with the satrap Tissaphernes. He was now free to focus his attention on the local Greeks, but they preferred to deal with Lysander. According to historian Xenophon, Lysander's former friends were overwhelming him with requests to intervene with Agesilaus to grant them their wishes, "and for this reason a very great crowd was continually courting and following Lysander, so that Agesilaus appeared to be a man in private station and Lysander king." Although Xenophon suggests that courting Lysander was the locals' idea, it is possible that he urged them to it. He probably hoped the intimidating display of influence would persuade Agesilaus to let him be in control—not of the campaign, but rather of Greek affairs in the region, through his network of friends and oligarchies, as the evidence

---

55. See the previous note, and Bommelaer 1981, 182–184; Krentz 1995, 182–183; Shipley 1997, esp. 116–121, 129–132.
56. Agesilaus and Agamemnon: Xen. *Agesilaus* 1; Plut. *Agesilaus* 6; Pausanias 3.9.1–5; cf. Xen. *Hellenica* 3.4.3–4.

suggests. Lysander was realist enough to know that ultimate power rested with the king, and he counted on their record of cooperation to keep him in Agesilaus' favor. The setting at Ephesus, his old base, was conducive for his liaison with the Greeks, and he also thought that his services in that role were indispensable. This was a mistake, as was his insensitivity to other people's honor. Like King Pausanias in Athens, Agesilaus pulled rank to overrule and insult Lysander. He rejected his advice and made Lysander's personal connections a liability by refusing, in his presence, all requests from his friends and granting those of Lysander's foes. To further humiliate Lysander, he reportedly appointed him royal meat carver and sarcastically advised petitioners to seek an audience with that functionary. Lysander is said to have told his friends not to use his name and recommendation if they wanted anything from Agesilaus. Plutarch justly opines that Lysander did not deserve such treatment. He was an experienced general with a record of success and a clear idea of how to run the empire, yet he was rejected on grounds of prestige. Though his enemies said he behaved more royally than the king himself, he did not defy royal authority or even try to subvert it. Instead he sought to patch up their relationship by essentially conceding defeat. Xenophon, a sympathizer of Agesilaus, tried to make the king look fair and suggests that Lysander himself asked to be sent away from the court. More likely it was the king who wanted to distance the general from his Greek friends and the Spartan camp when he sent him on an unspecified mission to the Hellespont. Lysander operated there as a diplomat and *agent provocateur*, helping a Persian nobleman defect from the satrap Pharnabazus. The deserter brought with him money, 200 much-needed cavalry, valuable intelligence about the enemy, and his very handsome son, with whom Agesilaus would become infatuated. There was something humiliating in Lysander's eagerness to bring prizes to Agesilaus, and in the king's display of royal pleasure with the veteran general. But whether their relationship was repaired (as Xenophon implies) or Lysander remained resentful (as Plutarch claims), he seems to have been given no other assignments. When his term as a royal adviser ended in 395, he returned home.[57]

There was one more battle for this man of war to fight. Lysander's campaign against Boeotia in 395 constituted an early phase of the Corinthian War between Sparta and a coalition of its former allies Thebes, Corinth, Athens, and Argos. The relationship between these states and Sparta had

57. Lysander's conflict with Agesilaus: Xen. *Hellenica* 3.4.7–9; Plut. *Lysander* 23; *Agesilaus* 7–8. His mission and return: Xen. *Hellenica* 3.4.10, 20; *Agesilaus* 3, 5; Plut. *Lysander* 24; *Agesilaus* 8, 20; *Oxyrhynchian Greek History* 21.

deteriorated since the end of the Peloponnesian war, and in 397, Persian subsidies strengthened the cause of anti-Spartans in Greece. The war itself originated from a local conflict between the central Greek states of western (or eastern) Locris and Phocis over disputed land. When Thebes, Locris' ally, invaded Phocis, the Phocians appealed to Sparta, which responded by declaring war on Thebes. Plutarch says his sources are divided about whose fault the war was: Thebes', Lysander's, or both. The biographer opts for Lysander as the driving force behind the Spartan decision to go to war, but this choice reflects Plutarch's tendency to privilege the role of his biographical hero. He says Lysander was old (he was presumably in his mid-sixties), ill tempered, and angry at the Thebans for complaining that the Spartans did not share the profits of the Peloponnesian War with them and for aiding the Athenian democratic exiles against the Thirty, in violation of Spartan instructions. But the silence of our other sources about Lysander's initiating the war and the fact that the Spartans shared his grievances against Thebes (and had others) suggest that he should not be held solely responsible for the decision. Indeed, there is no substantial evidence for opposition at home to the Boeotian campaign or, for that matter, for the scholarly reconstruction of two factions in Sparta: the imperialists, led by Lysander, and the more pacific Spartans, led by King Pausanias, both remarkably maintaining the same policy since the Peloponnesian War. As in the past, Lysander's personal agenda to revive his military career coincided with the Spartans' desire to punish Thebes and reduce its power.[58]

To some extent, the Spartan war plan resembled Lysander's and Pausanias' joint attack on the democrats in the Piraeus. As in the earlier campaign, Lysander was supposed to go first to the region to recruit a local army and then to join Pausanias at the head of a Peloponnesian army. Here again, Pausanias was in charge of operations. Taking a small force with him, Lysander went to Phocis, where he recruited troops. He added to them soldiers from in and around Heraclea Trachinia, a Spartan colony on the Thessalian border north of Boeotia. This took time, as did Pausanias' mustering of a Peloponnesian army

---

58. Lysander and the war: Plut. *Lysander* 27–28; but see also Xen. *Hellenica* 3.5.3–6; blaming Thebes, as does the *Oxyrhynchian Greek History*, 16–18; cf. Paus. 3.9.9–12. Plut. *Agesilaus* 20 and *Moralia* 212.52 claim that Lysander formed an anti-Agesilaus faction upon his return, yet the anti-Theban Agesilaus must have supported the Boeotian campaign; and see Athenaeus 12.550e on Lysander's praises of Agesilaus in Sparta. See also Hamilton 1979, 192–195 (alleges opposition by Pausanias); Westlake 1985; Cartledge 1987, 291–292, 359–360 (with Agesilaus' approval).

at Tegea in Arcadia, consisting of 6,000 men, including Lacedaemonians, mercenaries, and allied troops. The two leaders planned to meet on a designated day at Haliartus in western Boeotia, on the southern shore of the (now drained) Lake Copais (see Map 11, p. 169). Lysander was to arrive there from the northwest and Pausanias from the south after marching along the eastern shore of the Corinthian Gulf.[59]

Lysander accomplished quite a bit before arriving in Haliartus. In addition to recruiting an invading force, he succeeded in causing the surrender of the northern Boeotian city of Orchomenus without a battle. He was probably helped by its pro-Spartan residents, a resource he often used elsewhere, and the presence of his army nearby constituted an effective threat. An anecdotal story of this campaign reports that he asked undecided Boeotians if they wanted him to march through their land with spears held upright (in peace) or leveled. He also probably promised Orchomenus autonomy from Theban control, as he did later at Haliartus. Orchomenus was a significant acquisition. Around the time of Lysander's invasion, it was a member of the Boeotian confederacy, and its military contribution to the Boeotian army consisted of, or was expected to be, one or perhaps even two generals, 1,000 soldiers, and 100 cavalrymen. About this number must now have joined Lysander's army, and although their defection was not a devastating blow to the Boeotian cause, it did do military, political, and psychological damage to it. From Orchomenus, Lysander marched about 15 kilometers south to Lebadea, where he attacked and raided the city, presumably because it refused to join him. Lebadea, Haliartus, and Coronea together comprised another component district in the Boeotian confederacy, and Lysander accordingly continued from Lebadea to Haliartus. So far, his overall strategy resembled the one he and other Spartans had used against the Athenian empire. Before meeting the main adversary, Thebes, in a decisive battle, he intended to weaken it by tearing one member at a time away from its alliance.[60]

59. Xen. *Hellenica* 3.5.6–7, 17, 25; cf. Pausanias 3.5.6. Plut. *Lysander* 28, however, suggests that there was no prearranged time and place for their union. Haliartus' strategic advantages: Westlake 1985, 125. Pascual 2007, 40–41, surmises that the Spartan strategy was based on Athenian precedents, including Demosthenes' two-pronged attack (pp. 168–171 above), but Lysander's learning from his own experience is likelier.

60. Lysander, Orchomenus, Lebadea, and Boeotia: Xen. *Hellenica* 3.5.6; Plut. *Lysander* 28; Plut. *Lysander* 22; *Moralia* 229c. The Boeotian confederacy: *Oxyrhynchian Greek History* 19, and pp. 19–20 above. Orchomenus' contribution: Pascual 2007, 49.

What happened next became a subject of controversy. Lysander was killed near the walls of Haliartus, and King Pausanias, who was not there, was later held responsible for his death. He was put on trial for his conduct and decisions before and after the fighting in Haliartus, and even for his past policies and prior dealings with Lysander (see pp. 224–225 below). Post-factum recriminations and justifications influenced our sources, whose variant accounts of the events make their reconstruction challenging.[61]

The sources agree that Lysander reached Haliartus ahead of Pausanias. There is less clarity about whether Pausanias was late or Lysander came early, though the latter possibility is slightly likelier than the former. The king was then in Plataea, about 25 kilometers southeast of Haliartus, and Lysander asked him to join him, as he intended to approach the city's walls the next morning. The Thebans intercepted Lysander's messenger. To this point they seem to have taken no action, perhaps because they were waiting for reinforcements to arrive from Athens, with which they had secured a military alliance. Now they could risk going out in force, because Lysander's message told them Pausanias was not going to march on their city, and because an Athenian force under the veteran general Thrasybulus had arrived in Thebes. They hoped thus to save Haliartus for the confederacy before Lysander and the king joined forces. A combined Theban force of hoplites and cavalry left hastily in the night for Haliartus, about 20 kilometers away, and split upon arriving. One unit entered the city to ensure its loyalty, and the rest stayed to the west, hidden from Lysander's view.

Lysander camped on a ridge, presumably southeast of the city, and then made a disputed decision. He did not to wait for Pausanias but took a phalanx of hoplites and marched to the city walls, probably using the easier southern approach to the Acropolis. Our primary sources do not adequately explain his reasoning, if at all. They criticize Lysander for pressing on with the attack prematurely rather than waiting for Pausanias, as if the latter's arrival would have guaranteed success. They also ascribe to the general motives such as anger (about what?) and love of honor, whose relevance to this case is unclear, but which often stands for impetuosity. Yet Lysander's record shows that he

61. Xen. *Hellenica* 3.5.17–25; Plut. *Lysander* 28–30; Diod. 14.81.1–3, 89.1; Pausanias 3.5.3–7; 9.32.5; cf. Nepos *Lysander* 3; Plut. *Moralia* 408b; Westlake 1985; Cartledge 1987, 292, 358–359; Buck 1994, 36–39. Lysander's route in Boeotia and his station near Haliartus: Buckler 2003, 73–82; Pascual 2007, 51–58. For Cissusa Spring (below), see Frazer 1913, 5:165, whose identification is preferred here to that of Buckler 2003, 81n7.

was not the kind of a commander who let emotions determine his tactics or who rushed heedlessly into action.[62]

Lysander hoped to persuade the people of Haliartus to surrender with a promise of autonomy and the threat of his column of hoplites. For that purpose, he did not need Pausanias, and waiting for him would have spoiled the psychological advantage given by his first appearance near the city. But the Theban presence in Haliartus prevented its surrender. Lysander then opted for taking the city by storm before other Thebans and the Athenians arrived, as they later did. There are two versions of how he died. One says that a sortie from the city surprised him and his company outside the walls and ahead of his troops. The other suggests that he fell next to the walls, but at a later stage of the siege. Whenever exactly he was killed, it appears that he and his men were caught in a pincer movement between a party of Haliartians and Thebans coming out of the city and the Theban force that came from the Cissusa Spring north of the city and around the walls, attacking him from the rear. The credit for killing him was given to one Neochorus of Haliartus.[63]

Thus the general who had won his greatest victory in Aegospotami by surprising the enemy was taken by surprise himself. The deciding difference at Haliartus was his lack of adequate knowledge about events in the city and around it. The fall of a general was devastating to any army and could decide the battle, as it did here. Lysander's troops probably escaped toward the slopes of Mt. Libethrion, south of Haliartus. The Theban cavalry and infantry pursued them closely, and it was presumably at this stage that Lysander's men suffered most of their 1,000 casualties. Upon reaching rough terrain, Lysander's officers finally restored discipline and offered an effective opposition. They and their troops used their higher position to hurl projectiles and roll down rocks, breaking the enemy's cohesiveness and making them vulnerable to counter attacks. After losing between 200 and 300 men, the Thebans retreated. The Phocians and other allies of Lysander waited for night before fleeing for home.

King Pausanias heard of the defeat on his way from Plataea to nearby Thespia. He arrived at Haliartus the next day, ready to offer battle, but after

---

62. See the previous note. Anger: Plut. *Comparison of Lysander and Sulla* 4. Lysander reportedly suffered from melancholy or depression in his old age, but it is hard to see how it affected his decision at Haliartus: Aristotle *Problems* 30.1; Plut. *Lysander* 28.

63. Lysander's death: Xen. *Hellenica* 3.5.19 (both versions); Plut. *Lysander* 28 (by surprise); cf. Pausanias 3.5.3 (uniquely adding Athenians to the attackers). For the following events, see note 61 above.

another day, he decided in favor of a truce instead. The Thebans allowed him to collect Lysander's corpse and other dead for burial, on the condition that he withdraw from Boeotia. The sources tell that he was eager to get the bodies but was afraid to fight for them against what was (or would soon be) a joint force of Thebans and Athenians. Furthermore, the enemy's cavalry was superior to his own, Lysander's army had evaporated, and his troops were suffering from low morale. These apparently reasonable considerations will not be examined here, because they have little to do with Lysander's generalship. Yet, one episode involving a debate in the Spartan camp before Pausanias made his deal with the Thebans is relevant to Lysander's image. We are told that the king planned to ask the Thebans for a truce to collect the bodies of Lysander and other troops: a common request in Greek warfare, but also an admission of defeat. This angered elderly Spartans in his camp:

> Coming to the king, they protested that the body of Lysander must not be taken up under cover of a truce, but by force of arms, in open battle for it; and that if they conquered, then they would give him burial, but if they were vanquished, it would be a glorious thing to be dead with their general.[64]

The story evinces Spartan ethos and historical legacy: the elders were trying to save Spartan honor by recreating the scene of Leonidas' death at Thermopylae, where the general's loyal companions had fought to the death to protect his body from the Persians (pp. 51–52 above). At Haliartus, Lysander's troops actually ran away and left his body behind, but they were not Spartans. His countrymen were now given an opportunity to emulate the famous 300, while the Thebans, who refused to surrender Lysander's body and thus abused it, played the role of their old friends the Persians, who mutilated Leonidas' body. There was an irony in the elders' wish to return to traditional Spartanism in honor of a man who was charged with corrupting it. The pragmatist king Pausanias, however, refused their request—at heavy personal cost, as it turned out. On his return to Sparta, he faced charges about his no-show at Haliartus when Lysander was there, his refusal to fight for the bodies, and even his "pro-democratic" settlement in Athens in 403. In short, he was made to pay for Lysander's death. Rather than stand trial in such a hostile climate, he fled into exile. As for Lysander, although his reputation had diminished since the glory days of the Peloponnesian War, his death, as

64. Plut. *Lysander* 29.

was often the case, opened the gates for selective favorable memories, and he was greatly honored.[65]

Lysander was buried in friendly Phocian land across from the Boeotian border, where his monument was seen by Plutarch more than five centuries later. For the people of Haliartus, however, his fall was a proud moment in their history, and they claimed that he was buried in their land. Lysander would have smiled: he never minded being a subject of controversy.[66]

Conclusion

Plutarch thought Sparta gave Lysander the greatest commands and undertakings because his contemporaries considered him the first of the first men and the best of the best.[67] If Lysander with his mixed record was the best that Sparta could offer, his preeminence is a comment more on his city than on him. Not that he did not deserve much praise. He did an excellent job of rebuilding Spartan military power in the Aegean twice, each time after a heavy defeat. He made useful connections with powerful men, be they Cyrus or Greek oligarchs, who helped him assemble a large navy and later to maintain regional control. He took good care of his men, including foreign friends, officers (see his wish to settle them in Sestos), troops, and rowers. His tactics and use of surprise, which successfully exploited the enemy's deficiencies, resembled these of the general Demosthenes, and Lysander also shared some of Pericles' good qualities. Both Lysander and Pericles carefully prepared their men for battle, kept them well disciplined, and made sensible, cautious decisions about when to avoid and confront the enemy. They successfully commanded land and naval operations separately and in coordination. Yet Lysander was the better judge of psychology, both the enemy's and his own men's. He was also much luckier in benefitting from circumstances outside his control, such as Athenian and Persian internal politics and mistakes made by the enemy. Finally, Lysander was a better strategist than Pericles, because his preference for deciding the war in a major battle proved more effective than Pericles' way of defeating the enemy through physical and mental attrition.

---

65. Significantly, one source claims that Pausanias made a deal so as not to be surrounded by the enemy, as the Spartans had been at Thermopylae and Pylos: Pausanias, 3.5.5. Pausanias' trial: see note 61 above.
66. Lysander's grave: Plut. *Lysander* 29 (Phocis); Pausanias 9.33.1; cf. 3.5.5 (Haliartus).
67. Plut. *Comparison of Lysander and Sulla* 1.

Yet Lysander was also responsible for significant failures. His deficient military intelligence at Haliartus was uncharacteristic, but it led to his death and to the abortion of the Boeotian campaign. More significantly, the system of alliances he created for the Spartan rule in Greece proved unstable if not harmful, and had to be dismantled. Its failure appears to be connected with Lysander's view of relationships between individuals or states as based primarily on their relative power. Good allies and friends were those who were dependent on or subordinate to Lysander and Sparta. Athens could stay in the Spartan fold because the military power that had defeated it could be redeployed to keep it there. Force, intimidation, cruelty, and deception were justified means for attaining and maintaining a dominant position for Lysander and the state. Conversely, he fawned on Cyrus, and yielded when confronted with higher royal authority, even though he was "the first of the first men" at the time. There seems to have been something of the authoritarian personality in Lysander, a tendency to oppress inferiors and defer to his superiors. However unattractive such an attitude may seem to us, his career shows that it was compatible with good generalship.

CHAPTER 6

Dionysius I of Syracuse

The Evolution of a General

Dionysius' Syracuse and His Military Challenges

The tyrant Dionysius I, the Elder, of Syracuse (to distinguish him from his son and successor, Dionysius II, the Younger) lived c. 430–376, and was a man of strong build with blond or red hair and freckles. He is often depicted as cruel, manipulative, paranoid, and murderous in his treatment of family, citizens, and foes.[1] The following story illustrates his terrifying image.

> For (the historian) Timaeus relates in his sixteenth book that a certain woman of Himera (Sicily) saw herself in a dream coming into heaven and being led by someone to look upon the abodes of the gods. And there she saw Zeus sitting upon his throne, beneath which some ruddy, great man was bound by chain and collar. She asked the one leading him who he was, and he said, "He is the scourge of Sicily and Italy, and if he is released, he will destroy the lands." Arising from sleep a little while later she came upon the tyrant Dionysius with his spear-bearers. And looking upon him she shrieked, as this man was the scourge revealed then (in the dream).... And after three months the girl was no longer seen, having been done away with secretly by Dionysius.[2]

---

1. For the ancient sources on Dionysius, see the Bibliography, "The Main Ancient Sources," s.vv. "Diodorus of Sicily" and "Polyaenus," as well as Pearson 1987, esp. 19–30; Sanders 1987; Stylianou 1998, *passim* (favoring Ephorus as Diodorus' source).
2. Timaeus *BNJ* 566 F 29, Champion trans., slightly modified, and see the commentary there for additional versions. For the speculation that Dionysius presented himself as

This tale of dubious historicity tells only part of the story at best, for the hostile traditions surrounding Dionysius' name cannot easily be reconciled with his acts of kindness, long reign, and many accomplishments, especially in war. To be sure, his military record was not perfect, but in many ways Dionysius combines many of the merits of the Greek generals discussed in this book, some of whom he seems to have carefully studied. It is unfortunate, then, that his imprint on the Greek art of command is insufficiently recognized, probably because he operated in Sicily and southern Italy, whose history is often treated by Greek historians as peripheral to that of the Greek mainland.[3]

Syracuse, Dionysius' birthplace, was one of the larger cities in the ancient Greek world (Map 12, p. 173 above). Founded by Corinth around 734, it comprised an island, Ortygia, and the mainland town opposite it, which was connected to the island by a mole. The city had two harbors, the Small and the Great, and its wealth came largely from trade within and outside the island as well as agriculture. During the Archaic and Classical ages, Syracuse often pursued an expansionist policy, which brought it into conflict with local Sicels and other Greeks on the island. It also rivaled Greek and Etruscans cities in Italy, as well as Carthage, which dominated western Sicily (pp. 21–22 above). In contrast to fellow Greeks in the old country, the Syracusans often destroyed the cities they defeated and forcibly transplanted their populations, but they also granted generous enfranchisements. Syracuse's government was at first aristocratic, then democratic, then ruled by a prolonged tyranny of the Deinomenid family, and then (after the Deinomenids' fall in 466) democratic again. Thus, when Dionysius attained sole power in 406–405, the city had had a long experience of political changes, internal and external conflicts, and imperial growth and contraction.[4]

After Carthage's devastating defeat by the Syracusan ruler Gelon in the battle of Himera in 480, the Carthaginians long kept their involvement in Sicilian affairs to a minimum, renewing their military campaigns and expansion only around 409. By that time, they exerted a varying degree of control

the scourge of Carthage, and that his critics turned this image into that of a Greek bane, see Lewis 2000, 101; Prag 2010, 63–64. Dionysius' lifespan: Stylianou 1998, 476–477.

3. On Dionysius, see Stroheker 1958; Sanders 1987 (mostly on the ancient sources); Caven 1990; J. Champion 2010, 129–221; and various articles in Bonacasa et al. 2002.

4. Ancient Syracuse and Sicily: Drörgmüller 1969; Sjöqvist 1973; Asheri 1992; Lewis 1994; Evans 2009.

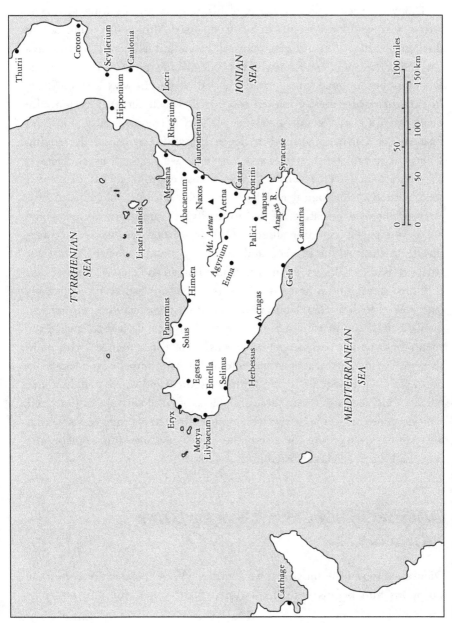

MAP 14 Ancient Sicily and Southern Italy.

over western Sicily, roughly to Panormus in the north and Selinus in the south. Syracuse's dominion extended intermittently to Mount Aetna in the northeast (Map 14).[5]

Dionysius spent the better part of his 38-year rule fighting Carthage, Greek cities, and local peoples in Sicily and Italy. Although it is not easy to distinguish among his military, political, and administrative activities, this chapter focuses on his performance as a general and strategist. In these roles, Dionysius encountered some formidable challenges. His wars with Carthage in particular were mostly uneven contests in which the enemy enjoyed a quantitative and at times qualitative superiority in troops, cavalry, ships, and finance. The Carthaginians also besieged and raided Syracuse, challenging Dionysius to provide that large city with effective land and naval defenses. These were massive, expensive, labor-intensive projects that demanded sophisticated technological and logistical solutions. When going to war, often on his own initiative, he had to justify his campaigns both at home and to foreigners, including allies. He led large armies and navies that were diverse in their ethnic makeup and in the types and proficiencies of their troops. His undertakings required sufficient human and material capital, and skillful allocation of military assignments. Dionysius had also to adjust his land warfare to different seasons, terrains, and settings, including open fields, fortified sites, and urban space. On several occasions, he had to engage the enemy both on land and sea simultaneously. He also contended with more than one conflict or threat at a time, finding himself compelled to make risky decisions about how to divide his limited resources and where to fight. Since not all of his campaigns were successful, he had to deal with the military and political consequences of defeat, which could threaten his rule. Nevertheless, his record of overcoming these and other problems makes him arguably the best of all the generals discussed in this volume.

Dionysius' Early Career Up to the Battle of Gela (405)

Dionysius, son of Hermocritus, was born c. 430, and the controversy that surrounds him begins with his ancestry. Sources describe him either as

---

5. Carthage: Huss 1992; Lancel 1995. Carthage and Sicily: Manni et al. 1982–1983; Tusa 1988; Asheri 1992, 157. Carthaginian army and navy: Introduction, pp. 21–22, 23. Carthage and Dionysius: Miccichè 2008 (up to 392), and the works cited in his 122n11.

the scion of a respected family or as a man of an undistinguished origins who started his career as a lowly scribe. Like Themistocles, he may have belonged to the ruling class but not to its top ranks. His first taste of war probably came in his teens, when the Athenians tried and failed to capture Syracuse in 415–413, but nothing is known about his role then. His first recorded military experience was in 406 at Acragas (Agrigentum) during the so-called First Carthaginian War (407–405). The Carthaginians had renewed their large-scale military operations in the island in 409. They put Acragas in western Sicily under siege in 406, and Syracuse came to its rescue with large infantry and cavalry forces. In spite of an initial victory and their subsequent harassment of the enemy with their cavalry, the Syracusans were unable to save Acragas. Dionysius is said to have shown exceptional courage in the campaign, although it is unknown under what circumstances. Personal valor would also characterize him later as a commander of troops.[6]

Dionysius rose to power in 406–405, but his ascendance tells nothing about his style of command as distinct from his artful politics. He charged his fellow generals with corruption and treason, accusations that found fertile ground in the Syracusans' expectation of a Carthaginian attack and disappointment with the city's military leadership. Dionysius was elected as supreme general (*strategos autokrator*), which perhaps remained his official title throughout his reign. Now and later, he used the conflict with Carthage to justify his rule, presenting himself as the only man who could win it. Among his first measures was to double the payment of the mercenaries, who had shown that their loyalty depended on timely payment, and to increase their numbers with additional men and exiles. To secure the city of Leontini, north of Syracuse, he called on Syracusans under forty years old to muster there, each with thirty days' provisions. The city was a Syracusan outpost full of political exiles and non-Syracusans, and lay potentially on Carthage's warpath. At home, Dionysius obtained a bodyguard of 600–1,000 men, whom he selected and armed, and appointed his own officers to the Syracusan armed forces. One source presents these and similar actions as designed to create a

---

6. Dionysius' respectable background: Cicero *Tusculan Disputations* 5.20.58; cf. 5.63; cf. Diod. 14.8.5. Undistinguished origins: Isocrates 5.65; Demosthenes 20.162; Diod. 13.96.4 (secretary); Polyaenus 5.2.2 (secretary to generals); Ambaglio 2008, 165; cf. Stroheker 1958, 37. The First Carthaginian War: Diod., 13.43.1–44.6, 54.1–62.6, 80.1–96.5, 114.1–3; Caven 1990, 45–77; Anello 2008, 81–84. Dionysius' courage: Diod. 13.92.1. It is unknown whether he fought in western Sicily in 408 with the exiled oligarch Hermocrates, whose daughter he later married: Diod. 13.63.1–6, 75.1–9.

personal cadre loyal to Dionysius and his tyranny. He was certainly looking to strengthen his position, but all his measures also made good military sense in preparation for a campaign against Carthage. His army would fight a very large and well-financed force, and Dionysius needed all the men, provisions, and good will he could get.[7]

Indeed, the Carthaginians had done very well up to this point. Under their aging general, Hannibal (an ancestor of his more famous name-sake), and his co-commander Himilco, they had destroyed Himera in the north and Selinus in the south, and had later captured Acragas in spite of substantial Syracusan help and even an initial defeat (above). In 406, Carthage reinforced its invading army with 120,000 infantry and cavalry (according to one account), or 300,000 men (according to another). Both figures appear inflated; modern estimates reduce the size of the entire force to 60,000, and that of the army that soon marched on Gela to 45,000. The sources report the origins of the new recruits, but not their capacities. Their use elsewhere suggests that the mercenaries from the Balearic Islands excelled as slingers, and those from Iberia served as infantrymen, while recruits and allies from North Africa joined the infantry and the cavalry. Carthage also sent 1,000 transport ships and ninety triremes, fifteen of which were destroyed by a Syracusan navy at the start of the invasion.[8]

(1) Around the spring of 405, a Carthaginian army led by Himilco (now in sole command after Hannibal's death) marched to southern Sicily against Gela, a close ally of Syracuse. Gela was built on a ridge near the shore. It was bounded to the east by the River Gela, whose outlet to the sea served the city's port, and by a fertile plain and the Gattano River (modern name) to its west. It appears that the Carthaginians arrived without their ships, whose absence, perhaps due to the lack of a safe anchorage, proved costly later. Historian Diodorus suggests that Himilco and his army set up camp on the river Gela, but this location cannot be reconciled with the movements and actions of Dionysius' forces in their later attack, which makes a site on

---

7. Diod. 13.95.1–96.2, 112.1–2; Anello 2008, 91; cf. Ambaglio 2008, 196. Date of Dionysius' assuming power: C. Champion, *BNJ* 556 F 110, commentary. His title: Stylianou 1998, 477–478.
8. Capture of Acragas: Diod. 13.80.5–81.3, 85.1–90.7. Carthaginian forces: Diod. 13.80.1–5, citing Timaeus for 120,000 men, and Ephorus, who usually gives higher numbers, for 300,000; cf. Xen. *Hell.* 1.5.21 (but see note 10 below); Caven 1990, 46; DeVoto 2000, 15n8. Naval reinforcements and battle: Diod. 13.80.5–7; Xen., *Hellenica* 1.5.37, mentioning 120 triremes, but the text is problematic: Krentz 1989, 108–110.

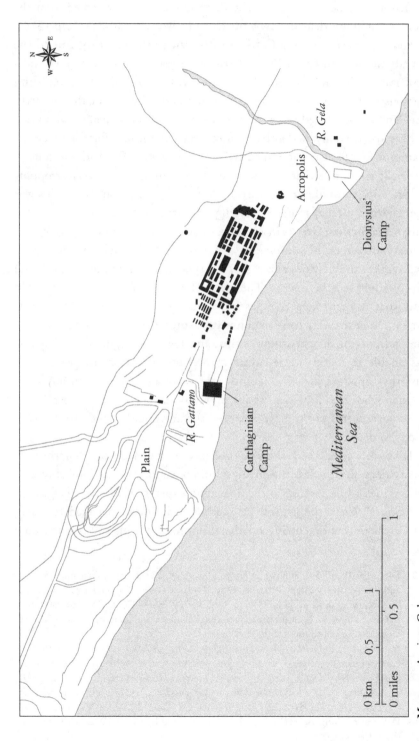

Map 15 Ancient Gela.

the River Gattano more likely. The Carthaginian camp stretched from the sea inland and was defended by a trench and a wooden palisade (Map 15).[9]

Soon after arriving, the Carthaginians raided the territory around the city all the way to Camarina and tried to breach the western city walls with rams. The Gelans defended themselves successfully by rebuilding portions of the wall and by attacking marauding units in the countryside. Their hopes of salvation rested, however, on the arrival of Dionysius and his army. Dionysius probably now presented himself as an all-Greek champion against the common Carthaginian enemy, if he had not done so earlier. It was a role that he continued to foreground, sincerely or opportunistically, throughout his career. When he arrived at Gela—he was later charged, perhaps unjustly, with procrastination—his army included Italian and Sicilian Greeks in addition to Syracusan recruits and his mercenaries. Altogether, he commanded 50,000 or 30,000 infantrymen, 1,000 cavalrymen, and fifty *cataphract* ships, a type of vessel whose top deck and screens sheltered the rowers. The year before he took power, a Syracusan army that went to help Acragas included 30,000 soldiers, 5,000 cavalrymen, and thirty triremes. Dionysius' army, if 30,000 strong, had the same number of infantry, more ships, and fewer cavalrymen. Perhaps he was unable to recruit more cavalrymen, who came from the well-to-do class that opposed him and would later rebel against him. In any case, the man who cried foul against the previous leaders of the war, especially in Acragas, seems not to have enlarged the army, and would also lead his troops to defeat.[10]

Dionysius camped by the sea, probably near Gela's port. For the first twenty days, he attacked the enemy's lines of supply, having probably gotten the idea while serving in the Syracusan expedition to save Acragas the year before. There the general Daphnaeus had almost managed to starve the Carthaginians by cutting off their supplies with his cavalry, and only

---

9. Diod. 13.108. 1–5, 110.3. Gela: Longo 2002, 224–227. Carthaginian ships' absence and the location of camp: Stroheker 1958, 46; Caven 1990, 59–60; DeVoto 2000, 15. The following description is closer to Stroheker 1958, 44–47, and DeVoto 2000, than to Caven 1990, 63–73, whose interpretation includes many conjectures and minimizes Dionysius' responsibility for the defeat.

10. Initial fighting at Gela: Diod. 13.108.5–9. Xen., *Hellenica* 1.5.21, claims that the Carthaginian siege lasted seven months, but the text is problematic and probably interpolated; cf. Krentz 1989, 108–110. Dionysius' pan-Hellenism: e.g. Sordi, 1992, 33–49; Prag 2010, 61–63. Dionysius' force: Diod. 13.109.1–2 (citing Timaeus for the lower estimate). Syracusan army in Acragas: Diod. 13.86.5; DeVoto 2000, 17. Delay in reaching Gela: Diod. 13.122.2, exonerated by Caven 1990, 62. Cataphract ships: Casson 1991, 90.

a Carthaginian seizure of Syracusan ships carrying provisions to Acragas reversed the situation, eventually leading to the evacuation of the city by its residents. Dionysius also sent out light-armed troops, cavalry, and ships to disrupt the Carthaginian lines of supplies by land and sea. The tactic carried little risk, but it also failed to achieve the success of Daphnaeus or to move the enemy to ease its pressure on Gela.[11] Dionysius then opted for a frontal attack on the Carthaginian camp that resembled the tactics of the Athenian general Demosthenes in its originality, ambition, and execution—and which failed for much the same reasons as Demosthenes'. Dionysius devised no fewer than four simultaneous prong attacks (Map 15, p. 233 above). Diodorus reports that he divided his infantry into three divisions: he told one, made up of Sicilian Greeks, to march to the enemy camp keeping the city to its left; the second, made up of Italian Greeks, was to go there along the shore with the city on their right. He was to take a mercenary group through the city towards where the Carthaginian siege engines were. His cavalry was to cross the River Gattano and overrun the plain, joining the fighting if successful or shelter battle refuges in case of a loss. His marines aboard the ships were to attack the camp as soon as the Italian Greeks (his second column) launched theirs.[12]

Dionysius could not or would not meet the Carthaginians in a pitched battle, because of his smaller force and his preference for other modes of combat, which we shall see again later. His plan aimed to overcome three main challenges: the enemy' superiority in numbers, its occupation of a well-protected camp, and the presence of additional enemy forces around Gela's walls. Accordingly, he split his army into four separate attacking units, in the hope that by keeping the Carthaginians busy in different places, he would create confusion and reduce Himilco's ability to send aid where it was needed. He also believed that a Syracusan victory in one place would have a rolling effect elsewhere because the victorious troops could join the fighting where it was successful, undecided, or difficult. It was an ambitious plan that showed a readiness to take risks and an urgent need to win.

The most problematical aspect of Dionysius' plan was its dependence on successful synchronization and coordination of the different units. These included hoplites, light infantry, cavalry, and marines, who were

---

11. Fighting over supplies at Acragas: Diod. 13.88.1–8, 92.1. Dionysius and supplies: Diod. 13.109.2–3; J. Champion 2010, 169.
12. Diod. 13.108.4–5. Caven 1990, 63, followed by Kern 1999, 173, attributes Dionysius' change of plan to frontal attack to pressure on him to fight from his troops, but no such pressure is attested.

spread over different locations. The plan's originality lay in dividing rather than concentrating his power. It called for assigning separate key missions to seconds in command, whom the sources leave anonymous, and on whose success Dionysius relied for victory. A multi-pronged attack also meant that he had to give up direct control of the entire battle. Instead, he settled for leading his mercenaries through the city in a surprise attack on the Carthaginian siege engines, probably near the western walls and gate. It was arguably the least difficult assignment in the plan.

At first, success smiled on the attackers. The Syracusan ships charged the unprotected part of the enemy camp on the beach and landed marines and probably other crewmembers. Himilco must now have sorely regretted his lack of ships to oppose the landing. The Carthaginians rushed to meet the disembarking soldiers, weakening the camp's line of defense and allowing the contingent of Italian Greeks, who must have hurried their march along the shoreline, to overcome the depleted enemy forces and enter the southern part of the camp. It was a short-lived victory, however, because the Carthaginians had enough soldiers of high quality to recover quickly. Himilco sent a large force led by Iberian and Campanian troops against the Italian Greeks, who were now pressed between a trench in front of the camp and an acute angle of the palisade. There was no help in sight. The Syracusans who had disembarked from the ships could not join them, probably because the enemy did not allow it. (Their hold on the beach was precarious anyway.) The Sicilian Greeks, who marched behind or on the ridge of Gela to the right of the city and into the plain, did well against their Libyan opponents and penetrated the northern part of the camp. They were even joined by many Gelans, and Dionysius' cavalry surely helped the effort by engaging enemy forces on the plain. Yet even these units could not come to the rescue of the Italian Greeks, because they arrived at their destination late and were busy fighting their opponents. Dionysius could provide no assistance either. He got stuck in the streets of Gela (he should have known better, having been there before), and even if he completed the mission of destroying the Carthaginian siege engines, it was too late to do anything else. Some of the Gelans tried to help the Italian Greeks, but, fearing for their walls, they would not venture beyond them. One thousand Italian Greeks fell, and the rest fled to the city under the protection of arrows that the ships' crews shot at their pursuers. Their escape freed the Campanians, Iberians, and other enemy combatants to return and help the Libyans against the Sicilian Greeks, who also retreated to Gela, after losing

600 men. The Syracusan cavalry, whose role was auxiliary to begin with, also fled to the city for shelter.[13]

The defeat was not heavy or even inevitable. Yet it took a great deal of youthful daring and optimism to assume that a coordinated attack of four separate forces could succeed despite the delicacy of their interdependence. A win at one point could not be sustained without a decisive victory at, and help from, another, and the whole scheme required, not just simultaneous attacks and good communication, but also an enemy who would become flustered and despondent. None of this happened. Dionysius underestimated the Carthaginians' ability to recover from a setback and to use reserves effectively (as they did earlier in 409 in a campaign against Himera). An anecdote related to the earlier battle of Acragas is illuminating. It tells how the Syracusan general Daphnaeus on the right wing of his phalanx heard a commotion on his left wing where the Italian Greeks were fighting. He hurried there, saw them losing, and ran back to the Syracusans on the right to tell them falsely that the Italians were winning. The message energized his soldiers, who went on to defeat the enemy. Even if the story is suspect, it highlights the importance of commander's presence at the scene of the fighting. But Dionysius was stuck in town.[14]

The defeat decided Gela's fate. As much as the Gelans (and even Dionysius, who could ill afford failing in his first lead command) may have wished to offer another battle, the unanimous opinion in his war council was that he should retreat. He organized a mass evacuation of the city by night, under a ruse designed to convince the enemy that he was still in the city. The trick was probably superfluous, because the Carthaginians must have been happy to take and despoil Gela without a fight. Ancient and modern critics have argued that Dionysius should have offered a more stubborn resistance and that he erred in evacuating Gela and then Camarina, whose people he told to move to Syracuse. But the later desertion of his Italian Greek allies suggests the defeat undermined his authority over the coalition army that he needed for a fight over both cities. Besides, Syracuse with its walls, army, and navy offered a better chance of withstanding the Carthaginian offensive.[15]

13. Diod. 13.110.1–7; Philistus *BNJ* 556 F 58. Dionysius' earlier visit to Gela: Diod. 13.93.1–5.
14. Daphnaeus in Acragas: Polyaenus 5.7.
15. Evacuating Gela: Diod. 13.111.1–2. Complaints against Dionysius: Diod. 13.112.2; 14.66.4. Wrong to leave Gela and Camarina: Diod. 13.112.2; DeVoto 2000, 20; cf. Lewis 1994, 134. The Italian Greeks left Dionysius at an uncertain date: Diod. 13.112.3.

Dionysius' defeat and the unpopular evacuations of Gela and Camarina encouraged members of the Syracusan cavalry to rebel against him. They burst into his house and gang-raped his wife, who subsequently killed herself. Dionysius rushed back to the city and, with the help of his bodyguard and mercenaries, put down the revolt ruthlessly. What saved him and Syracuse, however, was a recurrent plague in the Carthaginians' camp, which killed half their men. Cutting his losses, Himilco signed a peace treaty with Dionysius that confirmed Carthaginian control over western Sicily, allowed refugees from the cities Carthage had conquered to return as autonomous but tribute-paying residents, and arranged for the exchange of prisoners and captured ships. Dionysius was recognized, at least *de facto*, as the ruler of Syracuse. For some contemporary observers, the treaty begot or confirmed the idea that he used Carthage and the fear of it to become the lord of Syracuse and later of Sicily.[16]

The Buildup of Syracuse's Power

In spite of the peace with Carthage, Dionysius' hold on power was uncertain and his reputation at a low point. It must also have hurt this proud and very competitive man to live under the cloud of defeat. Yet historian Diodorus is at least partly wrong in attributing Dionysius' fortification of the island of Ortygia at Syracuse in 404 to his insecurity and desire to build a personal shelter for himself. Since neither Dionysius nor the Carthaginians could be trusted with keeping the peace, the fortification anticipated a siege and provided protection to many more people than just Dionysius and his group of friends and mercenaries. In essence, Dionysius converted Ortygia into a fortress island. He surrounded it with walls that included towers at close intervals and a second line of defense in the form of a fortified citadel. The latter site enclosed what was known as the Small Harbor, which provided anchorage for sixty triremes, with an entrance for only one ship at a time. Readers who recall Themistocles' and Pericles' fortification of the Piraeus or Pericles' difficulties in the war with Samos may appreciate Dionysius' preparations for an amphibious attack on the city.[17]

Dionysius also rewarded his friends and officers with choice lands, distributed land and homes to the people, and enfranchised others. But his acts of

16. Diod. 13.111.1–114.2; Plut. *Dion* 3. See Lewis 1994, 135, on the treaty, and Caven 1990, 74–75, for the parties' considerations of signing it.
17. Diod. 14.7.2–3, 8.5; Caven 1990, 78; Evans 2009, 25 (offering alternative interpretations of Diodorus).

patronage and generosity failed to gain him universal loyalty. When he went on a campaign against independent Sicels at inland Herbessus, the army rebelled, and he had to lift the siege. I shall avoid discussing the details of the failed revolt because it tells us little about Dionysius' generalship. He did not even take part in the battle that saved his rule, between the rebels and 1,200 mounted Campanian mercenaries whom he had allured with much money to desert Carthage and fight for him. But the revolt revealed aspects of his leadership that recurred later in his career. He was able to retain the loyalty of many of his commanders (though of fewer mercenaries), and he refused to give up even in very dire straits. When he finally left his shelter in Ortygia to confront the rebels, he timed the attack to when they were divided, and he used tactical deceptions and showed proficiency in urban warfare. Finally, he exercised leniency toward the defeated and toward political exiles, as he would do later when it suited him.[18]

(3)

After consolidating his power at home, and with the peace with Carthage holding, Dionysius could afford to go to war against some of Syracuse's old enemies. These campaigns, which probably lasted from 403 to 401–400, took place mostly in the eastern part of the island so as not to alarm Carthage in the west. At first, he marched inland to Aetna, a fortified refuge of Syracusan political exiles that he had weakened the year before by allowing some of them to return home. He took it now with ease. He then turned south to Leontini, which also harbored opposition to him. He hoped to scare the city into submission by displaying his army in battle formation, but the locals, who saw that he did not have siege engines, were unimpressed and stayed behind the walls. Dionysius settled for raiding their land, and learned the lesson that he had to use a more credible threat.

(4)

From Leontini, Dionysius marched to Sicel Enna in central Sicily. Here he hoped the local tyrant would betray the town, but when the ruler did not stick to their agreement, Dionysius encouraged the people to rebel against him. Just as he did with the Syracusan rebels, he then attacked the city when it was divided. With his light-armed soldiers, he rushed in through an unguarded place, seized the tyrant, and handed him over to the people. He did not occupy the city or destroy it, and Diodorus is probably right to suggest that he hoped thus to encourage trust and good will towards him in other places. Indeed, after failing to capture another Sicel town, he took Catana, which was delivered to him by a local general. He did no more than disarm the citizens and garrison the city, probably to avoid scaring off another collaborator, the general Procles of Naxos, with whom he had negotiated the

strategic

18. The mutiny against Dionysius: Diod. 14.7.4–9.9.

betrayal of his city. There are two versions on how he acquired Naxos. [One] makes Procles solely responsible for Dionysius' capture of the city, but [the other] credits it to Dionysius' ploy. The general approached the city with 7,000 soldiers, expecting its betrayal, but the Naxians were ready for him on the walls. He threatened to kill them all if they did not capitulate, and at the same time ordered one of his fifty triremes to enter Naxos' harbor with pipers pretending to signal time for many more ships. The frightened Naxians expected an attack by land and sea, and remembering Dionysius' threat, they surrendered. The two versions can be reconciled on the supposition that Procles helped to persuade his people to give up after Dionysius' stratagem. Undoubtedly, Dionysius' leniency toward Catana helped to assuage their fear. His coordinated movements on land and sea against Naxos were also reminiscent of his attack on the Carthaginian camp at Gela. Once he had Naxos, however, he treated it and then Catana in a way that resembled the Carthaginians' treatment of the vanquished, enslaving the residents and plundering and razing their cities—often his way of compensating his troops and gaining their favor. He similarly earned the friendship of local Sicels and of his Campanian mercenaries, giving them Naxian lands and Catana, respectively, as their new homes. He then returned to Leontini and besieged the city, this time with siege engines. When he offered the citizens the option of surrendering and moving to Syracuse, they accepted his terms, because he now had the capability to breach their walls, and because his terror tactics at Naxos and Catana had worked.[19]

The campaigns in eastern Sicily demonstrated Dionysius' versatility as a commander. He deployed a large army and smaller specialized units, and used carrots and sticks in dealing with his opponents. He both confronted the enemy directly and encouraged internal division before attacking it, using trickery and fifth columns. He also showed a persistence that treated setbacks as an incentive to try again or elsewhere. His treatment of the defeated could be lenient or very harsh, depending on the threat they posed to him and his city. In this flexibility, in his trickery, in his partnership with local leaders, and in his cruelty, he resembled Lysander and his methods of establishing a Spartan empire. Unlike Lysander's, however, his settlements tended to last longer. The result was that he extended Syracusan rule over a vast territory in southeastern Sicily. He also strengthened the army's loyalty to him through

19. Dionysius' campaigns: Diod. 14.14.1–15.4, 68.3. Chronology: Caven 1990, 84. Dionysius and Procles: Diod. 14.15.2. Stratagem in Naxos: Polyaenus 5.2.2. Moving people to Syracuse in this case and others also strengthened Dionysius' personal base in the city: cf. Zahrnt 1997.

an impressive winning record and substantial rewards. Many of the campaigns were self-financed through raiding and booty, and the city of Syracuse also benefited from the influx of war revenues and new residents.

In 399, Dionysius made peace with Messina (Messana) and Rhegium on both sides of the Straits of Messina after they failed to mount a joint attack on Syracuse. Uncharacteristically, he did not try to take advantage of their internal divisions in order to confront them. He probably thought that such a move would reunite them, and he had a greater objective in mind: a war against Carthage.[20]

Preparations for the Second Carthaginian War (397–392)

Dionysius' successful campaign against Syracuse's neighbors made him confident that he could drive the Carthaginians out of Sicily and become its lord. Carthage's dominion in Sicily provided his enemies and subjects with a shelter and even an alternative to his rule, and the competitor in him wanted to emulate a former Syracusan tyrant, Gelon, who had ruled most of the island after his victory over the Carthaginians in the Battle of Himera in 480.

In Gela and its aftermath, Dionysius had learned firsthand the harmful consequences of Carthaginian superiority in manpower and material resources. He tried to level the field by increasing his army and navy and by introducing new and improved instruments of war. Like Pericles before the Peloponnesian War, he must have believed that he had sufficient wealth to carry on the war through taxation, loans, and booty, and that he could replenish his resources with victories and raids. Unlike Pericles, he hoped to win, not by wearing down the enemy, but by defeating him on land and sea.[21]

But first he had to improve the city's defenses against a possible enemy attack. Syracuse was already walled and the island of Ortygia well protected, yet the Athenian invasion of 415–413 (pp. 173–180 above) proved that the natural barrier of Epipolae, a plateau west of the city, could be used to wall off the city and attack it. Sometime in 401–399, Dionysius fortified the Epipolae to deprive the enemy of this option and to provide shelter for war refugees. He

20. Messina and Rhegium: Diod. 14.40.1–7.
21. Diod. 14.18.1, 41.1; Lewis 1994, 141–142. Dionysius' revenues: Stroheker 1958, 161–162; Caven 1990, 163–166, and see p. 245 below.

first built a northern wall from the sea to the Euryalus Pass, and from there a southern wall to and around Neapolis and Achradina (see Map 12, p. 173). A fort at Euryalus was possibly built around 398–397.

Diodorus' description of the construction of the wall around the northern Epipolae shows Dionysius' excellent organizational and motivational skills, qualities less pronounced in the other commanders discussed in this book. He reportedly recruited 60,000 workmen from the country and divided them into groups of 200. Each unit was supervised by a mason and assigned to building a wall section roughly 30 meters long. Master builders were in charge of larger sections comprising six such segments. Building material was quarried and carted by thousands of men and animals. To motivate the builders, Dionysius awarded prizes for speedy construction. His hands-on approach was particularly effective: he and his friends spent all day with the workers, building their good will and enthusiasm by

FIGURE 14 *The Euryalus Gate, Syracuse*. The Euryalus fort controlled the way to Epipolae from the north. Its complex structure included ditches connected by underground passages, towers, walls that were originally 15 meters high, and water storage areas. The fort underwent constructions and modifications, which make it difficult to establish how it looked in Dionysius' time.
© *Getty Images, DEA/G. Dagli Orti.*

solving problems on the spot and helping out. (The Greeks looked down on manual labor, and the historian Diodorus thought Dionysius demeaned himself and his office by working with the builders.) We shall see that he would also share his soldiers' hardships while on campaign. Moreover, he turned the building of the walls into a communal project, replacing fear of punishment with rewards and camaraderie as means of control. Clearly, he had matured as a leader. The result was that it took the workers only twenty days to complete roughly 5.4 kilometers of a fairly high wall, including many towers.[22]

Dionysius used similar methods to manufacture large quantities of weapons. He actively recruited and generously paid expert craftsmen in and outside Sicily to produce arms. He also effectively divided the labor among workers and their supervisors, increased productivity through rivalry, and boosted the workers' morale and self-esteem by mingling with them, even inviting them to dinner. They responded with an impressive reported output of 140,000 shields, swords, and helmets, along with 14,000 sets of body armor for the cavalrymen, infantry commanders, and Dionysius' mercenary bodyguards. This plethora of arms enabled Dionysius to draft those who could not afford them and to replace lost and damaged weapons. In addition to men from Syracuse, he enlisted mercenaries in Sicily, Italy, and Greece, including Sparta. He even made sure that soldiers fought with the type of weapons they were used to. The variety of weapons with their corresponding ethnic units could be used to confound the enemy, and provided Dionysius with a variety of skills to choose from. In fear of uprisings, however, he did not allow citizens to keep their arms, but distributed them before battle and collected them afterward.[23]

Dionysius' organizational efficiency, employment of experts and his encouragement of competition among them produced innovations. Although the claim that Dionysius' men invented the catapult has been challenged, I subscribe to the view that he introduced it to the Greek world. The catapult was a hand-held crossbow capable of shooting arrows and other missiles with more power and from a greater distance than a regular composite bow (Figure 15). On first seeing a dart shot from a Syracusan weapon, probably a catapult, a Spartan king reportedly exclaimed that this was the end of

(handwritten margin note: assemble his Army (now TRAD))

---

22. Diod. 14.18.1–6, 45.1; 15.13.5; Stroheker 1958, 62–65; Garlan 1974, 185–189; Caven 1990, 88–91, 234; Kern 1999, 174–176; Mertens 2002. Later fortifications make it hard to uncover Dionysius' walls. Evans, 2009, 129, questions Dionysius' building of a fort at Euryalus.
23. Diod. 14.41.2–42.1, 43.1–3, 44.1–2, 45.5; Polyaenus 5.2.14; Kern 1999, 175–176.

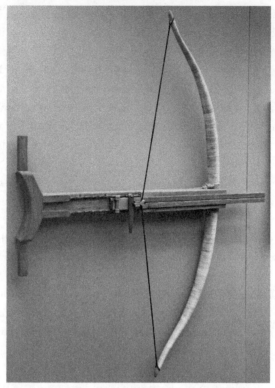

FIGURE 15 *A modern reconstruction of an early catapult.* The *gastraphetes* ("belly bow") was probably the earliest type of catapult, and the one used by Dionysius' men.

manly valor. For traditionalist Spartans, real courage belonged to hoplites fighting at close range, not to far-shooting archers. Yet the Spartan lament was misplaced. The catapult could do a lot of damage, but it could not decide battles.[24]

If Diodorus is to be believed, Dionysius was also responsible for the introduction of two types of battleships to Greek naval warfare: the "four" or *quadrireme* and the "five" or *quinquereme*. The quadrireme probably had two levels of more than 200 rowers on both sides of the ship, with two men pulling each oar. The quinquereme had two to three levels of about 300 rowers, with two men per oar on the upper levels and one rower per oar on the bottom. Both ships were bigger, steadier, and sturdier than

24. Catapult: Diod. 14.42.1, 43.3 (invented in Syracuse); Philo of Byzantium, *Construction of Catapults,* 56.14. Its history: Campbell 2003, 3–8; Cuomo 2007, 41–50; Rihll 2007, 26–45. Catapult and courage: Plut. *Moralia* 219a.

the trireme, and thus had an advantage in ramming power, especially frontally. They had a larger upper deck that allowed for more marines, possibly around ninety, who could grapple and board an enemy ship. The high deck also facilitated the use of projectiles, including catapults. Dionysius' organization of the shipbuilding was as exemplary as his other preparations. He sent woodcutters to Mount Aetna in Sicily and to Italy to fell fir and pine trees. Other teams were detailed to cart them to vessels already waiting for the cargo. At home he built 200 ships, re-equipped 110 existing ones, and built and repaired ship sheds in the Great Harbor that could more than accommodate his expanded fleet. Half of the rowers, pilots, and officers were from Syracuse, and the others were mercenaries.[25]

Dionysius' use of experts and his promotion of new military technology distinguished him from most contemporary Greek war leaders, who did not sufficiently recognize the potential of innovative technology and of the men who could develop it. Dionysius was more practical and much less set in his ways, if only because he needed new weapons and ships to compensate for his inferiority to Carthage in forces and resources. None of his innovations really changed the face of war or guaranteed victory, although they surely gave him an advantage in battle. In addition, the fortification of Syracuse, the mass manufacturing of weapons, the hiring of craftsmen and mercenaries, and the new inventions must have drained his treasury, and the sources provide undated tales about his repeatedly looking for new taxes and ways of cheating his subjects out of their money.[26]

Going to war against Carthage exposed Dionysius to threats from closer neighbors in Sicily and Italy, which he tried to neutralize through alliances. In 399, he secured peace with Messina and Rhegium (p. 241 above) and in 398–397, he strengthened his alliance with Messina by giving it a large territory on its border. Rhegium refused a closer tie by rejecting his request to marry a woman from the city. Instead, he took an aristocratic wife from his old ally to the east of Rhegium, the Locri Epizepherii, who could conceivably check Rhegium if it turned hostile. He also married Andromache, the daughter of Hipparinus, a close ally from Syracuse. The latter marriage

---

25. New ships: Diod. 14.41.3 (accepting the emendation from *triereis* [triremes] to *tetrereis* [quadriremes]), 42.2–5, 43.4. Their description here is a compromise among the views of Morrison 1990; Morrison and Coates 1996, 1–3, 268–271, 285; De Souza 2007, 357–360; and Murray 2012, 23–29.
26. Aristotle, *Economics* 2.1349a–1350a; and note 21 above.

probably endeared him to local patriots, and his bigamy (unusual among the Greeks) marked his special status.[27]

It was time now to declare war on Carthage. Both at home and abroad, even in Carthage, Dionysius presented his aggression as a campaign for Greek freedom against a barbarian enslaver. This characterization gave Syracuse, other Sicilian Greeks, and even the Sicels a common cause, and legitimized attacks on other communities that refused to join him. Dionysius also argued that the war was winnable because the Carthaginians were weakened by a plague. He whetted the Syracusans' and other Greeks' appetite for war by allowing them to start looting at home, giving them license to abuse resident Carthaginians in their cities and to pillage their possessions. Diodorus describes these pogroms as retribution for the Carthaginians' past cruelty to the Greeks, but they also validated hatred, xenophobia, and greed. Dionysius was surely encouraging the men who were about to serve in his army to expect more such incentives in the future.[28]

The Siege of Motya

In 397, Dionysius led his army toward the island of Motya, an important Carthaginian outpost in western Sicily. Along the way, he enlarged his army with troops from the Greek cities of Camarina, Gela, Acragas, Selinus, and perhaps Himera. The sources say that he led more than 3,000 cavalrymen and 80,000 infantry, figures which, if credible, must have included many mercenaries and light-armed soldiers. By now, Dionysius was one of the biggest employers of mercenaries in the Greek world, and their professionalism had an effect on his army. About 200 warships and 500 other vessels transporting war engines and supplies joined him at his new base near Motya. His first victory was bloodless. The size of his army and the absence of Carthaginian opposition convinced the city of Eryx, north of Motya, that it must join him. He then turned his full attention to Motya.[29]

27. Land grant to Messina: Diod. 14.44.3–4. Marriages: Diod. 14.44.3–8, 45.3; Plut. *Dion* 3, *Timoleon* 6 (unlikely tradition); Aelian *Historical Miscellany* 13.10; Stroheker 1958, 68; Caven 1990, 98–99; D'Angelo 2010, 41–50.
28. Dionysius' "national war:" Diod. 14.45.1–46.5, 47.2–3.
29. Diod. 14.47.4–7. Date (397): Caven 1990, 96; Lewis 1994, 142n94, but also Stroheker 1958, 70 (398). Caven 1990, 100, allows Dionysius only 40,000 infantrymen, on the basis of his smaller armies before and after Motya, but the circumstances then were different. Dionysius and mercenaries: Parke 1933, 63–71; Trundle 2004, 6–7, 45, 127–130.

246 | THE CLASSICAL ART OF COMMAND

MAP 16 Motya.

The tiny island of Motya, now S. Pantaleo, was located in a shallow lagoon about 6.5 kilometers long and about 3 kilometers at its widest (Map 16). The lagoon was bounded at its north and west by a peninsula, now the island of Aegithallus (Isola Grande or Lunga), and by the Sicilian shore to the east, with a southern exit to the sea, about 1.5 kilometers at its widest. Motya was surrounded by walls, in part as thick as 5.2 meters, dotted by towers. In preparation for the siege, the Motyans broke a causeway that connected the city's fortified north gate to a necropolis on the Sicilian shore, lest Dionysius use it. Motya's mixed population included Carthaginians and Greeks whose loyalty to Carthage was unshakable. Diodorus believed that their loyalties moved Dionysius to make them his first target, intending to destroy Motya in order to deter others from opposing him. There must have been additional reasons. Motya's wealth was a tempting prize, and Dionysius' large army and navy could easily surround the city and isolate it from outside help.[30]

30. Motya and its fortifications: Diod. 14.48.1–2, 49.3, 53.2–4; Whitaker 1921; Isserlin et al. 1974; Ciasca 1995; Holloway 2000, 141–142.

Dionysius instructed his troops to build a mole to the island and beached his ships in preparation for a prolonged, methodical siege. Our sources' unclearness about the exact locations of the mole, of Dionysius' camp, and of his ships complicates the reconstruction of events. A likely site for the camp of the large army was on the Sicilian shore, next to the necropolis and the broken causeway, which must have invited its restoration as a mole. Less certain is the whereabouts of Dionysius' beached warships. The sources locate them in relation to the "harbor" and its "entrance," but these terms can be variously interpreted, and the accounts of later events in both locations are not easily compatible. It has been reasonably suggested that Dionysius beached his warships around the northern part of the lagoon, needing their crews to build the mole and to conduct a campaign in the region. Beaching them also prevented the vessels from becoming waterlogged, and Dionysius seems mistakenly not to have expected the Carthaginians to arrive as soon as they did. His merchant ships anchored along a "beach," probably south of the lagoon and on the shore of the Bay of Lilybaeum. Dionysius then left his brother Leptines in charge of local operations and took his infantry to replace the Carthaginian hegemony in western Sicily. Most of the Sicel Sicani in the region joined him out of fear of his army or resentment of Carthage. Others offered resistance, and Dionysius raided their countryside, leaving forces to besiege inland Segesta and Entella. He then returned to Motya.[31]

The Carthaginians in the meantime made preparations to rescue Motya. Led by Himilco, Dionysius' old opponent, they recruited European mercenaries and even dispatched a small fleet of ten Carthaginian triremes, which sailed into Syracuse's Great Harbor by night and sank most of the ships anchored there. One source suggests that the goal was to ease the pressure on Motya and entice Dionysius to return home or to send forces back there. The naval intervention was also intended to demoralize the Syracusans. We are not told how many warships were lost, but the operation must have dealt a psychological blow to a city that the tyrant had made feel safe with his new fortifications and armament. Dionysius did not react, trusting Syracuse to sustain an even larger attack before he would have to come to its rescue.[32]

Himilco continued to score points in the contest of resourcefulness. He sailed by night with 100 triremes, first to Selinus and then to Lilybaeum,

---

31. Ships' location: Diod. 14.47.3–5, 51.3–4; Polyaenus 5.2.6; Whitaker 1921, 80–84; and below. Campaign inland: Diod. 14.48.4–5.
32. Diod. 14.49.1–3. Carthage's mobilization: Diod. 14.47.3, 54.4–5.

south of Motya. His military intelligence was far superior to Dionysius', who was now caught by surprise for the second time. Himilco, in contrast, knew the exact location of Dionysius' carriers and his 200 warships, which were beached in the northern lagoon. With his ships on land, Dionysius' naval superiority in number and size meant nothing when attacked by surprise, and Himilco hoped to do to the Syracusans what the smaller Carthaginian squadron had done to the ships in Syracuse's harbor. First, however, he rammed and burned an unreported number of Dionysius' merchant ships outside the lagoon, while the tyrant watched helplessly from the shore. The loss undermined the logistics of Dionysius' siege and reduced his ability to send men and equipment back to Syracuse if necessary. The Carthaginian general then entered the lagoon and arrayed his ships for battle, probably around the island of Motya, which provided him with land support. To protect his ships—both beached and in the water—Dionysius marched his infantry to the peninsula (Map 16, p.247: Aegithallus Island) so as to shoot at the enemy. But he had lost control over the lagoon and its exit, and needed to get his fleet out to the open sea. For this purpose, he used his advantage in manpower and engineering to haul the ships overland. The idea may have been inspired by the *diolkos* of Corinth, Syracuse' mother city, where ships and other loads were carried overland from the Saronic to the Corinthian Gulf. The topography around the Motya lagoon allowed such portaging: we are told that the (probably northern) side of the peninsula was flat and muddy. Dionysius constructed a wooden path on which men and animals reportedly wheeled eighty triremes to the sea. Himilco turned to meet Dionysius' first ships, which probably sailed around the exit into the lagoon before others joined them in closing him in. He was stopped by slingers and archers that Dionysius put on deck, as well as troops on land using catapults. Fearing being trapped in the harbor or losing to Dionysius' larger fleet on the open sea, Himilco sailed home. It is likely that Dionysius did not try to stop him.[33]

Thus Dionysius extracted himself from a difficult situation for which he bore full responsibility: the Carthaginian attack, apart from its timing, should not have come as a surprise. To his credit, however, he won the conflict, which was more about outmaneuvering than real battle. Thanks to a combination of brawn and brains, he made good use of his civil and military

33. Diod. 14.50.1–4; Polyaenus 5.2.6; Whitaker 1921, 75–91. Polyaenus claims that the ships were dragged over 20 *stades*, or 3.6 kilometers, but this is unlikely, and if the reconstruction suggested here is accepted, unnecessary: see Caven 1990, 103, *contra* Whitaker 1921, 81–83. The Diolkos and what it took to carry a trireme on land: Raepsaet and Tolley 1993; cf. Pettegrew 2011.

technology and massive manpower, and he effectively coordinated land and maritime forces. Himilco's leaving Motya in the lurch allowed him to focus his undivided attention on the siege.

The siege's lifeline was the mole that enabled troops and war engines to attack Motya's walls. In 332, when Alexander put the island of Tyre in Lebanon under siege, the besieged defenders used fire, boats, ships, and divers to obstruct the building of the mole. Dionysius was fortunate in the Motyans' failure to employ any of these means of interfering with his construction. He probably used the original causeway for the mole, which was about 1,500 meters long and more than 10 meters wide. Once it was completed, Dionysius brought in rams to destroy the city's walls, probably at their northern section, as well as catapults and wheeled siege towers. (There is archaeological evidence for the dismantling and removal of a block of stones from the walls.) Siege towers that offered platforms for shooting projectiles were not new to Sicily: in 409, the Carthaginian general Hannibal had used them in the siege of Selinus. In Motya, the towers showed how much the fighting depended on establishing an advantage or equality in height. The towers were six stories high, as tall as many Motyan buildings, and thus allowed Dionysius' archers, slingers, and other projectile throwers to shoot at the defenders (many arrows were found on the site). The Motyans countered by reaching for even greater heights through crow's nests attached to high masts, from which they rained fire on the siege engines. The Sicilian Greeks quickly extinguished the fire, probably thanks to prior training.[34]

Even when the walls were finally breached, the Motyans did not give up. They expected nothing better than death or slavery, and prepared a second line of defense made of the outer houses' walls and blocked alleys. The contest over who controlled the high positions continued. The defenders enjoyed the advantage of shooting missiles from tall houses, and Dionysius tried to dislodge them by bringing his towers close. His engineers devised bridges, which his troops used to reach the enemy positions, but the devices became death traps that constrained the movements and numbers of the attackers, allowing the resolute Motyans to kill them in hand-to-hand combat or throw them down to their death. After few days of futile attacks, Dionysius came up with a stratagem that may have been inspired by the Spartan general

---

34. Fighting over the walls: Diod. 14.51.1–3. Alexander, Tyre, and Motya: Whitaker 1921, 77n2; Sanders 1987, 48; Bosworth 1988, 65–76. Mole's size: Whitaker 1921, 84, 132. Siege towers in Selinus: Diod. 13.55.2–6, 55.3; and their inspiring Dionysius: Winter 1971, 314–316; and see also Garlan 1974, 163; Kern 1999, 51–52, 181–182; Campbell 2005, 26–28. Extinguishing the fire: Garlan 1974, 177–178.

Lysander. Since his rise to power, Dionysius had maintained excellent relations and communications with Sparta, and an admittedly uncertain tradition suggests that Lysander visited him, perhaps around the end of the fifth century. In any case, by the time of the siege, Lysander's stratagem at Aegospotami (405; pp. 202–204 above) must have been well known. Before that engagement, the Spartan commander arrayed his ships for battle daily but took no action for several days, accustoming the Athenian navy to think he would not attack them. Then he charged after they disembarked from their ships. Dionysius similarly got his troops and the enemy used to stopping the fighting in the evening, whenever the trumpet blew. One night, after both sides had retired, he sent forth an officer with picked soldiers, who used ladders to seize a commanding position in the city. With the line of defense thus breached, Dionysius could send in many soldiers.

The fighting turned now into mass slaughter and plunder. Dionysius' troops rushed from the camp over the mole and joined the fighting, killing anyone in sight. Dionysius was dismayed to see the death of so many potential slaves, but was unable to control his soldiers. He offered the survivors sanctuary in temples (inviolate to the Greeks), so that he could sell them later. He did not stop the plunder, however, because he couldn't and/or wouldn't: it was a form of payment for the soldiers that created expectations of similar rewards in the future. After the looters had had their fill, he recognized brave soldiers with public honors and paid tribute to the official Greek crusade by executing Greeks who fought on the enemy's side. Before returning to Syracuse, he made arrangements to defend his new acquisition. He left in Motya a Sicel garrison led by a Syracusan officer to prevent its reoccupation by Carthage. He also gave his brother Leptines 120 ships to stop an expected Carthaginian armada from reaching Sicily, and instructed him to continue the siege of neighboring Segesta and Entella.[35]

At Motya, Dionysius displayed skills that are recognizable from his past. He used his organizational capabilities and expertly applied war technology to the construction of the mole, the portaging of ships over land, and the operation of siege instruments. He effectively deployed light-armed soldiers and their weapons on land and sea. He also astutely picked Sicilian Greeks, who were highly motivated to fight the hated Carthaginians, for

success attack

35. Lysander's visit and contacts with Dionysius: Plut. *Lysander* 2; *Moralia* 229a; Hamilton 1979, 96–97; but Sansone 1981 doubts their historicity. Winning the siege: Diod. 14.51.4–53.5, 54.4. Greek opposition to Dionysius in Motya: Diod. 14.51.3–7, 52.3–7, 52.7–53.2.

dangerous missions such as protecting the towers or fighting on the gangways. Dionysius showed that he could get out of difficult situations by outwitting the enemy both in the lagoon and on the island. Despite these achievements, the fighting in Motya does not fully justify historians' praise of Dionysius for creating a "modern army." He achieved his final victory thanks, not to war technology, but to a ploy that used traditional infantrymen. There were also preventable failures. Himilco's attack revealed that Dionysius' military intelligence was deficient and that he too confidently exposed his ships to danger. The sack of Motya suggests an inability to control his soldiers. Finally, the Carthaginians' recapture of Motya in the following year showed that Dionysius was more a marauder than a conqueror, in spite of his well-deserved victory.[36]

Besieged in Syracuse

In the spring of 396, Dionysius plundered defenseless Carthaginian territory in Sicily while Himilco was preparing a larger expedition to the island. The reported numbers of the Carthaginian invaders are staggering and probably exaggerated: between 130,000 and 300,000 infantrymen, 4,000 cavalrymen, 400 chariots (whose deployment is never described), 400 warships, and 600 other ships that might also have been used in battle. A modern estimate cuts the troops' number to around 80,000. On his way to Sicily, Himilco outwitted Dionysius once again. With moderate losses of fifty ships, probably transports, his fleet evaded the fleet of Dionysius (or his brother Leptines) and made it to friendly Panormus in northwestern Sicily. The Carthaginian general wasted no time in regaining Eryx, Dionysius' first conquest the year before, and then Motya. Dionysius, who was besieging Segesta in western Sicily at the time, decided to return home. He suffered from short supplies, and the local Sicels could not be trusted. His control of territories in western Sicily and even in other regions was generally shaky because the Sicels remained loyal only as long as he stayed in their land and the Carthaginians were away from it.[37]

36. Dionysius' "new army": Stroheker 1958, 76; Caven 1990, 84. Carthage's recapture of Motya: Diod. 14.55.4. The island recovered from the destruction, but not fully: Famà 2008, 52–54.
37. The Carthaginian expedition: Diod. 14.54.5 (citing Timaeus and Ephorus, respectively); Caven 1990, 107; Stylianou 1998, 73–75. Fighting in western Sicily: Diod. 14.55.1–7; Polyaenus 5.2.9, 10.2. For Himilco's speculative route: Caven 1990, 107–108.

Himilco's strategy was to dismantle Dionysius' Sicilian rule and system of alliances before confronting the tyrant directly. His invading force moved on land and sea along the northern shore of the island, capturing cities and fortresses along the way, including the big prize, the city of Messina. Its occupation gave Himilco a harbor for his large fleet and enabled him to intercept maritime aid and reinforcements to Syracuse from Italy and Greece (in this, he was only partially successful). He then razed Messina because he did not think that he could trust it as an ally and safely use it as an outpost. Its destruction was also a warning to those who contemplated opposing him on his march to Syracuse.

Dionysius, the aggressor the year before, now adopted a defensive strategy. He dared not march to help his northern allies for fear of exposing Syracuse to a Carthaginian surprise attack. Instead he went around the countryside and the eastern Sicilian coast, preparing fortified sites for a siege and moving grain and people to them. The idea was to delay Himilco's advance, harass his army, and provide food reserves for Syracuse. But it seems that fear of the Carthaginians had severely depleted Dionysius' pool of local recruits. Neighboring Sicels deserted him, and, in what looks like an act of near desperation, he freed slaves to man sixty ships. He also requested 1,000 mercenaries from Sparta, probably to strengthen his hoplite contingent. A comparison with the army he took to Motya the year before suggests the decline in his fortunes. Then he had led 80,000 infantrymen, but now he prepared to meet Himilco with "just" 30,000 soldiers. His other forces were less affected. He had the same number of cavalrymen, 3,000, and the 200 warships he took to Motya were now reduced to 180, including a limited number of triremes.[38]

Himilco's next major destination was Catana, which had been evacuated by its inhabitants for a better shelter at Aetna. The Carthaginian general planned to reunite there with his fleet, led by the admiral Mago, but his march was delayed by a recent eruption of Mount Aetna, and other obstacles. The temporary separation of the Carthaginian navy and army weakened them, and Dionysius liked his enemy to be under such constraints. He rushed towards Catana with his army to take possession of the coast before Himilco arrived there, and instructed his brother Leptines to attack Mago

38. Himilco to Messina: Diod. 14.56.1–57.6, 58.3–4. Dionysius' defensive measures: Diod. 14.58.1–2; cf. Caven 1990, 111; Kern 1999, 184. Polyaenus' claim (5.2.9) that Dionysius instructed the men at the forts to surrender in order to force Himilco to deplete his army by garrisoning them is an unconvincing attempt to turn mere capitulation into a stratagem. Dionysius' forces in Motya and the year after: Diod. 14.47.6, 58.1–2; Stroheker 1958, 76; Caven 1990, 111.

with the Syracusan fleet. By occupying the shore, Dionysius hoped to deprive the enemy of a land base or shelter and generally to demoralize him. He was also providing a refuge for his own ships and their crews if defeated.

I shall not discuss the ensuing naval battle, which ended in a heavy Syracusan loss of more than 100 ships and of 20,000 men. Dionysius played no direct role in the defeat, and, according to Diodorus, it was all Leptines' fault. He reportedly ignored Dionysius' battle plan of retaining a compact line of ships and instead rushed against the larger enemy fleet with only thirty vessels. It is an open question whether this version of events is wholly or partially accurate or a product of later recriminations. Dionysius should not be faulted for not leading the charge in person, since he might have fared no better than Leptines. It is worth noting, however, that even though his fleet probably included the newly introduced quadriremes and quinqueremes (pp. 244–245 above), they failed against the better Carthaginian crewmen and their ships. Himilco even towed damaged ships to his base at Catana, repaired them, and added them to his fleet. In the end, regardless of who was responsible for the defeat, it became part of Dionysius' record.[39]

After a war council—and it was to Dionysius' credit that he often made decisions after hearing a variety of opinions—he marched back to Syracuse. That was his safest option, but it also meant giving up on trying to offset the defeat with a land battle, and abandoning his allies between Catana and Syracuse. Many of them switched sides, though not those who had given him hostages and their best units. Dionysius' concern was to get to Syracuse before Himilco's fleet. Upon his return, he requested Greek aid and mercenaries from Italy and Sparta and waited for the invaders.[40]

Himilco carefully staged his arrival in Syracuse, aiming to awe the city with the size of his expedition. Like Demosthenes coming to help the Athenians at Syracuse in 414 (p. 176 above), Himilco made a spectacle of his coming. Two hundred and fifty Carthaginian warships entered the Great Harbor, rowing in unison and decorated with the spoils of their recent victory at Catana. They were joined by a few hundred merchant ships, and it is reported that the sails of the vessels concealed the view of the harbor. As if this were not terrifying enough, the Carthaginian army of reportedly 300,000 soldiers (or

39. Himilco's and Dionysius' marches to Catana: Diod. 14.59.1–7; cf. Polyaenus 5.2.9. The naval battle: Diod. 14.59.7–60.7, 66.4; Freeman 1891–1894, 4:113; Caven 1990, 112–113.

40. Diod. 14.61.1–3, 62.1. Dionysius would later be accused of missing an opportunity to attack the enemy ships that were beached for two days because of a storm, but the criticism is biased on hindsight: Diod. 14.60.4, 68.6–7.

perhaps only a third of this number) and 3,000 cavalrymen marched into Syracuse's territory. The enemy camped about 2 kilometers away from the city, south of the River Anapos, where the Athenians had established their camp in 415. Himilco sacrilegiously converted the Olympeium, a temple of Zeus Urios, into his headquarters, and then offered land and naval battle. But there were no takers. For thirty days, he ravaged the countryside, reducing supplies to the city, depressing the morale of its residents, and rewarding his soldiers. The looting campaign was extended to temples and tombs, and Diodorus regards their desecration as the cause of a plague that visited the invaders later. In addition, Himilco set up a fort on the southern shore of the harbor at Plemmyrium, another at mid-shore, probably around Dascon, and a third on elevated Polichne, next to his headquarters (Map 12, p. 173). The two forts along the shore controlled traffic in and out of the harbor, and all three served as storage depots.

Winter was approaching, and Himilco arranged for a food supply to come from Libya and Sardinia in preparation for a long stay. It appears that he was looking for surrender or betrayal, because during the siege he made no attempt to breach the walls. At one time, he raided the Achradina quarter of Syracuse, probably in a seaborne attack, but overall Dionysius' fortification of the city before the invasion paid off. Dionysius' conservative strategy also made Himilco give up on enticing the Syracusans into a land or sea battle. After the disaster at Catana and the Carthaginians' previous gains, the tyrant could ill afford another defeat. He limited his engagements to (successful) skirmishes, and when he ventured out it was primarily to protect the maritime import of food to the city. A point of light was the arrival of the Spartan Pharacidas (possibly a mistake for "Pharax") with thirty warships, probably in the spring of 395, bringing an unknown number of mercenaries from the Peloponnese and Italy. After Catana, with his fleet reduced to around eighty ships and many of his local allies gone, Dionysius could use all the help he could get.[41]

Paradoxically, Dionysius nearly lost his power because of a Syracusan victory. While he was away protecting supply ships, a small naval skirmish

<hr>

41. Diod. 16.61.1–63.4, 70.5. Polyaenus 2.11; 5.8 (on a victory of Syracusan cavalry over a Carthaginian raiding party around Cape Pachynum in southeastern Sicily). Diodorus' text on the numbers of Himilco's ships (250) is corrupt; 14.62.2; cf. 14.54.5, 56.1, 59.7; Stylianou 1998, 73–75. Himilco's camp, the Olympeium, and its environs: Stroheker 1958, 208–209, n. 92; Dover in Gomme et al. (1945–1981), 4:478–484; Evans 2009, 37–38, 72–78. Pharax for Pharacidas: Beloch 1879, 124. Carthaginian forts: Evans 2009, 33. For the chronology of the siege, see Freeman 1891–1894, 4:123–125.

in the harbor evolved into a naval battle in which the Carthaginians were defeated and lost twenty-five ships. It was not a victory that could win the war, but when Dionysius returned home and convened a popular assembly, a cavalryman named Theodorus contrasted Dionysius' earlier defeats with the recent win and called on the people to depose him. But Dionysius had neutralized alternatives to his rule through cooption, executions, and exile. Furthermore, the Spartan Pharacidas, admiral of the Greek reinforcements, declined the offer to "free" the citizens and supported Dionysius instead. The tyrant later mollified the people with gifts, honors, and banquets.[42]

The threat to Dionysius' rule probably contributed to his change of strategy in the summer of 395. No longer waiting the enemy out and trying to avoid defeat, he now went on the offensive. Conditions were favorable because a plague of uncertain nature had spread through the enemy camp, but not to Syracuse.[43] It is claimed that 150,000 people died from the disease, and although the number is probably inflated, the plague must have impaired the enemy's military capability and morale. Dionysius now conceived his most ambitious plan of attack so far. It was based on surprise, and it recalls the battle at Gela in more than one respect.

As at Gela, the enemy's camp was secured by a palisade, a wall, and a river, here Anapus, that together with marshes along the coast added to its defense. (Unlike at Gela, however, a Carthaginian fleet anchored nearby.) Also as at Gela, Dionysius intended to surprise, confuse, and divide the enemy through separate but coordinated attacks. But this time, the movements were not interdependent, and Dionysius himself led the main attack and probably supervised others. His brother Leptines and the Spartan Pharacidas were sent with eighty ships to Dascon to attack the enemy ships at dawn. On land, Dionysius planned to charge the Carthaginians in more than one spot. First, he made an effort to avoid detection by picking a moonless night for the march and taking a circuitous route. He led his army (probably from the Euryalus Gate) and moved west and south, bypassing the Cyane temple (about two kilometers west of the Olympeium), until he arrived south of the enemy camp. He then split his force into three groups. A party of 1,000 mercenaries and a cavalry unit went to the western, inland end of the camp. Diodorus claims that Dionysius intentionally sent the mercenaries to their death because of their rebellious nature, and that he ordered the cavalry to

---

42. Diod. 16.64.1–70.3. None of the problems that Caven (1990, 116) finds with the Theodorus episode are critical enough to justify its rejection.
43. The plague: Diod. 14.76.2. Littman (1984) identifies it as smallpox, but a variant of typhoid is also possible, and perhaps both: Stroheker 1958, 210n98; Sanders 1987, 171nn96–97.

flee when the fighting commenced. This appears to be a hostile depiction of what was a diversionary tactic: having been blamed for failing to win the war, Dionysius is unlikely to have planned another defeat. He himself charged and captured the Carthaginian fort at Polichne that gave its occupier a strategic advantage in height. At the same time, his cavalry rode to Dascon, which in antiquity may have been closer to Olympeium than it is today. Their mission was to take the fort there and assist in the naval attack on the enemy ships. The multiple charges, aided by ineffective Carthaginian command, achieved the desired effect of confounding and splitting the enemy. It troops hurried in spontaneous, disorganized manner in an attempt to defend first the camp and the fort, and then the ships and their anchorage. Indeed, the ships were the Carthaginians' lifeline.

Caught unprepared at Dascon, the Carthaginians had to man the ships and fight at the same time, thus allowing the Greek ships to ram them repeatedly and their marines to board the decks of the disabled vessels and kill their crews. The sounds of the crashes and sight of the floating corpses must have thrown the Carthaginians into despair. Dionysius rushed in on horseback with his infantry and found forty beached penteconters (fifty-oared ships) and an uncertain number of triremes and merchant ships at anchor. He set the beached ships on fire, and the wind carried the flames to the anchored boats. Other ships whose anchor ropes caught fire collided with each other in the rough waters and strong wind. In the battle of Salamis, Themistocles had timed his attack on the enemy ships to coincide with the blowing of the wind, and it is permissible to think that Dionysius, too, planned the burning of the ships with the wind in mind. Soon the fighting was joined by men from the city, who were too young or too old for service but who now desired to share in the victory and the loot. Either spontaneously (so Diodorus) or answering Dionysius' call, they manned ships in the Small Harbor and sailed to despoil damaged enemy ships, towing intact ones to the city. Diodorus' description of the battle as seen from the city walls rises up in vividness with the flames:

> For from a distance the sight resembled a battle with the gods, such a number of ships going up in fire, the flames leaping aloft among the sails, the Greeks applauding every success with great shouting, and the barbarians in their consternation at the disaster keeping up a great uproar and confused crying.[44]

---

44. Dionysius' route: Evans 2009, 37. The battle: Diod. 14.72.1–73.5. Quotation: Diod. 14.74.1. Themistocles and the wind: p. 89 above.

It was Dionysius' greatest victory, and he won it deservedly, making excellent use of surprise and his knowledge of the terrain, and coordinating the
attacks by land and sea—no small feat, because it involved the simultaneous
deployment of infantry, cavalry, and ships. It is to his credit that his failure
at Gela did not deter him from a complicated plan of attack, but also that
he revised his earlier tactics in order to keep a victory or defeat in one sector
from influencing another. He managed the battle effectively, rendered aid
when it was required, and resourcefully effected the destruction of the enemy
ships. In all of this, he was helped by Himilco's decline in effectiveness since
Gela, perhaps attributable to the plague, but no less plausibly to the routine
of a relatively uneventful siege. Finally, Dionysius involved the entire citizen
body in the fighting, intentionally or not, making his victory a communal
achievement—as well as a personal triumph for a man who, after Catana,
needed to prove his prowess and winnability.

After his defeat, Himilco chose to beat a retreat home and ended the
campaign discreditably. He entered into secret negotiations with Dionysius,
offering 300 talents in return for safe evacuation of the invaders to Africa.
Dionysius refused to allow the entire army go but agreed that Carthaginian
citizens could leave unharmed. A deal was struck, and Dionysius took his
army back to the city.

Diodorus, or his source, claims that Dionysius followed the wishes
of the Syracusans and their allies in refusing to let the entire enemy
army go. The historian also alleges that Dionysius gave safe-conduct to
Himilco and the Carthaginians in order to keep the fear of Carthage alive,
thereby justifying his oppression of freedom at home. This hostile interpretation apparently originated in the opposition to Dionysius. It is more
likely that Dionysius, like the Athenian general Demosthenes in western
Greece, exploited Himilco's despair to weaken his army further and to
undermine Carthage's reputation in Sicily and even Africa. After his victory at Olpae in 426, Demosthenes had made a deal with the commander
of the defeated coalition army, secretly allowing only the Spartans and
their Peloponnesian allies a safe retreat. He had thus deprived the enemy
of its leadership and damaged the Spartans' credibility in the region (p.
151 above). Dionysius, who may have known about this episode, aimed
for similar results and obtained them. Himilco fled with forty triremes,
although Dionysius' Corinthian allies, uninformed of the deal, chased
him and sank vessels that lagged behind. On land, Himilco's local Greeks
allies fled home safely, but many of the Sicels were captured in ambushes
that Dionysius had set in advance. This plan, too, resembles Demosthenes'
use of ambushes to capture and eliminate men who fled the battle of

Idomene in western Greece. Other enemy soldiers surrendered, including Iberians who joined Dionysius' mercenaries. Rather than being upset with Dionysius for letting remnant Carthaginians escape, as Diodorus suggests, the Syracusans must have been grateful to him for the victory and for their profit from capturing prisoners of war and looting the enemy camp. As for Himilco, Diodorus recounts his punishment for sacrilege and hubris (but not treachery): the admiral is said to have walked around Carthage dressed in rags and full of self-recriminations until he starved himself to death.[45]

[handwritten margin notes: "won ch2 over" and "Brut. skilled challeng"]

Campaigns in Southern Italy (ca. 396–383)

During the next decade or so, Dionysius' military campaigns were directed chiefly against the Carthaginians in Sicily and the Greek cities in southern Italy, especially Rhegium (Map 14, p. 229 above). The sources claim that the tyrant wished to incorporate the Italian Greeks into his rule, yet it is uncertain if this was his ambition all along, or if the idea evolved over time. In general, he dealt with the Carthaginian threat first, and turned to Italy only when he felt secure in Sicily. Even in Italy, he seems to have been much occupied with safeguarding the Straits of Messina in order to protect Syracuse. After all, Himilco had invaded Syracuse from that direction. As often happened, his intervention in one place led to another elsewhere, and Dionysius had to increase his military involvement and stabilize his dominance in southern Italy. His means of control in Sicily and Italy included resettlements, garrisons, and making allies.[46]

In the following account, we shall not dwell on each of Dionysius' military engagements, but only on those that illuminate his art of command. Depending on the circumstances, he showed a fondness for surprise and deception, but also exercised tactical caution.

With Carthaginian fortunes temporarily at an ebb, Dionysius used colonization and alliances to consolidate his power in eastern and central Sicily, with varied success. The most significant of these moves was the

---

45. Himilco's deal with Dionysius: Diod. 14.75.1–9. Dionysius and Demosthenes: cf. Lewis 1994, 144, with n. 104. A large group of Dionysius' mercenaries, however, were unhappy with their remuneration and got Leontini from him as settlement: Diod. 14.78.1–3; and cf. Polyaenus 5.2.11; Champion 2010, 199. Himilco's death: Diod. 14.76.1–4.
46. Dionysius in Italy and the Straits: Sabattini 1986; Caven 1990, 136; Lewis 1994, 141, 144.

repopulation of Messina (destroyed by Himilco) and the installation of a mercenary garrison there. The Rhegians on the opposing mainland rightly suspected hostile intentions, since their city stood in Dionysius' way to control of the Straits, and he bore them a personal grudge. Rhegium had a history of opposing him, had sheltered Syracusans he exiled, was an enemy of his friends and its neighbors the Locrians, and had insulted him in 397 by offering him the daughter of an executioner when he sought a wife from their city. Dionysius left it in peace for a time, but after a failed Rhegian attack on Messina in 394, he tried to capture Tauromenium near Naxos, a post that would have strengthened his control of the Sicilian northeastern coast. We have described in the Introduction his failure to take the fortified city on a cold winter's night (pp. 5–6 above). Apparently his success in catching Himilco off guard near Syracuse had given him the confidence to try this tactic again at Tauromenium. His failure was exacerbated by the consequent exile of his friends from Messina and Acragas, but in 392, this commander who loathed giving up returned to Tauromenium and captured it.[47]

The Carthaginians' defeat at Syracuse did not stop them from renewing the war with Dionysius, and in 393, Mago, Himilco's former admiral, returned in force to the island. His campaign was cut short by the tyrant, who defeated him and killed 800 of his men in a battle near Abacaenum in northeastern Sicily. No other details of this event are known, but *if* it was a pitched battle, it would have been a first for Dionysius. The victory freed him to go against well-fortified Rhegium in Italy, which he hoped to capture by his trademark diversion and surprise. Arriving at night with a fleet of 100 triremes, he set the city gates on fire and tried to mount the walls at the same time. A group of Rhegians rushed to put down the fire, until Heloris, Dionysius' adopted father and now an exile and his bitter foe, warned them that they might save the gates but lose the city, because Dionysius could easily overcome their small number. The Rhegians then made the fire bigger, preventing Dionysius from entering the city and buying themselves time to organize a stronger defense. The attack failed, and Dionysius, who seemed unready or unwilling to put the city under siege, ravaged the countryside

---

47. Dionysius after Himilco's invasion and Messina: Diod. 14.78.4–7. Dionysius and Rhegium: Diod. 14.44.3–6, 107.3–4; Caven 1990, 131–132. Banishing his supporters from Acragas and Messina: Diod. 14.88.5. Messina came back later to Dionysius: Diod. 14.103.2. Caven 1990, 127–128, 131, ties Polyaenus 5.2.18 (on Dionysius' stirring up civil strife in Messina) to the city's change of policies, but an earlier context in 396 (Diod. 14.40.1–7) is possible too; cf. Lewis 1994, 145n108.

before making a one-year truce with the city. But the failures at Rhegium and Tauromenium did not dissuade him from making successful use of surprise later.[48]

Dionysius spent the summer of 392 meeting a new Carthaginian offensive. Mago returned with 80,000 soldiers but no navy to speak of, thus acknowledging Dionysius' naval supremacy. After drawing many of Dionysius' former Sicel allies to his side, he camped next to Agyrium in central-eastern Sicily. Dionysius drafted Syracusans and mercenaries into an army of "only" 20,000 soldiers, probably because he did not intend to decide the war on the battlefield. Instead he marched to Agyrium, which was ruled by Agyris, a powerful warlord with plenty of supplies. Agyris was an old ally, but in Sicily such loyalties could not be taken for granted. Displaying characteristic courage, Dionysius took the risk of visiting Agyris with just a small company and persuaded Agyris to renew their friendship, perhaps in the interest of fighting the common enemy. The alliance proved a very valuable asset, keeping Dionysius' army well fed while the much larger Carthaginian army suffered from a food shortage, and its foraging expeditions fell victim to Agyrian ambushes. The invaders' deteriorating conditions encouraged the Syracusans in Dionysius' army to press for battle. The tyrant resisted, knowing that an early clash would favor the enemy, whose situation was deteriorating. His inaction revived (or helped his enemies revive) the old suspicion that he wished to keep the Carthaginian danger alive in order to maintain his rule, and the angry Syracusans deserted him. Partly in order to punish them, partly out of necessity, Dionysius freed their slaves, who presumably joined his army. Then his patience paid off. Mago sued for a peace that preserved Carthaginian holdings in western Sicily but gave Dionysius the rest of the island, possibly including Selinus, Acragas, and other cities. Dionysius then returned the slaves to their owners and went to take Tauromenium, which was left in the lurch by its Carthaginian ally. Thus after a largely bloodless campaign, Dionysius won a very big reward. He did it by facing opposition from within and without and by wisely using his allies and the terrain. Moreover, he ranked self-restraint and caution over the surprise that was often an attractive tactic for a smaller army facing a larger one. From the inexperienced, daring leader of his youth he had grown into an expert, judicious general.[49]

48. Dionysius and Mago: Diod. 14.90.1–4. Attack on Rhegium: Diod. 14.90.4–7.
49. Agyris' alliance: 14.9.2, 78.7. The campaign: Diod. 14.95.1–96.5. Tauromenium: Diod. 14.96.4. For the peace terms, see Stylianou 1998, 206–227.

The peace with Carthage enabled Dionysius to campaign in southern Italy. He would attain dominion there through a combination of conquests, acts of friendship, and reliance on local allies.

In 390, he took 20,000 infantry, 1,000 cavalrymen, and 120 warships on a campaign against Rhegium. He landed first in allied Locri and then marched to Rhegium, where he punished the city and rewarded his soldiers by devastating its countryside. Yet Rhegium had strong allies, a circumstance that partly explains the large size of his army and fleet. According to Diodorus' chronology, by 393, the Greek cities in the region had already reacted to Dionysius' earlier attack on Rhegium by forming (or rather expanding a preexisting) mutual defensive alliance, the so-called Italiot League. They viewed Dionysius and the local Italian Lucanians as common enemies, and the city of Croton, which was their leader and the most active of them, also sheltered the largest number of Syracusan exiles. It now sent sixty ships to Rhegium's aid, and Dionysius sailed to meet them with only fifty, perhaps because his other ships were busy elsewhere. What happened next resembled in part the battle of Motya, but with the roles reversed. The Crotonian ships fled for shelter on Rhegian land, and Dionysius began towing them away. He had to give up and retreat, however, when Rhegian light-armed soldiers arrived and kept him at bay from the land with their missiles (at Motya, Dionysius had done the same to Himilco). Then a storm came, and because the Rhegians prevented Dionysius' fleet from landing, he lost seven ships and almost lost his quinquereme. One thousand five hundred of his crewmen drowned, and the Rhegians captured others who were swept to the shore. Winter was approaching, and Dionysius decided to call off the campaign. But it was not the season alone that influenced his decision. Indeed, winter had not prevented him from going on with the siege of Tauromenium. His failure at sea showed him that he could not fight both the Greek coalition and Rhegium at the same time. Before leaving, he made the Italian Lucanians his allies—wisely, as events proved.[50]

We hear next of a Lucanian raid on the territory of the Greek city of Thurii, which was a member of the League. Although Dionysius helped the Lucanians at a later stage, it is unclear if he encouraged them to initiate hostilities. The raid led to a battle between the Lucanians and the local Greeks, mostly from Thurii, that ended in a heavy defeat for the latter. At that moment, Dionysius' brother arrived on the scene with a fleet, after the

---

50. Diod. 14.91.1, 100.1–101.1, 103.4–5; Caven 1990, 133. Cf. Justin 20.1.1–4. Italiot League: Purcell 1994, 386–387. I follow Diodorus' not-undisputed chronology.

tyrant had sent him to help the Lucanians. Leptines, however, opted for local reconciliation. He treated the Greeks he captured kindly, arranged for the ransoming of other Greek prisoners of war, and then made a peace between the warring parties. Diodorus claims this conduct gained him much good will and esteem among the Greeks, but displeasure from Dionysius, who thought a local war that kept the Greeks busy could help his plan of mastering events in southern Italy. He therefore took away Leptines' command and gave it to Thearides, his younger brother. (Later, Leptines went into an exile in Thurii until he was recalled and fully reconciled with Dionysius.) But Dionysius would largely follow Leptines' conciliatory policy in his next campaign (below), and it is possible that he was angry, not just with Leptines' action, but also with his winning the Greeks' gratitude and adoration. As in Sicily, there could be only one benefactor and leader for the Greeks.[51]

In 389, Dionysius returned to Italy. He led 20,000 infantry, 3,000 cavalrymen, forty warships, and 300 transports that carried food and probably siege engines. This force was as large as the one he had commanded the year before in infantry, but smaller by eighty warships and larger by 2,000 horsemen, suggesting that, this time, his focus was on land operations. He stopped on the way at Messina, whence he sent his brother Thearides with a fleet to the Lipari Islands. Thearides came back with ten captured Rhegian ships, whose crews Dionysius put in chains. The prisoners' conditions probably contributed to the Rhegians' later decision to accede to his demands (p. 265 below). He then sailed to Caulonia on the eastern shore of the Italian "toe" and began assaulting its walls with his siege engines. We are not told why he attacked this city, but from Caulonia he could interrupt maritime traffic or aid from or to Croton, which had spoiled his last campaign. Caulonia's distance of "only" 40 kilometers or so north of his Locrian allies suggests they may have helped or even pressured Dionysius to besiege it.[52]

The Italiot League was moved to action, rightly suspecting that Dionysius would go on to attack other members after Caulonia. Once again, Croton took a leading role. Besides being the most populous city in the League, it was probably the most motivated to fight the invaders, since it hosted the largest number of Syracusan exiles and may have regarded Caulonia as its daughter colony. The Crotonians and their allies elected the

---

51. Diod. 14.101.1–102.3; 15.7.3–4. Pawnall (*BNJ* 556 T5c) argues that Leptines opposed Dionysius' aggression against the Italian Greeks.
52. Diod. 14.103.1–2. Caven 1990, 136, increases Dionysius' fleet to 70 ships. During the siege of Caulonia, 12 triremes under Aristides of Elis succeeded through a stratagem in evading Dionysius' fleet and getting in: Polyaenus 6.11.

exiled Syracusan leader Heloris to lead the coalition army. His prominent role and the presence of other Syracusan exiles in his camp broadened the conflict from a regional war to a struggle over the future of Dionysius' regime in Syracuse and Sicily. Heloris' army of 25,000 infantry and 2,000 cavalrymen marched to the river Eleporus, north of Caulonia. He planned to offer Dionysius battle there, forcing him to relax the siege and possibly exposing him to attack from Caulonia. Heloris himself and 500 of his best soldiers marched in the lead or were stationed in a vanguard position, perhaps planning an ambush or a commando strike. Yet their separation from camp proved to be their undoing, because Dionysius would catch them by surprise.[53]

Dionysius did lift the siege of Caulonia and marched with his army to a site 7 kilometers away from the enemy, where he camped for the night. It appears that the two armies were ignorant of each other until Dionysius learned from his scouts about the enemy's whereabouts. He fully exploited his intelligence advantage. He woke his soldiers at first light and was ready to attack at dawn. They surprised first Heloris and his men, who had little chance of survival, despite their quick recovery and heroics. Dionysius used his overwhelming numerical superiority to form a tight noose around their group. The surprise affected the rest of Heloris' army. Although Heloris sent men to alert his camp and many rushed to his aid, in the absence of his and others' guiding hands, they were scattered and disorganized, and thus easy prey for Dionysius' well-ordered phalanx, whose close formation was favored by the level ground. As in many other battles, the Greeks fled after hearing that their general had fallen.

Whether spontaneously or under recovered command, many of the fleeing Greeks found safety on a hill that could be easily defended. But it was summer, and they had no water, as Dionysius knew. He surrounded the hill with soldiers and waited, making sure that his guards stayed alert to prevent an escape by night. The next day, suffering from growing heat and the thirst, the Greeks proposed a ransom. Dionysius refused, demanding instead that they lay down their arms, surrender, and let him decide their fate. For a while they held on, but as in the case of his refusal to engage Mago's ill-nourished army in Sicily (p. 261 above), he knew that time was on his side. Later that day,

53. Caulonia and Croton: Dunbabin 1948, 27–28. Preparations for battle: Diod. 14.103.4–104.1. Scholars have identified the River Eleporus with the Stilaro (Walbank 1957–1979, 1:48) or Galliparo (Caven 1990, 137). Even if its identity were secure, it is unknown exactly where next to the river the armies met. For an elaborate but speculative reconstruction of the battle, see Caven 1990, 136–139; followed by Champion 2010, 205–206.

exhausted and parched, the Greeks accepted his terms. There were more than 10,000 of them and, in contrast to his brutal reputation, Dionysius' treatment of them earned Diodorus' praise as "probably the finest act of his life." ✳

He freed the prisoners without ransom, made peace with their cities, and left them autonomous. The Greeks reciprocated with gratitude and honored him with gold crowns. Dionysius' handling of the prisoners and their cities was in line with Leptines' policy of establishing supremacy through good will and patronage instead of destruction and occupation. If he opposed his brother's action before (p. 263 above), he now showed, as he did on other occasions, his ability to learn from his mistakes. His replacing Leptines in the Greeks' hearts was an added bonus. In the short run, the peace with the Greeks freed him to deal with cities that were on his immediate warpath, and in the long run it strengthened his hegemony in the Italian toe.[54]

The settlement produced immediate results. When Dionysius marched to besiege Rhegium, the city looked for a deal instead of offering resistance. The peace left it without allies, and Dionysius' harsh treatment of the captive Rhegians in Messina (p. 263 above) on one hand, and his moderate treatment of the defeated Greeks on the other, made the choice clear. Because Dionysius enjoyed unmatched superiority, he could drive a hard bargain. In return for raising the siege, he got 300 talents and the surrender of the Rhegian fleet of seventy ships, as well as 100 hostages. The historian Diodorus thinks he was aiming to weaken the city in preparation for his siege of it the next year, but that judgment looks like hindsight supported by the ruler's reputation for trickery. It is no less likely that, at this stage, a weakened Rhegium was all Dionysius needed for the security of the Straits and the isolation of his next targets.

He now returned to accept the surrender of Caulonia, which may have been following Rhegium's example and motives. But here he took harsher measures, destroying the city, giving its territory to the Locrians, and removing the residents to Syracuse, where he compensated them with local citizenship and five years' exemption from taxes. The year after, 388, he treated Hipponium on the other side of the peninsula similarly, and at an unknown but not much later date, he also gave Scylletium, a Crotonian colony north of Caulonia, to the Locrians. His settlements, as well as his undated, failed attempt to build a wall across the peninsula, suggest that he now aimed to incorporate this part of southern Italy into his realm. Indeed, around this time, young Dion, Dionysius' brother-in-law and Syracuse's future tyrant, wrote a letter to Plato describing Italy as part of Dionysius'

54. Dionysius' treatment of the Greeks: Diod. 14.104.1–105.4; cf. Polyaenus 5.3.2.

rule (*arche*). Moreover, Dionysius' treatment of conquered sites in southern Italy resembled his practice in Sicily, where he often settled conquered cities with mercenaries, exiles, or other dependent and allied groups. The wall was designed to protect the area from local Italians' incursions and especially to strengthen the Locrians, his allies, whom he tried to build up as a counter-power to the Italiot League. In that last strategy, he miscalculated: about six years later, the Locrians would join an Italian-Carthaginian coalition against him (p. 268 below).[55]

Dionysius returned to Rhegium to put it under siege in 388, after reportedly tricking it into breaking the peace with him, according to Diodorus. He first came to the Sicilian side of the Straits with land and naval forces, intending to cross the sea, and he asked the Rhegians for provisions, which he promised to replenish from Syracuse. He then extended his stay under various pretexts, causing the Rhegians to stop sending him supplies because they suspected (correctly, says Diodorus) that he wished either to justify a war against them or to deplete their resources before a siege. Dionysius' career had many examples to justify the Rhegians' conspiratorial interpretation of his conduct, but it was also true that they had first given him supplies and then refused them. Probably to show that he was acting in good faith, unlike the Rhegians, Dionysius released Rhegian hostages he had taken the year before.

In describing the siege, Diodorus focuses less on its military aspects than on the Rhegians' suffering and Dionysius' cruelty. The historian does tell us that Dionysius used huge siege engines (probably resembling those at the siege of Motya) to assault the walls daily. The Rhegians defended themselves successfully, setting the engines afire and venturing out to attack his troops. At one point, Dionysius, who had not shirked joining the fray in the past, was severely wounded in the groin by a spear. When his frontal attacks failed to produce results, he turned to a slow, methodical starvation of the city. As we have seen, waiting for a distressed enemy to give up suited his temperament as much as surprise attacks. His army and navy's control of Rhegium's perimeters forced the besieged to live on their dwindling supplies. Grain became prohibitively expensive: a bushel (*medimnos*) that cost 6 drachmas in Athens about this time was reportedly worth 500 in Rhegium. The Rhegians were reduced to eating horses and beasts of burden, then boiled skins and leather, and even the grass that grew around the walls.

---

55. Dionysius, Rhegium, Caulonia, and Hipponium: Diod. 14.106.1–107.5. Scylletium and the wall: Dion. Hal. *Roman Antiquities* 20.7.3–5; Strabo 6.1.10; Pliny, *Natural History* 3.15; Caven 1990, 136, 141–142. Dion on Dionysius in Italy: Plato *Letters* 7.327e. Securing conquered cities in Sicily: Diod. 14.15.1–4, 58.1–2, 78.5–6.

Dionysius is said to have grazed cattle at the walls to deprive the besieged even of this diet: a first use of cows as a siege weapon, if the story is true. (But didn't the Rhegians try to catch them?) Many residents died of hunger, and after eleven months, the city surrendered (387). The extent of its devastation was revealed when Dionysius was forced to make his way through piles of corpses in the streets; only 6,000 persons survived. He sent the prisoners to Syracuse, where those who could not come up with a ransom of 100 drachmas were to be sold into slavery. To Diodorus' disgust, Dionysius tortured the Rhegian general Python, physically and mentally, and then drowned him and his next of kin at sea. For Dionysius, the struggle for Rhegium was deeply personal.[56]

The fall of Rhegium bought Dionysius a period of peace around the Straits and in southern Italy. He was already at peace with Carthage, and could now apply his destructive energies to intellectual pursuits such as poetry and playwriting—with laughable results, if we are to believe his critics. He is also said to have grown increasingly paranoid and to have killed suspected rivals and exiled others, including his brother Leptines.

The Third and Fourth Carthaginian Wars (383–367)

Partly because of his relative inaction, partly because of our deficient sources, we are less informed about Dionysius' generalship in the last two decades of his life. In 386, he expanded his influence to northwestern Greece and the Adriatic Sea through alliances with the Illyrians and an Epirote claimant to the throne, as well as by founding colonies, but with only limited military intervention. By now, his fame as a general who favored surprise attacks and sacrilegious plunder was so firmly established that it contributed to an unfounded story that he planned a surprise landing around Epirus in order to rob the Temple of Apollo at Delphi. But in 384, he confirmed his reputation, taking sixty (or 100) triremes to the Etruscan city of Pyrgi, where, after landing by night, he attacked the few guards of a rich temple at dawn and

---

56. Diod. 14.108.1–4, 111.1–112.5. Price of grain in early-fourth-century Athens: Markle 2004, 126. Aristotle *Economics* 2.1349b states that, before selling the Rhegians into slavery, he squeezed them for ransom under false pretenses. For the meaning of punishment by drowning as "purging pollution and tyranny," see Lewis 2000, 103–104.

proceeded to pillage it. He then defeated a local army that came to meet him, captured prisoners, and wasted the land. The campaign yielded a huge haul of 1,500 talents, which he used to add mercenaries to his army and to prepare for his next Carthaginian war.[57]

In 383, after almost a decade of peace with Carthage, Dionysius felt confident enough to challenge its remaining hold on the island of Sicily. Syracuse and Carthage always competed over local Sicel alliances, and Dionysius encouraged Carthaginian allies to move to his side. After a failed negotiation, Carthage went to war. This time, the conflict extended into southern Italy, forcing Dionysius to fight on two fronts against the allied Italian Greeks and Carthaginians. It also required him to allocate military and economic resources judiciously and to make difficult decisions about where and how to meet the enemy and when to command in person.

Unfortunately, Diodorus' account of the Third Carthaginian War is too broad and beset with chronological difficulties. Other sources add disjointed episodes whose date is uncertain and that say little about Dionysius' art of command. I share the view that the war lasted from 383/382 to 375/374. In Italy, it included a campaign against the Locrians, who had defected to the Carthaginian side; a difficult war against Croton, which he captured by deception (in 379/378?) and held for twelve years; a Carthaginian resettlement of Hipponium in 379; and a maritime attack on Thurii that failed because of a storm. In Sicily, Dionysius captured Himera and a Carthaginian general who was betrayed to him.[58]

The war was concluded with two major land battles in Sicily, probably in 375. The first one was near Cabala, whose exact location is unknown, and ended in what could have been a decisive victory for Dionysius. More than 10,000 Carthaginian soldiers fell, including their general Mago, and

---

57. Dionysius after Rhegium: Diod. 15.6.1–7.4. Dionysius in the Adriatic Sea and his later dealings with mainland Greeks: Diod. 15.13.1–5; Stroheker 1958, 119–128; Caven 1990, 149–153, 202–212 (suggesting, not very convincingly, an ambition for a maritime empire). Plan to raid Delphi: Diod. 15.13.1; Stylianou 1998, 191–192. Raiding Pyrgi: Diod. 15.14.3–4; Strabo 5.2.8; Aelian *Historical Miscellany* 1.20; cf. Aristotle *Economics* 1349b, and Polyaenus 5.2.21, on how he robbed his troops of their loot. The lacunose text of Diod. 15.13.5 reports his building walls around Syracuse and preparing dockyards for 200 triremes in 385. If this story is not a duplication of an earlier account (Diod. 14.18.2–8, 42.5 and pp. 241–245 above), he could have been preparing the city for the war with Carthage; but see also Stylianou 1998, 81–82.

58. Third Carthaginian War: Diod. 15.15.1–2. Its duration: Beloch 1914, 2: 374–376. Locris: Plato *Laws* 1.638b; Justin 20.5.1; cf. Cicero *On the Nature of the Gods* 3.34 (a raid of a local temple). Croton: Livy 24.3.8; Dionysius Halicarnassus *Roman Antiquities*

about 5,000 were captured. The rest fled to a waterless, fortified hill. The situation resembles the aftermath of the battle of Eleporus in Italy (pp. 264–265 above), where Dionysius was able to dictate the terms of surrender. At Cabala, he raised the price, demanding that Carthage evacuate Sicily and pay the costs of the war.

The sources claim that the commanders of the defeated Carthaginians pretended to accept Dionysius' terms but said they lacked the authority to speak for their government. They requested a truce in order to confer with Carthage, and Dionysius agreed. According to one account, they asked first to move their camp next to their admiral, presumably on the coast, and then, freed of the siege, they rejected Dionysius' demands. Diodorus does not mention this episode, but he agrees that the request for a truce was a trick designed to buy the defeated army a few days to prepare for a second battle. Diodorus' version contracts events and makes little sense, and all reports are colored by the ancient stereotype of the Carthaginians as perfidious. It is possible that the defeated Carthaginians were sincere in accepting Dionysius' demands and in deferring the decision to higher authorities, which then rejected his terms. Dionysius agreed to the truce and negotiations because the Carthaginians' difficult conditions resembled those at Eleporus in 389, which led to the successful conclusion of the war against the Italiot League, and even those at Agyrium in 392, which ended the Second Carthaginian War (p. 261 above). It is also possible that his so-far-uninterrupted chain of military successes, including Cabala, made him think that he could take the risk of another battle because he was invincible.[59]

After the defeat, the Carthaginian home government appointed Mago's son (Himilco?) to command its forces in Sicily, and he trained and motivated them for the next clash with the tyrant. The opposing armies met at Cronium (location unknown), and the Carthaginians won resoundingly. Dionysius led one wing, and his brother Leptines, now back from exile, the other. Diodorus' depiction of the battle singles out Leptines' heroism, yet his courage was no compensation for his poor generalship (as on previous occasions), and he was

20.7.3; Justin 20.5.1–3; Athenaeus 12.541a–b (capture of a nearby temple of Hera). Hipponium: Diod. 15.24.1; Dionysius Halicarnassus *Roman Antiquities* 20.7.3. Attack on Thurii: Aelian *Historical Miscellany* 12.61. Taking Himera and a Carthaginian general: Polyaenus 5.2.10; Justin 20.5.10–12; cf. Aeneas Tacticus 10.22. For a sensible ordering of these events, see Caven 1990, 188–201.

59. Polyaenus 6.16.1 (pretend consultation); Diod. 15.15.3–16.1. Caven 1990, 197–198, suggests that the Carthaginian army escaped Dionysius' encirclement, but that interpretation contradicts our sources; see also Stylianou 1998, 204–6.

defeated and killed. The collapse of his wing nullified Dionysius' temporary victory on the other, and the Syracusan army fled. Either on orders or in rage, the Carthaginians went in for the kill: Dionysius reportedly lost more than 14,000 men, and the rest were saved by the dark of night and their fortified camp. The Carthaginians then marched to their main base of Panormus, probably because they were unready or reluctant to pursue the war all the way to Syracuse. It was now Dionysius' turn to accept their terms: they retrieved all their former holdings in western Sicily, in addition to Selinus and Acragas. At least in the short term, the loss wiped out many of Dionysius' gains in this region since 392.[60]

We know little of Dionysius' subsequent military activity apart from his sending soldiers to aid allies in Greece. His last battle was in 368/367, in a Fourth Carthaginian War, as might be expected. True to his old self, he timed his offensive to a moment when the enemy was in distress from a plague and a Libyan mutiny. His army reportedly included 30,000 infantrymen, 3,000 cavalrymen, 300 triremes, and many supply ships. In the past, Dionysius had drafted more infantry and cavalry, but never so many warships. His large navy now probably reflected his chief targets, the coastal towns in western Sicily, and his expectation of a battle with the Carthaginian fleet that would come to their rescue. He first took Selinus, then inland Entella (an old thorn in his side) and the northwestern city of Eryx, which he used as a temporary base. From there, he sailed south to Carthaginian Lilybaeum, whose proximity to Motya must have triggered fond memories. Yet Lilybaeum was larger and more populous than Motya, and he had to call off the siege. He then sent 170 triremes back home, keeping his best 130 ships in the harbor of Eryx. There was more than one reason for the reduction of the fleet. He had heard that the Carthaginian docks (more probably at home than in Panormus) had been destroyed in a fire, and he wrongly assumed (or was intentionally misinformed) that the fire had consumed the entire navy. Reducing his fleet also made economic sense.

60. Diod. 15.16.2–17.5. Peace terms: Stylianou 1998, 206–207. It is told that the Carthaginian general Himilco stole the city of Cronium from under the nose of Dionysius' generals, and that a Carthaginian fleet defeated Dionysius' ships (Polyaenus 5.10.5, 6.16.3), but dating both episodes between Cabala and Cronium is conjectural: Caven 1990, 1998–199; Stylianou 1998, 206. Stroheker (1958, 232n28) locates Cronium near Panormus. The evidence for Dionysius' betrayal of Leptines in battle is dubious: Plut. *Moralia* 338b; Aelian *Historical Miscellany* 13.45; cf. Aeneas Tacticus 10.21–22. For the possibility that the Carthaginian war lasted till 367, see Lewis 1994, 149.

An undated episode in our sources tells how the Carthaginian admiral Hanno tricked the Syracusan fleet into allowing him and his ships to escape. If it happened during this campaign, Dionysius had the right to be disappointed with the performance of his large navy. Not long after, Hanno returned with 200 ships, surprised Dionysius' idle, smaller fleet at Eryx, and towed away most of his triremes. The Carthaginians thus beat Dionysius in two domains that he had mastered in his prime: surprise attack and good intelligence. Diodorus also suggests that his successful campaign up to this point had made him sanguine and disdainful. The coming of winter encouraged both sides to sign a truce and retire to their home bases. Shortly thereafter, in 367, the sixty-three-year-old Dionysius died by conspirators' hands, according to one tradition, or after binge drinking, according to another. If the latter version is correct, he anticipated the most famous of all ancient generals, Alexander the Great, who both learned from him and died like him.[61]

 DEATH

Conclusion

Dionysius' last two wars with Carthage cost him great losses of men, equipment, and probably territory. These results raise the justified question of whether his lifelong conflict with Carthage was wise. Dionysius probably never asked himself that question; his nearly incessant campaigning suggests that he saw victory or defeat not as endpoints but as temporary signposts in an ongoing contest. Two personality traits shaped this attitude: perseverance and a wish to be recognized as the best. Since Dionysius' rule and generalship were essentially personal, such attributes played a large role in them.

There is a story (probably unfounded, but justly associated with Dionysius) of an oracle that predicted he would die after defeating his betters. He was a highly competitive man in politics and war, two traditional showplaces for

61. Dionysius' involvement in Greece: Xen. *Hellenica* 5.1.26, 6.2.33–36, 7.1.20–29; Diod. 15.47.7, 70.1. Caven 1990, 195, pre-dates a plague in Carthage followed by Libyan and Sardinian rebellions to the previous war (Diod. 15.24.1–3). Dionysius' last campaign: Diod. 15.73.1–5; cf. Justin 20.5.11–12. The 300 ships Dionysius took to Thurii were probably transports, unlike those in this campaign: Ael. *Historical Miscellany* 12.61. Hanno's trick: Polyaenus 5.9. Death by conspiracy: Justin 20.5.14–21.1.1; Plut. *Dion* 6; Nepos *Dion* 2. Death by alcohol: Diod. 15.74.1–4. Age at death: Champion *BNJ* 566, F 110, commentary. Alexander and Dionysius: Plut. *Alexander* 8; Sanders 1987, 48; Sanders 1990–1991.

arete: the attainment of excellence and fame by beating others. His ambition manifested itself in military aggression and a preference to strike first that gave him an advantage. It is seen in his personal courage in planning a battle or in joining the fray. His competitive character is indicated even in his naming one of his daughters "Arete" and in the contests of productivity and inventiveness he organized during the fortification of Syracuse. His people's expectations that he would excel are evinced by rebellions and discontent when he failed to achieve less than full victory.[62]

Dionysius' striving for preeminence was complemented by his tenacity. He rarely gave up after defeat, but continued the conflict after recovering, especially if the enemy was somehow disadvantaged or unprepared. His campaigns against Leontini, Tauromenium, and Rhegium show his tendency to return and complete the mission after failing to take a city.

If his courage, determination, and pursuit of excellence made Dionysius like Leonidas and the Spartans, he was very different from them in his ways of warfare. The traditional Spartans liked to keep war simple, preferring a pitched battle where their hoplites could fight their counterparts. Dionysius often took a more indirect or complex approach, as demonstrated, *inter alia*, by his fondness for surprise. As shown by his attacks on the Carthaginian camps at Gela and Syracuse, and by numerous smaller operations, he used specialized units or combinations of infantry, cavalry, and ships to confuse and surprise the enemy, and to strike him at multiple points of weakness. He learned to improve as a general, primarily from experience, but possibly also from other generals such as Lysander and Demosthenes. His attitude ranged from daring to caution and waiting for the enemy to give up. He was also open-minded, as is seen in his consulting others before making decisions and in his adopting new war technology on land and sea.

Not that Dionysius' generalship was free of faults or failures. His attack on the Carthaginian camp at Gela collapsed because of bad planning, and his record of naval combat was unimpressive. But the good qualities he showed as a commander and soldier are more characteristic of his career as a whole, inconsistent though they are with his hostile depiction in some sources as full of paranoia and quick to kill anyone on the slightest suspicion. Dionysius was surely suspicious, and he committed many crimes against individuals and communities who crossed his path. Yet his military record suggests no such

---

62. Oracle: Diod. 15.74.3–4. For more on Dionysius' search for *arete*, see Plut. *Dion* 5–6; Caven 1990, 155, 228, 236–238. It may be relevant to his anxiety about his name that he didn't like laughter: Aelian *Historical Miscellany* 13.18. Dionysius' personal rule: Sekunda 2013, 205.

fear and distrust. When he sneaked up the snowy mountain of Tauromenium with his troops at night, he showed no concern about the loyalty of those around him. Moreover, no ruler can rule alone, and there were scores of men he trusted, including lieutenants in divided missions and commands. And, although he was cruel and tyrannical, he climbed from a disappointing beginning to become one of Greece's best generals.[63]

63. Dionysius' suspiciousness and its manifestations: Plut. *Dion* 3, 9; Cicero *Tusculan Disputations* 5.57–62 (acknowledging, however, his self-restraint and many companions); *De Officiis* 2.25; Nepos *Of Kings* 2.2; Polyaenus 5.2.3, 13, 15–16; cf. Plato *Letters* 7. 321e–322d, 329b–c. See also Caven 1990, 224–233. His cooperative style: *pace* Caven 1990, 239–240.

| # Epaminondas and Pelopidas of Thebes
The Double-Edged Returns of Daring

Epaminondas and Pelopidas, Their Military Challenges and Their City

This chapter deals with two generals instead of one, because the careers of Epaminondas and Pelopidas provide a unique opportunity to observe two military leaders working in partnership, in addition to examining their individual performance. Both generals are rightly held responsible for making their city of Thebes the leading power in Greece, if only for a short period.[1]

Epaminondas, son of Polymis, came from a distinguished but relatively impoverished family. In his origins and in his refusal to profit materially from office, he resembled the Spartan Lysander. In his youth, he associated with Pythagorean philosophers, whose influence may account for his habit of helping others and sharing his possessions, but also for his arrogance. He was physically fit and learned discipline and rhythm from playing the flute and dancing. Before he came to prominence, he was engaged in intellectual pursuits that were interrupted by military duties.

Pelopidas, son of Hippocles, was an aristocrat in origins and attitude. He was fond of sports and hunting, married well, and spent his money on public

---

1. The ancient evidence for Epaminondas and Pelopidas: Bibliography, "The Main Ancient Sources," s.vv. "Cornelius Nepos," "Diodorus," "Pausanias," "Plutarch," and "Xenophon," as well as Cawkwell 1972; Westlake 1975; Buckler 1978, 1980; Hanson 1988; Georgiadou 1992; Stylianou 1998. For their careers, see in addition, Beck 1997; Georgiadou 1997; and the following notes.

causes. He was also a very courageous man on the battlefield. Both Pelopidas and Epaminondas were democrats.[2]

In the course of their military and political careers, Pelopidas and Epaminondas encountered significant challenges, individually and together. In several of their campaigns, the terrain constrained the deployment of the infantry and cavalry, while the enemy had a larger army that, in the case of Sparta, also enjoyed a better reputation than Thebes'. Pelopidas and Epaminondas had to transform demoralized soldiers into motivated, effective warriors and to lead coalition armies with heterogeneous units and different agendas. They had to adapt their leadership and warfare to pitched battles, fortified sites, and urban combat. In some battles, they were forced to make on-the-spot decisions that could decide the result. Both generals had to persuade and cajole fellow Thebans or colleagues, who could be divided or reluctant in their willingness to follow their military plans. Indeed, like the Athenian generals discussed in this book, they were legally accountable to the people for their actions, a fact that affected their careers. Both at home and away, they met with opposition to their efforts to build up Theban dominance in Greece, an enterprise involving alliances that required maintenance or active intervention. Finally, Epaminondas and Pelopidas often met the aforementioned challenges simultaneously. Although some of the military issues they encountered are recognizable from the careers of the other generals discussed in this book, Pelopidas and Epaminondas sometimes dealt with them in unique ways.

Thebes, Epaminondas' and Pelopidas' native city, was the chief city of the Boeotian League or Confederacy from at least the late sixth century.[3] Its government fluctuated between oligarchy and democracy, but the two factions shared a wish to maintain or increase Theban power in Boeotia. During the Persian invasion of Greece in 480–479, Thebes infamously joined the enemy, unlike Athens and Sparta. The city's independent, often selfish policy made it unpopular in Greece, although its powerful army and cavalry and its strategic location made it a desirable ally. Indeed, during the Peloponnesian War, Sparta allied with it. Their relationship worsened in the war's aftermath, though, partly because of Thebes' change to a more democratic (and hence pro-Athenian) government. In 395, the Spartans launched

---

2. Epaminondas and Pelopidas' background and character: Plut. *Pelopidas* 3–4; Nepos *Epaminondas* 2–4; Diod. 15.39.2; Plut. *Moralia* 583c; 585e; 799f; 808e; 809a.
3. Theban history: Buck 1979; Buckler 1980; Demand 1982. For the Boeotian League, see my Introduction, pp. 19–20, and for the following, e.g., Rhodes 2006, 188–251.

a campaign against Thebes in which Lysander died (pp. 219–225 above). Thebes was then joined by Athens, Corinth, Euboea, and Argos in the Corinthian War against Sparta, which ended in 387 in a general Greek peace known as the Peace of Antalcidas. Like other, similar agreements known as the King's Peace or the Common Peace, it suspended conflict between the Persian king and Greek city-states in the mainland and the Aegean, and was supposed to guarantee the autonomy of the Greek *poleis*. The Spartans were the enforcers of the peace and of Greek autonomy, a function they exercised selectively and to protect their power. Thus, when the Thebans wanted to swear to the peace of Antalcidas as representatives of Boeotia, the Spartan king Agesilaus invoked the autonomy of the individual members of the Boeotian confederacy and refused to allow it. He then forced Thebes to disband the confederacy under the threat of war. Two years later (385), Sparta similarly used the principle of autonomy among its reasons or pretexts for waging war on the Arcadian city of Mantinea, which it considered a threat. Mantinea was an amalgam of several settlements, and Agesilaus ordered it to disband into its original independent villages. The Mantineans resisted, and at Sparta's request, Thebes contributed a force including Pelopidas and Epaminondas to the campaign against Mantinea. It was their first attested cooperation under arms.[4]

Biographer Plutarch ascribes the beginning of their Homeric-style friendship to this shared battle experience. They fought as hoplites on the side of the Spartans, and even though the Spartans retreated, the Thebans closed ranks and repelled the attackers. Young Pelopidas reportedly suffered no fewer than seven frontal wounds before dropping almost dead on a pile of corpses. Epaminondas rushed to his help, received a frontal wound of his own, and was in great danger until the Spartan king Agesipolis came to their rescue.[5] The story cannot be authenticated or refuted, but it suggests themes that recur later in both men's careers. These include their doing better than the Spartans in battle, their exhibition of personal valor and sacrifice in spite of the odds, and Epaminondas' role as the friend in need.

Revolution in Thebes

In 382, Sparta supported an oligarchic, pro-Spartan coup in Thebes and even occupied its citadel of the Cadmeia with a garrison. (So much for Spartan

4. See note 3. Mantinea: Plut. *Pelopidas* 4; Pausanias 9.13.1; Georgiadou 1997, 80–82.
5. Plut. *Pelopidas* 4.

championship of Greek autonomy!) Many Theban democrats fled to Athens, including Pelopidas but not Epaminondas, whom the sources claim that the oligarchic government left alone because it was contemptuous of his poverty and his preoccupation with philosophy. Not explained, however, is why Epaminondas chose to stay under an oligarchic regime, although he was hardly the only democrat who did so. Perhaps he had protectors among the oligarchs, and living in exile was not an attractive option for a relatively poor man. Whatever his motives for staying, Epaminondas used his clout as an educator to incite Theban youth against Sparta in the name of local patriotism.[6]

The Theban oligarchy was overthrown by a conspiracy of exiles and their partners in the city.[7] The plan called for the assassination of oligarchic leaders in the city during a festival and the subsequent arrival of a force of exiles waiting near Eleusis in Attica. Pelopidas was in a selected group of twelve (or seven) exiles, mostly of distinguished background, who were supposed to sneak into the city. To avoid detection, they left Athens at night and tried to stay out of sight during the day, disguised as hunters. They also took the precaution of entering Thebes in the evening at different locations, and they were helped by bad weather that drove people off the streets. The exiles reunited at the house of the influential Charon, who had worked with other leading democrats to prepare the groundwork for the coup. Among the local conspirators was Phillidas, who served as secretary for oligarchic senior magistrates (polemarchs). He lured them to a banquet at his house with promises of wine and sex. Then came a scene worthy of a suspense novel or melodrama. Plutarch tells of an awkward moment when one magistrate wanted to investigate rumors about the presence of the exiles in the city and sent for Charon, in whose house the exiles were hiding. Under this challenge to his ability to keep a secret, Charon offered the exiles his son as a hostage to assure them of his loyalty, but the exiles tearfully and vehemently protested they were incapable of suspecting him. The mutual display of high-mindedness culminated in Charon's insisting

6. Plut. *Pelopidas* 5, 7; *Moralia* 576e–f; Nepos *Pelopidas* 4; Polyaenus 2.3.6.
7. The following reconstruction is based on the different, but not incompatible, accounts of Xen. *Hellenica* 5.4.2–12 (who does not mention Pelopidas and Epaminondas); Diod. 15.25.1–27.4, 81.1; Plut. *Pelopidas* 5, 7–12 (overemphasizing the conspirators' good luck); *Moralia* 575b–588b, 594a–598f (literary and philosophical renditions); Nepos *Pelopidas* 2–4 (resembles Plutarch); *Epaminondas* 10; cf. Polyaenus 2.3.1; 2.4.3. See DeVoto 1989; Buck 1994, 71–87; Georgiadou 1997, 5–11; Pelling 2010.

on leaving his son with the exiles, proclaiming that nothing was better than dying honorably.[8]

There were other close calls that almost exposed the plot, which succeeded largely because of luck and the oligarchs' errors of judgment. Finally, the exiles and forty-six other plotters split up into separate missions. Some disguised themselves as women and went to Phillidas' banquet, where they dispatched the drunk, lusty magistrates. Pelopidas (or Phillidas, according to Xenophon) and his group went to kill two other oligarchs, including their most prominent leader, Leontidas. Unlike the aforementioned magistrates, Leontidas was clever, physically strong, and sober. He was either asleep or relaxing after dinner with his wife when the conspirators entered his house under false pretenses. He gave them a good fight and killed or mortally wounded one of the assailants before dying in a wrestling and stabbing match with Pelopidas. Another oligarch was killed after a chase over the rooftops.

The next step, preplanned and executed by the local plotters, was taking control of the city. They armed their supporters, including men they had freed from prison, with weapons snatched from trophies and from sword and spear workshops. But their call for hoplites and cavalry to join them went nowhere, because the cautious Thebans waited for daylight to find out who was in charge. The conspirators were joined, however, by Epaminondas and another democratic leader, who arrived with armed young followers and older men. The plotters also sent for aid from the force of exiles in the Eleusis and from Athenian troops under two generals who were serving on the border.

It was now daylight, and the Thebans, both civilians and soldiers, learned that the oligarchic leadership had been eliminated. Combined with the arrival of the exiles' force, the *fait accompli* helped convince them that they should support the democrats. An assembly was called, in which Epaminondas introduced Pelopidas and his fellow exiles in the company of priests who held out garlands as if in supplication, and the people were exhorted to come to the help of their gods and country.

It was vital for the security of the new democracy to get rid of a Spartan garrison of 1,500 men in the citadel of the Cadmeia, a rather flat site that formed part of the city. Its Spartan commander had already sent for reinforcements from Sparta and nearby towns, but a Theban cavalry force defeated those who came to his aid from Boeotia. The arrival of Athenian units from the

---

8. Plut. *Pelopidas* 7; Diod. 15.81.1; Nepos *Pelopidas* 2, 4; *Epaminondas* 10.

Line drawing showing relative positions of figures on the amphora

FIGURE 16 *Leontidas' assassination?* A drawing of a scene on a fourth-century vase, which Borthwick (1976) claims describes Pelopidas and fellow conspirators knocking on Leontidas' door. A frightened servant opened it for them. The identification has been disputed by Griffith 1998, 44–49, who argues that it describes a comic scene.
Used with permission, Journal of Hellenic Studies.

border emboldened the Thebans to attack the Cadmeia without delay. They successfully asked Athens for additional help, and an Athenian army of 5,000 hoplites and 500 cavalry reportedly showed up at Thebes the next day. They were later joined by Boeotian sympathizers, who are said to have swelled the force to about 12,000 hoplites and 2,000 cavalrymen. Everyone, including the besieged, was expecting a Spartan army to arrive.

By this time, Pelopidas and four other democratic leaders had been appointed as *Boeotarchs* (generals). The sources suggest that he led the siege operations, which lasted perhaps close to a week. To motivate the soldiers and their commanders to risk their lives, large prizes were offered for the first men who would enter the fortress. It is even claimed that Epaminondas joined the front ranks, probably more for patriotic than for mercenary reasons. Pelopidas and his fellow commanders put constant pressure on the men in the citadel by attacking it from different directions, in relays and without a stop. The large number of soldiers in the city made such operations possible. The pressure proved too much for the garrison, which also suffered from dwindling provisions and dissention in its ranks. The Spartan commanders struck a deal that allowed them and their troops to leave Boeotia unharmed in return for evacuating the citadel. They were later punished harshly at home for not waiting for the Spartan army, which was already in Megara. The Thebans, however, were elated about completing the liberation of their city before the Spartans' arrival. They also proudly (though selectively) credited just a few exiles with the fall of Spartan power.[9]

That the affair belongs to Pelopidas' and Epaminondas' early career may explain their limited role in it. There seemed to be a division of labor in their partnership. Pelopidas was the military man of action, eager to be in the thick of things, while Epaminondas played a more political, even secondary role. During the coup, Pelopidas displayed determination, bodily fitness, and personal courage, and he used deception in what can be described as a commando operation in an urban setting. As he did later, he easily moved between the roles of fighter and commander, showing his capacity to plan and coordinate complex undertakings such as the siege. He was also lucky, especially in executing the plot, even if Plutarch exaggerates the role of fortune.

The Sacred Band and the Battle of Tegyra (375)

Because of the episodic nature of the evidence on Pelopidas' and Epaminondas' lives, their careers between the liberation of Thebes in 378 and the battle of Leuctra in 371 can be reconstructed only partially. During this period, the Thebans were largely busy defending Boeotia from Spartan invasions and reorganizing the Boeotian confederacy in a way that kept it under their domination. Both tasks involved military operations, and Pelopidas, who was elected Boeotarch almost every year until his death, probably played a role in them. It was also during this period that he took command of an elite infantry unit known as the Sacred Band.

Plutarch provides the most detailed description of this unit: He reports that the Theban military leader Gorgidas was the founder of the unit and that it consisted of 300 picked men, who were maintained and trained by the

9. See the last note, and Dinarchus *Against Demosthenes* 1.38–39; Isocrates 14.3; Aeschines 3.138–139; Schmitzer 1998; Parker 2007b, 17–18.

city and were camped in the Cadmeia. "Some say" that it was composed of homosexual couples. Plutarch suggests that the love between the lovers made the unity unbreakable, because the partners were ashamed to show cowardice before each other and so stood their ground to protect them. Plutarch then adds:

> It is said, moreover, that the band was never beaten, until the battle of Chaeronea (338); and when, after the battle, Philip (II of Macedonia) was surveying the dead, and stopped at the place where the three hundred were lying, all where they had faced the long spears of his phalanx, with their armor, and mingled one with another, he was amazed, and on learning that this was the band of lovers and beloved, burst into tears and said: "Perish miserably they who think that these men did or suffered aught disgraceful."

Plutarch goes on to say that Gorgidas distributed the sacred band among the front ranks of the hoplite phalanx and so "dissipated" their strength and quality. Pelopidas, however, kept them together as a unit after they they had demonstrated their valor at Tegyra (below), never divided them, and put them into the forefront of the greatest battles.[10]

Although Plutarch's description, and especially the erotic character of the group, have been questioned, the biographer's account is largely credible. Other Greek armies, including in Athens and Sparta, had elite units of identical number, and the Spartans similarly regarded homoerotic love between soldiers as conducive to their motivation and courage. More significant than the erotic nature of the unit, however, was its military character. Unlike the rest of the Theban army, it was kept and maintained by the state year-round and could be deployed for a variety of missions. Gorgidas, who commanded and (re)organized this force after the city's liberation, spread them in the front ranks, either to improve other soldiers' performance or because he counted on individuals and even pairs of soldiers to excel in the single combats that normally followed the clash of the phalanxes. Pelopidas changed this arrangement by making them into a separate crack unit that led the attack or served as a core for the rest of the heavy infantry. As we shall see, he used them most effectively in the battles of Tegyra and Leuctra.[11]

---

10. Sacred Band: Plut. *Pelopidas* 18–19, 23. See also Polyaenus 2.5.1; Plut. *Moralia* 761b–d; Athen. 13.561f, 602a (crediting Epaminondas with its creation).
11. DeVoto (1992), Leitao (2002), and Georgiadou (2006) are skeptical of the Sacred Band's erotic nature. Spartan erotics and war: Cartledge 2001, 90–105; Sprawski 2004, 17; Van Wees 2004, 59. Comparable Greek units: DeVoto, 1992, 5–7.

As opposed to Pelopidas' association with the Sacred Band, which is well documented, the case for his attempt in 378 to embroil Athens and Sparta in a conflict is much less certain. In that year, the Spartan king Cleombrotus invaded Boeotia, and although he accomplished little, it was the first of several similar campaigns. Athens also distanced itself from Thebes. Against this background, Pelopidas and a fellow democratic leader allegedly schemed to provoke a conflict between Athens and Sparta in order to relieve Thebes of Spartan pressure. They used a Theban agent to bribe and influence Sphodrias, a Spartan governor in the Boeotian town of Thespia, to make an attempt to capture the Piraeus. The raid failed and greatly worsened the relationship between Athens and Sparta. It also encouraged Athens to found the so-called Second Athenian League, a multi-Greek alliance that included Thebes and was designed to rival or check Spartan hegemony. Yet the story of a Theban conspiracy behind the Spartan raid is dubious. Sphodrias did not need a bribe or Theban persuasion in order to try to capture the Piraeus, which if successful would have made him a hero at home. According to one source (Diodorus), he was even given King Cleombrotus' blessing for the operation. More important, the consequent worsening of the Athens–Sparta relationship was due, not so much to the Spartan failed attack, as to the Spartan government's failure to punish Sphodrias for his attempt. It is hard to believe that Pelopidas could have foreseen this or other consequences of the raid, although he probably took the credit for them.[12]

The war between the invading Spartan armies and the Thebans continued until 375 with no decision. Sparta's financial constraints and its decision to change the focus of military operations temporarily from Thebes to Athens allowed the Thebans to extend their rule over several Boeotian cities. It was in the course of this expansion that Pelopidas won a victory over a Spartan force in the battle of Tegyra.[13]

Our sources for the battle, of which the most informative are Plutarch and Diodorus, are incomplete and at times contradictory. They agree that it resulted from Pelopidas' attempt to add the city of Orchomenus to the Boeotian league (Map 11, p. 169). Orchomenus had been pro-Spartan since Lysander made it so in 395 (p. 221 above), and it hosted a Spartan

12. Plut. *Pelopidas* 14; *Agesilaus* 24; cf. Xen. *Hellenica* 5.4.20–33; Diod. 15.29.5–7; Buckler 2003, 220–222 (who hypothesizes an unlikely co-conspiracy between the Thebans and Cleombrotus); Parker 2007, 23–24.

13. Spartan campaigns in Boeotia: Cartledge 1987, 228–232. The battle of Tegyra: Plut. *Pelopidas* 16–17; Diod. 15.37.1–2 (without naming the battle); cf. Xen. *Hellenica* 6.4.10; Pritchett 1971–1991, 4: 103–122; Georgiadou 1997, 142–153; Sprawski 2004; Buckler and Beck 2008, 99–110.

garrison of two *morae* in strength. At least up to 371, a *mora* comprised a sixth of the Spartan army, yet its exact size is unclear because it was subject to changes. Plutarch found in his sources three different estimates of its strength: 100, 500, and 900 men, of which 500 appears most consistent with the testimonies, and would make the size of the garrison in Orchomenus about 1,000 men. Spartan garrisons often included an unknown number of mercenaries under a Spartan commander.[14]

Pelopidas planned to capture Orchomenus when its garrison was away on a campaign in Eastern Locris. His military intelligence, however, lacked the knowledge that the Spartans had sent a replacement garrison there. He therefore believed he could take the city with a relatively small force. The sources are divided on its size, but it included at least 300 hoplites of the Sacred Band, a small contingent of cavalry, and perhaps 200 additional picked infantry. The route he took is puzzling, because Plutarch suggests that he approached Orchomenus, not from his Theban base in the south, but from the north, and that he even took the same route back. He may have been in the region on a different assignment (raiding pro-Spartan Phocis?) and decided to go to Orchomenus when he heard the Spartan garrison was away.

Pelopidas' plan failed. Like Lysander in his abortive attempt to capture Haliartus in 395 (pp. 222–223 above), he came upon a walled city in which foreign troops enforced loyalty. He may also have heard that the original Spartan garrison was on its way back. Pelopidas retreated toward Tegyra, which was probably near modern Polygyra, on the shore of Lake Copais 5 kilometers north of Orchomenus. There he ran into problems. The nearby River Melas flooded and forced him to take a pass over the foothills and through a plain. He could not see the returning Spartan garrison that came upon him from the north, because the foothills on one side and a rocky outcrop on the other blocked his view. The sudden appearance of the Spartans unnerved the soldiers, but not Pelopidas, who reportedly reacted with a defiant phrase. When informed that he and his troops had fallen into the enemy hands, he retorted: "Why any more than that they have fallen into ours?" The *bon mot* may be apocryphal, since it is also ascribed to Leonidas at Thermopylae, but it suggests Pelopidas' need to reassure his demoralized soldiers. After all, his march to Orchomenus and back included one unpleasant surprise after another, partly because of his poor military intelligence.[15]

14. *Mora*: Lazenby 1985, 5–12; Rzepka, commentary on "Kallisthenes of Olynthos," 124 F18 *BNJ*, forthcoming.
15. Pelopidas' route and force: Plut. *Pelopidas* 16; Diod. 15.37.1 (500 picked troops). Tegyra's location: Buckler and Beck 2008, 99–110. Pelopidas' and Leonidas' retorts: Plut. *Pelopidas* 17; *Moralia* 225b, 234b.

The circumstances called for quick action. The Spartans had numerical superiority, perhaps 1,000 hoplites to the Thebans' 500, but Pelopidas' soldiers were better trained and more desperate to win their way out. At first Pelopidas sent the cavalry protecting his rear to the front, to harass the enemy and confound its formation. He then positioned his hoplites in a close formation, both for their protection and in order to punch a hole in the enemy front, probably with the Sacred Band, so that his army could make its way to safety. It appears that he first took a defensive position, because the sources suggest that the Spartans were the first to advance. Once the opposing phalanxes clashed, however, each side sought to decide the battle by going for the enemy commanders, whose death often led to retreat or flight. Here Pelopidas was more successful when the Spartan commanders of the two *morae* fell. Their death and that of the men around them caused the enemy to change its tactics. Led by seconds-in-command, the Spartans apparently opened their files to allow Pelopidas a free passage, his original goal. Yet, by now, their lines had begun to disintegrate, and their maneuver, which split them even more, undermined their numerical advantage. Pelopidas decided to go for a full victory. He advanced through the cleared path and killed all those who still stood together and offered resistance. Soon the enemy took to its heels. Pelopidas pursued them for only a short distance, because he wished to avoid a second battle with a new force and the replacement garrison who were on their way to help the Spartans from nearby Orchomenus. He stayed long enough, however, to put up a trophy as a testimony to his victory.[16]

Plutarch must have been carried away when he equated Tegyra with the later Theban victory over Sparta at Leuctra, calling both the most illustrious and greatest of contests. Unlike Leuctra (below), the battle of Tegyra was neither big nor consequential. Nor did it constitute a major defeat for Sparta or lead to the capture of Orchomenus. But the sources appear to be correct in suggesting that battles such as Tegyra damaged the Spartans' reputation and assured the Thebans of their ability to beat them at their own game. Tegyra also demonstrated Pelopidas' qualities as a tactician. His victory was impressive because he started from an inferior position, facing topographical handicaps and a more numerous enemy. He was also trapped between hostile Orchomenus and the returning garrison.

16. Plut. *Pelopidas* 17 does not support Buckler and Beck's suggestion (2008, 109) that the Spartans opened a lane in order to attack Pelopidas from the rear. Conversely, Sprawski 2004, 22–24, may go too far in denying the maneuver altogether.

Nevertheless, he defeated the enemy by cooperation between cavalry and infantry (which would recur in the battle of Leuctra) and by the disciplined performance of his hoplites, who probably took their cue from the Sacred Band. Pelopidas also showed his ability to change goals and tactics in accordance with changing circumstances, taking advantage of the enemy's allowing him to pass through in order to attack it. He was fortunate in the Spartans' mistaken assumption that all he wanted was to escape. He and Epaminondas would continue to use the Spartans' battle array and plans against them at Leuctra and elsewhere.[17]

The Battle of Leuctra (371)

Our sources are largely silent about Pelopidas' and Epaminondas' activities until Epaminondas' participation in a peace conference at Sparta in 371. The two men were probably involved in the post-Tegyra expansion of Theban control over most of Boeotia, including the destruction of Thebes' old enemy, Plataea (373). In 371, both Athens and Sparta, with the Persian king's blessing, looked to put an end to their conflict and convened a meeting of interested Greeks, Thebes included, to discuss a common peace. There was the usual exchange of recriminations and solicitations that preceded an eventual agreement. According to Xenophon, its terms included "that all should withdraw their governors (and garrisons) from the cities, disband their armaments both on sea and on land, and leave the cities independent." Sparta signed the treaty in its own and its' allies' names, Athens and its allies signed it individually, and then the Thebans added their signature.[18]

The next day, the Thebans, probably led by Epaminondas, asked to change their signature from "Thebans" to "Boeotians," thus claiming the right to represent all of Boeotia with the sanction of the other Greeks' signatures. It is unclear why they did not sign or ask to sign as Boeotians in the first place. I suspect that Epaminondas used the common ploy of trying to

17. Tegyra's distinction, Theban self-confidence, and Pelopidas' reputation: Plut. *Comparison between Pelopidas and Marcellus* 1; Plut. *Pelopidas* 16, 18; *Agesilaus* 27; Diod. 15.37.2, 81.2.
18. Between Tegyra and the 371 peace conference: Buck 1994, 101–113. For the possibility that Pelopidas failed to take Phocian Elatea during this period, see Polyaenus 2.38.1; Georgiadou 1997, 161. The 371 peace conference: Xen. *Hellenica* 5.3.118 (quotation), 6.3.1–20; Plut. *Agesilaus* 27–28; Diod. 15.38.2–3, 50.4–6; Nepos *Epaminondas* 6; Pausanias 9.13.2; cf. Buckler 1980, 48–54; Keen 1996b; and see the next note.

change an agreement after it had been made, assuming that the signatories would be willing to make concessions to salvage the common peace they all desired. But his gamble failed. The Spartan king Agesilaus, who had never liked the Thebans, gave Epaminondas the option of either keeping the existing signature or taking it out. It was probably now that Epaminondas made the speech attributed to him justifying the Theban cause and denouncing Spartan hegemony, which he criticized as tyrannical and the cause of Greek suffering, equating peace, law, and justice with equality for all Greeks. The Greeks at the meeting loved his speech, not so much because it supported the Theban agenda, but out of resentment of Sparta. In response, Agesilaus used the treaty's provision for local autonomy to put Epaminondas in the wrong. He asked him if it was not just and lawful that the Boeotians be autonomous. Epaminondas countered by asking Agesilaus if it were not just that the Laconians be autonomous. Plutarch rightly praises Epaminondas for his courage: the Theban leader was probably the first Greek to tell the Spartans to their face and in their homeland that their disenfranchisement of local non-citizens such as peripoeci and helots was illegal and violated the principle of autonomy. His challenge to the foundations of the Spartan state could not be left unanswered. Agesilaus erased the Thebans' signature from the agreement, and Sparta began a war that would prove catastrophic for her.[19]

Epaminondas must have understood that his uncompromising stand could lead to war. A Spartan army under King Cleombrotus was already stationed in Phocis, east of Boeotia, either to protect Phocis from Boeotian raids or to threaten Boeotia with an invasion. Its presence was probably on both Agesilaus' and Epaminondas' minds when they threw "Greek autonomy" in each other's teeth. Yet Epaminondas trusted in the ability of the Boeotian army, especially its Theban contingents, to defeat Sparta and her allies if it came to open war. He also knew, or rightly guessed, that although Athens was concerned about Thebes' rising power, it preferred keeping Thebes as an ally over making war upon it with Sparta.

The few weeks that separated the meeting in Sparta from the battle of Leuctra were full of tension. There was domestic opposition to the war on both sides, although more in Thebes, for good reason. The Spartan alliance had a larger army and more resources, and by describing the Thebans as enemies of peace and autonomy, the Spartans had warned the other Greeks

---

19. It is generally agreed that Diod. 15.38.1–4 confuses Epaminondas' speech in a peace conference in 375 with the one he gave in Sparta in 371: e.g., Rhodes 2006, 128; *contra*: Stylianou 1998, 326–328.

away from helping them. The Spartans' military reputation also gave them a psychological advantage. Sparta accordingly took action first. It gave Thebes an ultimatum to grant the Boeotians autonomy, restore Plataea, let go of Thespia (whose walls Thebes had demolished), and return confiscated lands to their original owners. Like most ultimatums, it put its server on high moral ground and was designed to be rejected. The Theban response was in line with Epaminondas' statements in Sparta, equating the legitimacy of the Boeotian confederacy with that of Spartan state. The Spartans, he said, should not interfere in internal Boeotian affairs, just as the Boeotians did not concern themselves with Spartan affairs.[20]

The war of words was followed by military actions. The leader of the Spartan expedition was King Cleombrotus, whose military record was mediocre and who was accompanied by advisers to counsel and supervise him. The leadership of the Boeotian side consisted of a council of Boeotarchs, in which Epaminondas seems to have enjoyed a senior position, but with an authority dependent on persuading the other generals to agree with him. By now there were probably fewer Boeotarchs than the former eleven, and in 371, Pelopidas was not one of them. Indeed, Epaminondas appears to have replaced Pelopidas in public visibility and prominence, although their partnership did not suffer as a result.

The Thebans expected Cleombrotus to invade Boeotia from Phocis but were unsure what route he would take. They also assumed that his ultimate goal was Thebes. To prevent him from reaching it, the bulk of the Boeotian army under Epaminondas waited for him a few kilometers east of Coronea (western Boeotia), where the main road from Phocis passed between Lake Copais and Mount Helicon. The narrow passage worked against the king's superiority in numbers. A second Boeotian force went southward to guard a pass on Mount Helicon, where an alternative, circuitous route went toward the Corinthian Gulf. A third force guarded a pass on the mountain range of Cithaeron between Boeotia and Attica, in case troops from the Peloponnese arrived there to join the campaign.

At first Cleombrotus acted as expected. After mustering his army at Chaeronea in northwestern Boeotia, he marched to Coronea, only to find the road blocked by Epaminondas (see Map 11, p. 169). Since it made little sense to fight where the Thebans held the advantage, Cleombrotus retreated to Ambrossus in Phocis. From there, he took his army through the not

---

20. See the last note. Cleombrotus in Phocis: Xen. *Hellenica* 6.3.20, 4.1–2; Plut. *Ages.* 28; Stylianou 1998, 357–360. Spartan ultimatum: Diod. 15.51.3–4; cf. Xen. *Hellenica* 6.4.3.

excessively difficult route over Mount Helicon, eliminated the aforementioned Boeotian force that guarded a passage there, and descended on Thisbe in southeastern Boeotia. He then turned to coastal Creusis, where he captured ten to twelve triremes (presumably beached), thus clearing the way for troops and supplies to arrive from the Peloponnese by sea. The occupation of Creusis also opened the way to Thespia, a city that had been pro-Spartan in the past and was now a reluctant member of the Boeotian confederacy. At Leuctra, few kilometers south of Thespia, Cleombrotus found a plain that suited his large army and the Spartan style of fighting. He pitched his camp on a southern slope overlooking the plain, dug a ditch for its protection, and waited for the enemy. So far he was doing very well for the Spartans, and appeared to have caught Epaminondas ill prepared. Xenophon reports suspicions and uncertainty in the Spartan camp about the king's resolve to fight the enemy, but Cleombrotus' actions so far suggest no such reluctance.[21]

Epaminondas took his army to Leuctra, where his first task was to convince his fellow Boeotarchs that they should fight Cleombrotus then and there. Observing the larger Spartan army, some of his colleagues preferred to move to a better position, probably like the one they had held around Coronea. There was also talk of finding shelter behind Thebes' walls and sending the women and children to Athens. The division of opinions corresponded to an even greater divide within the Theban populace about the advisability of fighting the enemy. Even the house of Pelopidas was allegedly affected; his wife tearfully begged him not to risk his life, only to be rebuked with a declaratory aphorism: "This advice, my wife, should be given to private men; but men in authority should be told not to lose the lives of others." The sources are full of stories about omens portending ill to the Thebans if they fought, probably disseminated by those opposing the war. Like Themistocles in Athens (pp. 64–65 above), Epaminondas had to use all his persuasive powers both in the city and in camp in order to convince his audience of the wisdom of adopting his positive interpretation of the omens. He also produced encouraging prophecies and local traditions, including one that predicted a Theban vindication of an old Spartan wrong done precisely in Leuctra. He even motivated his men by the scary (but dubious) prospect that the Spartans would kill all male Thebans and enslave the rest if they won.

21. Theban defense and Cleombrotus' route: Xen. 6.4.3–5, 14; Diod. 15.52.1, 53.1–2; Pausanias 9.13.3; Burn 1949, esp. 321–322; Buckler 1980, 55–59; Tuplin 1987, 74–76; Sergent 1991.

The struggle over public opinion influenced the Theban war council. Reportedly, it was split evenly between three Boeotarchs who advocated retreat and three, including Epaminondas, who wanted battle. The conflict was resolved by a seventh Boeotarch, who was recalled from Mount Cithaeron with his force (Epaminondas needed all the soldiers he could get) and was persuaded by Epaminondas to cast his vote for battle. The story perhaps intentionally recalls similar debates and narrow decisions in the Athenian war council before the Battle of Marathon (490), or those involving Themistocles and fellow generals during the Persian War (pp. 75–77 above). Even if the similarity was evoked by the sources for the glory of Epaminondas, there is little doubt that he had to contend with considerable opposition to his policy, and that at Leuctra he put his own and his city's future on the line.[22]

The best clue to the site of the battle is the Boeotian monument (Figure 17) that commemorates it: a circular tower built on three steps with a frieze of nine large shields. The structure originally carried a bronze trophy in the form of a hoplite holding a spear on his shoulders. Its exact date is uncertain, but such monuments were often erected where the fiercest fighting and crisis of the battle took place.[23]

The position of the monument indicates that the battle was fought on a level plain that is less than 2 kilometers across at its widest. The Boeotian camp lay on a hill north of the plain, and the Spartan camp on a slope south of it. As is often the case, our sources disagree on the sizes of the opposing sides and on the course of the battle. The most reliable figures for the Boeotian and Spartan armies are those closest to the size of their armies in other large battles. Accordingly, Epaminondas had around 6,000 infantry and 400 cavalry (probably a low estimate), and Cleombrotus 10,000 infantry and 1,000 cavalry. Although the Spartan king enjoyed a clear numerical superiority, readers of this book know by now that such an advantage

---

22. Divided Thebes, war council, and omens: Diod. 15.52.1–7, 53.2–54.4; Xen. *Hellenica* 6.4.7–8; Plut. *Pelopidas* 20–22 (involving Pelopidas in the war of omens); *Moralia* 192e–193a; Cicero, *On Divination* 1.74–76; Pausanias 4.32.4–6; 9.13.4–7; Polyaenus 2.3.8, 12; Frontinus *Stratagems* 1.11.6, 16; 1.12.5. Diodorus' report of the arrival on the scene of the Thessalian warlord Jason of Pherae and its consequences is commonly rejected: Diod. 15.54.5–6; Sprawski 1999, 96; Stylianou 1998, 395–396.

23. The Leuctra monument: Stroszeck 2004, 305, 321–322. Battle of Leuctra: Xen. *Hellenica* 6.4.3–15; Plut. *Pelopidas* 20–23; Diod.15.52.1–56.4; Pausanias 9.13.3–12. The following battle reconstruction partly agrees with and partly differs from Wolters 1931; Anderson 1970, 192–220; Buckler 1980, 59–65; Lazenby 1985, 151–162; Tuplin 1987; Hanson 1988; Buckler 2003, 289–295; Buckler 2013.

FIGURE 17 *The Leuctra monument.*
Deutches Archaeologisches Institut, D-DAI-ATH-1985-0794. Used with permission.

was not decisive in itself. We have few details about the composition of the armies. Epaminondas' force consisted of the full complement of the Theban army, including Pelopidas and his Sacred Band, as well as Boeotian units whose loyalty varied. The core of the Peloponnesian army was four Spartan *morai* of men up to about fifty-five years old, perhaps over 2,000 in number. They were joined by mercenaries in the service of Sparta, Arcadian troops, and Phocian peltasts (lighter-armed troops). Their cavalry included Spartans, horsemen from Heraclea on the Thessalian border and from Phlius in the northern Peloponnese, and other units.[24]

24. Diod. 15.52.2, 81.2; Plut. *Pelopidas* 20; Xen. 6.4.15, 17; Pausanias 8.6.2; Polyaenus 2.3.8, 12; Frontinus *Stratagem* 4.2.6 (the last two provide unlikely numbers). See Anderson 1970, 196–198, 320n21; Stylianou 1998, 238, 287, 390; cf. Lazenby 1985, 154–155 (possibly around 4,800 Spartan troops); Tuplin 1987; Buckler 2013, 658–659 (11,000 men for Cleombrotus and 7,000 hoplites and 600 horse for Epaminondas).

On the day of battle, around mid-August in 371, Cleombrotus called a war council to discuss final arrangements while his soldiers fortified themselves with wine as an antidote to the usual fear of battle. On the Theban side, all noncombatants began leaving camp to avoid death or captivity in case of defeat. They were joined by Boeotian soldiers, especially from Thespia, who were reluctant to fight the enemy in the first place. In a courageous act born of necessity, like Leonidas' dismissal of the unwilling at Thermopylae (pp. 44–46 above), Epaminondas let them go, further reducing his already-outnumbered army. (In any case, their going home was better than their joining the enemy.) Cleombrotus thought he could take advantage of the departure to score a first win. He sent light-armed mercenaries, Phocian peltasts, and allied cavalry after the Boeotians, killing some and pushing the others back to their camp. Xenophon argues that their return allowed Epaminondas to enlarge his phalanx, suggesting that the attack was counterproductive. But it is unlikely that the contribution of these soldiers to the fighting was meaningful, because Epaminondas relied on his Thebans and the Sacred Band for victory.

After these preliminaries, the opposing armies prepared for battle. The Spartan plan was simple and predictable. In a typical hoplite battle, generals charged the enemy with their right wing, which contained their best soldiers. The weaker left wing might support the attack but was chiefly expected to hold on until the right wing prevailed. When this happened, both wings might join forces to complete the victory, while a loss for the right wing often meant defeat for the entire army. Cleombrotus also prepared to lead the attack from the right and to rely on his Spartan troops for victory. Xenophon says that each Spartan *enomata* (half a company, or one-sixteenth of a *mora* or division; p. 284 above) advanced in three files abreast, making the phalanx twelve men deep. The ranks of Cleombrotus' non-Spartan allies and mercenaries probably stretched to his left in a straight formation, possibly with small intervals between different units in order to maintain as much of a solid front as possible. Since his phalanx was larger and longer than the enemy's, the king expected his center and left to sustain the enemy attack and if possible to charge it at its vulnerable flank or rear. Cleombrotus placed the Spartan cavalry, not beside his wings, as was often the practice, but at the front, because the level plain favored it and perhaps because he wanted it to spoil the formation of the enemy phalanx.[25]

---

25. Preliminaries to battle: Xen. 6.4.8–9; Pausanias 9.3.18; Polyan. 2.3.3. Date: Sergent 1991. Spartan lines: Xen. *Hellenica* 6.4.10; Diod. 15.55.1–2, 81.2 (he mistakenly makes the Spartan prince Archidamus the commander of the left wing); Plut. *Pelopidas* 23. Buckler's suggestion (2013, 667–668) that Cleombrotus positioned his cavalry first

Little did Cleombrotus know that Epaminondas would break with the conventional arrangement of hoplite battles. He formed his lines to match the Spartans' formation and anticipated their moves by pitting, not a strong right wing against the enemy's weak left, but a stronger left wing against their strong right (Map 17, p. 294 below). His left wing was fifty men deep so that it could crush the opposition. He placed his Theban contingents—his best hoplites—at the front, and Pelopidas and his elite unit of the Sacred Band in the lead, across from the Spartan king, where quick and disciplined action would be required. His massive concentration of troops on the left deprived his right wing of men, and to compensate for the imbalance, Epaminondas either staggered units with gaps between them or formed continuous, thinner lines as far as possible. If he chose the latter expedient, the right wing was arranged in an oblique formation and slanted somewhat backwards to create a greater distance from the enemy and a shorter retreat towards the protected Boeotian camp. Epaminondas' expectations of the right wing were subordinated to the needs of his left. The right was to hold off Cleombrotus' center and left and prevent them from attacking the Boeotian left at its flank or rear, retreating to camp if unsuccessful. He also put his cavalry opposite that of the enemy.[26]

The opposing cavalry positioned in the front were the first troops to see action. Xenophon thought that the contest was uneven. The Spartan cavalrymen had had little practice and suffered from poor motivation and condition, while the Boeotian cavalry was better trained and more experienced. As a result, the Spartan cavalry was easily defeated, and their flight into their infantry (a common refuge for Greek horsemen in battle) upset the movement and performance of the hoplites. At the same time, the Thebans went on the attack. Scholars have long maintained that Epaminondas planned this sequence and have congratulated him on coordinating the charges of the cavalry and the infantry. Though such foresight is possible, because Pelopidas similarly used the cavalry to help his phalanx at Tegyra (above), it should be borne in mind that Xenophon's wish to excuse the Spartan defeat at Leuctra was served by scapegoating their cavalry. Despite the inferior quality of the Spartan horsemen, they enjoyed a numerical advantage and were bold enough to attack first, so that their failure was far from predestined. We may assume

at the flanks and that he ordered them to the front after he began moving to the right is unsupported by the evidence. Intervals between units: cf. Wheeler 2007, 204–205.

26. Xen. 6.4.8–12; Diod. 15.55.1–2; Plut. *Pelopidas* 23; Nepos *Pelopidas* 4. Right wing: Buckler 2013, 668–669.

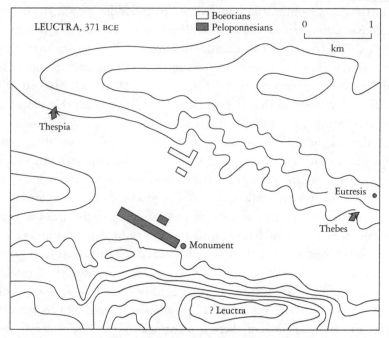

MAP 17 Leuctra Battle Plan. The Peloponnesians lines are close to the monument, and the Thebans are across the plain, with each cavalry stationed in front of its phalanx.

that Epaminondas took advantage of the confusion in the Spartan lines rather than created it.[27]

What decided the battle, however, was not the cavalry's action, but the fighting on the Spartan right wing. The Boeotian phalanx charged Cleombrotus and the men around him because this was where the enemy's strength was, and killing the commander could potentially decide the conflict. Epaminondas led his troops onward and to his left, a move that, along with the greater shortness and depth of the Theban front, was designed to induce Cleombrotus to try to meet and even outflank the phalanx by moving to his right. Epaminondas hoped the maneuver would disrupt the Spartan lines and create a gap between Cleombrotus' right and his center. The king reacted as expected, slanting to his right and forward, both to avoid the onslaught and in the hope of hitting the dense enemy phalanx on its less protected flank. He might even have hoped to surround it. (Diodorus' claim that the Spartans attacked in a crescent formation can be justified, with

27. Xenophon on the Spartan cavalry: *Hell.* 6.4.10–11. See also Lazenby 1985, 162, 202n22.

difficulties, if it describes this move.) The Spartans were well trained in such tactics and were supposed to keep their lines unbroken. They did not, and for more than one reason: Cleombrotus possibly moved too fast, the movement of troops and the cavalry's retreat into the files created confusion, and the swift Theban attack disrupted the king's plan. A gap was thus created between Cleombrotus' units and those to his left, and the Thebans were fast to exploit it. Plutarch describes what happened:

> But at this point Pelopidas darted forth from his position, and with his band of three hundred on the run, came up before Cleombrotus had either extended his wing or brought it back again into its old position and closed up his line of battle, so that the Spartans were not standing in array, but moving confusedly about among each other when his onset reached them. And yet the Spartans, who were masters at fighting while keeping solid formation ... since the phalanx of Epaminondas bore down upon them alone and neglected the rest of their force, and since Pelopidas engaged them with incredible speed and boldness, their courage and skill were so confounded that there was a flight and slaughter of the Spartans such as had never before been seen.[28]

Plutarch has telescoped or deleted events. Other sources say that the fighting was more even and prolonged, and that the Spartans withheld the attack for a while. But the combination of pressure by Epaminondas' phalanx, the quick deployment of Pelopidas and his Sacred Band against the Spartans in motion, and the fall of the Spartan king and other commanders decided the conflict. It is said that the allies on Cleombrotus' left retreated when they were under attack. If that is true, Epaminondas' right wing did more than defend its position.

Many of the battle accounts, however, focus on the fierce struggle over the body of Cleombrotus, who died of his wounds. The contestants probably included the Sacred Band and certainly Cleombrotus' 300 royal bodyguards, called "Cavalrymen," as well as the men who accompanied his second-in-command. For the Spartans, possession of the royal body was a matter of both pride and pragmatism. They had all grown up hearing the traumatic story of the contest over Leonidas' corpse at Thermopylae, and some probably remembered how they had more recently paid the Thebans a heavy price for Lysander's body (pp. 51–52, 224–225 above). At Leuctra the Spartans managed to

---

28. Plut. *Pelopidas* 23. See also Xen. *Hellenica* 6.4.13; Diod. 15.55.3–4; with Stylianou 1998, 404–407.

secure Cleombrotus' body and carried it to their fortified camp. This small victory in defeat was a consolation for them and their friends (including Xenophon). The body count told a different story, though. Of the divergent reports, Xenophon's figures appear the most reliable: nearly 1,000 Lacedaemonians died, including 400 full Spartan citizens out of the 700 who fought there. For a city with a shortage of citizens, this was a major blow. The Boeotians' reported losses ranged between 300, which seems too high unless they included those who left the Boeotian camp before battle (p. 292 above), and forty-seven, which is too low. Both the disparity in casualties and the consequences of the battle (below) arguably make Leuctra Sparta's worst defeat in its history.[29]

Xenophon described a "stiff upper lip" reaction to the disaster in Sparta, where the authorities behaved as if business were as usual, women's lamentations were banned, and the relatives of the dead walked about with cheerful faces and those of the living gloomy and downcast. Ignoring reality could go only so far, however, and those who were stuck in camp in Leuctra had to be rescued. The Spartans called for the muster of a Peloponnesian army at Corinth under Agesilaus' son, Archidamus, ordering it to sail to Boeotia. At the same time, the surviving Spartan generals in Leuctra were looking for a truce that would allow them to bury their dead and get their defeated army out of Boeotia. They met opposition from traditionalist Spartans, who refused to concede defeat and demanded a renewal of fighting to retrieve the bodies and prevent the Boeotians from setting up a trophy. The more realistic commanders silenced the protesters, afraid of adding more citizens to the roster of the fallen. They also had to deal with restive allies. The disproportional losses of Spartans in battle increased their dependence on the allies, who were demoralized and, according to some sources, happy with the Spartan disaster and looking to make a separate deal with the enemy. The truce depended on Epaminondas, who saw an opportunity to score a propaganda victory on top of the military one. When the Spartans asked his permission to collect the dead, he granted it only to their allies, who had few dead to bury because of their limited fighting, while 1,000 Spartans were left lying on the field. (They were easily recognizable by their red tunics and shields emblazoned with the letter lambda, Λ, for "Lacedaemonians.") It was only then that Epaminondas allowed the Spartans' burial. If the Spartans hoped to conceal the extent of their loss, Epaminondas' action advertised it.

29. Xen. *Hellenica* 6.4.13–15; Diod. 15.55.3–56.4; Plut. *Pelopidas* 23; *Agesilaus* 28; Pausanias 9.13.9–12.

He also humiliated them with the size of the defeat in front of the Boeotians and even the Peloponnesians.[30]

It remained to decide the fate of the troops in the Peloponnesian camp. The Thebans, probably including Epaminondas, wanted to go in for the kill. They also wished to give their war an all-Greek character and hurried to tell the Athenians of their victory in hopes that they would join them in the attack. The Athenians, unhappy with the prospect of a now-stronger Thebes, gave them the cold shoulder. The Thebans then requested help from their northern ally, the powerful Thessalian lord, Jason of Pherae. He arrived with cavalry and a mercenary force and was offered a role in a pincer-movement attack, in which he would descend on the Peloponnesian camp from above and the Boeotians would attack it from the front. But Jason had his own agenda and mediated a truce between the sides. Both parties were now amenable: the Spartans, who had wanted to get out of Boeotia all along, and the Thebans, who were growing more concerned about the prospective arrival of a Peloponnesian rescue force. Once again, Epaminondas exploited the situation to give preferential treatment to the Peloponnesian allies. He allowed them to leave first and let the Spartans go only after hearing that the Peloponnesian army had come closer to Boeotia. His twice driving a wedge between the Spartans and their allies was akin to his questioning the legitimacy of the Spartans' rule over non-Spartans in the peace conference that preceded the battle. Apparently he was quick to realize that Leuctra had opened the door to a new strategy for undermining the Peloponnesian League. He sent the Spartans home with the ominous statement that it was better to transfer the war from Boeotia to Sparta, a feat he eventually accomplished. The defeated Spartans hurried to Megara, where they united with their would-be rescuers, and the entire force disbanded in Corinth.[31]

It is remarkable that the Battle of Leuctra, which justifies the inclusion of Epaminondas among Greece's top generals, was also the first major battle in which he led an army. He displayed several high qualities there. Like Themistocles before Salamis, he combined courage, resolution, and ingenuity in persuading fellow Thebans and commanders to overcome their fear for their lives and of fighting a much superior enemy. His battle plan was based on a full understanding of the Spartans' tactics and state of mind, which enabled him to predict their moves if not provoke them. He also used

---

30. Reaction in Sparta: Xen. *Hellenica* 6.4.16–19. The Spartan camp and dead: Xen. *Hellenica* 6.4.14–15, 24; Pausanias 9.3.11–12; Plut. *Moralia* 193b.
31. Xen. *Hellenica* 6.4.19–25; Pausanias 9.3.9–12, 14.1; Plut. *Moralia* 193b. Jason: Sprawski 1999, 96–97.

original tactics when he matched the enemy's strength at the right with his own strengthened left wing. Although the Thebans had fought in deep formations before, no previous phalanx had been so deep as his. Once the quick action of Pelopidas and the Sacred Band had pinned down the enemy, it was only a matter of time before the weight of Epaminondas' massive phalanx and its ability to replenish losses would win the conflict.

Leuctra's outcomes made it one of the most important battles in Greek history. It established Theban dominance in Greece at the expense of Sparta, which never recovered her former dominion and military strength. A story about bad omens allegedly received by the Spartans before the battle illustrates their loss. It is said that wild, prickly weeds appeared suddenly on the head of Lysander's statue at Delphi, and that the golden stars in the Temple of Castor and Pollux commemorating his victory there disappeared. The suggestion is that Leuctra was the undoing of the triumph that had ushered in Spartan hegemony.[32]

Theban Supremacy and the First Invasion of the Peloponnese

Leuctra brought Epaminondas honor and fame, but he reportedly said that what pleased him most was that his parents were still alive when he defeated the Spartans there. It was a characteristic display of modesty with an implied put-down, this time of public accolades. He could get away with such an attitude because the battle had made him and Pelopidas the most influential leaders in Thebes and the Boeotian League. They had expanded its rule over Boeotian cities such as Thespia and Orchomenus, which could no longer rely on Sparta for aid. It is said that the Thebans wanted to enslave Orchomenus, much as the Spartans had allegedly wanted to do to Thebes, but that Epaminondas stopped them. The cost of the enslavement in Greek public opinion would have been too high, and it was possible to keep Thespia and Orchomenus in check by annexing them to their more loyal neighbors. Boeotia became even stronger when it acquired allies among its neighbors to the east, north, and west.[33]

---

32. Omens: Cicero *On Divination* 1.75. See Buckler 2003, 293n56, against Hanson's questioning (1988) of Epaminondas' tactical innovations, and Hanson's response: 2010, 114n7. Earlier deep Theban formations: Sprawski 2004, 16.

33. Epaminondas' glory and his reaction: Plut. *Pelopidas* 23; Plut. *Moralia* 193a. Thebes after Leuctra: Pausanias 9.4.2; Diod. 15.57.1, 62.3; Plut. *Comparison*

In the winter of 370–369, Epaminondas and Pelopidas led an army in an unprecedented invasion of Sparta, although that may not have been their original intention. Sparta's position had declined since Leuctra. It was unable to stop the Arcadian state of Mantinea from reuniting, or to keep several cities from forming an Arcadian league. Sparta could ill afford a strong, inimical Arcadia across its northern border, but its military campaigns there had accomplished little. Nevertheless, the Arcadian League was concerned for its safety, and together with Argos and Elis, old foes of Sparta, they asked Athens to join them in an anti-Spartan coalition. When the Athenians declined, the allies appealed to Thebes, which agreed to send a Boeotian army to the Peloponnese. It surely helped that Elis responded favorably to a Theban request for a ten-talent loan to cover the expenses of the expedition. The invading army included about 5,800 Thebans, allies from central and western Greece, and Thessalian peltasts and cavalry. Its leaders were Epaminondas and Pelopidas, although the sources' focus on the former suggests he was the senior partner. There are different versions of what the Theban generals hoped to achieve. The suggestion that they intended to defend the Arcadians against Sparta makes the best sense. Indeed, their leaving in early winter—normally the close of the campaigning season—and the fact that the generals' term of office was ending indicate that they expected a short, local campaign in or around Arcadia. Epaminondas, of course, would not have minded meeting the Spartans there again in a pitched battle.[34]

When the coalition partners met in Mantinea, the Peloponnesian generals pressed Epaminondas to extend the goal of the campaign from a rescue operation to an invasion of Sparta. They reasoned that, in contrast to the relatively small Spartan army, the coalition commanded a huge force: ancient accounts run from 40,000 hoplites to a total of 70,000 men, including light-armed and noncombatants, although modern estimates cut the figure to 30,000. The invaders had also the right kind of soldiers in terms of quality and specialization; namely, hoplites, peltasts, and cavalry, who could deal effectively with the Spartans and their terrain. We may imagine that the Peloponnesians mentioned the prospect of raiding the rich Spartan countryside as an added incentive. Other generals had

between *Pelopidas and Marcellus* 1; Xen. *Hellenica* 6.5.23; *Agesilaus* 2.24; Buckler 2003, 297–298.

34. Xen. *Hellenica* 5.1–22 (helping Arcadia); Diod. 15.62.1–5; Demosthenes 16.12, 19; Plut. *Pelopidas* 24; cf. Nepos *Epaminondas* 7; Buckler 1980, 138; Stylianou 1998, 426.

adjusted their plans or aims in accordance with local recommendations (see, e.g., pp. 148–149 above), yet our sources say the Theban generals were hesitant, even divided. Some Boeotarchs wanted to go home because the enemy was no longer there, winter was coming, and their term in office was approaching its end. The Thebans also learned that the Spartans had blocked the roads to their country in narrow places where the invaders' numerical advantage would be neutralized, and they expected the Spartans to fight especially hard for their homeland. Epaminondas and Pelopidas, who had showed their readiness to take great risks in the past, disagreed. There was an important consideration in favor of the invasion. Local perioeci, the underclass residents of Sparta, told the Thebans about an undefended passage. They also promised an open revolt if the army came, and claimed that many perioeci were already evading the draft. Epaminondas was receptive to their message because it conformed to his strategy of isolating the Spartans from other residents of the country. He and Pelopidas succeeded in persuading their colleagues to follow them. No one knew at the time that this would be the first of four invasions of the Peloponnese.

It has been argued that Epaminondas' attack on Sparta constituted a preemptive strategy designed to eliminate the threat of a Spartan invasion of Boeotia. The evidence, however, suggests a fear, not for Thebes, but for its allies in the Peloponnese. Epaminondas' offer of military help and encouragement of democratic governments among them shows that he wished to expand Theban influence there rather than defend Boeotia. Hence, invading Sparta was more a means than the goal of his policy; he did not originally plan to attack the city, neither now nor in his fourth invasion of the Peloponnese (below).[35]

Having decided to invade Sparta, the Theban generals sat together with their Peloponnesian colleagues to plan the campaign. Entering Sparta at one place with the whole coalition army would have played into the defenders' hands, as well as entailing the logistical problems of keeping a very large and diverse army together and on the march. It was much more effective to approach in four separate columns from four different directions, preferably at the same time. The invaders calculated that the small Spartan army,

---

35. War council and invasion: Xen. *Hellenica* 6.5.23–25; Diod. 15.62.5 (50,000 soldiers), 81.2 (70,000); Plut. *Agesilaus* 30; *Pelopidas* 24 (40,000 hoplites and up to 70,000 men, c. 5,800 Boeotians); cf. *Moralia* 346b. 30,000 men: Cartledge 1987, 232. See Wiseman 1969; Hamilton, 1991, 220–231; Stylianou 1998, 423–444. Preemptive strategy: Hanson 2010; cf. Hanson 1999, 72–94.

not yet reinforced by its Peloponnesian allies, could not possibly defend the unwalled city *and* all four routes simultaneously. Accordingly, Epaminondas and the Boeotians marched on the main road from Tegea to Sparta, passing Caryae, which revolted for them as the perioeci had promised. The Argives used a route to Epaminondas' east, and the Arcadians and the Eleans took one to his west. While the Boeotians and the Eleans met no resistance, both the Argives and the Arcadians had to overcome local guards, including a Spartan commander who insisted on imitating Leonidas' last stand at Thermopylae, with identical results. The four armies reunited at Sellasia, about 13 kilometers north of Sparta.[36]

The invaders burned and plundered Sellasia. It was the first of many such depredations on local houses and settlements. Raiding and looting were well-tried ways of warfare, and in this case had the added value of humiliating the Spartans, who often boasted that they had never seen enemy smoke in their country. And yet Sellasians and other victims of the raids included perioeci or helots, whom Epaminondas regarded as potential partners in his plan of isolating Sparta. Apparently they and many other locals remained loyal to Sparta. In any case, he could not control his Peloponnesian allies, who intended to maximize their profits.[37]

From Sellasia, the invaders advanced toward Sparta and marched along the eastern bank of the River Eurotas, which bordered the town. Epaminondas wanted to cross over to the city, but it was winter, and the river was swollen. Besides, Spartan hoplites were waiting for the invaders at a bridge. Epaminondas opted to continue to Amyclae, an important Spartan cult center about 5 kilometers south of the city. The march to the town and its capture were accompanied by heavy looting. After crossing the river at Amyclae, Epaminondas turned back north to the city of Sparta.

The invasion provoked a crisis in Sparta that King Agesilaus tried to manage. We hear about Spartan women, famous for their toughness, being made hysterical by the enemy's nearness. There were conspiracies of citizens and non-citizens, and helots and perioeci switched sides. Some Spartans, captives of their own reputation, called unhelpfully for a confrontation with the enemy, regardless of the consequences. Agesilaus overcame these challenges

36. Roads to Sparta: Diod. 15.63.3–64.5; Xen. *Hellenica* 6.5.25–26; Buckler 1980, 77–79, and see Map 2, p. 27.
37. Sellasia: Xen. *Hellenica* 6.5.26; Cartledge 2002, 86, 161. Diod. 15.64.1, however, says that it defected, perhaps after the destruction; cf. Xen. *Hellenica* 7.4.12. Strategy of destruction and pillaging: Hanson 1998. Spartan boasts: Plut. *Agesilaus* 31; *Moralia* 192c.

and adopted a defensive policy of avoiding a pitched battle against a greatly superior enemy. He spread his soldiers among easily defensible places and tried to augment his army by promising freedom to helots. Six thousand helots reportedly volunteered for service. Peloponnesian states still loyal to Sparta sent about 4,000 soldiers, who evaded the invaders and reached the city. But the odds were clearly in Epaminondas' favor.

What happened next is something of a puzzle. Epaminondas approached Sparta but left after a few insignificant clashes. Why didn't he seek a decision? Part of the answer lies in the Spartan countermeasures. In spite of Theban taunts or threats, the Spartans declined to give him a second Leuctra. The now-reinforced Spartan army had a deterrent power, and attacking the well-defended Spartan positions meant turning the war into a protracted struggle, in which Epaminondas could see no advantage to be gained. But these were all secondary considerations, because he had the forces to win a battle on the field or in the city. We have to conclude that his primary wish, and probably that of his Peloponnesian partners, was not to ruin Sparta, but merely to raid its territory and weaken and humiliate it. There was no need to conquer Sparta in order to establish Theban supremacy in Greece. Epaminondas had a better idea: creating a Spartan nemesis in the form of the city of Messene.[38]

It is said that when Agesilaus saw Epaminondas, he took a long look at him and said, "O man who is capable of great deeds!" The foundation of Messene was considered proof of Epaminondas' greatness, though Agesilaus would have strongly protested. Before founding the city, Epaminondas plundered his way to the southern port of Gythium in an attempt to destroy this Spartan outlet to the sea (with an unclear outcome). A few weeks later, he founded Messene on Mount Ithome, an ancient Messenian political and spiritual center that resonated with the glory of past rebellions against Sparta. The site allowed Epaminondas to legitimize the new city as a re-foundation of an old one. He granted citizenship to Greeks of Messenian descent as well of other origins, including helots and perioeci. The city's territory included lands previously owned by Spartans. The foundation, in short, dealt a severe blow to Sparta's infrastructure, security, and overall system. The Spartans regarded Messene as a permanent threat, as Epaminondas had intended. Their stubborn refusal to accept Messene's autonomy isolated them in the

---

38. Xen. *Hellenica* 6.5.27–31; 7.2.2–3; Diod. 15.64.6–65.6 (mentions only 1,000 volunteer helots and unlikely large-scale conflicts with the invaders); Plut. *Agesilaus* 31–33; *Pelopidas* 24; Polyaenus 2.1.27 and Frontinus *Stratagems* 1.10.3 (on a successful Spartan ambush); Polyaenus 2.1.29; Xen. *Agesilaus* 2.24; Cartledge 2002, 253–255.

FIGURE 18 *The Arcadian Gate, Messene.* This was the main western entrance into the city. Messene's walls and towers were well built, in places reaching 7–9 meters, and defended the city and its countryside.
Gianni Dagli Orti/The Art Archive at Art Resource, New York

Greek world, just as Thebes had been isolated before Leuctra. But there was not much the Spartans could do about it at the time, because they had to recover from a destructive invasion, and Epaminondas had left a garrison in Messene for its protection. He may even have initiated the building of its impressive walls (Figure 18). He could now add to his growing list of honors the high distinction of being the founder of a city.[39]

The entire invasion lasted about three months, part of which was spent wintering in Arcadia. But it had already begun to disintegrate at Sparta. Epaminondas' Peloponnesian partners were independent-minded, and although they accepted his military leadership, there were tensions, if not disharmony, in headquarters. Many Arcadians left for home because they were anxious to save their loot and because an Athenian force based in

39. Gythium: Xen. *Hellenica* 6.5.32. Epaminondas' greatness: Plut. *Ages.* 32; Diod. 15.66.1. Messene: Diod. 15.66.1–67.1; Pausanias 4.26.3–27.9; 9.14.5; Plut. *Agesilaus* 34; *Pelopidas* 24; Isocrates *Archidamus* 28; Nepos *Epaminondas* 8; Luraghi 2008, 209–229.

Corinth, led by the talented general Iphicrates, had invaded their country. (Athens had promised to help Sparta in its distress.) Furthermore, the winter and plunder had exhausted local resources and made it difficult to maintain the large army. In early spring of 369, Epaminondas led the Boeotians back home. His way was blocked at a passage in the Megaran Isthmus by an Athenian force led by Iphicrates, but he evaded it by a different route and even killed twenty Athenian cavalrymen on the way. He then defiantly marched by Athens, and although some Athenians wanted to confront him, cooler heads prevailed. He disbanded the army and went home to Thebes.[40]

According to our sources, instead of receiving a hero's welcome, Epaminondas, Pelopidas, and their colleagues were put on trial for illegally extending their command (p. 300 above). The charge was politically motivated, and Epaminondas reportedly volunteered to take all the blame. When it was his turn to face the judges, he stood up and said that

> his actions were his best speech, but if anything at all were to be answered to the judges, he entreated them, if they put him to death, to write his fault on his tombstone that the Greeks might know that Epaminondas compelled the Thebans against their will to plunder and burn Laconia, which in 500 years had never suffered the like, to build Messene 230 years after it was sacked, to unite the Arcadians, and to restore freedom to Greece; for those things were done in that expedition.

It is said that the judges burst out laughing and acquitted all the generals, or did not even bother to issue a sentence.[41]

The anecdote illustrates Epaminondas' courage; yet there was something disagreeable about his statements, especially as the case against him had legal merit. Though he clearly deserved high praise for his accomplishments, his resentment of not being properly appreciated was mixed with arrogance and contempt toward the people. He also did not achieve his victories single-handedly. This point came up in a different trial involving his good friend

---

40. Plut. *Pelopidas* 24–25; *Agesilaus* 32–33 (rightly questions the claim that the Spartans bribed the enemy to leave); *Moralia* 817f; Diod.15.67.1; Aelian *Historical Miscellany* 13.42; Wiseman 1987, 177–180. Iphicrates: Xen. *Hellenica* 6.5.33–52; Diod. 15.63.2 (predating events, *pace* Stylianou 1998, 426–429); Plut. *Pelopidas* 24; Pausanias 9.14.6–7; Polyaenus 3.9.28; and for a different interpretation: Buckler 1980, 89.

41. Quotation: Plut. *Moralia* 194b. For the trial, see also Plut. *Pelopidas* 25; *Moralia* 540e, 817f; Nepos *Epaminondas* 8; Aelian *Historical Miscellany* 13.42; Appian *Syrian Wars* 41; Buckler 1978; 1980, 137–142.

Pelopidas, who argued there that military victory was the work of the entire people, not of individual generals. It was a fine democratic principle, but it is unlikely that he or Epaminondas applied it to themselves.[42]

The Second Invasion of the Peloponnese

From at least 369, Pelopidas and Epaminondas seem to have operated in different regions: Pelopidas in northern Greece and Epaminondas in the Peloponnese. With Epaminondas' blessing, Pelopidas led an army to Thessaly, where he expanded Theban patronage and alliances to include the city of Larissa, countering the ambitions of Alexander, the Thessalian ruler of Pherae. The latter was portrayed as a tyrant, and Pelopidas used the ideals of democracy and freedom to justify the campaign. He must also have strengthened his personal connections in the region, because he later appeared as the patron of the Thessalians in Thebes (below). As with Lysander, his personal and public activities were compatible. Pelopidas also extended Theban influence to Macedonia, where he supported King Alexander II against a rival. To ensure the king's loyalty, Pelopidas took the king's brother Philip with him to Thebes as a hostage. Had he foreseen the future, he would have considered other treatment for the Macedonian prince. Philip (II), the future king of Macedonia, would greatly reduce Thebes' power, and his son, Alexander the Great, would raze it to the ground.[43]

In 369, envoys from Thebes' Peloponnesian allies Argos, Arcadia, and Elis asked Epaminondas to lead a second joint campaign in the Peloponnese. This time the targets were Corinth, Sicyon, and other northern Peloponnesians who were these pleaders' enemies, and allies of Sparta. Epaminondas and the Thebans agreed to attack them because a hegemonic state was expected to keep its allies satisfied if it wanted to maintain its position, and because the campaign could weaken the Spartan alliance. Indeed, Sparta was now allied with Athens, which was highly concerned about a powerful Thebes on its border. An added incentive must have been the prospect of replicating the profitable raids of the last invasion. In the summer of 369, Epaminondas took 7,000 Boeotian infantry, 600 cavalrymen, and an unknown number of light infantry to the main road to the Peloponnese, where they were supposed to rendezvous with their allies.

42. Pelopidas' statement: Plut. *Pelopidas* 25; cf. Roisman 2014, 280–281.
43. Plut. *Pelopidas* 26; Diod. 14.67.3–4, 71.2; Polybius 8.35.6–7; Georgiadou 1992, 4235–4238.

Unlike the last invasion, this one found the enemy prepared. A coalition of Athenians led by the talented general Chabrias gathered in Corinth with troops from Sparta, Corinth, and Achaean Pellene, to a total number of 20,000. In spite of their numerical advantage, they did not seek a pitched battle with Epaminondas, probably because after Leuctra and the invasion of Sparta, his military reputation and that of Boeotia were deterrents. The anti-Theban coalition instead took the safer course of trying to defend the Isthmus. There Mount Oneion stretched to the eastern shore, and limited the path into the Peloponnese to a western way by the well-defended citadel Corinth and an eastern coastal way by Cenchreae. The anti-Theban forces divided strategic high positions on the mountain among themselves, with the Spartans and the Pelleneans guarding the easier passage on its northeastern slope, where they surrounded themselves with fences and trenches and waited for the enemy.

Epaminondas learned about their preparations while on the march. When he reached a plain about 5 kilometers from the mountain, he offered battle. It is hard to imagine that he thought that the enemy would give up their advantage in safety and topography by accepting the challenge, but his dare and their refusal bolstered his soldiers' morale. He then set about dislodging the Spartans and the Pelleneans from their fortifications, choosing this task because their position made them the easiest to attack, and because the Spartans were his arch-enemies. His planning recalls the tactics of Lysander and Dionysius of Syracuse. Like Lysander at Aegospotami (pp. 202–203 above) and Dionysius at Motya (pp. 250–251 above), he habituated the enemy to a routine, in this case one of night attacks by light-armed troops, repeatedly recalling the attackers at daybreak. He also carefully observed the enemy's dispositions and movements in order to use the knowledge against them. Then he charged at dawn, when the enemy was least prepared. With a punctuality that involved computing the time it took to get from his camp to the enemy, he surprised the defenders exactly when the night watch was over and the soldiers were rising for their daily chores. The "best of the Thebans" (probably the Sacred Band) led the charge. After fierce fighting, the attackers breached the enemy's defenses and put them to the sword or to flight. The Spartan survivors, led by their officer (polemarch), retreated to higher ground nearby. Then the two sides made a deal that allowed the Spartans to leave and the Thebans to continue their march. The historian Xenophon thought that the Spartan officer should have held his position, because he could have called for reinforcements from other contingents on the mountain and for supplies from

Cenchreae. Xenophon also suggests, much too optimistically, that the Thebans even contemplated going back because of the Spartan threat to their march. Yet his critique in hindsight is based on the unlikely premise that Epaminondas would have allowed human and material aid to reach the Spartans. Equally retrospective and invalid is the charge, made later in Thebes, that Epaminondas could have killed many of the enemy. In fact, the goals of the Thebans and the Spartans happened to coincide. The Spartans wanted to avoid losing soldiers to death or capture in a disaster like Pylos (pp. 155–162 above), while Epaminondas had no wish to linger on the mountain. Each party then went its separate way.[44]

After uniting with Argive, Arcadian, and Elean forces somewhere south of Corinth, Epaminondas led the army west of the city, where he made significant gains, forcing the cities of Pellene and Sicyon to change sides. Now or later, Sicyon received a Boeotian garrison, which ensured its loyalty, at least temporarily. Epaminondas and Thebes' means of hegemonic control—a friendly government and a garrison— thus resembled those used by Athens and Sparta.[45]

An episode associated with a town near Sicyon illustrates Epaminondas' character and *modus operandi*. He had captured a group of Boeotian exiles and there was a Theban standing order to kill all Boeotian prisoners of war as opposed to other captives who could be exchanged for ransom. Epaminondas had a different idea: he gave them a non-Boeotian identity and then freed them. It was the second time he bent the rules. In his first invasion of the Peloponnese, he had illegally prolonged the term of his own and his colleagues' office so that he could lead the campaign, and his acquittal in a trial for the action must have given him the confidence that he could do it again. Yet the incident showed more than a disdain for regulations or a sense that he knew better than the people what was good for them. Epaminondas believed that moderation could work just as well as punishment in the exercise of power, as he showed in stopping the Thebans from enslaving Orchomenus and even in sparing Sparta in the previous invasion and its troops on Mount Oneion. His aversion to unnecessary

44. The present description tries to reconcile Xen. *Hellenica* 7.1.15–17, 2.5, with Diod. 15.68.1–5, 72.1–2. See also Frontinus *Stratagems* 2.5.26; Polyaenus 2.3.9; Pausanias 9.15.4 (mislocating the fighting). Stylianou 1998, 446–451, dates the invasion to 368.

45. Xen. *Hellenica* 7.1.18–22, 44–47, 2.11, 3.8–11; Diod. 15.69.1–70.3. Polyaenus 5.16.3 describes how Sicyon's harbor was taken by a stratagem; cf. Aeneas Tacticus 29.12.

bloodshed distinguished him from such generals as Demosthenes, Lysander, and Dionysius.[46]

From Sicyon, Epaminondas marched southeast against the cities of Epidaurus and Troezen. Argos, the nearest of his allies to these cities, may have recommended the move. He failed to take both objectives because their garrisons were too strong, and he settled for raiding and destroying their property outside the walls, as he had done in the first invasion. From there, he turned to the big catch, Corinth. Besieging it was an unattractive option, since the city and its ports were well defended by strong fortifications and by local and allied troops. At first, the Corinthians and their allies did what Epaminondas hoped they would, coming out in force to meet him and suffering defeat. Epaminondas saw an opportunity to storm the city and ordered the Sacred Band to lead the charge on its southern gate. A number of Theban soldiers got inside, but the Athenian general Chabrias, who was in the city, saved the day. He repelled the attack with his Athenians and used light infantry to occupy high spots near the walls, including burial mounds, giving his projectile-launchers an advantage in elevation and easy access to ammunition and shelter in the city. In spite of the invaders' repeated charges and numerical superiority, they suffered heavy losses and were forced to retreat "under fire." It was Epaminondas' and the Sacred Band's first recorded loss. Moreover, the Corinthians, perhaps learning from the master himself, used the enemy dead as a weapon, dragging them next to the walls and giving them back only under truce. Epaminondas was forced to admit defeat in front of his allies. Though he reportedly mocked Chabrias for erecting a trophy over only a few Theban dead, such ridicule fails to diminish the Athenian's achievement.[47]

Epaminondas' next step followed a familiar course of action: unsuccessful in taking the city, he turned into devastating its countryside. Units of his army spread over the plain southwest of Corinth to destroy houses, crops, and trees. Once again, the Corinthians were rescued by their allies. Twenty triremes arrived from their old friend Dionysius I, the tyrant of Syracuse, carrying Celtic and Iberian mercenaries and fifty cavalrymen. The Corinthians were happy to let the newcomers do the fighting, which they managed with great skill and success. Xenophon takes special notice of the Sicilian cavalry, which split into small groups that used hit-and-run tactics to attack the enemy with their javelins. Epaminondas had no better solution than to

46. Pausanias 9.15.4.
47. Xen. *Hell*. 7.1.18–19; Diod. 15.69.1–4 (Chabrias in Corinth); Plutarch *Moralia* 193f.

close the infantry ranks and charge back or to send cavalry against them, but the Sicilians were too good at retreating and then charging again. Not long afterwards, the invading army dissolved into its constituent contingents and went home.[48]

In spite of the failure at Corinth, Epaminondas' second invasion of the Peloponnese had some successes. He expanded the anti-Spartan coalition at the expense of the Peloponnesian league, inflicted damage on Spartan allies, and enriched his soldiers. But he failed to capture Epidaurus, Troezen, and Corinth, and his defeats at the hands of Chabrias' light infantry and the Sicilian cavalry suggest that he had difficulties dealing with skilled specialists and unfamiliar tactics. His lack of success must have angered and disappointed his countrymen. The Thebans had grown accustomed to an uninterrupted series of victories, and not everyone approved his lenient treatment of the Boeotian exiles. His opponents, including his old enemy Menecleides, impeached him for allowing the Spartans on Mount Oneion to escape unharmed, claiming that he had done it as a personal favor to the Spartans. (Prioritizing personal over public interest was a common charge in democracies.) If Epaminondas tried again to shame his judges into acquitting him, it did not work. The court found Epaminondas guilty, deposed him from his Boeotarchy, and perhaps fined him.[49]

Pelopidas' Missteps in Thessaly

Epaminondas' colleague Pelopidas fared no better. His previous political settlements in Thessaly and Macedonia were near collapse, partly because they relied on weak allies. Thebes' Thessalian friends repeatedly complained about the expansionist ambitions of the Thessalian ruler, Alexander of Pherae, and Pelopidas, their friend and patron, went to their rescue. Unlike Epaminondas, he was unable or thought it unnecessary to take an army with him. Instead, he and a fellow envoy, Ismenias, went to northern Greece in 368 with a small company, believing that they were protected by the ancient Greek version of diplomatic immunity and by the might of Boeotia they represented. When in Thessaly, Pelopidas learned that the Macedonian nobleman Ptolemy had become the ruler of his country after killing its king, Alexander (II), Thebes' ally. The danger to Theban influence in Macedonia

48. Xen. *Hell.* 7.1.20–22; Diod. 15.70.1–2.
49. Epaminondas' trial: Diod. 15.72.1–2; Nepos *Epaminondas* 7; Plut. *Pelopidas* 25, 28; Wiseman 1969, 186–192; Buckler 1980, 142–145.

was compounded by an Athenian intervention in support of the new regime. Pelopidas collected a mercenary force in Thessalian Pharsalus (probably paid by local friends) and marched to Macedonia. Although Ptolemy succeeded in luring away Pelopidas' mercenaries, the two leaders made a deal that returned Macedonia to the Theban fold. Pelopidas went back to Thessaly and collected a small force in order to punish the turncoat mercenaries by capturing their families in Pharsalus. But then Alexander of Pherae spoiled Pelopidas and Ismenias' good work of restoring Theban power. Alexander arrived at Pharsalus with an army, and when Pelopidas and Ismenias went out to meet with him without taking precautions for their safety, Alexander seized them and put them under arrest. His motives are unclear and may have included a mixture of revenge and provocation. Besides, the two Thebans made ideal bargaining chips. Pelopidas was criticized in antiquity for showing poor judgment in trusting the tyrant, and the criticism does not seem inaccurate.[50]

Stories of uncertain historicity about Pelopidas' stay with Alexander in Pherae show the two men behaving as less than perfect host and guest. At first Alexander allowed Pelopidas to interact freely with the locals, a privilege Pelopidas took advantage of in order to accuse Alexander of tyranny, of killing innocent citizens, and of being hated by the gods. The story aims to show Pelopidas as a courageous, free man and a sworn enemy of tyranny, but it also suggests the excessive confidence that got him into trouble in the first place. Alexander then put Pelopidas in chains and solitary confinement, although he did not prevent Thebe, Alexander's wife, from visiting Pelopidas. The two spent long hours hating Alexander, yet it is doubtful if he cared. He was much too busy making preparations for an upcoming Theban invasion, including a defensive alliance with Athens, which sent him thirty triremes with 1,000 soldiers aboard.[51]

The Thebans were naturally upset about the kidnapping of their delegates and planned to get them back by force or by negotiation backed by an invading army. They put up a force of 8,000 hoplites and 600 cavalrymen and sent it to Thessaly. Both the size of the army and its mission of rescuing two Thebans were exceptional, yet the prominent politicians Ismenias and

---

50. Plut. *Pelopidas* 27; Diod. 15.71.1–2; Nepos *Pelopidas* 5; Pausanias 9.15.1; Polybius 8.35.6–7 (criticizing Pelopidas); Plut. *Moralia* 194d; Georgiadou 1997, 196–199. There is no evidence for Buckler's speculation (1980, 116–17) that Pelopidas reconstituted the Thessalian federal army.

51. Pelopidas in Pherae: Plut. *Pelopidas* 28; *Moralia* 194d. Athens–Alexander alliance: Demosthenes 23.120; Diod. 15.71.3–4.

Pelopidas, the latter the hero of Tegyra and Leuctra, were not ordinary citizens. Furthermore, saving both men legitimized and personalized a campaign whose other goal was to reduce Alexander's power. Epaminondas joined the expedition as a regular soldier, either because he failed the annual election to the Boeotarchy or because he was temporarily barred from it. For him, saving Pelopidas was an act of patriotism and personal friendship, and he would not miss it.

The Boeotian army marched to rendezvous with Thessalian allies around friendly Larissa or further north at Pharsalus, where they intended to offer battle to Alexander. The tyrant had more horsemen, but the Boeotians and the Thessalians had many high-quality hoplites and cavalry to justify the risk. The odds soon changed. For unknown reasons, the Thessalian allies left for home, while Alexander was joined by his Athenian and other allies. The Boeotian invaders found themselves hard-pressed for water and supplies, probably because of harassment by Alexander's cavalry, and their commanders decided to call the campaign off. They led the way home in the direction of Thermopylae, but Alexander would not let them go in peace. His cavalry attacked them, especially on flat terrain, and his light-armed troops shot at them from a safe distance. Although the Theban generals had horsemen and light-armed soldiers who could repel the attackers, they apparently used them ineffectively, if at all. Casualties mounted, and dissatisfaction with the generals grew when Alexander surprised them on rough terrain somewhere north of Thermopylae. Once again in Epaminondas' career, formal procedures gave way to pressing military needs. Although he had no rank, the soldiers elected him as their general. He restored order among the hoplite files and put them at the head of his column. He himself protected the rear with cavalry and light infantry, who checked or pursued Alexander's men. According to one report, he also used the stratagem of a smokescreen in order to cross a bridge over the River Spechius, which was watched by Thessalian enemies. There was nothing remarkable or novel about his tactics. What made the difference was the leadership he provided, the confidence he inspired in the soldiers, and his effective use of available units. He made it safely home, where the original leaders of the expedition were put on trial and heavily fined. He may have taken part in their prosecution.[52]

---

52. Boeotian invasion: Diod. 15.71.3–7; Pausanias 9.15.1–2; Nepos *Epaminondas* 7; *Pelopidas* 5; Plut. *Pelopidas* 29; Polyaenus 2.3.13 (the bridge crossing, which Buckler 1980, 127, dates to Epaminondas' next expedition); cf. Plut. *Moralia* 193d; 680b; 797a–b.

Epaminondas returned with an army to Thessaly the next year, 376, this time as a general, to perform a delicate balancing act familiar from other hostage situations. He wanted Pelopidas and Ismenias alive but could not force his way into Pherae for fear they would be harmed. He also knew that Alexander wanted a settlement and that he would not harm the hostages unless forced to. Therefore, in spite of local Thessalian pressure to confront Alexander in battle and, reportedly, the desire of Alexander's subjects to get rid of him, Epaminondas bided his time. He put pressure on the tyrant by moving around with his army, making preparations for battle and then delaying it, engaging all the while in negotiations with him. The two eventually struck a deal: Alexander gave back the hostages in return for a thirty-day truce and a Boeotian retreat. It was a compromise in which both sides won and lost a little. Alexander did not get peace with Thebes but lost no territory or power, while Epaminondas got the hostages back but was unable to change the status quo in Thessaly. The freed Pelopidas declared his gratitude to Alexander, a notoriously cruel and faithless man, for finding out in prison that he (Pelopidas) had the courage not only to fight but also to die. His self-discovery, however, came at a heavy price in Boeotian casualties and expenditures. Furthermore, his and Epaminondas' interventions in northern Greece show the limited, reactive nature of Theban policy there. It was as if they went to Thessaly or Macedonia only to put out fires that others had started.[53]

Even Pelopidas' next assignment that year (367) came in response to others' initiatives, this time from Sparta and Athens. The two states sent envoys to the Persian king Artaxerxes II to seek his support against Thebes. The Boeotians and their Peloponnesian allies responded by sending the king a delegation that included the two former hostages, Pelopidas and Ismenias, as well as Arcadian and Elean ambassadors. Pelopidas' diplomatic and military experience highly qualified him for the mission, and his winning record against Sparta, which he touted in Persia, endeared him to Persians who remembered Spartan aggression against them. Xenophon, who favored Sparta over Thebes, claims that Pelopidas gained the king's good will by recounting all the good deeds that Thebes had done Persia in the past, including its infamous betrayal of the Greeks in the Persian War (480–479). He even reportedly belittled his fellow Peloponnesian envoys by boasting that they could not face up to Sparta without Thebes at their

---

53. Plut. *Pelopidas* 29; *Moralia* 194d; Diod. 15.75.2; cf. Buckler 1980, 126. I share the scholarly view that Epaminondas was not involved in the Arcadian foundation of Megalopolis concluded in 368: e.g., Hornblower 1990, 73–77.

side. We can imagine that Pelopidas was more tactful. He also left Persia with a very good deal for his city. The king approved his request that Greek states—in particular Messene, Sparta's bane—should be independent, that Athens deactivate its navy, and that the Greeks wage war against any state that opposed the agreement. After his return, a draft of this common peace was brought up for approval by a Greek congress that met in Thebes, the first such gathering there. It was rejected, and anti-Theban Xenophon glee-fully notes: "Thus it was that this attempt on the part of Pelopidas and the Thebans to gain the *arche* (hegemony) came to its end." But the effort was not a complete failure. Thanks to Pelopidas' diplomacy and persuasive pow-ers, Thebes could now present itself as the successor to Athens and Sparta as the leader in Greek international politics, its position confirmed by the Persian king and even by the Greeks' presence at the congress. Naturally, the Thebans would have loved for the Greeks to accept their leadership, but it is doubtful that they considered the Greeks' refusal to do so a major defeat.[54]

The Third Invasion of the Peloponnese and the Naval Bill

In 366, Epaminondas took an army to the Peloponnese for the third time. His target was the Achaean League in the northern Peloponnese, for sev-eral reasons. Adding Achaea to the Boeotian alliance would have expanded its supremacy in the Corinthian Gulf, weakened Achaea's ally Sparta, and threatened neighboring Corinth, which had led the opposition to the last invasion and to the recent Theban attempt at a common peace. A friendly Achaea could also replace the Arcadians, formerly Thebes' chief ally in the Peloponnese, with whom Thebes' relationship had soured. Finally, Achaea could play a role in Epaminondas' grand plan of turning Thebes into a mari-time power (below).

The road to Achaea went through the Isthmus and Mount Oneion, where Epaminondas had fought his way through before (pp. 306–307 above). In prob-able anticipation of his march, a guard made up of Athenians and mercenaries in Sparta's pay occupied the mountain. Once again, the Theban general proved to be a skilled planner and coordinator. He arranged for a force of 2,000 hoplites

54. Xen. *Hellenica* 7.1.33–40; Plut. *Pelopidas* 30–31; *Artaxerxes* 22; Nepos *Pelopidas* 4; Diod. 15.81.3.

from Argos to occupy a hill overlooking Cenchreae overnight, about where he had marched the last time. Their arrival from the south utterly surprised the guard on the mountain, which was waiting for Epaminondas to come from the north. The Argives had brought with them seven days' supplies, and Epaminondas timed his arrival to occur within that period. He thus was able to march through the Isthmus without trouble. He then joined forces with local allies, including perhaps the Argive force, and went to Achaea, a region embroiled in political conflicts. Many Achaean cities had oligarchic governments that were neutral or pro-Spartan, while Epaminondas' natural allies were the democratic opposition. Nevertheless, he did not initiate or support a change of government, but made a deal with the oligarchs that kept them in power in return for their cities' allegiance to Thebes. He correctly reasoned that a bloodless agreement was preferable to war or sieges, which would have ended in the same result, even if successful. But his domestic rivals and the Arcadian and Achaean enemies of the Achaean rulers strongly disagreed, and when Epaminondas returned home, they complained that his settlement was good for Sparta and its Achaean friends. Epaminondas lost the debate, and the Thebans sent governors and presumably garrisons to Achaea, who acted with local democrats to banish the oligarchs from the cities. The oligarchs had powerful followers and friends, however, and succeeded in effecting their return by force. They now became unequivocal supporters of Sparta, whose enmity to Thebes and Arcadia they shared. Though Epaminondas was ostensibly wiser than those opposed to him, it is impossible to judge whether or not his original arrangement would have outlasted its strong opposition. He also erred in thinking he had enough authority at home to get his nonpartisan settlement approved.

More successful was his removal of Achaean garrisons from Naupactus and Calydon on the Corinthian Gulf, and from Dyme at its entrance. These operations diminished the scope of Achaean power and gained Thebes friends against Athens and Corinth, which were active in the region. Furthermore, Dyme and Naupactus in particular could serve as bases for a Boeotian navy if its presence was required in and around the Gulf.[55]

Possibly during the year of the invasion, 366, Epaminondas also initiated a major Boeotian shipbuilding program of 100 triremes. Landlocked Thebes had never been a naval power, nor did it have a good harbor or the resources required for one. It was both audacious and ambitious on Epaminondas' part, then, to try to rival Athens' dominance on the sea. Nevertheless, there was

---

55. Xen. *Hellenica* 7.1.41–43; Diod. 15.75.2, and possibly Ephorus *BNJ* 70 F 84. Friends on the Gulf: *pace* Buckler 1980, 189–191.

the Spartan example to show that it could be done. In persuading the Theban assembly to approve his project, Epaminondas reportedly used Sparta's control of the joint Greek navy against Xerxes as an example of a state that had a small navy, but whose land power gave it the right to command the much larger Athenian fleet. A better example would have been Sparta after the Peloponnesian War, a city that actually ruled both the Greek mainland and the Aegean. The project involved significant logistical and organizational challenges and was very expensive. It required obtaining material for the ships, constructing 100 triremes (which may be only an approximate number), building facilities for them, and training and paying the crews. Yet these were not insurmountable difficulties. As suggested by scholars, the Boeotian harbors of Larymna and Aulis, across from Euboea, provided good bases for a fleet operating in the Aegean. The Theban invasions of the Peloponnese, especially the first one, had mitigated financial difficulties by producing surplus revenues. Boeotia must have also had rich individuals who, as at Athens, could help defray some of the cost, and Thebes may also have gotten Persian subsidies for the program. Training or hiring expert rowers could furnish the skilled men needed to operate the ships, and the Thebans also relied on cooperation with the navies of Aegean states such as Rhodes, Chios, and Byzantium, which they hoped shared the Theban desire to curtail Athens' power. Finally, there was Epaminondas' infectious belief in Thebes' ability to become a dominant power in Greece. It was not difficult for a man who had destroyed the Spartan myth of invincibility on land to imagine doing the same to Athens at sea. But he was not contemplating the conquest of Athens, except in the nightmares of the Athenians, one of whose orators spoke of Epaminondas' wish to move the Propylaea, the magnificent main gates to the Acropolis, to the Theban citadel of the Cadmeia.[56]

In 366 Epaminondas represented his state twice in international arenas— once successfully, winning an arbitration process between Thebes and Athens that won the border town of Oropus for Boeotia, and another time unsuccessfully, when he failed to dissuade the Arcadians from becoming Athens' allies. Yet these achievements paled in comparison to one of Thebes' greatest gains that year. The city of Corinth, one of Sparta's oldest and most important friends, was at war with Argos. Since Sparta was unable to help it, and

56. Diod. 15.78.4–79.1 (who dates both the naval bill and its fruition to 364; but building a large navy would have taken longer); Aeschines 2.105 (Propylaea); Isocrates 5.53; Roesch 1984; Buckler and Beck 2008, 180–198. The sources are more amenable to postulating Persian subsidies for the Theban program than to assuming the Persians initiated it.

Corinth's relationship with its former close ally, Athens, had deteriorated, Corinth asked Thebes for a peace treaty. The Thebans welcomed the request and wanted to make Corinth an ally, which meant that it was supposed to follow Thebes to war, even against Sparta. The Corinthians insisted that they wanted only peace and got it. They then went to Sparta and won its approval, even getting permission for other allies to make peace with Thebes. For the Spartans, such consent was preferable to a mass desertion or defiance by their allies. At least two other states, Phlius and Epidaurus, joined the peace with Thebes. We are not told if Epaminondas was involved in the negotiations, and he clearly could not claim sole credit for their results. But the Peloponnese was his "brief," and he probably contributed to the process. He must have supported the idea of a friendly Corinth that would not block his march to the Peloponnese if it came to that. In addition, it is hard to imagine that what was in essence the beginning of the end of the Peloponnesian league could have happened without his victory at Leuctra and his subsequent invasions of the Peloponnese. The race to obtain peace from Thebes confirmed its status as the most powerful state in Greece and of Epaminondas as the architect of its success.[57]

Nothing is reported about Epaminondas' activity until his naval expedition in 364, and even then the information is meager. He took a fleet whose exact size is unknown but was big enough to deter a large Athenian navy that tried to stop it. He sailed to Byzantium, perhaps hoping, like Lysander (p. 200 above), to control the Athenian grain supply from the Black Sea. The historian Diodorus even says that he "made the cities Thebes' own," but the meaning of the phrase is uncertain. Moreover, the evidence suggests that Byzantium, Chios, and Rhodes, on whom the Thebans had set their hopes of an alliance, did not withdraw from the Second Athenian League. Other Aegean cities appeared to follow a similar policy, and there is even a case where Epaminondas declined a local request to interfere in domestic affairs. Finally, an inscription reveals that he received the honorary title of a *proxenus* ("guest-friend") and the (personal) right to sail in and out of Cnidus on the southern coast of Asia Minor. Altogether, the evidence suggest that his expedition yielded little, and one source lamely excuses it on the grounds that Epaminondas did not want to turn the Thebans from "steadfast hoplites to

57. Oropus: Xen. *Hellenica* 7.4.1; Agatharchidas *BNJ* 86 F 8. Arcadia: Nepos *Epaminondas* 6; Plut. *Moralia* 194c–d. Theban alliances: Xen. *Hellenica* 7.4.4–11; Isocrates 6.91; Roy 1994, 200. If Diod. 15.76.3 is credible, a common (and as usual, fleeting) peace sponsored by Persia concluded the war between Thebes and Sparta. Its historicity has been questioned, but see Cawkwell 1961; Stylianou 1998, 485–489.

corrupt marines." On the positive side, the Theban show of power scared the Athenians and staked a claim to a Theban presence in what was largely an Athenian sea. But Thebes did not follow up it achievement, and the value of Epaminondas' experiment, with all its expense and effort, is questionable.[58]

Pelopidas' Last Battle

It appears that Epaminondas and Pelopidas never said proper goodbyes to each other: Pelopidas went to his last battle in Thessaly while Epaminondas was sailing the Aegean. In the summer of 364, Thessalian envoys came to Thebes to protest once again against Alexander of Pherae, who was doing better than usual in defeating and establishing control over towns in southeastern Thessaly. His adversaries asked for Pelopidas, their friend and Alexander's personal enemy, to come to their aid with an army. The envoys and Pelopidas made a good case for the campaign in the Boeotian assembly, which voted to send Pelopidas to Thessaly as a Boeotarch, his thirteenth time in that role. An army of 7,000 men was ready to march when a solar eclipse happened on July 13, 364. The phenomenon was commonly interpreted as a foreboding omen, and the soldiers refused to go, encouraged by doom-predicting seers and probably by Thebans who opposed the campaign. The situation called for a Themistocles, a Lysander, or even an Epaminondas, who could have turned a bad sign into a favorable one, but Pelopidas did not have their cunning and skills. He left for Thessaly with a small force of 300 volunteer horsemen and some mercenaries. What the Thessalians needed was not cavalry, which they had in abundance and good quality, but infantry, in which they were deficient. Yet Pelopidas was unable or forbidden to enlist Boeotian hoplites. Instead, he took mercenaries, whose number and paymaster are unknown, but who were presumably salaried by the Thessalians.

Pelopidas defied public opinion and went to war for a number reasons. He felt obliged to help his Thessalian friends and save his own and Theban influence in the region. He saw his personal hatred of Alexander as consistent with the Theban interest in defeating him. He was also confident in his ability to win without the Boeotian army, then the best in the Greek world. Finally, fighting

---

58. Diod. 15.78.4–79.1; Isocrates 5.35; Plut. *Philopoemen* 14 (turning Theban hoplites to sailors); Justin 16.4 (Heracleia's request that Epaminondas intervene). Buckler and Beck 2008, 199–210 (Cnidian inscription), and see also 174–175, 180–198. Ruzicka (1988) believes, however, that Epaminondas precipitated the Social War between Athens and its allies in 357.

Alexander made good international politics. Pelopidas held the banner of liberation from tyranny, while Thebes' enemies, Athens and Sparta, cultivated good relations with tyrants such as Alexander and Dionysius of Syracuse.[59]

Pelopidas went to Pharsalus, where the Thessalian coalition against Alexander was gathering. Alexander's army is said to have numbered 20,000 men, mercenaries included. He had as twice as many hoplites as the Thessalians, but probably fewer cavalry. Alexander's superiority in hoplites and his good intelligence about Pelopidas' strength and whereabouts may have influenced his decision to choose Cynoscephalae as his battlefield. Cynoscephalae (lit. "dog heads," from the formation of the ridges there) lay north of Pharsalus and east of Pherae, comprising a plain that formed part of the valley of the Enipeus River, cut from south to north by parallel ridges. Both the plain and the heights favored Alexander's advantage in hoplites. It is said that when Pelopidas was informed of the larger size of the enemy, he reacted with typical bravado: "All the better, for we shall defeat the more numerous." A similar line is attributed to him in the battle of Tegyra (p. 284 above), and the similarity of battles did not stop there.[60]

The exact location of the fighting is a matter of debate that cannot easily be resolved. Scholars offer different but almost equally convincing identifications of key sites there. Alexander first occupied the Thetideion (Temple of Thetis), which was located on a ridge where the modern Ayios Athanasios church now stands, according to John Buckler, who seems to manipulate the evidence least (Map 18 below). The main fighting revolved around the nearby ridge of Bekhides west of the Thetideion. Both sides wished to occupy it because it could be used to outflank the opposition and because it gave a height advantage over men in the plain. Defensively, it privileged its occupiers against attackers from below. Alexander apparently advanced with his phalanx toward Bekhides, leading the right wing, with his left wing stretching to the plain. Pelopidas, coming from the west, arranged his army on the western side of Bekhides, presumably leading the left wing. His position there resembled Epaminondas' at Leuctra, largely because of the topography and his response to Alexander's arrangement and movements. There is no evidence that he imitated Epaminondas in adding depth to his left.

---

59. Thessalian request and the eclipse: Plut. *Pelopidas* 31, 34; Diod. 15.80.1–3.
60. Size of the armies: Diod. 15.80.4, 81.3; Plut. *Pelopidas* 31; Hammond (1988, 77) believes the figures to be exaggerated. Cynoscephalae's topography and the battle: Plut. *Pelopidas* 32; Diod. 15.80.4–5; Nepos *Pelopidas* 5 (different in details); Kromayer 1903–1907, 2:118–122; Pritchett 1965–1992, 2:114–119; Buckler 1980, 175–182; Hammond 1988a, 67–68, 77–80.

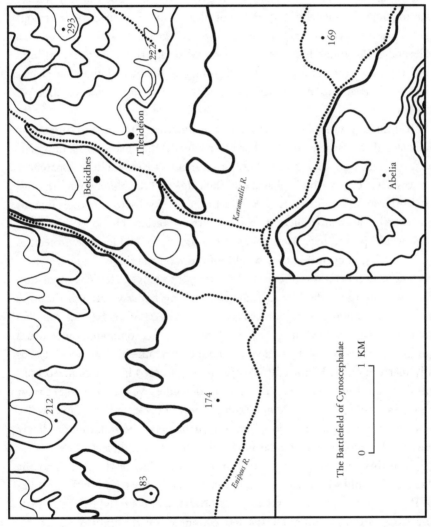

The Battlefield of Cynoscephalae

0   1 KM

MAP 18 Cynoscephalae: The Battlefield (elevations in meters).

Because our sources' attention, like a movie camera, largely follows Pelopidas wherever he went, it is hard to reconstruct what happened outside his field of action. It appears that the fighting took place on the ridges and spilled into the adjacent plain. Pelopidas sent his cavalry against Alexander's horsemen, who were positioned on the ridge and to Alexander's left. As at Tegyra, Pelopidas planned to harass the enemy and expose it to his infantry attack. Enjoying an advantage in numbers and skill, his Thessalian cavalry sent Alexander's cavalry into flight all over the plain. But the real contest was for the ridge of Bekhides, and Pelopidas lost it, either because his troops had more distance to cover or because he and they were slower to act than Alexander. Pelopidas' hoplites then tried to dislodge the enemy from its high positions, but the terrain and the climbing only allowed them to charge piecemeal, enabling Alexander's men to kill their forerunners and repel the rest.

It is unclear where Pelopidas was at this juncture. The modern suggestion that he led the cavalry attack is hard to reconcile with his record and preferences, which were exclusively those of an infantry commander. Apparently, he was advancing with his phalanx on the ridge and the plain, trying to push back Alexander's hoplites. At first he sent for his cavalry to stop their pursuit and attack the enemy where it still kept its formation. He hoped his horsemen would prevail over Alexander's left wing, which had lost the protection of its cavalry, or even that they would join him on the ridge.

The situation on the ridge was dire enough to move Pelopidas to pick up his shield and join the fray as a hoplite, making his way through the lines to the front. From a battle director he now changed to his favorite role of a soldier-general who led the charge in person. When a commander was forced to show personal valor in order to encourage or rebuke his followers, it usually meant a crisis. Reportedly, Pelopidas transformed his demoralized hoplites into bold and tenacious warriors. The defenders were able to repel two or three waves of attack, but Pelopidas kept coming back, and when his cavalry returned and were about to join him, the enemy gave ground, though slowly and hardly in a panic. Pelopidas now controlled the heights.

From his vantage point, he had an excellent view of the plain and the enemy. He could see Alexander's troops in retreat, barely resisting the pressure of Pelopidas' phalanx and probably his cavalry, and confused by the retreating troops from the hills. He spotted Alexander on the right wing, trying to encourage his mercenaries and restore order among them. Pelopidas then made a decision that cost him his life: he would attempt to kill the tyrant with his own hands. The biographer Plutarch admired Pelopidas' valor but was also critical of what he regarded as his imprudent impetuousness:

And when Pelopidas saw Alexander ... , he could not subject his anger to his judgment, but, inflamed at the sight, and surrendering himself and his conduct of the enterprise to his passion, he sprang out far in front of the rest and rushed with challenging cries upon the tyrant.[61]

Plutarch's description of Pelopidas' reaction is too one-dimensional: there was more to his conduct than an emotional outburst against a hated foe or a wish to imitate raging Homeric heroes. Killing the enemy leader made perfect military sense because it could lead to the kind of general defeat Pelopidas had witnessed at both Tegyra and Leuctra. As it happened, it was Pelopidas who would die at Cynoscephalae, and the impact of his fall was an exception to the rule.

We are told that he rushed towards Alexander and challenged him to a duel. Alexander prudently retreated to his mercenary bodyguard, an act that the sources portray as cowardly, but in fact was hardly unusual and surely justified. It left Pelopidas, and presumably the few men who accompanied him, facing Alexander's front-line mercenaries. Pelopidas killed many of them, but his position ahead of his troops made him an easy target. Probably on Alexander's orders, the mercenaries threw javelins at him from a distance and mortally wounded him. By the heroic code of close-range battle, this, too, was an act of cowardice.

Pelopidas' Thessalian troops and cavalry could not tell if he was dead and rushed to his rescue. Their determined effort to save him can be compared to the Spartans' struggle over their fallen king at Leuctra, but with a very different outcome. Either because Alexander's phalanx was already in disarray or because the new attack caused it to flee, a rout took place in which Alexander lost more than 3,000 men.

Pelopidas' generalship at Cynoscephalae has been described as a tactical masterpiece. It certainly showed that he could contend with difficult terrain and improvise moves on the spot. He also successfully led an army far less familiar to him than his Boeotian troops and with infantry of lesser quality. But Pelopidas allowed the enemy to frame the battle. It was Alexander who came first and chose the field, who initiated and won the race for the contested ridge, and who made Pelopidas recall his cavalry from their pursuit of the fleeing enemy. Pelopidas responded well to these challenges, but some of them were preventable with greater speed and preparedness. Moreover, the final victory was achieved by his subordinate officers and soldiers, who get no

61. See the previous note. Quotation: Plut. *Pelopidas* 32.

credit in our sources or the scholarship. Finally, Pelopidas' death tarnished the Thessalians' victory and his own. These considerations suggest that his performance at Cynoscephalae may stand not as his finest achievement but as a summation of his generalship. His experiences at Tegyra and Leuctra had taught him how to deal with an enemy that had more hoplites, as well as how to send in the cavalry before using it in conjunction with infantry. As in those battles, he charged the leader of the enemy at Cynoscephalae and mixed personal bravery with his command of troops. Although his victory was less than perfect, it confirmed Pelopidas' place among Greece's leading commanders.[62]

The Thessalians certainly thought he deserved lavish honors. Plutarch artfully uses their archaic ways of mourning him to pay him a tribute. When the Thessalians returned from battle, he says, they did not strip out of their arms or tend to themselves but went straight to Pelopidas' corpse and heaped captured enemy weapons around it, as if he were still alive to witness their victory. They shaved their hair and the manes of their horses, did not eat or drink, and sat in silent agony. Later, delegations arrived from Thessalian cities carrying trophies, wreaths, and golden armor to his funeral. They got the Thebans' permission to prepare his body and carry it to burial, as gestures of gratitude to him and his city. They also put up his statue at Delphi and gave lands to his children. These honors moved Plutarch to apply to Pelopidas the old Greek notion that a life can be judged happy only at its end. By that criterion, Pelopidas achieved supreme happiness in death.

His arch-enemy, Alexander of Pherae, could bask only briefly in the honor of killing Pelopidas. The Thebans invaded Thessaly in a campaign that combined revenge with reestablishing and even expanding their authority in the region. Alexander gave up most of his Thessalian acquisitions and became an obedient follower of Thebes—a result that was good enough for Thebes and probably for Epaminondas, who, unlike Pelopidas, did not seek his death. That goal was left to Alexander's wife and her brothers, who murdered him in 358.[63]

Epaminondas' Last Battle

While Pelopidas and Epaminondas were away in Thessaly and the Aegean, respectively, an anti-Theban conspiracy was exposed in Orchomenus (364),

---

62. Battle's results: see note 60. Pelopidas' tactical masterpiece: Buckler 1980, 180.
63. Plut. *Pelopidas* 33–35; Diod. 15.80.6; Nepos *Pelopidas* 5; Georgiadou 1997, 216–226; Ma 2013, 5.

a city with a long history of bad blood with Thebes. The Thebans reacted mercilessly, executing the many conspirators, selling the other residents into slavery, and razing the city. Epaminondas is said to have later condemned this treatment in the harshest terms, and some have speculated that Pelopidas also would have tried to prevent it. Both the destruction and the lack of any attested attempt by Epaminondas to rebuild the city suggest the limits of his power.[64]

We hear nothing of Epaminondas until the busy final year of his life (362). By that time, the coalition of alliances he had built in the Peloponnese seemed to be falling apart. The Arcadian League and Elis, both Thebes' allies, were at war with each other, and Elis turned to Sparta for help and alliance. In addition, the Arcadians were divided between the oligarchic city of Mantinea and a group of southern Arcadian communities centered on democratic Tegea. In 362, the Arcadians made peace with pro-Spartan Elis and complained in Thebes about the conduct of a Theban governor in Tegea. Epaminondas, then a Boeotarch, rebuffed them in the same accusatory and haughty manner that he displayed on other occasions. He supported the Theban governor and rebuked the Arcadians for making peace with Elis without consulting Thebes first, equating the act with treason. He also threatened to march on Arcadia. As a result, the Tegean bloc reaffirmed its alliance with Thebes, while Mantinea looked for allies to protect it from a fourth invasion by Epaminondas.[65]

In addition to Boeotian infantry and cavalry, Epaminondas' army included forces from Euboea and Thessaly, and even of the old enemy-turned-ally, Alexander of Pherae. Other troops arrived from Thessaly's southern neighbors: Achaea Phthiotis, Locris, Malis, and Aenis. Evidently, Pelopidas' activities in and around Thessaly were paying dividends. The Phocians refused to join in, claiming that their alliance with Thebes was exclusively for defensive purposes, and Epaminondas did not press the point. There were enough allies waiting for him in the Peloponnese, such as the southern Arcadians, Messene, Sicyon, and Argos. The opposing Mantinean coalition included other Arcadians and troops and horses from Peloponnesian Achaea, Elis, Sparta, and Athens. The stage was thus set for a confrontation like Leuctra.

Epaminondas took his army through the Isthmus. This time no attempt was made to block his way, because Corinth and other neighboring

---

64. Diod. 15.79.3–6; Pausanias 9.15.3; Plut. *Comparison between Pelopidas and Marcellus* 1.
65. Xen. *Hellenica* 7.4.28–5.1; Diod. 15.82.1–3; Buckler 2003, 343–345.

states were now his friends. He then led a quick march to Nemea, south of Corinth, which was a former mustering ground for him and the Peloponnesian allies. There he hoped to forestall and confront an Athenian army that was supposed to help Mantinea. If successful, this move would have been a major blow to the enemy, but apparently the Athenians got wind of it and planned to transport their troops by sea to Spartan territory and march to Mantinea from there. When Epaminondas learned about their change of plan, he went south to Tegea. His departure allowed the Athenians to return to their original route and march from Eleusis through the Corinthiad toward Mantinea. There is no need to assume that their first change of plan was a ruse designed to dupe Epaminondas into allowing them to go through Nemea. They simply chose their march according to the changing circumstances.[66]

Both the attempt to stop the Athenians at Nemea and its abortion suggest that Epaminondas possessed good intelligence about the Athenian plans. He had equally good information on his Peloponnesian opponents, knowing that they had gathered in Mantinea, that they had asked the Spartans to come there, and that the eighty-two-year-old king Agesilaus and his Spartan army were in Pellana, less than 20 kilometers north of Sparta, and on their way to Mantinea. Xenophon grudgingly praises Epaminondas for staying behind the walls of Tegea, where he was well protected and provisioned. There he could wait for defections from the coalition, observe the enemy's movements, and launch an attack at a moment of his choice. But perhaps Xenophon's praise is unwarranted, because Epaminondas was in an offensive rather than defensive frame of mind. He planned to take advantage of the enemy's presence at the gathering point of Mantinea and of the departure of the Spartan army in order to capture undefended Sparta by surprise. It is easy to imagine how such a bold move, if successful, would have crippled the anti-Theban coalition. Sparta was a bigger catch than Mantinea, and its capture could have led to its withdrawal from the war or even to Theban victory in the entire campaign. The humiliation of the capture for the Spartans—the sort of thing Epaminondas always enjoyed inflicting on them—would have been an added bonus.

He planned his surprise attack carefully, taking only part of his army and concealing his goal even from his soldiers. He told them only to eat an early

---

66. The opposing armies: Xen. *Hellenica* 7.5.4–5; Diod. 15.84.4–85.2. Athenian plans: Xen. *Hellenica* 7.5.6–7; Plut. *Moralia* 346 d–e, and p. 327 below. Athenian trickery: Buckler 1980, 208.

dinner and to leave camp when darkness fell, pretending that he intended to occupy a suitable battleground. In fact he took them on a quick and strenuous march of more than 50 kilometers to the city of Sparta. In spite of his efforts at secrecy, he found the Spartans ready for him: an informant had told Agesilaus about Epaminondas' plan. From his base in Pellana, the king dispatched a messenger to warn the Spartans and sent the Spartan cavalry, three out twelve infantry battalions (*lochoi*), and his mercenaries to Mantinea, while he himself rushed with the remaining troops back to Sparta to organize its defense. He arrived before Epaminondas and blocked the entrances to the city's narrow alleys with earth, with debris made of houses he destroyed, and even with tripods taken from shrines. He also stationed soldiers in different positions that could impede the enemy's advance into or around the city. Finally, he posted Spartans who were above and under active-duty age on the rooftops and told them to pelt the enemy with everything they had. Although there were fewer defenders than attackers, the urban fighting worked to the Spartans' benefit. They knew its layout of narrow alleys and could force the enemy to engage in the small-scale, face-to-face fighting in which the Spartans excelled. The bombardment of the attackers with stones, tiles, and other objects from the rooftops would put them in mortal danger.[67]

When Epaminondas arrived, he tried to make the best of the situation. Like Demosthenes on Sphacteria (p. 161 above) or Dionysius I in the Battle of Motya (p. 250 above), he sought to gain the height advantage by seizing hills either on the eastern bank of the river or, no less probably, in the northern part of the city. From these heights, he descended on Sparta, attacking enemy positions at several places simultaneously. The Spartans defended themselves vigorously and even ventured out on the attack. We hear of Prince Archidamus, who ran from one street to another to render help where it was necessary, and led 100 Spartans up the hill to score a minor victory against the invaders.

Plutarch tops it with a story that intertwines Ares and Eros. He tells of a Spartan youth, the very attractive Isidas, who, armed with a spear, sword, and only oil on his bare skin, charged the enemy and smote anyone he encountered. Miraculously, he survived without a scratch. He gained the admiration

---

67. The sources differ on the details of the invasion, but Xenophon's version is generally preferable: Xen. *Hellenica* 7.5.9–14, 18; Diod. 15.82.84.1; Plut. *Pelopidas* 34; *Agesilaus* 34; *Moralia* 346b–c; Polybius 9.8; Aeneas Tacticus *How to Survive under Siege* 2.2 (blocking streets); Justin 6.7.1–7; Polyaenus 2.3.10. Size of Epaminondas' force: Just. 6.7.4 (15,000 men); Xen. 7.15.18 (a large hoplite force).

of both sides, although the regulations-conscientious Spartans put a garland on his head and fined him 1,000 drachmas for risking his life without armor.[68]

Ever since Leuctra, the Spartans had hoped to reverse that defeat and the damage it had done to their prestige. Archidamus' victory on the hill and the tale about Isidas served this agenda. Xenophon joins in by mocking the defeated Thebans on the hill as "conquerors of the Spartans" and "fire breathers," as if the wheel of history had turned. In fact, although Archidamus and his troops killed and repelled Epaminondas' front men and were even joined by Spartans from the city, the Thebans recovered and inflicted losses on the defenders. The pro-Spartan Xenophon and the sources that followed him liked to believe that the valiant resistance of the few against the many saved Sparta and made Epaminondas call off the attack. Without denying their heroism, it should be noted that these "few" were in fact three-quarters of the full Spartan army. An even weightier concern for Epaminondas was the expected arrival of Arcadian troops from Mantinea (and probably the Spartan units sent there, too), about which he learned from a captive. Together with the Spartans in the city, they would have made the contest much more difficult. Historians have suggested that Epaminondas' march on Sparta was in fact a diversionary tactic designed to deprive the enemy coalition in Mantinea of the full strength of the Spartan army, or that it aimed to draw forces away from Mantinea to Sparta so that Epaminondas could rush there and take it in their absence. This interpretation risks deducing aims from later events. It is more consistent with the evidence to assume that he simply changed his mind. Epaminondas went to Sparta because there was an opportunity to capture it with little effort. When the fighting got harder and threatened to escalate into a greater conflict too large for his partial army, he left and tried to capture Mantinea by surprise, just as opportunistically. If this failed, too, it was always possible to fall back on a pitched battle. We may also consider the possibility that Epaminondas, like the Athenian general Demosthenes, lacked tenacity and tended to give up after an initial failure.[69]

Epaminondas tried now to get to Mantinea without delay and in secret. The Spartans thought he would plunder their lands as he had done in the last invasion, and Epaminondas may have encouraged the expectation. He even ordered a few cavalrymen to tend the campfires through the night

---

68. Fighting in Sparta: see the previous note and Isocrates *Letters* 9.4 (Archidamus the hero). Isidas: Plut. *Agesilaus* 34; cf. Aelian *Historical Miscellany* 6.3.
69. See note 67. Xen. *Hellenica* 7.5.11–14. See also Anderson 1970, 222 (Epaminondas aimed to keep the Spartans away from Mantinea); Buckler 1980, 209–213; Cartledge 1987, 235 (diversionary tactic); cf. Shipley 1997, 369–370.

while he and his army left on a forced march. On reaching Tegea, he rested and fed his very tired and hungry hoplites, but ordered his Theban and Thessalian cavalry to continue the rest of the way north to Mantinea, about 15 kilometers. Their mission was to seize the summer crops, the cattle, and the Mantinean residents, slaves, and children who were harvesting outside the walls. The captured people and property could have been used to force the city into surrender.

Clearly, Epaminondas demanded a lot of his soldiers, and they complied without complaint, even with enthusiasm. Xenophon, who could be critical of the general, was impressed:

> But that he had brought his army to such a point that the troops flinched from no toil, whether by night or by day, and shrank from no peril, and although the provisions they had were scanty, were nevertheless willing to be obedient, this seems to me to be more remarkable.[70]

What happened next justified the sources' judgment that Epaminondas was a good general and planner who ran into bad luck. His cavalry was supposed to have little trouble looting outside Mantinea's wall, but was forestalled by a force of Athenian cavalry perhaps 300–400 strong. The Athenians had left Eleusis with 6,000 infantrymen under the general Hegesilaus and fought their way through the Corinthiad. The cavalry then hurried ahead of the infantry and reached Mantinea or its neighborhood just before Epaminondas' cavalry arrived. Epaminondas either did not know about their coming or thought that his cavalry (considered the best in Greece) could handle them. Yet when the Mantineans spotted his cavalry, they prevailed upon the Athenians to save the people and the property outside the walls, even though the Athenians and their horses would have to skip breakfast. Xenophon lovingly describes how the outnumbered Athenian horsemen valiantly stood up to the larger force of better enemy cavalry and saved everything outside the walls. He fails to say that Epaminondas' cavalry must have been more tired than their opponents after their forced march from Sparta. Since both of Xenophon's sons, Diodorus and Gryllus, fought in the Athenian force, and since Gryllus died there, we may question the historian's glorification of

70. The march on Mantinea: Xen. *Hellenica* 7.5.14. Quotation: Xen. *Hellenica* 7.5.19 (in the context of the ensuing battle). Diod. 15.84.1–2; Frontinus *Stratagems* 3.11.5 (Epaminondas' repeated use of the campfires trick). See, however, Buckler 1980, 212–213, and Stylianou 1998, 511–512, who deny that Epaminondas marched on the city.

the cavalry's performance as the sole cause of the Mantinea's salvation. The Athenians who truly saved it were Hegesilaus and his 6,000 infantrymen, who arrived shortly after the cavalry. Epaminondas also hurried to Mantinea in the hope of getting there before the Athenians. His vanguard was close as 1.3 kilometers from the city when Hegesilaus and the Athenian army appeared on a mountain above it. The Athenians entered Mantinea and organized its defense with the locals. It now looked less likely that Epaminondas could take it by storm or by treason, and the arrival of the Mantinean and Spartan armies at the scene laid the idea to rest.[71]

Although a pitched battle appeared inevitable, Xenophon implies that Epaminondas was solely responsible for it. He depicts him as a man under pressure to offer battle because his term of office was ending and because leaving without a fight would have exposed his allies to danger and tarnished his name. Moreover, victory or even death in battle could have salvaged a reputation damaged by his failures in Sparta and Mantinea.[72] Epaminondas was surely an ambitious man who cared about his name, yet Xenophon's emphasis on his love of honor (*philotimia*) is speculative and misplaced. Epaminondas' original mission was to preserve the Theban influence in the Peloponnese by helping his Arcadian allies against Mantinea, and he showed no signs of giving it up. It is questionable that he regarded what happened at Sparta and Mantinea as significant setbacks that had to be reversed. If there was a personal motive behind his wish to do battle, it was his confidence that he could replicate his success at Leuctra. At Mantinea, his opponents were equally eager for a fight.

The plain between Tegea and Mantinea, where the battle was fought in the summer of 362, has the unique distinction of being the site of two other major battles: one between the Spartans and an Argive coalition in 418, and another in 207 between Sparta and the Achaean League. Its terrain ranges from flat ground to elevations and low places. It includes hills and mountains, and is bounded by mountains to the north, east, and west. The ancient evidence allows no certainty about the exact locations and movements of the forces. Many scholars follow the military historian J. Kromayer, who

71. The Athenian forces: Xen. *Hellenica* 7.5.14–19; Diod. 15.85.1; Plut. *Moralia* 346c–e. During the 370s–350s, the Athenians employed about 300–400 cavalrymen in battle: Spence 1993, 85, 138. Epaminondas' tired cavalry: Kromayer 1903, 1:44. Xenophon's sons: Pausanias 8.1.6, 9.5, 10; Ephorus *BNJ* 70 F 85. For Gryllus' alleged killing of Epaminondas in battle, see also Westlake 1975, 35–37.
72. Xen. *Hellenica* 7.5.18–19.

places the lines of the Mantinean alliance from west to east where the plain is at its narrowest (about 2 kilometers), between Mount Mytikas and Mount Kapnistra. There are other locations further north in the valley that are also possible, but in any case, topography seems not to have played a significant role in the battle (Map 19 below).[73]

Epaminondas made the first move, arranging his troops south of the enemy as if for battle as he watched the enemy doing the same. He then marched in a column northwest to the mountains on the edge of the plain, seized the high spots, and grounded arms, as if his work were done and he was going to camp there. He also ordered 1,600 cavalrymen to ride back and forth in front of his column to hide his movements with a cloud of dust. The sources agree that his moves and pretended encampment were stratagems, but differ about their purpose. They suggest that he wished to mislead the enemy into thinking that he did not intend to fight that day, causing many of them to disarm, leave their positions, and relax their mental readiness for battle. The sources also think that he intended to seize higher ground in order to surprise the enemy infantry at its rear. He probably sought all of the above advantages, as well as shelter for his infantry at the slopes in case of defeat. Provoking the enemy into positioning its troops for battle also gave him a good idea of how to organize his own lines and tactics.[74]

The historian Diodorus is our only source for the sizes of the opposing armies and for many of their composite units. He mentions more than 20,000 soldiers and around 2,000 cavalrymen for the Mantinean coalition, while granting about 30,000 foot soldiers and no fewer than 3,000 cavalrymen to Epaminondas. Lack of additional evidence hinders us from supporting or disputing his figures, even though his likely source, the lost historian Ephorus, was criticized in antiquity for his deficient account of the battle. Less controversial is Diodorus'

73. None of the ancient landmarks on the actual battleground is certain: Pausanias 8.11.5, 10 (a grove called Pelagos, "Sea"); Pausanias 8.11.7 (Epaminondas' dying place, Scopos); Pausanias 8.11.8, 12.1 (Epaminondas' grave). Topography of the battlefield: Kromayer 1903–1931, 1:27–55; Pritchett 1965–1992, 2:37–62; Buckler 1980, 213–216.

74. Epaminondas' actions: Xen. 7.5.21–22; Frontinus *Stratagems* 2.12; Polyaenus 2.3.14 (mistaking Tegea for Mantinea). For the battle, see primarily Xen. *Hellenica* 7.5.19–27; Diod. 15.84.1–87.6; Kromayer 1903, 1:27–123, which influenced Pritchett 1965–1992, 2:63–66, and Buckler 1980, 213–219; Buckler 1985. The differences between Xenophon's and Diodorus' accounts do not justify dismissing the latter, as is done by, e.g., Anderson 1970, 326n1; Buckler 1980, *ibid*.

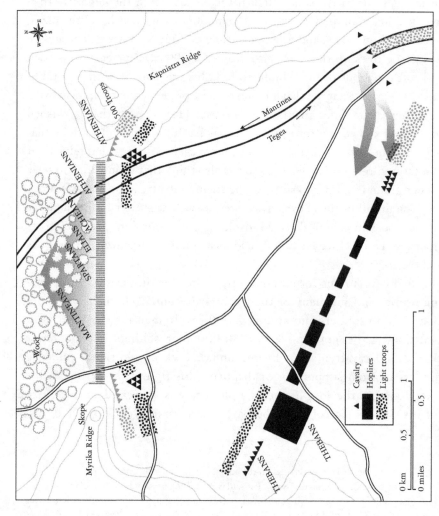

MAP 19 Mantinea Battle Plan.

description of the positions of the opposing lines. The right wing of the anti-Theban coalition included Mantineans, Arcadians, Spartans, Eleans, and (Peloponnesian) Achaeans. Their center was made of weaker units of various allies, and the Athenians occupied the left wing. Epaminondas' lines suggest a plan, like Leuctra's, in that he aimed to win with a strong left wing under his command. He beefed it up with units from his right and center that moved behind the lines for their protection, creating a deep, dense phalanx. At its front were Boeotian hoplites backed by picked Arcadian units. Epaminondas' weaker center was made up of troops from Sicyon, Messene, Euboea, and states north of Boeotia such as Locris, Malis, Aenis, and Thessaly. The units of the northern states probably also contributed light-armed troops. Epaminondas' right wing consisted of Argive units. He also sent a group of cavalry and hoplites to seize hills or the slopes of a mountain (Mount Kapnistra), both south of the Athenian wing. Their mission was to threaten the enemy rear so as to prevent the Athenians from helping units to their left, where Epaminondas was to attack. The cavalry of both sides were stationed on the flanks of their wings. Their component units generally reflected those of the infantry in their wings, except that Epaminondas split his Theban and Boeotian cavalry between his right and left wings and added Thessalian cavalry to his left. The evidence suggests that his adversaries stationed at least one cavalry unit from Elis at the back, probably to protect their rear. The cavalry on both sides were accompanied by light-armed troops (Map 19 above).[75]

Epaminondas' battle array reflected his numerical and (where possible) qualitative advantage over the enemy. He entrusted the main fighting in the left wing to the Theban infantry and cavalry, who had proved their ability to defeat the Arcadians and the Spartans in the past. He used other infantrymen to create a deeper and larger phalanx than the enemy's. His placing of Theban and Thessalian cavalry on the right wing suggests he hoped to win there, but otherwise, the right was expected to withstand the enemy until the commander's presumed victory on the left, or until he came to their rescue, if that proved necessary.

75. Armies' size: Diod. 15.84.4, 85.2. Ephorus: Polybius 12.25f.1–6 = Ephorus *BNJ* 70 T 20. The substance of Polybius' criticism of Ephorus is lost, but he elsewhere criticizes other historians for their incongruity about the number of troops, their positions, and battleground space; cf. 12.19–21. Kromayer 1903, 1:114–123, defends Diodorus' version, and Stylianou 1998, 513, questions the figure of the alliance's cavalry. Battle lines: Diod. 15.84.3–85.8; Xen. *Hellenica* 7.5.22; Arrian *Tactical Manual* 11.2.

Xenophon implies that Epaminondas enjoyed an advantage in morale, too:

> For at the time when he gave his men the last order to make ready, saying that there would be a battle, the horsemen eagerly whitened their helmets at his command, the hoplites of the Arcadians painted clubs upon their shields, as though they were Thebans, and all alike sharpened their spears and daggers and burnished their shields.[76]

It was not easy to create a common cause among units of diverse origin and military skills. The pre-battle enthusiasm in Epaminondas' army spoke volumes for their appreciation of him and for his hortatory powers.

Our primary sources for the battle, Xenophon and Diodorus, ignore the fighting in the center and focus on the wings, which were the stages for the chief actors: Epaminondas, the Athenians, and the Spartans. The two historians' depictions of the fighting on both wings read like almost like the accounts of two different battles. We shall begin with events on Epaminondas' right and then move to his left.

Xenophon claims that Epaminondas succeeded in misleading the enemy into believing that he would not fight that day, and when he actually advanced they were caught unprepared and fumbled to arm themselves and take up positions.[77] Yet Xenophon's and Diodorus' actual descriptions of the battle suggest that surprise played little role in it, particularly on Epaminondas' right wing, where the Athenian cavalry apparently soon reorganized and were even able to charge their opponents first. Their attack failed because the Theban and the Thessalian cavalry was more than a match for them in numbers and skill, and especially because of the contribution of the *hamippoi* in the Boeotian and Thessalian ranks. These were light infantrymen who came from states around Thessaly and who fought alongside the horses. They included skilled peltasts, slingers, and javelin-throwers who hid among or behind the riders when approaching the enemy. The slingers hit their targets from a distance, while the javelin-throwers and other light-armed troops fought at closer range and took part in hand-to-hand combat with their swords and spears. Epaminondas was fortunate in having such expert soldiers, who excelled their counterparts on the Athenian side and were thrice their number. The casualties and the injuries they inflicted and the

---

76. Xen. *Hellenica* 7.5.20.
77. Epaminondas' stratagem: Xen. *Hellenica* 7.5. 22–23.

pressure put on the Athenian horsemen by the Theban cavalry forced the former to retreat around their phalanx.[78]

Yet, from this point on, things went badly for the Thebans, for several reasons. First, the Athenian cavalry did not seek shelter in their phalanx in a way that disrupted its formation, as the Spartan cavalry had done at Leuctra. Second, because the Theban cavalry did not pursue the fleeing horsemen but charged the Athenian phalanx, the Athenian cavalry was able to regroup and recover. Third, it was while in flight or shortly after that, the Athenian horsemen encountered and eliminated a force of Euboean and mercenary peltasts and light-armed troops who had been sent to block the Athenians' retreat by seizing high ground or to help the Theban forces there against a forthcoming Elean attack (below). It was a minor victory that the Athenians later used to put themselves on a par with the victorious Boeotians.

The flight of the Athenian cavalry deprived their phalanx of protection and exposed its flanks to attacks from the Theban cavalry and its light-armed troops. The attackers probably also charged the Athenian phalanx at the front in an attempt to spoil its formation, expecting that the Argives on Epaminondas' right would finish the job while the cavalry proceeded to help Epaminondas' left wing. Cavalry and light-armed troops often used hit-and-run tactics, to which the hoplites responded in short pursuits. Such fighting exhausted the Athenian infantrymen, and with no cavalry to help them, they began to flee. But then an anonymous commander of a cavalry unit from Elis that was stationed at the rear came to their rescue. His appearance caught the Thebans by surprise, and he killed many of them. Diodorus' assertion that he reversed the defeat is surely exaggerated, because no such claim to a convincing victory is attested elsewhere. Indeed, the battle was decided on Epaminondas' left wing.[79]

Epaminondas planned on the left to pit the Boeotian and Thessalian cavalry on his flanks against the smaller Arcadian and Spartan cavalry on the flank of their right wing. There was a chance that putting the cavalry to flight would induce the infantry to follow them, because such spontaneous reactions were not uncommon in other battles. At the same time, Epaminondas was ready to engage the infantry lines with his slower, larger, and denser phalanx.

---

78. *Hamippoi*: Xen. *On the Cavalry Commander* 8.9; Lippelt 1910, 73–74; Spence 1993, esp. 21, 58–59; van Wees 2004, 81–85.

79. Reversal on the right wing: Diod. 15.85.3–8, 87.3; Xen. *Hellenica* 7.5.25.

In anticipation of the cavalry battle, he arranged his horsemen in a wedge formation that facilitated quick turns and cutting through the ranks of the enemy. The opposing cavalry, probably in a countermeasure, positioned themselves in the quasi-phalanx formation of a quadrangle six rows deep. Once again, the light infantry that was mixed with the cavalry made the difference. The Arcadian and the Spartan horsemen had either less of them or none at all, a deficiency that allowed Epaminondas' slingers to hit them from a comfortable distance. At the same time, his javelin throwers and the peltasts helped his cavalry inflict losses and injuries on the enemy. The better-skilled and more numerous attackers prevailed, and the enemy cavalry retreated into their phalanx. Xenophon suggests that the infantry followed the cavalry in flight, yet Diodorus' more detailed description indicates that Xenophon skipped over how the battle reached this point.[80]

Epaminondas' phalanx must have arrived hard on the heels of the cavalry. He shaped it like a blunt wedge, putting his best soldiers, the Boeotians, at the head, and his worst soldiers at the rear, so as to increase the impetus of the charge and its ability to penetrate enemy lines. (Xenophon likens its movement to that a trireme plowing the waves, ram first.) The back of the phalanx probably kept in line with the center and the rest of the army, which thus moved obliquely. The plan worked well against the Mantinean infantry, and their collapse enabled Epaminondas' cavalry to join in the pursuit of the fleeing infantry and horsemen. But the Spartan phalanx stationed next to the Mantineans held firm, and the sources tell of a fierce battle between them and the Boeotians. Diodorus even takes artistic license and suggests that their clash started with an "exchange of spears in which most were shattered by the very density of the missiles." Soon the group fighting disintegrated into hand-to-hand, individual combats with no clear victor.[81]

What happened next became the stuff of patriotic and heroic tales on both sides. It appears that Epaminondas, who was all this time in the thick of things, decided to take matters into his own hands in an attempt to break the impasse. He gathered around him "his best men," perhaps the Sacred Band, and formed them into a cohesive unit, which expedited their penetrating the enemy's midst and eliminating the opposition. According to Diodorus, Epaminondas led the charge and hit the Spartans' commander

---

80. Wedge formation: Arrian *Tactical Manual* 16; Spence 1993, 103–104. Epaminondas' charge: Diod. 15.86.2–87.2; Xen. *Hellenica* 7.5.25–27; Nepos *Epaminondas* 9.

81. See the last note.

with his javelin. He was joined by his men who broke through the Spartan phalanx that withdrew under the weight of the attackers. The Boeotians kept up the pressure and reached the rear, killing many on their way. Epaminondas kept running ahead in a cloud of missiles, which he dodged, repelled, or pulled out of his body. It was a performance in the style of Pelopidas, although no source criticizes Epaminondas for recklessly risking his life. But at last he received a mortal wound from a spear that, probably by design, broke on contact and left its iron head buried deep in his body. (He did not die on the spot; below.) As one might expect, there was more than one claimant for the fateful blow. The Mantineans said it was delivered by one of their own, Machaereion. The Spartans insisted it was their man, Anticrates, who stabbed Epaminondas with a sword, suggesting a closer and more honorable encounter. One Spartan tradition makes King Agesilaus responsible for Epaminondas' death, though it is doubtful that he was there. (Allegedly, he instructed his troops in Mantinea to do their best to kill Epaminondas, whom he regarded as the only intelligent man in Thebes.) Similarly unreliable is the Athenian and Theban tradition that the slayer was Gryllus, Xenophon's son, who probably died before the battle (p. 327 above) and, if present, ought to have been fighting on the other wing with his fellow Athenians. The Spartan claim is strengthened by the circumstances of Epaminondas' injury.

Undoubtedly, the Spartans and their coalition partners regarded Epaminondas' fall as a major accomplishment. Xenophon, who shared their desire to diminish the Theban victory at Mantinea, even depicts the Theban cavalry as despondent after Epaminondas' collapse, abandoning their pursuit of the fleeing enemy and sneaking back to camp like frightened men. In fact, the Boeotians won the battle convincingly, and the Spartans fled the field, even after Epaminondas fell.[82]

There are several descriptions of Epaminondas' last hours, all of them extolling him and his patriotism. The dominant tradition is that he was carried to a place overlooking the battlefield called *Scope* ("Lookout," on Mount Mytika). He watched the fighting knowing that he would die when the spearhead in his body was pulled out. But he was anxious to know what had happened to his shield, which he must have dropped when he was hit, and

---

82. The fighting: Diod. 15.86.4–5. Epaminondas' slayers: Pausanias 8.11.5 (Mantinean); Plut. *Agesilaus* 35 (Spartan); Plut. *Moralia* 214c–d (Agesilaus; cf. Polybius 9.8, but also Plut. *Agesilaus* 34–35; Anderson 1970, 222); Pausanias 8.11.6; 9.15.5 (Gryllus); cf. Justin 6.7.11–8.1. The Thebans lost two additional commanders: Aelian *Varia Historia* 12.3. Alleged Theban retreat: Xen. *Hellenica* 7.5.25. For a different interpretation, see Pritchett 1994, 135–136.

FIGURE 19 *"The Death of Epaminondas" by Louis Gallait* (1810–1887).

In his early career the Belgian painter Louis Gallait was influenced by the Neoclassical movement, and the "Death of Epaminondas" was his first major work in this style. The Death of Epaminondas (c.418–362 BC) (oil on canvas), Gallait, Louis (1810–87)/Musée des Beaux-Arts, Tournai, Belgium/Bridgeman Images

he asked his shield-bearer about it. Apparently the thought of an enemy, especially a Spartan, boasting of having his shield or displaying it in a temple was more painful than the wound. He was assured that the shield had been retrieved. He then wanted to know who had won, and was told of the Boeotian victory. Only now did he ask for the iron to be pulled out. His friends tried to dissuade him, reminding him that he would die childless. (He had never married and had had two male lovers.) Epaminondas retorted that he left behind two daughters, Leuctra and Mantinea, his victories. In control to the last, he then chose his time and place of death by ordering the spearhead to be extracted. He was buried in a tomb on the battlefield, which became a pilgrimage site for dignitaries from Greece and Rome.[83]

Like Pelopidas' fall in his last battle, Epaminondas' death weakened the Boeotian claim to victory and contributed to a dispute over the battle's results. Since requesting one's dead from the enemy was an admission of defeat, both sides fought over the possession of bodies. After the battle, there was a mutual holding off of requests for the dead in anticipation that the other side would ask first. It was the Spartans who finally yielded, having already shown their anxiety to bring the dead to burial at Leuctra and after Lysander's death in Haliartus (pp. 223–225, 296–297 above). The Athenians, on the other hand, used their possession of enemy corpses and their cavalry's win over an enemy unit to claim victory. According to one story, they even deterred the Mantineans from asking for their dead, so as not to concede defeat. Amid these rival claims to prestige, Xenophon refuses to grant either side a victory that made it the leading power in Greece. Concluding his *Greek History* at this point, he invites others to continue it up to a more decisive event. In fact, Mantinea was not so inconsequential as Xenophon pretends. It was Epaminondas' last battle, and it marked the height of Thebes' power, never to be reached again.[84]

Conclusion

More than two centuries after the battle of Mantinea, the Greek historian Polybius credited Thebes' success and fame to Pelopidas and Epaminondas alone. This was not a compliment, but rather a way of claiming that Thebes'

---

83. Epaminondas' death: Diod. 15.87.5; Nepos *Epaminondas* 9–10; *Pelopidas* 3; Justin 6.7.11–13; Pausanias 8.11.7 (Scope); Plut. *Moralia* 194c; 761d; Theopompus *BNJ* 115 F 247. His tomb: Pausanias 8.11.8.
84. Xen. *Hellenica* 7.5.26–27; Diod. 15.87.1–3; Polyaenus 2.32.

accomplishments were transitory and accidental, attributable to fortuitous exploitation of the Spartans' mistakes and the resentment they aroused. "For the success of Thebes grew, attained its height, and ceased with the lives of Epaminondas and Pelopidas." Polybius' judgment is both unfair and inaccurate. It ignores the contribution of other Thebans and Boeotians to Thebes' success and the fact that its decline came, not with Epaminondas' death, but later, after Thebes' involvement in the Third Sacred War of 356–346. But Polybius was only one of many ancient and modern observers who expressed appreciation of both Theban generals, and of Epaminondas in particular.[85]

There was much in the personalities of Pelopidas and Epaminondas to account for their successes and failures as generals and politicians. The aristocratic origin of both men was reflected in a code of behavior that regulated their leadership. Sayings attributed to Epaminondas suggest he was haughty, judgmental, and contemptuous of those who did not meet his standards, but that he also subscribed to the ideals of simplicity, disdain for wealth, moderation, and physical fitness.[86] Ironically, these were traditional values in Sparta, a city that he and Pelopidas weakened and humiliated more than any other Greek city. The Theban generals even out-Spartaned the Spartans in valor. Their courage, which at times bordered on rashness, explains their willingness to face an army superior in numbers and reputation, but also their disrespect for democratic procedures. It took personal and political bravery to go on with the conspiracy against the Theban oligarchy in spite of the risk of betrayal, and to confront the Spartans with the assertion that autonomy began at home. On the field, they both valiantly experimented with novel and unusual tactics, including coordinated cavalry and infantry attacks.

Especially daring was Epaminondas' greatest innovation in Leuctra: inviting outflanking of his smaller phalanx so that he could use a strengthened left wing against the traditionally strong enemy right wing. Valor, infectious battle enthusiasm, and the belief that they could personally make a difference led both to risk their lives in battle. They paid the ultimate price, although our sources unjustly fault only Pelopidas for what they deem his thoughtless risk-taking.

In his biography of Pelopidas, Plutarch considered Epaminondas the intellectual and Pelopidas the man of action, but in truth both were excellent planners, physically fit, and eager to brandish a spear. At Tegyra,

85. Polybius' judgment: 6.43.5–7; cf., e.g., Diod. 15.81.1–4; 88.1–4; Pausanias 8.11.9; Just. 6.8.1–13; Cawkwell 1972, 274–275 (on Epaminondas' ancient admirers); Hanson 2010, 93–94 (on his modern admirers).
86. Epaminondas' sayings: Plut. *Moralia* 192c–194c.

Leuctra, Cynoscephalae, and Mantinea, they effectively combined the charges of the cavalry and infantry, and at Leuctra they both worked in harmony when Pelopidas fronted the phalanx with the Sacred Band, commanded by Epaminondas. Operations such as Epaminondas' attacks on positions on Mount Oneion show that he could calculate movements with perfect timing. In their campaigns, they made an effective use of different specialized forces, be they hoplites, light-armed troops, or cavalry. The two generals were also quick to seize opportunities, as when Pelopidas turned on the Spartans who opened a way for him in Tegyra, or when Epaminondas rushed on what he hoped were defenseless Sparta and Mantinea. Beyond tactics or strategy, Pelopidas at Cynoscephalae and Epaminondas at Mantinea easily moved between the roles of battle director and warrior. Finally, both generals were great motivators who made their soldiers eager to fight (as at Mantinea) and could pull them out of despair (as at Tegyra and in retreat from Thessaly).

In spite of their similarities, cooperation, and friendship, the two Theban generals differed from each other in performance and results. Epaminondas was usually the more senior politician and general, and he came to Pelopidas' rescue three times: once in Mantinea (385) and twice in Thessaly. His seniority does not make him a better general, though. Epaminondas had a checkered record as a besieger, partly because he lacked the perseverance required for that kind of warfare. He had no good answer to skilled specialists such as the light infantry and Sicilian cavalry he met in his second invasion of the Peloponnese. He was also much fonder than Pelopidas of surprise attacks, which did not always work for him. Conversely, Epaminondas seems to have possessed better military intelligence than his colleague (as at Leuctra and during his invasions), probably because he worked harder to get it. Both men were very self-assured, yet it is hard to imagine Epaminondas committing Pelopidas' mistake of trusting Alexander of Pherae. Strategically, Epaminondas made extensive use of raiding as a means of war, unlike his colleague. Epaminondas also created alliances that were designed to build up Theban power and weaken Sparta, but he refrained from destroying the latter. Pelopidas similarly formed pro-Theban alliances against Alexander of Pherae in Thessaly and Macedonia, but his vengeful anti-Alexander policy stood in contrast to Epaminondas' moderate treatment of enemies, including Sparta. Conversely, Pelopidas' success in persuading the Persian king to support Thebes in 367 proves him a better and less confrontational diplomat than Epaminondas at the 371 peace conference in Sparta, or later with the Arcadians.

Both men had their share of failures. Thebes' foreign policy under their direction was often reactive, and many of their campaigns were initiated by allies from the Peloponnese or Thessaly. Moreover, the alliances they formed tended to be unreliable and to require frequent military interventions. Epaminondas bore the lion's share of responsibility for his novel yet overconfident idea that Thebes could rival Athens in naval power. A similar overconfidence led him to assume wrongly that he could persuade the Thebans to accept his Achaean settlement. There was also a measure of arrogance and selfishness in Epaminondas' and Pelopidas' belief that they could personally decide their last battles or at least die trying. But it would be unfair to blame them for qualities that contributed equally to their failures and accomplishments.

Finally, of the two generals, Epaminondas is credited with leaving a great impact on future military leaders. The most prominent of them was Philip II, king of Macedonia, who spent time as a hostage in Thebes (probably 368–365) while Epaminondas was active. It has been claimed since antiquity that he studied Epaminondas' art of war, and he seemed to have borrowed tactics from the Theban. Like Epaminondas, Philip employed a deep phalanx, élite heavy infantry, and cavalry units, sometimes coordinating cavalry with infantry. His army and cavalry were well drilled and on frequent active duty, like the Thebans'. In truth, however, none of these characteristics was unique to Epaminondas, and Philip is not known to have used the original tactics of Epaminondas at Leuctra and Mantinea. The Macedonians were already combining cavalry and infantry attacks in the fifth century, and the wedge formation of their cavalry more probably came from Thrace, Macedonia's eastern neighbor, than from Boeotia. It is equally hard to detect Epaminondas' influence on two other Greek generals said to have admired him: Timoleon, who ruled Syracuse from the 340s to the 330s, soundly defeated the Carthaginians and expanded his city's power, and Philopoemen, who led the Achaeans in 223–183 and was considered a champion of Greek freedom. Readers should not feel disappointed by the dearth of imitators; it was rare for a Greek general to research battles fought before his times. The contribution of Epaminondas and Pelopidas to the Greek art of command lies not in their legacy, but in their performances.[87]

---

87. Philip in Thebes: Plut. *Pelopidas* 26; Diod. 15.76.6; 16.22.2–3; Just. 6.9.7; Hammond and Griffith 1979, 205. Epaminondas' impact on Philip: e.g., Hammond and Griffith 1979, 2:204–206, 425; Ashley 2004, 22–23. Macedonian precedent: Thuc. 4.124.3–4. Epaminondas, Timoleon, and Philopoemen: Plut. *Timoleon* 36; *Philopoemen* 3.

Conclusion

A NCIENT MILITARY WORKS—handbooks, histories, and even semi-fictional narratives—tried to educate their readers in the ways of good generalship, often by providing examples of how generals exercised their trade, and giving the reasons for their success and failure. This Conclusion examines eight of the most prominent Greek generals of the Classical age in a similar spirit. Their careers illustrate the complexity of Greek generalship and the factors that contributed to its various forms, including the general's personality, which tends to be under-appreciated in modern studies of Greek warfare. I shall limit the summary to broad observations on the art of command of the generals discussed here. To avoid a deluge of cross-references to the earlier chapters, it is assumed here that the reader is familiar with their contents.

Before describing how the eight generals distinguished themselves, something should be said about their traits in common with other generals' of the Classical age. As might be expected, they all readied their armies or navies for campaigns, planned how to employ them, directed their movements in battle, and joined the fighting as individual combatants. Their leadership included a multitude of tasks and overlapped with their civilian activity. Hence, the modern view that Greek generals became more professional during the Classical age should be qualified: they rarely demonstrated expertise in particular types of warfare. Except for Pelopidas and perhaps Epaminondas, all generals discussed here fought on both land and sea. They all commanded large armies but also smaller special units, including on commando-like operations. They all fought on the open field in large-scale battles and put cities under siege, while Demosthenes, Dionysius, Pelopidas, and Epaminondas also engaged in urban combat. In short, the eight generals resembled their contemporaries in that they were expected to be military all-rounders, regardless of how well qualified or experienced they may have been in a particular mode of fighting.

The Art of Command: Planning, Management, and Tactics

The Greek art of command began with preparation. Training, planning, and logistics were among the yardsticks of Greek generalship. Pericles and Dionysius worked hard to prepare their cities for a long struggle with their respective enemies based on their estimation of the two rivals' capabilities, resources, and even characters. Both leaders dominated public life for a long time and were thus able to plan their wars in advance rather than in reaction to others' initiatives or to unforeseen events, as was the case with many Theban campaigns under Pelopidas and Epaminondas.

Part of preparing a city for war was developing a general strategy, for the Greek art of command encompassed more than leading unrelated campaigns. Themistocles, Pericles, Lysander, Dionysius, and Epaminondas all formulated strategies or visions that framed their cities' military policy. (Leonidas, in contrast, made no significant contribution to Greek tactics or strategic thinking.) The aforementioned Athenian and the Syracusan generals believed that protecting a city with fortifications enabled it to be aggressive elsewhere. Demosthenes hoped to keep the Spartans preoccupied with self-defense by setting up a well-protected enemy base in its territory, and Epaminondas extended and improved on the idea by founding the polis of Messene on formerly Spartan territory, which significantly weakened Sparta.

In addition to taking offensive initiatives, our generals also designed strategies for the preservation of their cities' hegemonies. They used a variety of means for this purpose, including alliances (below) and the founding of settlements away from home. They also relied on friendly local governments, which they set up or supported, and which were dependent on them and/or their cities (thus, Pericles, Lysander, Dionysius, Pelopidas, and Epaminondas). Generals of hegemonic states tended to repress revolts harshly, or go out frequently on campaigns that were required for the maintenance or expansion of their cities' rule. Dionysius' efforts to improve his army and navy are just one example of how generals developed these forces on which their hegemonies depended.

The ancients, however, judged the eight generals of this book and fellow military leaders less on their strategy and more on their management of campaigns and their tactics. Their performance was inconsistent, and their handling of complex operation illustrates the vicissitudes of their generalship.

There were times when our generals coordinated movements of forces that came from different directions and managed operations that called for cooperation among land and maritime forces or units of different proficiencies. The evidence shows that success depended more on the general's goals and planning than on his management skills, because, as Demosthenes or Dionysius showed, the same general could do well in leading a combined attack on one occasion and poorly on another. Moreover, there was nothing wrong with the tactics employed in such operations, but they became effective only when they were supported by a realistic expectation of what the force was capable of and its suitability to the particular mission.

In broad terms, our generals planned their campaigns with three sometimes-overlapping aims in mind: exploiting their advantage over the enemy, putting the enemy at a disadvantage, and curtailing the enemy's advantage by making the most of available resources. Of these three, an obvious, though not guaranteed, path to success was trying to capitalize on one's superiority over the enemy, as happened when Pericles overwhelmed Samos, and Lysander, Athens, with their greater navy, manpower, and resources. On a smaller scale, Demosthenes' and Epaminondas' advantage in mobility and the "firepower" of their light infantry helped them win over their respective opponents in Pylos and Mantinea. Pericles and Dionysius introduced innovative technologies to warfare, which did not, however, decide the conflict. Indeed, our generals' frequent wins over a superior enemy show that size and other advantages did not always insure victory.

Using one's strengths against the enemy often depended on making alliances. Practically every general in this book recognized that the foundations of hegemonic states rested largely on their allies. They tried, accordingly, to add them, retain them, and to detach them from rival hegemonies. Some generals bound allied states with close personal connections, or used sophisticated means of driving a wedge between the enemy and its own allies. Most of our generals also led coalition armies that included allies, whose contribution could be highly significant. Thus, it would have been impossible for Demosthenes in western Greece, Dionysius in the Third Carthaginian War, or Epaminondas in Mantinea to win the conflict without the services of their allies. The ability to recruit and effectively use allied troops, then, was a measure of the general's acumen. But the relationship between a commander and the allies were not one-sided. Dependence on allies made it necessary to accommodate their interests and sometimes to change plans. Working with allies forced commanders to be more inclusive and to broaden their outlook beyond that of their native cities.

The tactical art of command also included stripping the enemy of its advantages. One way of doing so involved using the layout of the land, maritime straits included, for both defensive and offensive purposes, as shown by Leonidas, Themistocles, and Demosthenes. Although topography could be a double-edged weapon—as Demosthenes' various campaigns showed—the careers described here make clear the importance of studying topography for a successful generalship. Our eight generals also illustrate the use of deception as a means of overcoming a superior opponent. Themistocles and Dionysius excelled in this art, and even the straightforward Leonidas feigned a retreat in Thermopylae. Surprise attacks could include deception, and our generals used it freely in positions of both power and weakness, with mixed results. Demosthenes resorted to surprise in all of his campaigns, as if it were an article of faith, with careful preparations and good military intelligence making the difference between success and failure (below). This held true for other generals, who, unlike Demosthenes, did not wholly condition the success of their campaigns on surprise. Thus Lysander, Dionysius, and Epaminondas excelled in creating the conditions for surprise by accustoming the enemy to a certain routine and then breaking it. A related tactic relied on the predictability of the enemy's conduct in order to ambush him (Demosthenes) or by anticipating his manner of fighting and reaction to attack (Epaminondas). Several generals similarly illustrate the effectiveness of catching the enemy at a disadvantage; say, when it was unprepared (Lysander), or disunited and under duress (Dionysius and Pelopidas). Indeed, many ancient military authors regard seizing the moment as a mark of good generalship.

Some of the above-mentioned tactics depended on acquiring good intelligence about the enemy and the battlefield, which could mean the difference between success and catastrophe. Among the generals of this book, Dionysius seems to have been the best collector of pre-battle intelligence. It is hard to imagine some of his victories over the Carthaginians or the Italiot Greeks without his accurate information about their whereabouts and conditions. Conversely, inadequate information contributed to the defeats of Demosthenes in Aetolia and Syracuse, and Lysander in Boeotia. Even Dionysius' record was imperfect, as when he was surprised twice by the Carthaginian navy. It would be unrealistic to expect Greek generals to have good military intelligence at all or even most times, yet it would be equally wrong to relieve them of the duty of making a sincere effort to obtain it. Thus it is not to Leonidas' credit that he learned about the path that bypassed Thermopylae only when he arrived there.

The examination of tactics and the art of command would not be complete without drawing attention to our generals' innovative tactics that produced noteworthy results. These included the effective deployment of light infantry against hoplites (Demosthenes), of a crack unit in battle (Pelopidas), and of tightened cooperation between infantry and cavalry in battle that yielded better results than the customary use of each arm separately (Pelopidas and Epaminondas). Epaminondas also changed the formation of the Boeotian phalanx and its place in battle in such a way that it won over the enemy. All these tactics were used against a larger or more skilled force and turned an initial inferiority into an advantage. They also displayed the generals' resourcefulness and original thinking, illustrating the importance of personality in the art of command.

The Art of Command: Personality

As we have seen, the ancients refused to separate the general's personality and image from his duties and performance. We, too, must deal with these factors, especially in view of the modern inclination to treat generalship mostly from structural and functional perspectives.

The most common popular expectation of Greek leaders at war was that they would be courageous, and all the generals of this book displayed bravery in one form or another. A commander's show of courage when he joined the fighting set an example for his troops, improved morale and solidarity among them, and could demoralize the enemy. It also supported his taking risks when they were called for. But courage was also deeply personal. All our commanders must have read Homer, and the actions of some of them suggest a wish to emulate the mental and physical prowess of his heroes, and attain the prestige accorded to those who fought and even died in battle. Leonidas exemplified traditional military valor in the service of his state and Greece, but a more individualistic, Homeric courage can be seen in the fighting of Demosthenes, Dionysius, Pelopidas, and Epaminondas. The last two gave in to Achillean battle fury when they led the charge, and paid for it with their lives. The sources' ambivalence about their deaths reflects the Greeks' distinction between wise courage and recklessness, but even their reproach seems mixed with reserved admiration.

Our generals' courage was often accompanied by other characteristics of Homeric heroes, such as the desire for honor (*philotimia*) and excellence (*arete*).

Classical Greeks praised these ambitions when they were directed toward producing public instead of personal good, and when they did not lead to unhealthy competition.[1] Once again, Leonidas' stand at Thermopylae was an exemplary manifestation of these motives, and though Themistocles and Lysander were criticized by their contemporaries for their love of personal honor, it did not interfere with their generalship and may even have spurred them to victory. At the same time, strong ambition for honor and excellence, often characteristic of a general in his early career, probably encouraged Demosthenes and Dionysius to underestimate the challenges they faced, and they suffered humiliating defeats. Similarly, overconfidence in one's own and one's followers' ability to win the conflict was responsible for bad decisions on the field (Demosthenes in Syracuse) or on the strategic level (Dionysius in Italy, Epaminondas' maritime venture, and perhaps even Pericles in the Peloponnesian War).

The personalities of the generals affected their relationships with the troops. Generals such as Leonidas and Epaminondas were able to motivate and inspire their followers to perform above expectations. The troops' loyalty to our generals was also based, sometimes primarily, on the expectation of being led to victory and material gain, and generals such as Themistocles, Pericles, Lysander, and Epaminondas were well aware of this. Indeed, the Greek art of command answered both instrumental and affective expectations.

The generals' authority and personality could also affect discipline. Good discipline as opposed to its absence in the enemy's camp significantly accounted for the victories of Lysander in Aegospotami and Dionysius against the Carthaginians near Syracuse and the Italiot Greeks on the River Eleporus. Needless to say, the troops' obedience was not blind, and the general's authority had limits, especially when it came to looting. Neither Dionysius nor Epaminondas could stop their soldiers from pillaging, even when it was against the general's interests or policy.

Relations with the troops were also influenced by the leaders' persuasive skills, natural or acquired, although there is more evidence for their use in the city and in military headquarters than in haranguing assembled armies. In all these situations, the generals had to counter their listeners' fear of meeting a superior enemy, and to prevail upon them to make difficult decisions (e.g., Themistocles before Salamis and Epaminondas before Leuctra). Their means of persuasion included the standard evocations of freedom, justice, courage, fame, and self-sacrifice, as well as praising their men's capabilities

1. See, generally, Adkins 1960; Whitehead 1983.

and belittling those of the enemy (especially, Pericles). At times, our generals resorted to the psychology of fighting fear with a greater fear when they scared their listeners into following them so as to avert a devastating fate, real or imagined (thus, Themistocles and Epaminondas). It was clearly advantageous for a general to have persuasive and political skills, and Themistocles, Pericles, and Epaminondas were the most successful in our group at blurring the lines between general and politician. Naturally, success was not guaranteed, and Demosthenes' failure to persuade his colleagues to retreat from Syracuse illustrates the problem of a divided military leadership that ended in tragic results.

A general's personality could also affect the style and even the orientation of his leadership. We have noted how personal ambition drove some to miscalculations and grandiose plans, though even the more ambitious commanders could also be circumspect. Caution, restraint, and limited engagement with the enemy or outnumbering its forces in order to reduce the risk characterized the leadership of Pericles and Lysander. Even the bold Demosthenes (in Pylos) and Dionysius (against Carthaginian and Italiot armies) learned to wait for the right conditions before launching an attack or bringing the opposition into submission. Perseverance was also a personal asset for generals who reacted to failure by trying again. Themistocles and Dionysius regarded losses as no more than first rounds in contests they would win in the end. In their patience, they differed from Demosthenes and possibly Epaminondas, both of whom prematurely called off their missions after an initial setback.

Persistence could go hand-in-hand with open-mindedness and the ability to adjust plans and be receptive to others' ideas. Presumably, all eight generals practiced consultation before making a decision, and the process was especially prevalent among Athenian and Theban commanders, who were members of boards of generals. Yet Themistocles and Dionysius seem to have been more welcoming of different views than others, and Pericles, voluntarily or under pressure, modified his strategy of prioritizing the security of the Athenian empire over that of his city.

Readiness to listen to others was complemented by the ability to learn from experience. Our commanders could have learned much about the art of command from contemporary and past generals and even from non-Greek leaders or literary works. Dionysius was probably the most ready to learn from other Greek commanders, yet the evidence suggests that, for almost all the generals in this book, personal experience, be it of victory or defeat, was the main teacher. For example, Epaminondas duplicated in Mantinea his successful battle formation in Leuctra, while Dionysius learned from his failure in Gela to better manage the fighting against the Carthaginians near Syracuse and make his attack less intricate.

Finally, the personality of the eight generals affected the way they treated the vanquished or handled defeat. Pericles, Lysander, and Dionysius could be cruel toward the conquered and repressive in settling their affairs. Epaminondas, by contrast, treated the defeated more leniently. Neither temperament or policy proved more effective than the other, because each failed to prevent former enemies from renewing hostilities later. The general's personality also influenced his conduct following a setback that tested his mental strength and judgment under adversity. The offensive-minded Demosthenes could not really handle losses or prevent his army from coming apart, but Epaminondas turned a disorganized and perilous retreat into a safe return home. Dionysius showed an impressive capability to recover and even to increase his power after defeat.

A general's personality, then, had much to do with the substance and the character of his art of command. Our examination of eight leading Greek generals has endeavored to draw attention to the importance of personal traits among the many other aspects of military leadership in the Classical age. Although none of these commanders had an unblemished record of meeting the high expectations of their jobs, they succeeded in leaving an indelible imprint on Greek military history.

BIBLIOGRAPHY

A. The Main Ancient Sources

Aeschylus, c. 525–455: Aeschylus was one of Athens' greatest tragic poets. His tragedy *Persians*, performed in Athens in 472 under the sponsorship of Pericles, is a near-contemporary account of the naval battle of Salamis between the Greeks and the Persians (480). It is commonly assumed that the poet's description of the battle is fairly accurate, but the reliability of his account should not be overstated, since neither the poet nor his audience expected a full reconstruction of the battle.[1]

Cornelius Nepos, c. 100–124: A Roman author who composed a large collection of short biographies entitled *On Illustrious Foreign Commanders*. Twenty-three of them survive, including the lives of Themistocles (no. 2), Epaminondas (no. 15), and Pelopidas (no. 16), which are largely admiring, unoriginal, and riddled with errors.[2]

Diodorus of Sicily, first century: His *Library* was a history of the Greco-Roman world from the mythical age to the first century. Fifteen books of the original forty survived, and the rest are in fragments. Diodorus often used one or two main sources, and for the history of Greece in the period under discussion, he relied on Ephorus of Cyme, a fourth-century author of a no-longer-extant universal history from mythical times to 340. His *Library*, Books 13–15, is our most informative source on Dionysius I, although more on the first half of his career (406/5–387) than on its second. On the whole, his depiction of Dionysius is more negative than favorable. Among Diodorus' ultimate or immediate sources on Dionysius was

---

1. Aeschylus' *Persians*: Pelling 1997; Harrison 2000; Rosenbloom 2006; Garvie 2009; Bosher 2012 (suggesting that the play was first performed in Syracuse).
2. *Cornelius Nepos*: Geiger 1985.

Ephorus, and the now-lost history of Philistus of Syracuse, whose depiction of Dionysius was largely positive. Philistus was a friend and supporter of the ruler until his exile around 384. Diodorus' other major source on Dionysius was Timaeus of Tauromenium, Sicily (c. 350–260), who wrote the now-lost history of Sicily and Italy that was critical of tyranny.[3]

Ephorus of Cyme: see Diodorus of Sicily; and for his problematic version of events in Thermopylae, see Chapter 1.

Herodotus of Halicarnassus, c. 484–420: His *Histories* is a monumental work that encompasses tales about Greeks and non-Greeks from mythical times onward, but its major theme is the conflict between the Greeks and the Persians that culminated in the great Persian War of 480–479. Herodotus' sources included written accounts, oral traditions, eyewitness testimonies, and his own observations. His account of Leonidas and his stand at Thermopylae was influenced by their later heroic legacy. Herodotus is arguably our most informative source for Themistocles and includes conflicting traditions that reflect Herodotus' mixed opinion of the general.[4]

Justin: A third–fourth-century CE author who wrote an epitome of the Augustan historian Pompeius Trogus' Greek history (*Historiae Phillipica*).[5]

"Oxyrhynchian Greek History": A papyrus from Oxyrhynchus, Egypt, partially preserved a Greek history, commonly known as *Hellenica Oxyrhyncha*, which covers events in Greece and Asia Minor from 407 to 395. Its fourth-century author is unknown, but his account is fairly reliable and supplements our information on Lysander and early fourth-century Boeotia.[6]

Pausanias, second-century CE: A Greek author of *Description of Greece* in ten books that is a trove of information about sites and monuments on the mainland and Ionia, and the history and culture that are related to them. His sources included his own investigations and earlier, similar travelogues. It is often assumed that his flattering account of Epaminondas is based on Plutarch's lost biography of the general.[7]

---

3. Diodorus: Rubicam 1987; Sacks 1990; Stylianou 1998; Green 2006, 1–47. Ephorus: Pearson 1984; Barber 1993; Pownall 2004, 113–142. Philistus: Pownall, "Philistos" *BNJ* 556; Timaeus: C. Champion, "Timaios" *BNJ* 566, both citing earlier works.
4. The literature on Herodotus and the Persian War is very extensive. See, e.g., Gould 1989; Lateiner 1989; Bakker, de Jong, and van Wees 2002; Luraghi 2001; Dewald and Marincola 2006; Baragwanath 2008; Munson 2013, vols. 1–2. *Themistocles in Herodotus:* Blösel 2001; Blösel 2004; Baragwanath 2008, 289–324.
5. Justin and Pompeius Trogus: Goodyear 1992; Yardley 2003.
6. McKechnie and Kern 1988; Bruce 1967.
7. Pausanias: Frazer 1913; Habicht 1998; Pretzler 2007; and see Tuplin 1984 against Pausanias' use of Plutarch on Epaminondas.

Philistus of Syracuse: see Diodorus of Sicily.

Plutarch of Chaeronea, c. 45–120 CE: A biographer and essayist, who wrote his *Lives* of important Greek and Roman leaders in pairs. Of direct relevance to my book are his biographies of Themistocles, Pericles, Lysander, and Pelopidas, while his biography of Leonidas is either lost or was never written, and that of Epaminondas is lost (but see "Pausanias" above). His *Life* of Aristides, Themistocles' rival, includes important information on the latter, while his biography of the Athenian general Nicias informs on the last chapter of Demosthenes' career. Similarly, his biography of the Athenian leader Alcibiades supplements our information on Lysander, and that of the Spartan king Agesilaus, on the careers of Lysander and Epaminondas. Plutarch looked to elucidate the protagonists' characters, and he left out details that military historians find valuable, but he was also a well-read, conscientious writer. He also wrote *On the Malice of Herodotus*, where he criticizes the historian for his negative portrayal of the Greek city of Thebes in Boeotia. He adds information not found in Herodotus, but his bias in favor of his fellow Boeotians creates problems with relying on his version.[8]

Polyaenus, second-century CE: a Macedonian author who collected military stratagems, mostly from the Greek world and from Greek historians, which he hoped that commanders could use. He has useful information on Dionysius I, though the historical accuracy of his anecdotes varies widely.[9]

Thucydides, son of Olorus, c. 460–395: The historian's magnum opus, *The Peloponnesian War*, is an incomplete history of the war (431–404) and the events that preceded it that stops in 411. Thucydides was careful and critical in his use of the evidence, which comprised eyewitness accounts, documentary records, and written and oral traditions. Yet he could be judgmental (implicitly more than explicitly), and his literary ambitions, selective perspective, and political and intellectual agendas could affect his narrative. He is an important source for Themistocles' career after the Persian War, although his view of the general as a farsighted strategist and the initiator of Athenian maritime power colored his account. He is also the most authoritative source on Pericles' and Demosthenes'

8. Plutarch and his biographies: Duff 1999; Pelling 2002. Plutarch's *Themistocles*: Frost 1998; Marr 1998; Duff 2010. Plutarch's *Pericles*: Stadter 1989. Plutarch's *Lysander*: Di Maria et al. 1997. Plutarch's *Pelopidas*: Georgiadou 1997. Plutarch on Herodotus: Plut. *Moralia* 854e–874c; Bowen 1992; Keaveney 1996, esp. 42; cf. Hershbell 1993, 159–160. Plutarch's Life of Leonidas: *Moralia* 866b; of Epaminondas: *Agesilaus* 28.
9. Polyaenus: Krentz and Wheeler, 1994, 1:vi–xxiv; Brodersen 2010.

careers. His using Pericles as a yardstick for other leaders questions the scholarly view that he criticized him. Similarly, the view that he under-appreciated Demosthenes' accomplishments is belied by his account of them.[10]

Timaeus of Tauromenium: see Diodorus of Sicily.

Timotheus of Miletus, c. 450–360: A poet who composed the poem "Persians" on the Battle of Salamis. It survives in a fragmentary form, and scholars are fairly unanimous in warning against its derivative and perhaps pro-Spartan character.[11]

Xenophon, son of Gryllus, of Athens, c. 430–354: A prolific author who spent many years in exile, serving as a soldier of fortune in the army of the Persian prince Cyrus the Younger (later writing about the experience in his *Anabasis*) and then in the employment of Sparta. He lived in the Peloponnese, where he enjoyed the patronage of the Spartan king Agesilaus (II) until he returned to Athens c. 369. His *Hellenica*, or *Greek History*, covers events from 411 to the (second) Battle of Mantinea in 362. He is an important source for the careers of Lysander and Epaminondas, but less so of Pelopidas. Xenophon relies on written accounts as well as memories of contemporaries, whose critical views of both leaders and Thebes he sometimes shares (although they do not completely dominate his narrative, as some have maintained).[12]

10. The literature on Thucydides is too vast to be cited here: see the bibliography in Rengakos and Tsakmakis 2006, 839–882. Of special note are Gomme et al. 1956–1981; Hornblower 1991–2008; and see also Connor 1984; De Romilly 1988; Stahl 2003. Themistocles in Thucydides: Blösel 2012. On Thucydides' approval of Pericles (including criticism of it), see, e.g., Vogt 2009 (originally 1956 in German); Will 2003; Luginbill 2011. Thucydides' critique of Pericles: Monoson and Loriaux 1998; Ober 2001; Foster 2010; Taylor 2010. Pericles as a yardstick for leadership: Thuc. 2.65.1–13. See also Westlake 1968, 23–42; Christodoulou 2013. For Demosthenes and Thucydides, see Roisman 1993b, Preface, 11–22.
11. Timotheus: Hordern 2002; Rosenbloom 2006, 148–154.
12. Xenophon and the *Hellenica*: Anderson 1974; Gray 1989; Krentz 1989–95; Dillery 1995; Tuplin 2003.

B. Modern Sources

Adcock, F. E. 1923–1925. "On Thucydides III, 17." *Cambridge Historical Journal* 1:319–322.

Adkins, A. W. H. 1960. *Merit and Responsibility: A Study in Greek Values*. Oxford.

Albertz, A. 2006. *Exemplarisches Heldentum. Die Rezeptionsgeschichte der Schlacht an den Thermopylen von der Antike bis zur Gegenwart*. Munich.

Allison, J. W. 1989. *Power and Preparedness in Thucydides*. Baltimore, MD.

Ambaglio, D. 2008. *Diodoro Sicolo. Biblioteca Storica Libro XIII. Commento storico*. Milan.

Ameling, W. 1993. *Karthago: Studien zur Militär, Staat und Gesellschaft*. Munich.

Anderson, J. K. 1970. *Military Theory and Practice in the Age of Xenophon*. Berkeley, CA.

———. 1974. *Xenophon*. London.

Andrewes, A. 1971. "Two Notes on Lysander." *Phoenix* 25:206–226.

———. 1978. "The Opposition to Pericles." *JHS* 98:1–8.

———. 1982. "Notion and Kyzikos: The Sources Compared." *JHS* 102:15–25.

———. 1992. "The Spartan Resurgence." *CAH*[2] 5:464–498.

———. 2007 (repr. 1966). "The Government of Classical Sparta." In M. Whitby, ed., *Sparta*. Edinburgh, 49–68.

Anello, P. 2008. "Punici e Greci del 405/4 a.C. all'età timoleontea." In M. Congiu, C. Miccichè, et al., eds., *Greci e Punici in Sicilia tra V e IV secolo a.C.* Rome, 81–100.

Asheri, D. 1992. "Sicily, 478–431." *CAH*[2] 5:149–170.

Ashley, J. R. 2004. *The Macedonian Empire: The Era of Warfare under Philip II and Alexander the Great, 359–323 B.C.* Jefferson, NC.

Asmonti, L. A. 2006. "The Arginusae Trial, the Changing Role of *Strategoi* and Relationship Between the *Demos* and Military Leadership in Late Fifth-Century Athens." *Bulletin of the Institute of Classical Studies* 49:1–21.

Azoulay, V. 2014. *Pericles of Athens*. J. Lloyd, trans. Princeton, NJ.

Badian, E. 1993. *From Plataea to Potidaea. Studies in History and Historiography of the Pentecontaetia*. Baltimore, MD.

Bakker, E. J., I. J. F. de Jong, and H. van Wees, eds. 2002. *Brill's Companion to Herodotus*. Leiden.

Baragwanath, E. 2008. *Motivation and Narrative in Herodotus*. Oxford.

Barber, G. L. 1993. *The Historian Ephorus*, 2nd ed. Chicago.

Basch, M. L. 1969. "Phoenician Oared Ships." *Mariners' Mirror* 55:139–162, 227–246.

Bearzot, C. 2004. "Lisandro tra due modelli: Pausania l'aspirante tiranno, Brasida il generale." In C. Bearzot and F. Landucci, eds., *Contro le "leggi immutabili." Gli Spartani fra tradizione e innovazione*. Milan, 127–160.

Beck, H. 1997. *Polis und Koinon. Untersuchungen zur Geschichte und Struktur der griechischen Bundesstaaten im 4. Jahrhundert v. Chr.* Stuttgart.

Beloch, K. J. 1879. "Due Nauarchie in Sparta." *RhM* 34:117–130.

———. 1914. *Griechische Geschichte*, 2nd ed., Vol. 2. Strassburg.

Berktold, P., J. Schmid, and C. Wacker, eds. 1996. *Akarnanien. Eine Landschaft im antiken Griechenland*. Würzburg.

Best, J. G. P. 1969. *Thracian Peltasts and Their Influence on Greek Warfare*. Groningen.

Blamire, A. 2001. "Athenian Finance, 454–404 B. C." *Hesperia* 70:99–126.

Bleckmann, B. 1998. *Athens Weg in die Niederlage. Die letzten Jahre des peloponnesischen Kriegs*. Stuttgart.

Bloedow, E. F. 1987. "Pericles' Powers in the Counter-Strategy of 431." *Historia* 36:9–27.

———. 1994. "Pericles and Athens' Alliance with Corcyra." *Classica et Mediaevalia* 45:51–69.

———. 2011. "Pericles' Early Career." *Athenaeum* 99:379–397.

Blösel, W. 2001. "The Herodotean Picture of Themistocles: A Mirror of Fifth-Century Athens." In N. Luraghi, ed., *The Historian's Craft in the Age of Herodotus*. Oxford, 179–197.

———. 2004. *Themistokles bei Herodot: Spiegel Athens im fünften Jahrhundert. Studien zur Geschichte und historiographischen Konstruktion des griechischen Freiheitskampfes 480 v. Chr.* Stuttgart.

———. 2012. "Thucydides on Themistocles: A Herodotean Narrator?" In E. Foster and D. Lateiner, eds., *Herodotus and Thucydides*. Oxford, 215–240.

Boedeker, D. 2003. "Pedestrian Fatalities: The Prosaics of Death in Herodotus." In P. Derow and R. Parker, eds., *Herodotus and His World*. Oxford, 17–36.

Boëldieu-Trévet, J. 2007. *Commander dans le monde grec au Ve siècle avant notre ère*. Besançon.

Boersma, J. S. 1970. *Athenian Building Policy from 561/0 to 405/4 BC*. Groningen.

Bolmarcich, S. 2005. "Thucydides 1.19.1 and the Peloponnesian League." *GRBS* 45:5–34.

Bommelaer, J.-F. 1981. *Lysandre de Sparte: histoire et traditions*. Paris.

Bommeljé, S., and P. K. Doorn et al., eds. 1987. *Aetolia and the Aetolians: Towards the Interdisciplinary Study of a Greek Region*. Utrecht.

Bonacasa, N., L. Braccesi, and E. De Miro, eds. 2002. *La Sicilia dei due Dionisî Atti della settimana di studio, Agrigento, 24–28 febbraio 1999*. Rome.

Borthwick, E. K. 1976. "The Scene on the Panagjurischte Amphora. A New Solution." *JHS* 96:148–151.

Bosher, K. 2012. "Hieron's Aeschylus." In K. Bosher, ed., *Theater Outside Athens. Drama in Greek Sicily and South Italy*. Cambridge, 97–111.

Bosworth, A. B. 1988. *Conquest and Empire. The Reign of Alexander the Great*. Cambridge.

———. 1995. *A Historical Commentary on Arrian's History of Alexander*, Vol. 2. Oxford.

Bosworth, A. B. 2000. "The Historical Context of Thucydides' Funeral Oration." *JHS* 120:1–16.

Bowden, H. 2005. *Classical Athens and the Delphic Oracle. Divination and Democracy.* Cambridge.

Bowen, A. 1992. *Plutarch. The Malice of Herodotus (de malignitate Herodoti).* Warminster.

Bowie, A. M. 2006. "Herodotus on Survival: City or Countryside?" In R. M. Rosen and I. Sluiter, *City, Countryside, and the Spatial Organization of Value in Classical Antiquity.* Leiden, 119–137.

————. 2007. *Herodotus Histories, Book VIII.* Cambridge.

Braund, D. 2005. "Pericles, Cleon and the Pontus. The Black Sea in Athens c. 440–421." In D. Braund, ed., *Scythians and Greeks: Cultural Interactions in Scythia, Athens and the Early Roman Empire (Sixth Century BC–First Century AD).* Exeter, 80–99.

Briant, P. 2002. *From Cyrus to Alexander: A History of the Persian Empire.* Trans. P. T. Daniels. Winona Lake, IN.

Brock, R. 2009. "Did the Athenian Empire Promote Democracy?" In J. Ma, N. Papazarkadas, and R. Parker, eds., *Interpreting the Athenian Empire.* London, 149–166.

Brodersen, K., ed. 2010. *Polyainos: neue Studien—Polyaenus: New Studies.* Berlin.

Brown, A. R. 2013. "Remembering Thermopylae and the Persian War in Antiquity." In C. Matthew and M. Trundle, eds., *Beyond the Gates of Fire: New Perspectives on the Battle of Thermopylae.* Barnsley, 100–116.

Bruce, I. A. F., ed. 1967. *An Historical Commentary on the Hellenica Oxyrhynchia.* Cambridge.

Brunt, P. A. 1953–1954. "The Hellenic League Against Persia." *Historia* 2:135–163.

————. 1965. "Spartan Policy and Strategy in the Archidamian War." *Phoenix* 19:255–280.

Buck, R. J. 1979. *A History of Boeotia.* Edmonton.

————. 1994. *Boiotia and the Boiotian League, 432–371 BC.* Edmonton.

Buckler, J. 1978. "Plutarch on the Trials of Pelopidas and Epaminondas (369 BC)." *Classical Philology* 73:36–42.

————. 1980. *The Theban Hegemony 371–362 BC.* Cambridge, MA.

————. 1985. "Epaminondas and the Embolon." *Phoenix* 39:134–143.

————. 2003. *Aegean Greece in the Fourth Century BC.* Leiden.

————. 2013. "Epaminondas at Leuctra, 371 B.C." In B. Campbell and L. A. Tritle, eds., *The Oxford Handbook of Warfare in the Classical World.* Oxford, 657–670.

Buckler, J., and H. Beck. 2008. *Central Greece and the Politics of Power in the Fourth Century BC.* Cambridge.

Bugh, G. 1988. *The Horsemen of Athens.* Princeton, NJ.

Burckhardt, L. 1996. *Bürger und Soldaten. Aspekte der politischen und militärischen Rolle athenischer Bürger im Kriegswesen des 4. Jahrhunderts v. Chr.* Stuttgart.

Burn, A. R. 1949. "Helikon in History: A Study in Greek Mountain Topography."
   BSA 44:313–323.

———. 1984. *Persia and the Greeks. The Defense of the West c. 546–478 B.C.*, 2nd ed.
   London.

Busolt, G. 1850–1920. *Griechische Geschichte bis zur Schlacht bei Chaeroneia.* 3
   vols. Gotha.

Campbell, D. B. 2003. *Greek and Roman Siege Machinery 399 BC–AD 363.* Oxford.

———. 2005. *Ancient Siege Warfare: Persians, Greeks, Carthaginians and Romans
   546–146 BC.* Oxford.

Campbell, J. B. 1987. "Teach Yourself How to Be a General." *Jornal of Roman
   Studies* 77:13–29.

Carawan, E. 2013. *The Athenian Amnesty and Reconstructing the Law.* Oxford.

Carey, C. 2000. *Democracy in Classical Athens.* Bristol.

Cartledge, P. A. 1982. "Sparta and Samos: A Special Relationship?" *CQ*
   32:243–265.

———. 1987. *Agesilaos and the Crisis of Sparta.* London.

———. 2001. *Spartan Reflections.* Berkeley, CA.

———. 2002. *Sparta and Lakonia: A Regional History 1330–362 BC*, 2nd ed.
   London.

———. 2004. *The Spartans. The World of the Warrior-Heroes of Ancient Greece.*
   New York.

———. 2006. *Thermopylae. The Battle That Changed the World.* Woodstock, NY.

Casson, L. 1991. *The Ancient Mariners: Seafarers and Sea Fighters of the Mediterranean
   in Ancient Times,* 2nd ed. Princeton, NJ.

Caven, B. 1990. *Dionysius I. War-Lord of Sicily.* New Haven, CT.

Cawkwell, G. L. 1961. "The Common Peace of 366–365 BC." *CQ* 11:80–86.

———. 1972. "Epaminondas and Thebes." *CQ* 22:254–278.

———. 1975. "Thucydides' Judgement of Periclean Strategy." *Yale Classical
   Studies* 24:53–70.

———. 1997. *Thucydides and the Peloponnesian War.* London.

———. 2005. *The Greek Wars. The Failure of Persia.* Oxford.

Champion, Craige B., "Timaios (566)," in: *Brill's New Jacoby*, Editor in Chief:
   Ian Worthington (University of Missouri). Consulted online on 29 June 2016
   <http://dx.doi.org/10.1163/1873-5363_bnj_a566>

Champion, J. 2010. *The Tyrants of Syracuse: War in Ancient Sicily. Volume I: 480–367
   BC.* Barnsley.

Charles, M. B. 2011. "Immortals and Apple Bearers: Towards a Better
   Understanding of Achaemenid Infantry Units." *CQ* 61:114–133.

Christ, M. R. 2001. "Conscription of Hoplites in Classical Athens." *CQ*
   51:398–422.

Christodoulou, P. 2013. "Thucydides' Pericles. Between Historical Reality and
   Literary Presentation." In A. Tsakmakis and M. Tamiolaki, eds., *Thucydides
   Between History and Literature.* Berlin, 225–254.

Ciasca, A. 1995. "Il sistema fortificato di Mozia (Sicilia)." In M. H. Fantar and M. Ghaki, eds., *Actes du IIIe Congrès international des études phéniciennes et Puniques. Tunis, 11–16 novembre 1991.* Tunis, 1:271–278.

Constantakopoulou, C. 2007. *The Dance of the Islands. Insularity, Networks, the Athenian Empire, and the Aegean World.* Oxford.

Conwell, D. H. 2008. *Connecting a City to the Sea: The History of the Athenian Long Walls.* Leiden.

Connor, W. R. 1984. *Thucydides.* Princeton, NJ.

Crane, G. 1998. *Thucydides and the Ancient Simplicity: The Limits of Political Realism.* Berkeley, CA.

Crowley, J. 2012. *The Psychology of the Athenian Hoplite: The Culture of Combat in Classical Athens.* Cambridge.

Cuomo, S. 2007. *Technology and Culture in Greek and Roman Antiquity.* Cambridge.

Dandamaev, M. M., and V. G. Lukonin. 1989. *The Culture and Social Institutions of Ancient Iran.* Trans. P. L. Kohl and D. J. Dadson. Cambridge.

D'Angelo, I. 2010. "Locri Epizefirii e Dionigi I di Siracusa." *Aevum* 84:41–60.

David, E. 1979/1980. "The Influx of Money into Sparta at the End of the Fifth Century B.C." *Scripta Classica Israelica* 5:30–45.

Debnar, P. 2001. *Speaking the Same Language. Speech and Audience in Thucydides' Spartan Debates.* Ann Arbor, MI.

Demand, N. H. 1982. *Thebes in the Fifth Century: Heracles Resurgent.* London.

Demont, P. 2013. "The Causes of the Athenian Plague and Thucydides." In A. Tsakmakis and M. Tamiolaki, eds., *Thucydides Between History and Literature.* Berlin, 73–88.

De Romilly, J. 1988. *Thucydides and Athenian Imperialism.* Trans. P. Thody. Oxford.

Desmond, W. 2006. "Lessons of Fear: A Reading of Thucydides." *CPh* 101:359–379.

De Souza, P. 2003. *The Greek and Persian Wars, 499–386 BC.* Oxford.

———. 2007. "Naval Forces." In P. Sabine, H. van Wees, and M. Whitby, eds., *The Cambridge History of Greek and Roman Warfare.* Cambridge, 357–367.

Develin, R. 1989. *Athenian Officials 684–321 BC.* Cambridge.

DeVoto, J. G, 1989. "The Liberation of Thebes in 379/8 B.C." In R. F. Sutton, ed., *Daidalikon, Studies in Memory of Raymond V. Schoder, S.J.* Wauconda, IL, 101–116.

———. 1992. "The Theban Sacred Band." *AncW* 23:3–19.

———. 2000. "Dionysius and Himilkon at Gela." *AHB* 14:14–21.

Dewald, C., and J. Marincola, eds. 2006. *The Cambridge Companion to Herodotus.* Cambridge.

Dillery, J. 1995. *Xenophon and the History of His Time.* London.

———. 1996. "Reconfiguring the Past: Thyrea, Thermopylae and Narrative Patterns in Herodotus." *AJP* 117:217–254.

Di Maria, G., A. Bertinelli, M. Manfredini, L. Piccirilli, and E. G. Pisani, eds. 1997. *Plutraco Le Vite Di Lisandro E Di Silla.* Milan.

Drögemüller, H.-P. 1969. *Syrakus: Zur Topographie und Geschichte einer griechischen Stadt*. Heidelberg.

Ducat, J. 1990. *Les Helotes*. Paris.

Due, B. 1987. "Lysander in Xenophon's *Hellenika*." *Classica et Mediaevalia* 38:53–62.

Duff, T. 1999. *Plutarch's Lives. Exploring Virtue and Vice*. Oxford.

———. 2010. "Plutarch's Themistocles and Camillus." In N. Humble, ed., *Plutarch's Lives: Parallelism and Purpose*. Swansea, 45–86.

Dunbabin, T. J. 1948. *The Western Greeks*. Oxford.

Evans, J. A. S. 1964. "The 'Final Problem' at Thermopylae." *GRBS* 5:231–237.

———. 1969. "Notes on Thermopylae and Artemision." *Historia* 18:389–406.

———. 1991. *Herodotus. Explorer of the Past. Three Essays*. Princeton, NJ.

Evans, R. J. 2009. *Syracuse in Antiquity. History and Geography*. Pretoria.

Famà, M. L. 2008. "Mozia tra il V e il IV sec. a.C." In M. Congui, C. Miccichè, et al., eds., *Greci e Punici in Sicilia tra V e IV secolo a.C.* Rome, 47–67.

Fields, N. 2007. *Thermopylae 480 BC. Last Stand of the 300*. Oxford.

———. 2008. *Syracuse 415–413 BC. Destruction of the Athenian Fleet*. Oxford.

Figuera, T. J. 1990. "Aigina and the Naval Strategy of the Late Fifth and Early Fourth Centuries." *RhM* 133:15–51.

———. 2006. 'The Spartan *Hippeis*." In S. Hodkinson and A. Powell, eds. *Sparta and War*. Swansea. 57–84.

Finley, M. I. 1979. *A History of Sicily: Ancient Sicily to the Arab Conquest*. New York.

Flower, H. 1992. "Thucydides and the Pylos Debate (4.27–29)." *Historia* 41:40–57.

Flower, M. A. 1991. "Revolutionary Agitation and Social Change in Classical Sparta." In M. A. Flower and M. Toher, eds., *Georgica: Greek Studies in Honour of George Cawkwell*. London, 78–97.

———. 1998. "Simonides, Ephorus and Herodotus on the Battle of Thermopylae." *CQ* 48:365–379.

———. 2002. "The Invention of Tradition in Classical and Hellenistic Sparta." In A. Powell and S. Hodkinson, eds., *Sparta beyond the Mirage*. London, 191–217.

Flower, M. A., and J. Marincola, eds. 2002. *Herodotus Histories Book IX*. Cambridge.

Fontenrose, J. 1978. *The Delphic Oracle: Its Responses and Operations*. Berkeley, CA.

Fornara, C. W. 1971. *The Athenian Board of Generals from 501 to 404*. Wiesbaden.

———. 1983. *Archaic Times to the End of the Peloponnesian War*, 2nd ed. Cambridge.

Fornara, C. W., and D. M. Lewis. 1979. "On the Chronology of the Samian War." *JHS* 99:7–19.

Fornara, C. W., and L. J. Samons II. 1991. *Athens from Cleisthenes to Pericles*. Berkeley, CA.

Forsdyke, S. 2005. *Exile, Ostracism and Democracy: The Politics of Expulsion in Ancient Greece*. Princeton, NJ.

Foster, E. 2010. *Thucydides, Pericles, and Periclean Imperialism*. Cambridge.

Foster, E. 2012. "Thermopylae and Pylos, with Reference to the Homeric Background." In E. Foster and D. Lateiner, eds., *Thucydides and Herodotus*. Oxford, 185–214.

Foxhall, L. 1993. "Farming and Fighting in Ancient Greece." In J. Rich and G. Shipley, eds., *Warfare and Society in the Greek World*. London, 134–145.

Frazer, J. G. 1913. *Pausanias' Description of Greece*. 6 vols. London.

Freeman, E. A. 1891–1894. *The History of Sicily from the Earliest Times*. 4 vols. Oxford.

Frost, F. J. 1998. *Plutarch's Themistocles. A Historical Commentary*. Revised edition. Chicago.

Gaebel, R. E. 2002. *Cavalry Operations in the Ancient Greek World*. Norman, OK.

Gainsford, P. 2013. "Herodotus' Homer: Troy, Thermopylae and the Dorians." In C. A. Matthew and M. Trundle, eds., 2013. *Beyond the Gates of Fire: New Perspectives on the Battle of Thermopylae*. Barnsley, 117–137.

Garlan, Y. 1974. *Recherches de poliorcétique grecque*. Paris.

Garland, R. 1987. *The Piraeus from the Fifth to the First Century BC*. London.

Garvie, A. F., ed. 2009. *Aeschylus Persae*. Oxford.

Geiger, J. 1985. *Cornelius Nepos and Ancient Political Biography*. Stuttgart.

Gengler, O. 2009. "Leonidas and the Heroes of Thermopylae: Memory of the Dead and Identity in Roman Sparta." In H. Cavanagh, W. Cavanagh, and J. Roy, eds., *Honouring the Dead in the Peloponnese. Proceedings of the conference held in Sparta, 23–35 April 2009*. Nottingham, 151–163. Available at http://www.nottingham. ac.uk/csps/documents/honoringthedead/kokkorou-alevras.pdf.

Georges, P. 2000. "Persian Ionia under Darius: The Revolt Reconsidered." *Historia* 49:1–39.

Georgiadou, A. 1992. "Bias and Character-Portrayal in Plutarch's *Lives of Pelopidas and Marcellus*." *Aufstieg und Niedergang der römischen Welt* 2.33.6:4222–4257.

———. 1997. *Plutarch's Pelopidas. A Historical and Philological Commentary*. Stuttgart.

———. 2006. "The Wanderings of the Sacred Band: Uses and Abuses of Erotic Tradition." *Millennium* 3:125–141.

Geske, N. 2005. *Nikias und das Volk von Athens im Archedamischen Krieg*. Stuttgart.

Giraud, J.-M. 2001. "Lysandre et le chef idéal de Xénophon." *Quaderni di Storia* 53:39–68.

Gomme, A. W., A. Andrewes, and K. J. Dover, eds. 1945–1981. *A Historical Commentary on Thucydides*. 5 vols. Oxford.

Goodyear, F. 1992. "On the Character and Text of Justin's Compilation of Trogus." In K. Coleman, J. Diggle, J. Hall, et al., eds., *F. R. D. Goodyear: Papers on Latin Literature*. London, 210–233.

Gorman, V. B. 2001. *Miletos. The Ornament of Ionia. A History of the City to 400 B.C.E.* Ann Arbor, MI.

Gould, J. 1989. *Herodotus*. London.

Graham, A. J. 1996. "Themistocles' Speech Before Salamis: The Interpretation of Herodotus 8.83.1." *CQ* 46:321–326.

Graninger, D. 2010. "Plutarch on the Evacuation of Athens (*Themistocles* 10.8–9)." *Hermes* 138:308–317.

Gray, V. J. 1987. "The Value of Diodorus Siculus for the Years 411–386 BC." *Hermes* 115:72–89. 1989. *The Character of Xenophon's Hellenica*. Baltimore, MD.

Green, P. 1970. *Armada from Athens*. London.

———. 1991. "Rebooking the Flute-Girls." *AHB* 5:1–16.

———. 1996. *The Greco-Persian Wars*. Berkeley, CA.

———, ed. 2006. *Diodorus Siculus Books 11–12.37.1. Greek History, 480–431 BC—The Alternative Version*. Austin, TX.

Griffith, J. G. 1988. *Festinat Senex. Essays on Greek and Latin Literature and Archaeology*. Oxford.

Grundy, G. B. 1901. *The Great Persian War and Its Preliminaries: A Study of the Evidence, Literary and Topographical*. London.

———. 1948. *Thucydides and the History of His Age*, 2nd ed. Oxford.

Haas, C. J. 1985. "Athenian Naval Power before Themistocles." *Historia* 34:29–46.

Habicht, C. 1961. "Falsche Urkunden zur Geschichte Athens im Zeitalter der Perserkriege." *Hermes* 89:1–35.

———. 1998. *Pausanias' Guide to Ancient Greece*, 2nd ed. Berkeley, CA.

Hale, J. R. 2009. *Lords of the Sea: The Epic Story of the Athenian Navy and the Birth of Democracy*. New York.

Hamel, D. 1998. *Athenian Generals: Military Authority in the Classical Period*. Leiden.

———. 2015. *The Battle of Arginusae. Victory at Sea and Its Tragic Aftermath in the Final Years of the Peloponnesian War*. Baltimore, MD.

Hamilton, C. D. 1979. *Sparta's Bitter Victories. Politics and Diplomacy in the Corinthian War*. Ithaca, NY.

———. 1991. *Agesilaus and the Failure of Spartan Hegemony*. Ithaca, NY.

Hammond, N. G. L. 1936–1937. "The Campaign in Amphilochia during the Archidamian War." *The Annual of the British School at Athens* 37:128–140.

———. 1966. *Epirus: The Geography, the Ancient Remains, the History and Topography of Epirus and Adjacent Areas*. Oxford.

———. 1973. *Studies in Greek History*. Oxford.

———. 1988a. "The Campaign and the Battle of Cynoscephalae in 197 BC." *JHS* 108:60–82.

———. 1988b. "The Expedition of Xerxes." *CAH*² 4:518–591.

———. 1996. "Sparta at Thermopylae." *Historia* 45:1–20.

Hammond, N. G. L., and G. T. Griffith 1979. *A History of Macedonia*. Vol. 2. Oxford.

Hands, A. R. 1965. "On Strategy and Oracles, 480/79." *JHS* 85:56–61.

Hansen, M. H. 1975. *Eisanglia: The Sovereignty of the People's Court in Athens in the Fourth Century BC and the Impeachment of Generals and Politicians*. Odense.

———. 1981. "The Number of Athenian Hoplites in 431." *Symbola Osloenses* 56:19–32.

———. 1991. *The Athenian Democracy in the Age of Demosthenes: Structure, Principles and Ideology*. Trans. J. A. Crook. Oxford.

Hanson, V. D. 1988. "Epaminondas, the Battle of Leuctra and the Revolution in Greek Battle Tactics." *ClAnt.* 7:190–207.

———, ed. 1991. *Hoplites. The Classical Greek Battle Experience*. London.

———. 1998. *Warfare and Agriculture in Classical Greece*. Revised edition. Berkeley, CA.

———. 1999. *The Soul of Battle. From Ancient Times to the Present Day, How Three Great Liberators Vanquished Tyranny*. New York.

———. 2004. *Wars of the Ancient Greeks*. Washington, DC.

———. 2005. *A War Like No Other: How the Athenians and Spartans Fought the Peloponnesian War*. New York.

———. 2009. *The Western Way of War: Infantry Battle in Classical Greece*, 2nd ed. Berkeley, CA.

———. 2010. "Epaminondas the Theban and the Doctrine of Preemptive War." In V. D. Hanson, ed., *Makers of Ancient Strategy. From the Persian War to the Fall of Rome*. Princeton, NJ, 93–117.

Harrison, T. 2000. *The Emptiness of Asia: Aeschylus' Persians and the History of the Fifth Century*. London.

Henderson, B. W. 1927. *The Great War between Athens and Sparta*. London.

Henry, M. M. 1995. *Prisoner of History. Aspasia of Miletus and Her Biographical Tradition*. Oxford.

Hershbell, J. P. 1993. "Plutarch and Herodotus—The Beetle in the Rose." *RhM* 136:143–163.

Hignett, C. 1963. *Xerxes' Invasion of Greece*. Oxford.

Hodkinson, S. 2000. *Property and Wealth in Classical Sparta*. London.

———, ed., 2009. *Sparta. Comparative Approaches*. Swansea.

Holladay, A. J. 1978. "Athenian Strategy in the Archidamian War." *Historia* 27:399–427.

———. 1979. "Thucydides and the Plague at Athens." *CQ* 29:282–300.

———. 1987. "The Forethought of Themistocles." *JHS* 107:182–187.

Holland, T. 2005. *Persian Fire. The First World Empire and the Battle for the West*. London.

Holloway, R. R. 2000. *The Archaeology of Ancient Sicily*, 2nd ed. London.

Hope Simpson, R. 1972. "Leonidas' Decision." *Phoenix* 26:1–11.

Hordern, J. 2002. *The Fragments of Timotheus of Miletus*. Oxford.

Hornblower, S. 1990. "When Was Megalopolis Founded?" *BSA* 85:71–77.

———. 1991–2008. *A Commentary on Thucydides*. Oxford, 3 vols.

Hornblower, S. 1992. "The Religious Dimension to the Peloponnesian War; or, What Thucydides Does Not Tell Us." *Harvard Studies in Classical Philology* 94:169–197.

——. 2000. "Sticks, Stones, and Spartans: The Sociology of Spartan Violence." In H. van Wees, ed., *War and Violence in Ancient Greece*. London, 57–82.

Howie, J. G. 2005. "The Aristeia of Brasidas: Thucydides' Presentation of Events at Pylos and Amphipolis." In F. Cairns, ed., *Papers of the Langford Latin Seminar*. 12:207–284.

Humble, N. M. 1997. "Xenophon's View of Sparta: A Study of the *Anabasis, Hellenica* and *Respublica Lecedaemoniorum.*" Unpublished dissertation. McMaster University.

Hunt, P. 2006. "Arming Slaves and Helots in Classical Greece." In C. L. Brown and P. D. Morgan, eds., *Arming Slaves from Classical Times to the Modern Age*. New Haven, CT, 14–39.

Hunter, J. H. 2005. "Pericles' Cavalry Strategy." *Quaderni Urbinati di Cultura Classica*, 81:101–108.

Hunter, V. G. 1973. *Thucydides the Artful Reporter*. Toronto.

Huss, W., ed. 1992. *Karthago*. Darmstadt.

Hutchinson, G. 2000. *Xenophon and the Art of Command*. London.

Isserlin, B. S. J., and J. Du Plat Taylor. 1974. *Motya. A Phoenician and Carthaginian City in Sicily*. Leiden.

Jacoby, F. 1947. "Some Remarks on Ion of Chios." *CQ* 41:1–17.

Jameson, M. H. 1960. "A Decree of Themistokles from Troizen." *Hesperia* 29:198–223.

Johansson, M. 2001. "The Inscription from Troizen: A Decree of Themistocles?" *Zeitschrift für Papyrologie und Epigraphik* 137:69–92.

Jordan B. 1988. "The Honors for Themistocles after Salamis." *AJP* 109:547–571.

Jung, M. 2011. "'Wanderer, kommst du nach Sparta . . .' Die Bestattung der Perserkämpfer Leonidas und Pausanias im Heiligtum der Athena Chalkioikos." In M. Haake and M. Jung, eds., *Griechische Heiligtümer als Erinnerungsorte: von der Archaik bis in den Hellenismus. Erträge einer internationalen Tagung in Münster, 20.–21. Januar 2006. Alte Geschichte*. Stuttgart, 95–108.

Kagan, D. 1969. *The Outbreak of the Peloponnesian War*. Ithaca, NY.

——. 1974. *The Archidamian War*. Ithaca, NY.

——. 1981. *The Peace of Nicias and the Sicilian Expedition*. Ithaca, NY.

——. 1987. *The Fall of the Athenian Empire*. Ithaca, NY.

——. 1991. *Pericles of Athens and the Birth of Democracy*. New York.

——. 2005. "Pericles as General." In J. M. Barringer and J. M. Hurwit, eds., *Periklean Athens and Its Legacy: Problems and Perspectives*. Austin, TX, 1–9.

——. 2010. "Pericles, Thucydides and the Defense of the Empire." In V. D. Hanson, ed., *Makers of Ancient Strategy: From the Persian Wars to the Fall of Rome*. Princeton, NJ, 31–57.

Kagan, D., and G. F. Viggiano. 2013. "The Hoplite Debate." In D. Kagan and
   G. F. Viggiano, eds., 2013. *Men of Bronze: Hoplite Warfare in Ancient Greece.*
   Princeton, NJ, 1–56.

Kallet, L. 2001. *Money and the Corrosion of Power in Thucydides. The Sicilian Expedition
   and Its Aftermath.* Berkeley, CA.

Kallet-Marx, L. 1989. "Did Tribute Fund the Parthenon?" *ClAnt* 8:252–266.

———. 1993. *Money, Expense, and Naval Power in Thucydides' History 1–5.24.*
   Berkeley, CA.

———. 2008 (1994 repr.). "Money Talks: *Rhetor, Demos*, and the Resources
   of the Athenian Empire." In P. Low, ed., *The Athenian Empire.* Edinburgh,
   185–210.

Karavites, P. 1985. "Enduring Problems of the Samian Revolt." *RhM* 128:40–56.

Keaveney, A. P. 1996. "Persian Behaviour and Misbehaviour: Some Herodotean
   Examples." *Athenaeum* 84:23–48.

———. 2003. *The Life and Journey of Athenian Statesman Themistocles (524–460
   B.C.?) as a Refugee in Persia.* Lewiston, NY.

Keegan, J. 1988. *The Mask of Command.* New York.

Keen, A. G., 1996a. "Lies about Lysander." *Papers of the Leeds International Latin
   Seminar* 9:285–296.

———. 1996b. "Were the Boiotian Poleis Autonomoi?" In: M. H. Hansen and K.
   Raaflaub, eds., *More Studies in Ancient Greek Polis.* Stuttgart, 113–125.

Kelly, T. 1982. "Thucydides and the Spartan Strategy in the Archidamian War."
   American Historical Review 87:25–54.

Kennell, N. M. 2010. *Spartans: A New History.* Malden, MA.

Kern, P. B. 1999. *Ancient Siege Warfare.* Bloomington, IN.

Khorasani, M. M. 2010. *Lexicon of Arms and Armor from Iran: A Study of Symbols and
   Terminology.* Tübingen.

Koon, S. 2011. "Phalanx and Legion: The 'Face' of Punic War Battle." In D.
   Hoyos, ed., *A Companion to the Punic Wars.* Malden, MA, 77–94.

Kowerski, L. M. 2005. *Simonides on the Persian Wars: A Study of the Elegiac Verses of
   the "New Simonides."* London.

Krentz, P. 1982. *The Thirty at Athens.* Ithaca, NY.

———. 1984. "The Ostracism of Thukydides, Son of Melesias." *Historia*
   33:499–504.

———. 1985a. "Casualties in Hoplite Battles." *GRBS* 26.1:13–21.

———. 1985b. "The Nature of Hoplite Battle." *ClAnt* 4:50–61.

———, ed. 1989. *Xenophon. Hellenika I–II.30.* Warminster.

———, ed. 1995. *Xenophon. Hellenika II.3.11–IV.2.8.* Warminster.

———. 2002. "Fighting by the Rules: The Invention of the Hoplite *Agôn*."
   Hesperia 71:23–39.

———. 2007. "War." In P. Sabin, H. van Wees, and M. Whitby, eds., *The
   Cambridge History of Greek and Roman Warfare.* Cambridge, Vol. 1:147–185.

Krentz, P. 2010. "A Cup by Douris and the Battle of Marathon." In G. G. Fagan
and M. F. Trundle, eds., *New Perspectives on Ancient Warfare*. Leiden, 183–204.

Krentz, P., and E. L. Wheeler, eds. 1994. *Polyaenus: Stratagems of War*. 2 vols. Chicago.

Kromayer, J. 1903–1907. *Antike Schlachtfelder in Griechenland. Bausteine zu einer
Kriegsgeschichte*. 2 vols. Berlin.

LaForse, B. 1998. "Xenophon, Callicratidas and Panhellenism." *AHB* 12:55–66.

Lancel, S. 1995. *Carthage. A History*. Trans. A. Nevill. Oxford.

Lateiner, D. 1977. "Pathos in Thucydides." *Antichthon* 11:42–51.

———. 1989. *The Historical Method of Herodotus*. Toronto.

Lazenby, J. F. 1985. *The Spartan Army*. Warminster.

———. 1993. *The Defense of Greece, 490–479 BC*. Warminster.

———. 1998a. *Hannibal's War: A Military History of the Second Punic War*.
Norman, OK.

———. 1998b. "Review of Szemler, G. J., Cherf, W. J., and Craft, J. C., 1996,
Thermopylai. Myth and Reality in 480 B.C." *CR* 48:521–522.

———. 2004. *The Peloponnesian War. A Military Study*. London.

Legon, R. P. 1981. *Megara: The Political History of a Greek City-State to 336 BC*.
Ithaca, NY.

Lehmann, G. A. 2008. *Perikles. Staatsmann und Stratege im klassischen Athen*. Munich.

Leitao, D. 2002. "The Legend of the Theban Sacred Band." In M. C. Nussbaum
and J. Sihvola, eds., *The Sleep of Reason: Erotic Experience and Sexual Ethics in
Ancient Greece and Rome*. Chicago, 143–169.

Lenardon, R. J. 1978. *The Saga of Themistocles*. London.

Lendon. J. E. 1994. "Thucydides and the 'Constitution' of the Peloponnesian
League." *GRBS* 35:159–177.

———. 2005. *Soldiers and Ghosts. A History of Battle in Classical Antiquity*. New
Haven, CT.

———. 2010. *Song of Wrath. The Peloponnesian War Begins*. New York.

The Leonidas Expedition: http://www.300spartanwarriors.com/
theleonidasexpeditions.html.

Lengauer, W. 1979. *Greek Commanders in the 5th and 4th Centuries B.C., Politics and
Ideology. A Study of Militaism*. Warsaw.

Leutsch, E. L., and F. G. Schneidewin, eds. 1958. *Corpus Paroemiographorum
Graecorum*. 2 vols. Hildesheim.

Lewis, D. M. 1977. *Sparta and Persia*. Leiden.

———. 1992a. "Mainland Greece, 479–451 B.C." *CAH*² 5:96–120.

———. 1992b. "The Archidamian War." *CAH*² 5:370–432.

———. 1992c. "The Thirty Years' Peace." *CAH*² 5:121–148.

———. 1994. "Sicily, 413–368 B. C." *CAH*² 6:120–155.

———. 2004 (1963 repr.). "Cleisthenes and Attica." In P. J. Rhodes, ed., *Athenian
Democracy*. Oxford, 287–309.

Lewis, S. 2000. "The Tyrant's Myth." In C. Smith and J. Serrati, eds., *Sicily from
Aeneas to Augustus*. Edinburgh, 97–106.

Lippelt, O. 1910. *Die griechischen Leichtbewaffenten bis auf Alexander den Grossen.* Jena.

Littman R. J. 1984. "The Plague at Syracuse, 396 B.C." *Mnemosyne* 37:110–116.

———. 2009. "The Plague of Athens: Epidemiology and Paleopathology." *Mt. Sinai Journal of Medicine* 76:456–467.

Llewellyn-Jones, L. 2013. *King and Court in Ancient Persia 559 to 331 BCE.* Edinburgh.

Loening, T. C. 1987. *The Reconciliation Agreement of 403/2 B.C. in Athens: Its Content and Application.* Stuttgart.

Longo, F. 2002. "Gela." In L. Cherchia, L. Jannelli, and F. Longo, eds., *The Greek Cities of Magna Graecia and Sicily.* Los Angeles, 224–229.

Loraux, N. 1995. *The Experiences of Tiresias. The Feminine and the Greek Man.* Trans. P. Wissing. Princeton, NJ.

Lotze, D. 1964. *Lysander und der peloponnesische Krieg.* Berlin.

Low, P. 2006. "Commemorating the Spartan War-Dead." In S. Hodkinson and A. Powell, eds. *Sparta and War.* Swansea. 85–109.

———, ed. 2008. *The Athenian Empire.* Edinburgh.

———. 2011. "The Power of the Dead in Classical Sparta: The Case of Thermopylae." In M. Carroll and J. Rempel, eds., *Living through the Dead: Burial and Commemoration in the Classical World.* Oxford, 1–20.

Luginbill, R. D. 1999. *Thucydides on War and National Character.* Boulder, CO.

———. 2004–2005. "Thucydides on Peloponnesian Strategy at Pylos." *American Journal of Ancient Historians* 3–4:39–57.

———. 2011. *Author of Illusions: Thucydides' Rewriting of the History of the Peloponnesian War.* Newcastle upon Tyne.

Luraghi, N., ed. 2001. *The Historian's Craft in the Age of Herodotus.* Oxford.

———. 2008. *The Ancient Messenians: Constructions of Ethnicity and Memory.* Cambridge.

Luraghi, N., and S. E. Alcock, eds., 2003. *Helots and Their Masters in Laconia and Messenia: Histories, Ideologies, Structures.* Washington, DC.

Ma, J. 2013. *Statues and Cities. Honorific Portraits and Civic Identity in the Hellenistic World.* Oxford.

Ma, J., N. Papazarkadas, and R. Parker, eds. 2009. *Interpreting the Athenian Empire.* London.

McDonald, J. 1994–1995. "Supplementing Thucydides' Account of the Megarian Decree." *Electronic Antiquity* 2.3. Retrieved from http://scholar.lib.vt.edu/ejournals/ElAnt/V2N3/mcdonald.html, April 27, 2014.

McGlew, J. F. 2006. "The Comic Pericles." In S. Lewis, ed., *Ancient Tyranny.* Edinburgh, 164–177.

McInerney, J. 1999. *The Folds of Parnassos: Land and Ethnicity in Ancient Phokis.* Austin, TX.

McKechnie, P., and S. J. Kern, eds. 1988. *Hellenica Oxyrhynchia.* Warminster.

Macleod, C. 1983. *Collected Essays.* Oxford.

Macan, R. W., ed. 1908. *Herodotus, the Seventh, Eighth and Ninth Books.* 2 vols. London.

Mann, C. 2007. *Die Demagogen und das Volk. Zur politischen Kommunikation im Athen des 5. Jahrhunderts v. Chr*. Berlin.

Manni, E., et al. 1982–1983. "I Cartaginesi in Sicilia all'epocha dei due Dionisi." *Kokalos* 28–29: 127–277.

Marinatos, S. 1951. *Thermopylae. An Historical and Archaeological Guide*. Athens.

Marincola, J. 2007. "The Persian Wars in Fourth-Century Oratory and Historiography." In E. Bridges, E. Hall, and P. J. Rhodes, eds., *Cultural Responses to the Persian Wars: Antiquity to the Third Millennium*. Oxford, 105–126.

Markle, M. M. 2004 (1985 repr.). "Jury Pay and Assembly Pay at Athens." In P. J. Rhodes, ed., *Athenian Democracy*. Oxford, 95–131.

Marr, J. L. 1995a. "The Death of Themistocles." *G&R* 42:159–167.

———. 1995b. "Themistocles and the Supposed Second Message to Xerxes: The Anatomy of a Legend." *Acta Classica* 38:57–69.

———, ed. 1998. *Plutarch: Life of Themistocles*. Warminster.

Matthew, C. A. 2013. "Was the Defense of Thermopylae in 480 BC a Suicide Mission?" In C. A. Matthew and M. Trundle, eds., *Beyond the Gates of Fire: New Perspectives on the Battle of Thermopylae*. Barnsley. 60–99.

Matthew, C. A., and M. Trundle, eds. 2013. *Beyond the Gates of Fire: New Perspectives on the Battle of Thermopylae*. Barnsley.

Meiggs, R. 1972. *The Athenian Empire*. Oxford.

Mertens, D. 2002. "Le lunghe mura di Dionigi I a Siracusa." In N. Boncasa, L. Braccesi, and E. De Miro, eds., *La Sicilia dei due Dionisî. Atti della Settimana di Studio (Agrigento, 24–28/2/1999)*. Rome, 243–252.

Miccichè, C. 2008. "Tra Siracusa e Cartagine. La realtà sicula fra il 405 e il 392 a.C." In M. Congui, C. Miccichè, et al., eds., *Greci e Punici in Sicilia tra V e IV secolo a.C*. Rome, 121–132.

Moles, J. L. 1994. "Xenophon and Callicratidas." *JHS* 114:70–84.

Monoson, S., and M. Loriaux. 1998. "The Illusion of Power and the Disruption of Moral Norms: Thucydides' Critique of Periclean Policy." *American Political Science Review* 92:285–297.

Moore, R. 2013. "Generalship: Leadership and Command." In B. Campbell and L. A. Tritle, *The Oxford Handbook of Warfare in the Classical World*. Oxford, 457–473.

Moreno, A. 2007. *Feeding the Democracy: The Athenian Grain Supply in the Fifth and the Fourth Centuries BC*. Oxford.

Morrison, J. S. 1990. "Tetrereis in the Fleets of Dionysius I of Syracuse." *Classica et Mediaevalia* 41:33–41.

Morrison, J. S., and J. F. Coates. 1996. *Greek and Roman Oared Warships*. Oxford.

Morrison, J. S., J. F. Coates, and N. B. Rankov. 2000. *The Athenian Trireme: The History and Reconstruction of an Ancient Greek Warship*, 2nd ed. Cambridge.

Morrison, J. V. 2006. "Interaction of Speech and Narrative in Thucydides." In A. Rengakos and A. Tsakmakis, eds., 2006. *Brill's Companion to Thucydides*. Leiden, 251–277.

Munn, M. 2006. The *Mother of the Gods, Athens, and the Tyranny of Asia. A Study of Sovereignty in Ancient Religion*. Berkeley, CA.

Munson, R. V. 2001. *Telling Wonders: Ethnographic and Political Discourse in the Work of Herodotus*. Ann Arbor, MI.

————, ed. 2013. *Herodotus: Volume 1. Herodotus and the Narrative of the Past.* Oxford.

————, ed. 2013. *Herodotus: Volume 2. Herodotus and the World.* Oxford.

Murray, M. W. 2012. *The Age of Titans: The Rise and Fall of the Great Hellenistic Navies*. Oxford.

Ober, J. 1985a. *Fortress Attica: Defense of the Athenian Land Frontier, 404–322 B.C.* Leiden.

————. 1985b. "Thucydides, Pericles, and the Strategy of Defense." In J. W. Eadie and J. Ober, eds., *The Craft of the Ancient Historian: Essays in Honor of Chester G. Starr*. Lanham, MD, 171–188.

————. 1996. *The Athenian Revolution: Essays on Ancient Greek Democracy and Political Theory*. Princeton, NJ.

————. 2001. "Thucydides Theôrêtikos/Thucydides Histôr: Realist Theory and the Challenge of History." In R. D. McCann and B. S. Strauss, eds., *Democracy and War: A Comparative Study of the Korean War and the Peloponnesian War*. Armonk, NY, 273–306.

Obst, E. 1913. *Der Feldzug des Xerxes*. Klio Beihaft 12.

Ogden, D. 1996. *Greek Bastardy in the Classical and Hellenistic Periods*. Oxford.

Osborne. R. 2000. *The Athenian Empire*. London.

————, ed. 2004. *The Old Oligarch: Pseudo-Xenophon's Constitution of the Athenians*. London.

Ostwald, M. 2002. "Athens and Chalkis: A Study in Imperial Control." *JHS* 122:134–143.

Papadopoulos, J. K. 2008. "The Archaic Wall of Athens: Reality or Myth?" *Opuscula* 1:31–46.

Papazarkadas, N. 2009. "Epigraphy and the Athenian Empire: Reshuffling the Chronological Cards." In J. Ma, N. Papazarkadas, and R. Parker, eds., *Interpreting the Athenian Empire*. London, 67–88.

Parke, H. W. 1933. *Greek Mercenary Soldiers from the Earliest Times to the Battle of Ipsus*. Oxford.

Parker, V. 2007a. "Herodotus' Use of Aeschylus' *Persae* as a Source for the Battle of Salamis." *Symbolae Osloenses*. 82:2–29.

————. 2007b. "Sphordias' Raid and the Liberation of Thebes: A Study of Ephorus and Xenophon." *Hermes* 135:13–33.

Pascual, J. 2007. "Theban Victory at Haliartus (395 B.C.)." *Gladius* 27:39–66.

Paul, G. M. 1987. "Two Battles in Thucydides." *Echos du Monde Classique/Classical Views* 31:307–312.

Pearson, L. 1984. "Ephorus and Timaeus in Diodorus: Laqueur's Thesis Rejected." *Historia* 33:1–20.

Pearson, L. 1987. *The Greek Historians of the West: Timaeus and His Predecessors.* Atlanta.

Pelling, C. 1997. "Aeschylus' *Persae* and History." In C. Pelling, ed., *Greek Tragedy and the Historian.* Oxford, 1–19.

———. 2002. *Plutarch and History: Eighteen Studies.* Swansea.

———. 2006a. "Homer and Herodotus." In M. J. Clarke, B. G. F. Currie, and R. O. A. M. Lyne, eds., *Epic Interactions: Perspectives on Homer, Virgil, and the Epic Tradition Presented to Jasper Griffin by Former Pupils.* Oxford, 75–104.

———. 2006b. "Speech and Narrative in the Histories." In C. Dewald and J. Marincola, *The Cambridge Companion to Herodotus.* Cambridge, 103–121.

———. 2007. "Plutarch's Persian Wars." In E. Bridges, E. Hall, and P. J. Rhodes, eds., *Cultural Responses to the Persian Wars. Antiquity to the Third Millennium.* Oxford, 145–164.

———. 2010. "The Liberation of Thebes in Plutarch's *De genio Socratis* and *Pelopidas.*" In H.-G. Nesselrath, ed., *Plutarch, On the* Daimonion *of Socrates: Human Liberation, Divine Guidance and Philosophy.* Tübingen, 111–127.

Pettegrew, D. 2011. "The Diolkos of Corinth." *AJA* 115:549–574.

Piccirilli, L. 1995. "L'ideale spartano della morte eroica: Crisi e trasformazione." *Annali della Scuola normale superiore di Pisa* 25:1387–1400.

Platias, A. G., and C. Koliopoulos. 2010. *Thucydides on Strategy. Athenian and Spartan Grand Strategies in the Peloponnesian War and Their Relevance Today.* New York.

Podlecki, A. J. 1975. *The Life of Themistocles: A Critical Survey of the Literary and Archaeological Evidence.* Montreal.

———. 1976. "Athens and Aegina." *Historia* 25:396–413.

———. 1998. *Perikles and His Circle.* London.

Pomeroy, S. 2002. *Spartan Women.* Oxford.

Potter, D. 2006. "Review of R. T. Wallinga, *Xerxes' Greek Adventure: The Naval Perspective.*" *Bryn Mawr Classical Review* 2006.3.29.

Powell, A. 2006. "Why Did Sparta Not Destroy Athens in 404, or 403 BC?" In S. Hodkinson and A. Powell, eds., *Sparta & War.* Swansea, 287–303.

Pownall, F. A. 2004. *Lessons from the Past: The Moral Use of History in Fourth-Century Prose.* Ann Arbor, MI.

———. "Duris of Samos (76)," in: *Brill's New Jacoby,* Editor in Chief: Ian Worthington (University of Missouri). Consulted online on 29 June 2016 <http://dx.doi.org/10.1163/1873-5363_bnj_a76>

———. "Philistos (556)," in: *Brill's New Jacoby,* Editor in Chief: Ian Worthington (University of Missouri). Consulted online on 29 June 2016 <http://dx.doi.org/10.1163/1873-5363_bnj_a556>

Prag, J. R. W. 2010. "Tyrannizing Sicily: The Despots Who Cried 'Carthage!'" In A. Turner, K. O. Chong-Gossard, and F. Vervaet, eds., *Private and Public Lies: The Discourse of Despotism and Deceit in the Graeco-Roman World.* Leiden, 51–71.

Prentice, W. K. 1934. "The Character of Lysander." *AJA* 38:37–42.

Pretzler, M. 2007. *Pausanias: Travel Writing in Ancient Greece.* London.

Pritchard, D. M. 2010. "The Symbiosis between Democracy and War: The Case of Ancient Athens." In D. M. Pritchard, ed., *War, Democracy and Culture in Classical Athens*. Cambridge, 1–62.

Pritchett, W. K. 1965–1992. *Studies in Ancient Greek Topography*. 8 vols. Berkeley, CA.

———. 1971–1991. *The Greek State at War*. 5 vols. Berkeley, CA.

———. 1994. *Essays in Greek History*. Amsterdam.

Purcell, N. 1994. "South Italy in the Fourth Century." *CAH*² 6:381–403.

Quinn, T. J. 1981. *Athens and Samos, Lesbos and Chios: 478–404 B.C.* Manchester.

Raaflaub, K. A. 1994. "Democracy, Power, and Imperialism in Fifth-Century Athens." In J. P. Euben, J. R. Wallach, and J. Ober, eds., *Athenian Political Thought and the Reconstruction of American Democracy*. Ithaca, NY, 103–146.

Raepsaet, G., and M. Tolley. 1993. "Le Diolkos de l'Isthme à Corinthe: son tracé, son fonctionnement." *Bulletin de Correspondance Hellénique* 117:233–261.

Rapp, G. R. 2013. "The Topography of the Pass at Thermopylae circa 480 BC." In C. Matthew and M. Trundle, eds., *Beyond the Gates of Fire: New Perspectives on the Battle of Thermopylae*. Barnsley, 39–59.

Rawlings, L. 2007. *The Ancient Greeks at War*. Manchester.

Ray, F. E. 2009. *Land Battles in the 5th Century B.C. Greece: A History and Analysis of 173 Engagements*. Jefferson, NC.

Rengakos, A., and A. Tsakmakis, eds. 2006. *Brill's Companion to Thucydides*. Leiden.

Rey, F. E. 2010. "Weapons, Technological Determinism, and Ancient Warfare." In G. Fagan and M. Trundle, eds., *New Perspectives on Ancient Warfare*. Leiden, 21–56.

Rhodes, P. J. 1993. *A Commentary on the Aristotelian* Athenaion Politeia. Oxford.

———. 1994. *Thucydides History III*. Warminster.

———. 1999. *Thucydides History IV.1–V.24*. Warminster.

———. 2006. *A History of the Classical Greek World 478–323 BC*. Malden, MA.

———. 2007. "Democracy and Empire." In L. J. Samons II, ed., *The Cambridge Companion to the Age of Pericles*. Cambridge, 24–45.

———. 2011. *Alcibiades: Athenian Playboy, General and Traitor*. Barnsley.

Rihll, T. E. 2007. *The Catapult. A History*. Yardley, PA.

Robertson N. 1976. "The Thessalian Expedition of 480 B.C." *JHS* 96:100–120.

Robinson, E. W. 2014. "What Happened in Aegospotami? Xenophon and Diodorus on the Last Battle of the Peloponnesian War." *Historia* 63:1–16.

Roesch, P. 1984. "Un décret inédit de la ligue thébaine et la flotte d'Épaminondas." *Revue des Études Grecques* 97:45–60.

Roisman, J. 1987. "Kallikratidas—A Greek Patriot?" *Classical Journal* 83:21–33.

———. 1988. "On Phrynichos' Sack of Miletos and the Phoinissai." *Eranos* 86:15–23.

———. 1993a. "The Background of the Battle of Tanagra and Some Related Issues." *AC* 62:69–85.

———. 1993b. *The General Demosthenes and His Use of Military Surprise*. Stuttgart.

Roisman, J. 2014. "Persuading the People in Greek Participatory Communities." In D. Hammer, ed., *A Companion to Greek Democracy and the Roman Republic.* Malden, MA, 277–293.

Roisman, J., and Ian Worthington. 2015. *Lives of the Attic Orators: Texts from Pseudo-Plutarch, Photius, and the* Suda. Oxford.

Roisman, J., ed. and J. C. Yardley, trans. 2011. *Ancient Greece from Homer to Alexander: The Evidence.* Malden. MA.

Romilly, J. de. 1956. "La crainte dans l'oeuvre de Thucydide." *Classica et Mediaevalia* 17:119–127.

Rood, T. 1998. *Thucydides: Narrative and Explanation.* Oxford.

Rosenbloom, D. 1993. "Shouting 'Fire' in a Crowded Theater: Phrynichus' *Capture of Miletos* and the Politics of Fear in Early Attic Tragedy." *Philologus* 137:159–196.

———. 2006. *Aeschylus: Persians.* London.

Roux, G. 1974. "Eschyle, Hérodote, Diodore, Plutarque racontent la bataille de Salamine." *Bulletin de correspondance hellénique* 98:51–94.

Roy, J. 1994. "Thebes in the 360s BC." *CAH*² 6:187–208.

Rubicam, C. I. R. 1987. "The Organization and Composition of Diodorus' *Biblioteke*." *Échos du monde classique* 31:313–328.

———. 2003. "Numbers in Greek Poetry and Historiography: Quantifying Feeling." *CQ* 53:448–463.

Russel, F. S. 1994. "A Note on the Athenian Defeat at Notium." *AHB* 8:35–37.

———. 1999. *Information Gathering in Ancient Greece.* Ann Arbor, MI.

Rusten, J. S., ed. 1989. *Thucydides: The Peloponnesian War, Book II.* Cambridge.

Rutter, N. K. 1973. "Diodorus and the Foundation of Thurii." *Historia* 22:155–176.

Ruzicka, S. 1988. "Epaminondas and the Genesis of the Social War." *CPh* 93:60–69.

Rzepka, J. "Kallisthenes of Olynthos." 124 *BNJ*, forthcoming.

Sabattini, C. 1986 "Aspetti della politica di Dionisio in Italia: note sul testo diodoreo." *RSA* 16:31–48.

Sabin, P., H. van Wees, and M. Whitby, eds. 2007. *The Cambridge History of Greek and Roman Warfare.* Vol. 1: *Greece, The Hellenistic World and the Rise of Rome.* Cambridge.

Sacks, K. S. 1990. *Diodorus Siculus and the First Century.* Princeton, NJ.

Saïd, S. 1992–1993. "Pourquoi Psyttalie ou comment transformer un combat naval en défaite terrestre." *Cahiers du GITA.* 7:53–69.

Sage, M. M. 1996. "*Warfare in Ancient Greece: A Sourcebook.* London.

Ste Croix, G. E. M. de. 1972. *The Origins of the Peloponnesian War.* London.

———. 2004. "Herodotus and King Cleomenes I of Sparta." In G. E. M. de Ste Croix, *Athenian Democratic Origins and Other Essays.* D. Harvey and R. Parker, eds., Oxford, 421–440.

Samons II, L. J. 2006. "Thucydides' Sources and the Spartan Plan at Pylos." *Hesperia* 75:525–540.

———. 2007. "Introduction: Athenian History and Society in the Age of Pericles." In L. J. Samons II, ed., *The Cambridge Companion to the Age of Pericles*. Cambridge, 1–23.

Sánchez, P. 2001. *L'Amphictionie des Pyle et de Delphes*. Stuttgart.

Sánchez Moreno, E. 2010. "La ruta Anopea, talón de Aquiles de los griegos en Termópilas." In A. J. Domínguez Monedero and G. M. Rodríguez, eds., *Doctrina a magistro discipulis tradita: Estudios en Homenaje al Profesor Doctor don Luis García Iglesias*. Madrid, 59–75.

Sanders, L. J. 1987. *Dionysius I of Syracuse and Greek Tyranny*. London.

———. 1990–1991. "From Dionysius to Augustus: Some Thoughts on the Nachleben of Dionysius I of Syracuse." *Kokalos* 36–37:111–137.

Sansone D. 1981. "Lysander and Dionysius (Plut. Lys. 2)." *CPh* 76:202–206.

Schmitzer, U. 1998. "Sieben Thebaner gegen Theben: Bemerkungen zur Darstellungsform in Xenophon, *Hell.* 5,4,112." *Würzburger Jahrbücher für die Altertumswissenschaft* 22:123–139.

Schreiner, J. H. 2004. *Two Battles and Two Bills: Marathon and the Athenian Fleet*. Oslo.

Schubert, C. 1994. *Perikles*. Darmstadt.

Schubert, C., and D. Laspe. 2009. "Perikles' defensiver Kriegsplan: Eine thukydideische Erfindung?" *Historia* 58:373–394.

Schwartz, A. 2009. *Reinstating the Hoplite: Arms, Armour and Phalanx Fighting in Archaic and Classical Greece*. Stuttgart.

Sealey, R. 1976. "Die spartanische Nauarchie." *Klio* 58:335–358.

Sekunda, N. 1992. *The Persian Army 560–330*. Oxford.

———. 2013. "War and Society in Greece." In B. Campbell and L. A. Tritle, eds., *The Oxford Handbook of Warfare in the Classical World*. Oxford, 199–215.

Sekunda, N. V., and B. Burliga. 2014. *Iphocrates, Peltasts and Lecaheum*. Gdansk.

Sergent, B. 1991. "La date de la bataille de Leuctres et celle de la fête des Gymnopaidiai." *RSA* 21:137–143.

Sheldon, R. M. 2012. *Ambush. Surprise Attack in Ancient Greek Warfare*. Barnsley.

Shepherd, W. 2010. *Salamis 480 BC. The Naval Campaign That Saved Greece*. Oxford.

Shipley, D. R. 1997. *A Commentary on Plutarch's Life of Agesilaos*. Oxford.

Shipley, G. 1987. *A History of Samos 800–188 BC*. Oxford.

Sinclair, R. K. 1988. *Democracy and Participation in Athens*. Cambridge.

Sjöqvist, E. 1973. *Sicily and the Greeks: Studies in the Interrelationships between the Indigenous Populations and the Greek Colonists*. Ann Arbor, MI.

Smarczyk, B. 1990. *Untersuchungen zur Religionspolitik und politischen Propaganda Athens im Delisch-Attischen Seebund*, Munich.

Smith, R. E. 1948. "Lysander and the Spartan Empire." *CPh* 43:145–156.

Sordi, M. 1992. *La Dynasteia in Occidente (Studi su Dionigi I)*. Padova.

Spence, I. G. 1990. "Perikles and the Defense of Attika during the Peloponnesian War." *JHS* 110:91–109.

———. 1993. *The Cavalry of Classical Greece. A Social and Military History with Particular Reference to Athens*. Oxford.

———. 2010. "Cavalry, Democracy and Military Thinking in Classical Athens." In D. M. Pritchard, ed., *War, Democracy and Culture in Classical Athens*. Cambridge, 111–138.

Sprawski, S. 1999. *Jason of Pherae. A Study on History of Thessaly in Years 431–370 BC*. Cracow.

———. 2004. "Battle of Tegyra (375 BC). Breaking Through and the Opening of the Ranks." *Electrum* 8:13–26.

Stadter, P. A, ed. 1989. *A Commentary on Plutarch's* Pericles. Chapel Hill, NC.

Stahl, H-P. 2003. *Thucydides. Man's Place in History*. Swansea.

———. 2006. "Narrative Unity and Consistency of Thought: A Composition of Event Sequences in Thucydides." In A. Gengakos and A. Tsakmakis, eds., *Brill's Companion to Thucydides*. Leiden, 301–334.

Strassler, R. B. 1988. "The Harbor at Pylos, 425 BC." *JHS* 108:198–203.

———. 1990. "The Opening of the Pylos Campaign." *JHS* 110:110–125.

Strauss, B. S. 1983. "Aegospotami Reexamined." *AJP* 104:24–35.

———. 1987. "A Note on the Topography and Tactics of the Battle of Aegospotami." *AJP* 108:741–745.

———. 2004. *The Battle of Salamis. The Naval Encounter That Saved Greece—and Western Civilization*. New York.

Stroheker, K. F. 1958. *Dionysios I. Gestalt und Geschichte des Tyrannen von Syrakus*. Wiesbaden.

Stroszeck, J. 2004. "Greek Trophy Monuments." In S. des Bouvrie, ed., *Myth and Symbol II. Symbolic Phenomena in Ancient Greek Culture*. Bergen, 303–332.

Stylianou, P. J. 1998. *A Historical Commentary on Diodorus Siculus, Book 15*. Oxford.

Szemler, G. J., W. J. Cherf, and J. C. Craft. 1996. *Thermopylai. Myth and Reality in 480 B.C.* Chicago.

Taylor, M. C. 2010. *Thucydides, Pericles, and the Idea of Athens in the Peloponnesian War*. Cambridge.

Thomas, C. G. 1973. "On the Role of the Spartan Kings." *Historia* 23:257–270.

Thorne, J. A. 2001. "Warfare and Agriculture: The Economic Impact of Devastation in Classical Greece." *GRBS* 42:225–253.

Tompkins, D. 2013. "The Language of Pericles." In A. Tsakmakis and M. Tamiolaki, eds., *Thucydides between History and Literature*. Berlin, 447–464.

Tracy. S. V. 2009. *Pericles: A Source Book and Reader*. Berkeley, CA.

Treu, M. 1956. "Der Stratage Demosthenes." *Historia* 5:420–447.

Tritle, L. A. 2010. *A New History of the Peloponnesian War*. Malden, MA.

Trundle, M. 2004. *Greek Mercenaries from the Late Archaic Period to Alexander*. London.

Tsetskhladze, G. R. 1997. "Plutarch, Pericles and Pontus: Some Thoughts." In
C. Schrader et al., eds., *Plutarco y la historia. Actas del V simposio español sobre
Plutarco, Zaragoza, 20–22 de junio de 1996*. Zaragoza, 461–466.

Tuplin, C. 1984. "Pausanias and Plutarch's Epaminondas." *CQ* 34:346–358.

———. 1987. "The Leuctra Campaign: Some Outstanding Problems." *Klio*
69:72–107.

———, ed. 2003. *Xenophon and His World. Papers from a Conference held in Liverpool
in July 1999*. Stuttgart.

Tusa, V. 1988. "The Punics in Sicily." In S. Moscati, ed., *The Phoenicians*. Milan,
186–205.

Van de Maele, S. 1980. "Démosthène et Cléon à Pylos (425 av. J.-C.)." In J.-B.
Caron, M. Fortin, and C. Maloney, eds., *Mélanges d'études anciennes offerts à
Maurice Lebel*. Quebec, 119–124.

Vanderpool, E. 1974. "The Date of the Pre-Persian City-Wall of Athens." In
D. W. Bradeen and M. F. McGregor, eds., *Φόρος: Tribute to Benjamin Dean Meritt*.
Locust Valley, NY, 156–160.

Van Wees, H. 1992. *Status Warriors: War, Violence and Society in Homer and History*.
Amsterdam.

———. 2004. *Greek Warfare. Myths and Reality*. London.

Viggiano, G. F., and H. Van Wees. 2013. "The Arms, Armor, Iconography of
Early Greek Hoplite Warfare." In D. Kagan and G. Viggiano, eds., *Men of
Bronze: Hoplite Warfare in Ancient Greece*. Princeton, NJ, 57–73.

Vogt, J. 2009 (trans. from German, 1956). "The Portrait of Pericles in
Thucydides." In J. Rusten, ed., *Thucydides. Oxford Readings in Classical Studies*.
Oxford, 220–237.

Walbank, F. A. 1957–1979. *A Historical Commentary on Polybius*. Oxford. 3 vols.

Wallace, P. W. 1980. "The Anopaia Path at Thermopylae." *AJA* 84:15–23.

Wallinga, H. T. 1993. *Ships and Sea-Power before the Great Persian War: The Ancestry
of the Ancient Trireme*. Leiden.

———. 2005. *Xerxes' Greek Adventure. The Naval Perspective*. Leiden.

Waters, M. W. 2010. "Applied Royal Directive: Pissouthnes and Samos." In
B. Jacobs and R. Rolinger, eds., *Der Achämenidenhof/The Achaemenid Court*.
Wiesbaden, 817–828.

Wecowski, M. 2013. "In the Shadow of Pericles: Athens' Samian Victory and
the Organization of the *Pentekontaetia* in Thucydides." In A. Tsakmakis and
M. Tamiolaki, eds., *Thucydides between History and Literature*. Berlin, 153–166.

Westlake, H. D. 1936. "The Medism of Thessaly." *JHS* 56:12–24.

———. 1945. "Seaborne Raids in Periclean Strategy." *CQ* 39:75–84.

———. 1968. *Individuals in Thucydides*. Cambridge.

———. 1969. *Essays on the Greek Historians and Greek History*. Manchester.

———. 1975. "Xenophon and Epaminondas." *GRBS* 16:23–40.

———. 1983. "The Progress of Epiteichismos." *CQ* 33:12–24.

Westlake, H. D. 1985. "The Sources for the Spartan Debacle at Haliartos." *Phoenix* 39:119–133.

Wet, B. X. de. 1969. "The So-called Defensive Policy of Pericles." *Acta Classica* 12:103–119.

Whatley, N. 1964. "On the Possibility of Reconstructing Marathon and Other Ancient Battles." *JHS* 84:119–139.

Wheeler, E. L. 1983. "The Hoplomachoi and Vegetius' Spartan Drillmasters." *Chiron* 13:1–20.

———. 1991. "The General as Hoplite." In V. D. Hanson, ed., *Hoplites*. London, 121–170.

——— 2007. "Battle: A. Land Battles." In P. Sabin, H. van Wees, and M. Whitby, eds., *The Cambridge History of Greek and Roman Warfare.* Cambridge. 1:186–223.

Whitaker, J. I. S. 1921. *Motya, a Phoenician Colony in Sicily*. London.

Whitehead, D. 1983. "Competitive Outlay and Community Profit: *Philotoimia* in Democratic Athens." *Classica et Mediaevalia* 34:55–74.

———. 2001. *Aineias the Tactician. How to Survive under Siege*, 2nd ed. Bristol.

Whitby, M., ed. 2002. *Sparta*. Edinburgh.

Will, W. 2003. *Thukydides und Perikles. Der Historiker und sein Held*. Bonn.

Wilson, J. 1979. *Pylos 421 B.C.: A Historical and Topographical Study of Thucydides' Account of the Campaign*. Warminster.

Winter, F. E. 1971. *Greek Fortifications*. Toronto.

Wiseman, J. 1969. "Epaminondas and the Theban Invasions." *Klio* 51:177–199.

Wolpert, A. 2001. *Remembering Defeat: Civil War and Civic Memory in Ancient Athens*. Baltimore, MD.

Wolters, J. 1931. "Die Schlacht bei Leuktra." In J. Kromayer and G. Veith, eds., *Antike Schlachtfelder im Griechenland*. Berlin. 4:290–316.

Wood, N. 1964. "Xenophon's Theory of Leadership." *Classica et Mediaevalia* 25:33–66.

Woodcock, E. C. 1928. "Demosthenes, Son of Alcisthenes." *Harvard Studies in Classical Philology* 39:93–108.

Wycherley, R. E. 1978. *The Stones of Attica*. Princeton, NJ.

Wylie, G. 1986. "What Really Happened at Aegospotami?" *AC* 55:125–141.

———. 1993. "Demosthenes the General—Protagonist in a Greek Tragedy." *Greece & Rome* 40:20–30.

———. 1997. "Lysander and the Devil." *AC* 66:75–88.

Yardley, J. C. 2003. *Justin and Pompeius Trogus: A Study of the Language of Justin's Epitome of Trogus*. Toronto.

Zahrnt, M. 1997. "Der Demos von Syrakus im Zeitalter der Dionysioi." In W. Eder and K.-J. Hölkeskamp, eds., *Volk und Verfassung im vorhellenistischen Griechenland, Beiträge auf dem Symposium zu Ehren von Karl-Wilhelm Welwei in Bochum, 1–2 März 1996.* Stuttgart, 153–175.

INDEX

democracy and government of, 58, 98, 102–103, 210–215

empire of, 19, 98, 102–103, 105–106, 108, 111–143, 189–210, 215

and finances, 112–113, 118, 123–125, 133, 139–141, 142, 153

fourth-century alliances and foreign affairs of, 222, 278, 283, 299, 304–305, 316, 317, 323

fourth-century campaigns of, 219, 222–224, 277, 304, 306, 308, 310–311, 313–314, 323–324, 327–337

and generalship, 12, 19, 58, 114, 150, 153, 155, 276

navy of, 1, 4–5, 59, 65–67, 70–91, 97, 122–142, 151, 153–160, 170–172, 175–176, 180–181, 188, 191–205, 208, 310, 316

and the Peloponnesian War, 121–210

and the Persian War, 32, 33, 63–93

and the Piraeus, 50, 61, 81, 84, 94, 97–99, 109, 133–134, 200, 208–209, 210, 212–213, 220, 238, 283

resident aliens (metics) in, 19, 22, 134

and the Sicilian Expedition, 173–185, 189, 231, 254–255

walls of, 64–65, 94–98, 108, 123, 208–210, 212

Attica. *See* Athens

Attic-Delian League. *See* Athens, empire of

Aulis, 218, 315

Ayios Georgios, 84

Balearic Islands, 232

battle, general characteristics of on land, 5, 14–15, 51
naval, 22–23, 90, 180–181

battleships, 22–23, 63, 76, 89, 157, 192, 234, 244–245, 254, 257, 262. *See also* Athens, navy of; Carthage, navy of; Dionysius I, navy of; Persia, navy of; Sparta, navy of

Bekhides, 318, 320

Black Sea, 105–106, 120, 124, 132, 141, 200, 206, 316

Boeotarch, 12, 19–20, 221, 280, 281, 288–290, 299–300, 309, 311, 317, 323

Boeotia, Boeotian confederacy, 3, 12, 19–20, 36, 55, 74, 104, 106–108, 124, 128, 146–149, 163, 166, 167–172, 174, 179, 188, 214, 218, 219–225, 276–277, 279–281, 283, 286–298, 300, 301, 304, 306, 307, 309, 312–313, 315, 317, 322–323, 333, 337, 340, 344, 350, 351

army, troops and cavalry of, 17, 19–20, 167–172, 178, 221, 280, 287, 290–296, 299–309, 311–312, 323–337 (*see also* Boeotarch; Epaminondas; Lysander, Boeotia; Pelopidas; Thebes)

booty, 50, 134, 136, 202, 200, 201, 205, 211, 327, 241, 246, 251, 255, 259, 301, 303. *See also* raids

Brasidas, 157, 166–168, 187

Brea, 106

Buckler, J., 318

Burial. *See* war dead

Byzantium, 113, 118, 120, 206, 315–316

Cabala, 268–269

Cadmeia. *See* Thebes, and the Cadmeia

Calchedon, 206

Callicratidas, 188, 195–197

Calydon, 314

Camarina, 234, 237, 238, 246

Neochorus, 223
Neocles, 60
Nepos, Cornelius, 67–68, 349
Nicias, 128, 160, 172, 174–176,
    179–184, 351. *See also* Peace,
    of Nicias
Nicomedes, 61
night attack. *See* surprise, military
Nike, 163
Nisaea, 108, 134, 163–168
Notium, 146. *See also* Lysander, and
    the battle of Notium

Odysseus, 58
Oeniadae, 104, 141, 148
Oenoe, 126
Oeta, Mt., 38
officers, 17, 18, 19, 31, 161, 206, 203,
    236, 238–239, 243, 251, 273,
    284–285, 295, 306, 321
"Old Oligarch" (Ps. Xenophon), 129
Olpae. *See* Demosthenes, and the battle
    of Olpae
Olympeium. *See* Syracuse, and
    Olympeium
Olympia, 163
Oneion, Mt., 306–307, 309,
    313–314, 339
Onosander, 11
oracle, 28, 47, 63–64, 72, 97, 105,
    217, 267, 271, 298
Orchomenus, 221, 283–285, 298, 307,
    322–323
Oropus, 128, 315
Ortygia. *See* Syracuse, and Ortygia
ostracism, 58, 60, 63, 66, 73, 99, 109
Oxyrhynchian Greek History, 350

Palara, 130
Pamphylia, 84
Panormus. 230, 252, 270
Paralus, 204
Patroclus, 52

Patton, George, 4
Pausanias, author, 53, 184, 350
Pausanias, king, 208, 212–215, 219,
    220–224
Pausanias, regent, 53
peace, of 404, 209–210
    of Antalcidas, 277
    common, 277, 286–287, 312–313
    of Nicias, 162, 172
    Thirty Years, 108–109, 122, 134
    Pegae, 104, 108, 163
Pellana, 324–325
Pellene, 306–307
Pelopidas, 3, 10, 12, 19–20,
    275–277, 337
    and allies and friends, 300, 309–310,
        312, 317–322, 339–340, 342
    ancient evidence on, 310, 320, 338
        (*see also* Diodorus; Nepos; Plutarch;
        Xenophon)
    army and cavalry of, 282–286, 291,
        293–295, 299, 317–322
    and authority, persuasion and
        leadership, 276, 280–281, 284,
        287, 289, 300, 312–313, 317,
        320–321, 338–339
    and the battle of Cynoscephalae,
        317–322, 339
    and the battle of Leuctra, 282,
        285, 291, 293–295, 311,
        321–322, 325
    and the battle of Tegyra, 282–286,
        293, 311, 318, 320–322, 338–339
    challenges of, 276, 321
    death and burial of, 321–322, 337
    and diplomacy, 309–310,
        312–313, 339
    and Epaminondas (*see* Epaminondas,
        and Pelopidas)
    honors received, 322
    image of, 310, 318, 337–338
    and military intelligence, 284,
        300, 339